FROM CRADLE TO CROWN

BRITISH NANNIES AND GOVERNESSES
AT THE WORLD'S ROYAL COURTS

CHARLOTTE ZEEPVAT

SUTTON PUBLISHING

*For Sue – without whose encouragement,
company and first-rate research skills this
book might have foundered a long time ago*

First published in the United Kingdom in 2006 by
Sutton Publishing Limited · Phoenix Mill
Thrupp · Stroud · Gloucestershire · GL5 2BU

British Library Cataloguing in Publication Data
A catalogue record for this book is available from the British Library.

ISBN 0-7509-3074-8

Typeset in 10.5/14pt Sabon.
Typesetting and origination by
Sutton Publishing Limited.
Printed and bound in England by
J.H. Haynes & Co. Ltd, Sparkford.

Contents

List of Plates		iv
Picture Credits		vi
Acknowledgements		vii
Introduction		ix
One	Two Beginnings	1
Two	'Yesterday a Nanny Arrived . . .'	20
Three	'A Lady-like Form of Suicide'	43
Four	'A Little World of its Own'	63
Five	'A War Dance on a Wet Afternoon'	88
Six	'The King Came Up to Tea'	110
Seven	'Candles in Open Air'	130
Eight	'Her Only Crime'	150
Nine	'Like a Poor Little Sparrow'	174
Ten	'Alone at Night without a Revolver'	195
Eleven	'A Wonderful Fifth Column'	217
Twelve	'It's Only Bombs, Dear'	238
Thirteen	Living with the Memory	263
Appendix	*Nurses and Governesses*	285
	Notes	301
	Bibliography	326
	Index	331

List of Plates

Emma Hobbs with Princess Charlotte of Prussia.
Mary Anne Thurston and Princess Beatrice.
Mrs Clark holding Princess Victoria of Hesse.
Marjorie and Susan Chapman with the Connaught and Battenberg children and Prince Waldemar of Prussia.
Elizabeth Francklin and Grand Duchess Olga Alexandrovna.
Frances Fry with Grand Duchess Maria and Grand Duke Dmitri.
Margaretta Eagar and Mary Ann Orchard with the Russian Grand Duchesses.
Margaretta Eagar and her four little Grand Duchesses.
Princess Elisabeth of Hesse and her father Grand Duke Ernst Ludwig.
Lilian Wilson with the Hereditary Grand Duke Georg Donatus of Hesse.
Norlander Lilian Eadie with Prince Ludwig of Hesse.
'Georgie' and 'Lu' of Hesse outside the playhouse at Wolfsgarten.
Prince Louis Ferdinand of Prussia.
Princes Moritz and Heinrich of Hesse-Cassel.
Prince Michael of Romania.
'Georgie' and 'Lu' with their toys.
Charlotte Bill, Princess Mary and Prince Henry of York.
Norlander Beatrice Halls with Prince Berthold of Baden.
Miss Brompton and the Italian royal children.
Saxton Winter.
Queen Wilhelmina of the Netherlands.
'Erzsi', Archduchess Elisabeth Marie of Austria.
May T.
Archduke Karl Stefan of Austria and his family.
The sons of Kaiser Wilhelm II.
Ada Leslie, governess to the three eldest Princes.
Mary Ann Orchard with Princess Alix of Hesse.
Prince Friedrich Wilhelm, 'Fritzie' of Hesse and his elder sisters.
Fritzie's deathbed.
The York children.

Lalla Bill with Prince John.
Winifred Thomas and her father Frederick, *c.* 1916.
Signed photograph of Prince John.
Princes Sigismund, Waldemar and Heinrich of Prussia.
Beatrice Todd in retirement.
Eliza Creak and Princess Alice of Albany.
Helene, Duchess of Albany with her children.
The children of King Alfonso XIII and Queen Ena of Spain.
Norlander Irene Collenette with Prince Alvaro of Orléans-Borbón.
Crown Princess Marie of Romania and children.
'Nana' Green with Princess Elizaveta and Marie of Romania.
Kate Fox, Princesses Olga and Elizabeth of Greece.
Emily Roose, Princesses Margarita and Theodora of Greece.
Marian Burgess's charges, Princesses Marie and Kira of Russia.
Margaret Alison with Princesses Olga, Marina and Elizabeth.
Marian Burgess with Prince Vladimir Kirillovich of Russia.
Irene Collenette with Prince Vladimir.
'Emily and her 4 Babys, St Moritz, Sep. 10th, 1917'.
Prince Tadashige Shimadzu as a child.
Tadashige and his brothers.
Khedive Ismael Pacha of Egypt with his son, the Grand Pacha Ibrahim.
Princess Zeyneb, the Khedive's daughter.
Anna Leonowens in later life.
Norland nurse Anne Chermside.
Rosalind Ramirez with King Faisal II of Iraq.
The Princess of Stolberg-Wernigerode with her children.
Mrs Hull in a bath chair given to her by Queen Victoria.
Lalla Bill aged 76.
Kate Fox in retirement, with Princesses Elizabeth and Marina, Princess Alexandra and Prince Michael of Kent.

Picture Credits

Royal Archives © Her Majesty Queen Elizabeth II: Mrs Thurston; Mrs Clark; the Chapmans; Eliza Creak; 'Emily and her 4 Babys'; 'Old May' Hull; Lalla Bill aged 76

Copyright Reserved: Kate Fox in retirement

© Staatsarchiv Darmstadt: Emma Hobbs; Margaretta Eagar, Mrs Orchard in carriage; Margaretta and children; Lilian Wilson; Lilian Eadie; 'Georgie' and 'Lu' (both pictures); Mrs Orchard and Princess Alix; 'Fritzie' album page

© The Royal Library, Copenhagen, Department of Maps, Prints and Photographs: Elizabeth Francklin with Grand Duchess Olga

© Royal House Archives, The Netherlands: Saxton Winter

© Orléans-Borbón Archives – Descendants of the Dukes of Montpensier: Irene Collenette with Prince Alvaro (ref. 12.05.006 EXENTO-11. *c.* 'Sep 1913'.Rosenau), with Prince Vladimir (ref. 12.05.0051.12)

© Brotherton Library, University of Leeds: Frances Fry with Maria and Dmitri

Norland College: Sigismund, Waldemar and Heinrich of Prussia; Beatrice Todd; Kate Fox with Olga and Elizabeth; Anne Chermside; Stolberg-Wernigerodes

Graf Heinrich von Spreti: 'Fritzie' of Hesse with his two sisters

Anne Sharp Collection: Winifred Thomas; signed photo of Prince John

Mr Konstantin Eggert: Rosalind Ramirez

Mr Francis Barnard: Ada Leslie

Private collection: all other photographs

Acknowledgements

I wish to thank Her Majesty The Queen for graciously allowing access to documents in the Royal Archives at Windsor and for permitting extracts from these documents to be published; also TRH The Duke of Kent and Princess Alexandra for allowing the use of Kate Fox's papers; HRH The Landgraf Moritz of Hesse for making documents available from the Hesse Family Archive in Darmstadt, and HRH Prince Philip, Duke of Edinburgh for looking kindly on the use of letters from that archive by Emily Roose, his nurse; also Princess Beatriz of Orléans-Borbón for photographs of Nurse Irene Collenette. I am grateful to Mr Robert Dimsdale, Mrs Anne Sharp, the Rt Hon. Lord Gisborough, Ms Sarah Williamson and Mr Thomas Murray, Mr Francis Barnard, Mrs Sylvia Parrett, Mr Colin Worley and Mr William Lyall, for allowing the use of material relating to their families and for providing information I could not have found otherwise.

The staff of a number of libraries and institutions have helped with documentary material. I would like to thank everyone at the Royal Archives for their friendliness, knowledge, encouragement and patience, tea, biscuits and birthday cakes; especially the Registrar, Pam Clark, Jill Kelsey and Allison Derrett, for fielding all sorts of obscure questions, Jenny Hurley for bringing out trolley-loads of documents, Frances Dimond, Curator of the Photograph Collection, and her assistant Lisa Heighway, for their help with illustrations. Professor E.G. Franz of the Hesse Family Archive in Darmstadt was equally helpful with this project and I look back with pleasure on a week spent in Darmstadt, nanny-hunting through the packets, boxes and albums he produced.

Larisa Kryachkova of the State Archive of the Russian Federation found some amazing material on the nurses in Russia; I'm grateful to her, also to Mrs Charlotte Eymael of the Koninklijk Huisarchief in the Netherlands for help with Saxton Elizabeth Winter, to Juan José Alonso and Rafael Villarreal of the Royal Archives in Madrid who answered my initial enquiries about Annie Dutton and produced mountains of information on nurses and governesses I had never even heard of. Jørgen Bjerregaard of the Ballerup Egnsmuseum in Denmark and Anne Dhyr of the Royal Danish Library in Copenhagen came up trumps with photographs of Elizabeth Francklin; and Richard Davies of the Leeds Russian Archive provided valuable information relating to Frances Fry.

I am grateful to the Trustees of the Bodleian Library for the use of letters from Queen Elisabeth of Romania to Professor Max Müller; to Mrs Anne Griffiths, Librarian to HRH The Duke of Edinburgh; to Christine Klössel, Archivist at Schloss Fasanerie and to P. Boswell Gibbs, the Archivist at Harrow School; to Dr Barbara Mortimer for permission to use her unpublished thesis on nurses in Edinburgh; to Professor Anthony Crosse for alerting me to his splendid articles on the earliest British nurses and governesses in Russia and to Gillian Long of the School of Slavonic and East European Studies for copying them for me; to Mrs K.M. Crosse, Principal of the Norland College and to Rebekeh Yeomans of Norland; to Helen Peacock of the Nord Anglia College for information on Princess Christian's, and to Miss Deborah Jenkins of the London Metropolitan Archive for help with the papers of the Governess's Benevolent Institution. Also, special thanks to cataloguer Keith Austin, whose knowledge of the GBI proved invaluable.

Material preserved by nurses and governesses to royalty often finds its way onto the market and a number of collectors and dealers have contributed to this book. I would like to thank Konstantin Eggert for material relating to Rosalind Ramirez, also Graf Heinrich von Spreti, John Wimbles, Ian Shapiro and Argyll Etkin, Helen Berger, Sophie Dupré and Harold Brown. Thanks too to Jörg Geller, Gerhard Hackelboerger and other German collectors for their cooperation with letters to Miss Byng; the accidental closure of an email account robbed me of their names but I still owe them my thanks.

Many people have offered help along the way. I am especially grateful to Ricardo Mateos Sainz de Medrano, Gerardo Kurtz, Ana Maria de Sagrora and José Luis Sampredo in Spain; to Olga Barkovets, Elena Yablochkina and Jane Sawyer for material from Russia; to Kirsti Sund in Finland; to Karen Roth-Nicholls, Marion Wynn, Coryne Hall, Diana de Courcy-Ireland, Geoffrey Swindells, David Horbury, Paul Minet, Robert Golden, Trond Norén Isaksen, Marianne Teerink, Arturo Beeche and Ilana Miller; Sue Woolmans and Katrina Warne must have photocopied every nanny reference in every book they own. I'd also like to thank Katrina for searching for information on Lilian Eadie and I'm more grateful to Sue for coming with me on research trips and undertaking others on her own. Thanks too to my mother for living with this book for so long; to my agents, Sheila Watson and Sugra Zaman, and my editors Jaqueline Mitchell and Alison Miles. And finally, because he doesn't believe I'll say it, thank you to John Osborn for keeping the grass cut so that I could go on writing. Without him, this house would be surrounded by impenetrable jungle!

Introduction

Where to begin? In reading about the royal families of the nineteenth and early twentieth centuries, it is hard to escape the English governess and the English nurse. Wherever you went in the world, it seems, from India to Russia, Spain to Japan, to the remote mountain kingdoms of the Balkans, there she was, dishing out the same plain diet of rice pudding, mutton and baked apples to her little princes and princesses; instilling the same simple precepts, insisting on the same standards, and noted the world over for her love of fresh air. She could be thousands of miles from home, cut off from home for the rest of her life, perhaps, but it didn't matter. 'Home' and all it stood for was a part of her being. She was calm, loving and strict. She stood no nonsense from anyone; Elizabeth Francklin, who was 'Nana' to a little Grand Duchess of Russia, thought nothing of leaning out of the palace window and ticking off a Russian general if he barked out his orders in too loud a voice – and they always obeyed. The English nurse or governess at her best provided a cushion of stability no matter what was happening around her. Royal authors would often refer to the 'inevitable' English nurse (or governess), as if not having one was unthinkable.

They intrigued me, these women. Who were they? Why did they go so far and what was it like for them to inhabit a world so different from anything their own backgrounds could have prepared them for; a world of kings and queens and royal Courts and children who, in some parts of the world, held the power of life or death over adult slaves. And what was so special about them that people who could afford the very best in childcare looked to Britain to provide it? Even today, many women would hesitate to go abroad alone, yet the nurses and governesses crossed continents, long before the advent of modern communications (or plumbing). The practical difficulties alone must have been overwhelming, never mind the loneliness and the danger. It was to satisfy this curiosity that I started collecting anecdotes, photographs, references, names; then published memoirs by the women themselves, and once you start . . .

All research is a journey and it is wise not to be too sure of the destination at the outset. This book was to have included the pooled experience of sixty-eight women, all of whom worked at Courts overseas. But the further I went, the wider and deeper the pool became and women who worked at the British Court were inexorably drawn in. Today there are nearly 250 nurses and governesses treading water in it and who knows? I'm certain there are many families in this country with memories of a relative who was nurse or governess to someone royal. Some may preserve photographs and letters along with the memories and someone out there probably knows the answers to questions about individual nurses and governesses that have defeated me, but finding them? That journey could last a lifetime.

In drawing together stories from the pool, published accounts were a good starting point, giving a broad picture of the lives and experiences of royal nurses and governesses. But a starting point only: beyond these the royal side of the story is supplied by letters; letters sent home, letters written by the nurse or governess to her royal employer in the course of her duties, which say so much about their work and about the children they cared for. Then there are letters written by a royal family to their nurse or governess. The convention used to be that such correspondence was returned to the writer on the recipient's death and adherence to this has allowed the survival of some fascinating material: the letters of the Waldeck family to 'Nana' Smith, for example, or the suitcase of royal correspondence treasured by the redoubtable Kate Fox and bequeathed by her to her princesses. Kate's letters from Princess Nicholas of Greece provide a running commentary on the royal nurseries of Europe in the early twentieth century, on nurses, parents and children. Where the convention was not adhered to, other documents have found their way onto the open market as the generation that understood and valued them died away; these are preserved today in private collections.

Then there are official papers. At larger royal Courts records of salaries, travel expenses, pensions and so on were kept by the relevant offices. Where these papers survive they supply another important aspect of the story of working for royalty. Details of how any individual found her employment are rare, so it was exciting to find that the State Archive in Moscow holds a complete file on the nurse Margaretta Eagar, even including her letters of reference.

But from the outset it seemed important to move away from the royal story into the private worlds of the nurses and governesses, to answer the questions of identity and background. For this there is no alternative to the standard sources of family history: the registers of births, marriages and deaths kept by the General Register Office in England and Wales since 1837; parish registers;

the England and Wales census returns from 1841 to 1901; newspapers, directories and the like. These things have been made more accessible by the rising popularity of family history and a corresponding rise in internet sites offering resources for researchers. At one time it was impossible to find someone on a census unless you had some inkling of where they lived; the steady increase of census surname indexes is making the task much easier now and it is possible to check findings from the census against other sources to give some form of confirmation. Attempting to trace the families of over 200 women was probably insane, but it did turn up some fascinating stories.

Family history is a chancy business, though. Some individuals and families are easy to trace, some never give up their secrets. It has been possible to establish basic family histories for many of the leading characters in this book and for a few minor ones, but others continue to tantalise. I would love to know more about Nana Bell, for example, whose long career in royal service started in Russia and Greece in the early 1900s and continued in Yugoslavia in the 1920s. In 1931 she was still overseas and still angling for a new royal position, though she was said to be in her early sixties. She had a house in Harrogate, but was that where she came from? Without a Christian name it proved impossible to find out. The governess Ethel Howard eluded me too, though she left what should have been ample clues to her background, and all attempts to pin down the identity of May T – who published an anonymous account of her adventures in Poland, Hungary, Austria and Italy – proved futile.

All research has its frustrations and the language we use poses problems of its own – as Ethel Howard discovered when she tried to introduce five young Japanese princes to the custom of afternoon tea. She raised each article on the table, speaking its name clearly for the boys to repeat, but made the mistake of adding 'sit up, don't fidget' as she lifted the teacup. It took her months to dispel the notion of the 'teacup–sit-up–don't-fidget'. Extra sensitivities attach to language now that she would never have recognised. When a prospective employer overseas looked for an 'English' nurse or governess in the nineteenth or early twentieth century she did not necessarily want someone from England. Scottish and Irish women were equally prized for their skills in childcare. In other countries they were invariably referred to as 'English', but no insult was intended or taken and they were never expected to deny their own special heritage. Modern sensitivities require the use of 'British' but it would be wrong to read any darker significance into the old usage.

Language changes with time. Today we automatically use 'nanny' for the woman who cares for children. The correct term in the nineteenth century, and back into the very roots of English, was 'nurse'. 'Nanny', or more usually

'Nana', was used informally in families as a pet name and my guess is that, like 'Mama' and 'Papa', it came from the children's first attempts to speak to the person in charge. 'Nanny' took over gradually, as hospital nursing developed and its members claimed 'nurse' for themselves. Throughout this book I have used 'nurse' because that is what the women themselves would have used and some, particularly the college-trained nurses of the early twentieth century, actively disliked being called 'Nanny'.

Countries change too. Siam, where Anna Leonowens taught the children of a king, is Thailand now, Emily Payne's Burma is Myanmar – names they would not understand. And the names and titles of royalty pose another set of problems. Writing about the Russian imperial family in previous books I've used the accurate translation of titles favoured by recent Russian writers: 'Grand Prince' and 'Princess' instead of the older and more accepted 'Grand Duke' and 'Duchess'. Here though, because the book is written from a very 'English' point of view, that became too unwieldy. The nurses and governesses used 'Grand Duke' and so have I – while retaining the Russian name forms, 'Mikhail' for 'Michael' and so on – to help identify the country concerned. But British women in Germany tended to write of the 'Kaiser' and 'Kaiserin', not the 'Emperor' and 'Empress' and again I have followed them, though this dictates that Queen Victoria's eldest daughter must end her life as 'Kaiserin Friedrich' instead of the more familiar 'Empress Frederick'. For the same reason, all dates in the text are given according to the modern Western calendar, though this was not in use at the time in all of the countries concerned.

Some may question the exclusion of two familiar names from recent British history: Clara Knight, who was nurse to Queen Elizabeth II and her sister (and to their mother before them) and Marion Crawford, 'Crawfie', their governess. This happened naturally because at the outset this book was about British nurses and governesses to foreign royalty. Queen Victoria and her daughters and granddaughters were drawn in because they were so active in employing these women and in finding places for them at other Courts: until the First World War the network of royal nurses and governesses was worldwide and proved too closely entwined to separate Britain out. But during that war and as a consequence of it the British royal family set themselves apart and the nurses and governesses they employed afterwards seem to me to be part of another network, that of the British aristocracy. I found two points of contact only: Kate Fox, who in later life had an interest in the nurseries of 'her' children's children, including the young Kents in England; and Rosalind Ramirez, nursery governess to the present Duke of Gloucester and his elder brother Prince William: she who was previously governess to King Faisal II of Iraq.

In the 1860s Emma Bailie went to Darmstadt in Germany as under-nurse to the great-nephews and nieces of the Grand Duke of Hesse. She would have been about twenty-five years old. In 1872 she was taken on by the Grand Duke's niece Marie, Princess Gustav of Erbach-Schönberg. Emma cared for all the Princess's four children but her principal charge was the second son Maximilian, 'Maxi', a profoundly handicapped boy who was bedridden all his life. Maxi never spoke, never smiled, never showed the least sign of recognition and was subject to recurrent fits, but his mother adored him. When he died at the age of thirteen she appointed Emma, his faithful nurse, as her housekeeper. The two women stayed together until the death of the Princess's husband in 1908, after which she could no longer afford her large household and many servants were pensioned off. Emma, then in her sixties, went back to England but found that neither she nor the Princess could bear the separation. So she returned to Germany and kept house for her Princess as before. She remained through the First World War, an Englishwoman abroad obeying a human loyalty deeper than the ties of nationhood. She endured the increasing privations and food shortages suffered by all Germans and finally died from their effects in 1919, in her seventy-fourth year.

This book is not about the British nation or British officialdom imposing its values on the world; it traces something infinitely more human and more subtle. The nurses and governesses were stubbornly individual. Officialdom had no say in where they went or what they did. When it tried to muscle in, very late in the day, it was treated with the same stern disdain as Mrs Francklin's loud Russian general. And though the women who worked overseas were and remained adamantly 'English', in their sense of the word, they also received and responded to influences from the places where they went and the people they worked among, often without their knowing. They developed new affections and new ties. In the world of men there is a relationship said to be quintessentially English, a profound friendship and understanding born of mutual dependence which crosses the barriers of class and status: the gentleman and his valet, the officer and his soldier-servant. We recognise it in history, particularly in personal accounts of Britain's wars, and in literature, in such diverse partnerships as Jeeves and Wooster or Frodo and Sam. Look at Emma Bailie and the Princess of Erbach-Schönberg, and others like them, and you have the precise equivalent in the world of women, but often crossing nationalities as well as classes.

This book is about those women: about royal women, obliged by custom and convention to hand their children into others' care from the moment of birth, and so forced to share their children's affections, and about the ordinary women who took on that care and received that affection. But the parallel is closer than it might appear because many of the ordinary women, particularly the nurses, had themselves been obliged to entrust their children to others in order to earn a living. At least two were brought up in orphanages because their own mothers, left widowed at an early age, could not afford to care for them. Two more grew up overseas because their grandfather's disgrace left their father disinherited. Their background was aristocratic; they might have expected to employ nurses in adult life but instead they became nurses themselves. The story of the royal nurses and governesses turns out to be a kaleidoscope of women's lives.

Charlotte Zeepvat
Sussex, 2006

ONE

Two Beginnings

THE FIRST NURSES – AND A FEW
GOVERNESSES TOO

St Petersburg, Friday 13 March 1891; in the fading light of the northern afternoon a procession drew out of the Winter Palace and onto Palace Square, turning down towards the Admiralty Embankment. It was a funeral. The hearse emerged first from the Palace's high, ornamental gates; horse-drawn, glass-sided, with the coffin hidden beneath a mountain of flowers, which made a vivid splash of colour on an otherwise leaden day. In the Russian winter, with snow still lying on the ground, the sight of those flowers, imported from the south, or taken from the imperial hothouses, would have been enough to make passers-by pause and wonder: the appearance of the chief mourners would have frozen them where they stood. They were led by the Tsar himself, His Imperial Majesty Alexander III, Emperor and Autocrat of all the Russias, flanked by his four brothers: Grand Duke Vladimir, Governor of the city and Commander of the Military District of St Petersburg; Grand Duke Alexei, Admiral-General of the Russian Fleet; Grand Duke Sergei, Commander of the Preobrazhensky Regiment and soon to be appointed Governor-General of Moscow; Grand Duke Pavel, Commander of the Grodno Hussars – four of the wealthiest and most powerful men in the world, on foot, walking with bowed heads through the snow. It was a rare thing to see them together, like this, in the open. Ten years ago to the day their father, Tsar Alexander II, was assassinated by a terrorist not a mile from the spot and the security surrounding his family had been rigorous ever since. But for this funeral they took the risk, and not the men only: behind, in carriages, came their wives, sisters and daughters, the Tsaritsa and the Grand Duchesses of Russia. Who could have been held worthy of such a tribute? A member of the imperial family? A minister, perhaps, or high-ranking courtier?

No. The hearse contained the remains of an ordinary Englishwoman, Catherine 'Kitty' Strutton; a bricklayer's daughter from Hackney who had nursed Alexander III and his younger brothers and sister from the day of his birth. Twice in her life Kitty Strutton was carried to church unaware by those who loved her, but when George Strutton and his wife Elizabeth took their baby daughter to St John's Church in Hackney for her christening, in October 1811, they could not possibly have imagined how and where her life would end. They might have laughed if anyone suggested it; to them, the Tsar's Court in St Petersburg would have been as remote and unreal as Hy-Bresil or the Gardens of the Hesperides. Yet Kitty lived in that Court over half her life. She brought up a generation of princes and knew them as no one else could, and they loved her as one of their own.

Russian Court memoirs of the 1840s and '50s contain innumerable glimpses of Kitty at work, separating squabbling princes, tending their ailments and bathing the babies. In some ways the children's lifestyle was extraordinary; a watercolour of 1858 shows the only girl among Kitty's charges, five-year-old Grand Duchess Maria Alexandrovna, on an outing in the park at Tsarskoe Selo. The little girl rides in a child-sized replica of an open landau, detail-perfect with its brass lamps and quilted upholstery, drawn by a miniature pony. She holds the reins but real control is exercised by two liveried grooms, one on each side, each with a firm grip on the pony's collar. A palace footman, also in livery, walks behind, and a woman, possibly Kitty but more likely the child's aristocratic governess, Countess Tolstoy, looks down and speaks to her. Few five-year-olds would have taken the air in such state, but Kitty was in the privileged position of seeing the private world behind the façade, where the imperial family was just like any other family. Anna Tiutcheva, the Empress's maid-of-honour, described a typical evening. She was sitting with her mistress when Kitty brought in the baby: 'Maria Aleksandrovna, chirping like a little bird. . . . The Tsar came in, the little darling stretched out her arms to him, and he picked her up tenderly. It was heart warming,' Anna said, 'to see them so kind and loving . . . to see them made of the same human clay.'[1]

When Kitty retired, the imperial family provided her with an apartment of her own in the Winter Palace and a little house near to their country residence at Tsarskoe Selo. In this way, they could look after her and she could get to know new generations of 'her' children. But she never forgot where she came from. At Maria's wedding in 1874, Alexander II told Queen Victoria's representatives about his family's 'excellent English nurse', who 'was so overjoyed when she heard that her darling was to marry an English Prince!'[2] Kitty maintained an interest in the nurseries too. In 1876 she found a position at Court for her great-niece Millicent Crofts in the nursery of Grand Duke Vladimir's children and she may well have done the same for other relatives. Tsaritsa Maria Feodorovna, Alexander III's wife, mentioned the presence of

Kitty's nephews and nieces at the funeral in a letter to her son. Millicent nursed the Vladimir children for ten years. Then she vanished, during Christmas week at the palace of Gatchina. One minute she was there, the next . . . The children were told nothing except that she would come back, though she never did. But Kitty knew. On 27 December 1886 she sent their mother a formal – too formal – letter of thanks for a gift, adding, 'I shall be pleased to receive poor Millie.'[3] For the rest it remained a mystery for twenty-five years.

Kitty Strutton lived to be almost eighty. When she died in her bed at the Winter Palace the news even reached the Court Circular in *The Times*, which noted, 'Their Imperial Majesties were unremitting in their personal and affectionate attentions to the deceased.'[4] And the imperial family were not the only prominent people to attend Kitty's funeral in St Petersburg's English Church. Lady Morier, the British Ambassador's wife, was there with her daughter, as were the embassy staff and leading members of the British community. Their presence signalled the importance of a woman whom, in other circumstances, they would never have noticed at all. No official report mentioned the members of Kitty's own family who attended the funeral; the Tsar and his brothers were the chief mourners who accompanied Kitty on her last journey, to the Smolenska Cemetery on Vassilevsky Island. 'How many cherished memories go to the tomb with her,' Alexander III remarked to his brother Sergei when she died; 'a whole era of our lives. . . . I am terribly sad.'[5]

Kitty's story is a vivid illustration of the opportunities childcare could offer to a woman in the early years of the nineteenth century. No other career could have taken a bricklayer's daughter so far or allowed her to experience and achieve so much. But the path that took her from Hackney to the Court of the Tsar is lost. Kitty was thirty-four when she arrived at the Winter Palace and she must have been an experienced nurse whom someone important was willing to recommend – vacancies in royal nurseries were almost always filled by word of mouth. She had received an elementary education at least: her letter to Grand Duchess Vladimir is in a perfectly formed and regular hand, straight from the copybook, though her youngest brother could not even sign his name.[6] It seems likely that she went into service in her early teens, as a nursery maid or under-nurse. Her elder brother William Strutton, Millicent's grandfather, was a grown man when Kitty was still a little girl and he worked as a coachman in one of the wealthier parts of London. He may have found her a good place; from this, or from whatever first position she had, her advancement would have been a matter of skill, hard work, and the willingness to snatch the opportunity when it came.

Kitty's career as a royal nurse began on 10 March 1845, the day Grand Duke Alexander Alexandrovich, the future Alexander III, was born. She succeeded another Englishwoman, a Miss Isherwood, who was nurse to his elder brother, Grand Duke Nikolai. Miss Isherwood died in service; the boys' elder sister, Grand Duchess Alexandra Alexandrovna, was nursed by a Miss Hughes, and both women seem to have come from the British community resident in St Petersburg. An intriguing pair of entries in the register of the English Church points to this and may also explain what became of Miss Hughes. On 24 January 1852 baby twins Thomasina and Jane Alex Isherwood were baptised in the church with the six-year-old Grand Duke Alexander as Thomasina's godfather. Jane Alex was sponsored even more regally: Empress Alexandra Feodorovna, wife of Tsar Nicholas I, and her nineteen-year-old son, Grand Duke Mikhail Nikolaevich, stood as her godparents. The twins' parents were Thomas Isherwood and his wife Margaret, born Margaret Hughes; the imperial presence at the christening suggests that Margaret may have been Miss Hughes the imperial nurse, married to a relative of her former colleague.

Miss Hughes, Miss Isherwood and Kitty Strutton were part of a long tradition. There were English nurses at the Russian Court over half a century before their time, in the late 1700s: Grand Duke Alexander Pavlovich, the future Tsar Alexander I, and his brother Konstantin were nursed by sisters Pauline Gessler and Sarah Nichols. These two, probably the first English nurses at any overseas royal Court, seem to have been the daughters of John Primrose, a grandson of the first Lord Rosebery. When John's father Archibald Primrose was executed for his part in the Jacobite rebellion of 1745 and his estates forfeit, John was forced to take his family and seek service overseas; like many 'English' nurses and governesses who came after them, Pauline and Sarah were actually from Scotland.[7]

Pauline took care of Alexander, who was born in 1777. She married his valet, Johann Gessler, and both were held in very high esteem at the Russian Court. Alexander's tutor La Harpe called Pauline 'a woman of rare quality who . . . inspired in Alexander the first of those good habits that set him apart'.[8] Both sisters were described in the journal of Baroness Elizabeth Dimsdale, who visited Russia with her husband in the summer of 1781. Baron Thomas Dimsdale was a doctor and a pioneer in the technique of inoculation against smallpox, and this was his second visit. In 1768 he had been asked to inoculate Catherine the Great, on the strength of a book he had written on the subject. The inoculation was a success; he performed the same operation on her son, the future Tsar Paul, and was awarded the hereditary title 'Baron of Russia'. He returned in 1781 to inoculate her grandsons Alexander and

Konstantin and he and his wife spent a month at Court, where Elizabeth became very friendly with the two nurses, particularly Pauline, whom they called 'Polly' or, in Russian, 'Prascovia Ivanovna'.

The little Grand Dukes lived in considerable state. Their younger brother Grand Duke Nikolai Pavlovich, the future Tsar Nicholas I, recalled, with unconscious irony, 'Our childhood was much like that of any other child, apart from the matter of court etiquette. . . . From the moment of birth, each child was allotted a nanny, two night maids, four chambermaids, a nurse, two valets, two footmen, eight domestic servants and eight drivers.'[9] There was no mention of a nursery as such: three-year-old Alexander and Konstantin, who had just turned two when the Dimsdales visited Russia, each had their own apartments. According to Elizabeth Dimsdale the annual clothing allowance for each boy was 30,000 roubles – about £6,000 in the values of the day. If she was right about this figure it is quite extraordinary. At the same time, she says, an army colonel received 300 roubles a year and an ordinary soldier 7, 4 of which went to buy his uniform.

The children's toys that were shown to Elizabeth Dimsdale, 'were really beyond any thing that can be imagined for Expence. There were two silver Barges with Clockwork in the inside, and two Men in the middle to appear as if they were rowing, after they were wound up they would swim upon the Water for a considerable time, and there were a great many expensive things, some all Gold, that I am certain if I were to say they cost two thousand Pounds I very much under value them, and the Empress is continually giving them more, she is excessively fond of them and cannot refuse them any thing they ask for.'[10] But in the midst of all this outrageous luxury were two very normal, appealing little boys whose mother had given an order that they were never to be addressed by their titles 'as she said Pride would come fast enough without encouraging it'.[11]

That was about as far as the mother's authority went, for the Empress had assumed complete control of her grandsons' lives. She gave instructions on every aspect of their upbringing and even designed clothes for them. Elizabeth Dimsdale watched Pauline Gessler undress Alexander one evening and thought his outfit 'very clever' – presumably there was something unusual in the way it was fastened or arranged. When the Dimsdales were preparing to leave, Pauline offered to give the Baroness one of Alexander's best outfits, 'and to add to the value of it, she put it in Prince Alexander's hand, desiring him to give it to me himself with a kiss,' Elizabeth said. 'I likewise had his Cap, and Prince Constantine's Coat in the same manner.'[12] The Empress wrote books of history and stories to be used in her grandchildren's education. She consulted Thomas

Dimsdale on the upbringing of other royal children, especially in England. When he returned home he spoke to Mrs Cheveley, who was nurse to the younger daughters of George III and had been wet nurse to their brother Prince Ernest; with her help he produced a detailed description of the English royal nursery's routines for the Empress.

It seems almost certain that it began with Catherine the Great, the idea that English (and Scottish and Irish) women provided the best childcare money could buy. In the course of the next century it would take the world by storm, but the little Grand Dukes of Russia seem to have been the very first foreign royal children to be nursed by British women. Catherine employed 'English' governesses for her grandchildren too: Alexander and Konstantin's sisters were taught English and Italian by a Miss Ramsbottom, who left them to marry Reverend Kennedy, one of the chaplains at the English Church. She would return to Court later as a widow, after the Empress's death, to nurse the youngest brother, Grand Duke Mikhail Pavlovich. These appointments were in tune with Catherine's whole policy of modernising her country by attracting to Russia the best practitioners of medicine, sciences and the arts that Europe could offer. She gave positive encouragement to foreign business people and industrialists too, and she seems to have had a particular liking for the British. Baroness Dimsdale certainly thought so. 'It is said the Empress is very partial to the English, and I really am of that Opinion from her having so many English in her Service', she observed, going on to note the British people she had met during her visit: the Empress's physician Dr Rogerson, the Governors of Kronstadt and Riga, the imperial nurses, the gardener, artists, even the imperial watchmaker.[13] And where the Empress led, others followed.

Alexander and Konstantin were in their late teens when their mother produced Nikolai, her third son, born in the last months of his grandmother's life. Catherine the Great took over his upbringing for those few months and for him too she chose an 'English' nurse (from Scotland), Jane Lyon, known in Russia as 'Evgenia Vasilevna'. In later years Nikolai would call her his 'lioness'. Jane was the daughter of a sculptor who worked under Catherine's architect Charles Cameron, and there must have been something very striking about her. She was only seventeen when the Empress appointed her, far too young to have had any experience to offer. What she did have was courage, a clear sense of right and wrong and the determination to stand up to anyone in Nikolai's interest – a quality that would become famous in later generations of British nurses.

Nikolai was still a baby when his grandmother died and his father became Tsar Paul. His mother, Empress Maria Feodorovna, finally in control of her own children, introduced some changes to his routine. For all her desire to discourage pride in her elder sons, Maria Feodorovna retained a keen sense of who and what her offspring were, and she insisted that Nikolai be treated as a child apart – an emperor's child. Twice a day Jane had to lead him to his mother in a stately procession with a full retinue of Court ladies and servants in attendance, among them the formidable Countess Lieven, the aristocratic governess of the imperial children and Jane's immediate superior. The Empress had given orders that Nikolai should not mix with ordinary children; one day, on his way to his mother, he spotted an older boy, the son of one of the ladies, and broke ranks to grab hold of his hand. Countess Lieven was horrified and tried to separate them but Nikolai threw such a tantrum that Jane Lyon stepped in, 'took all responsibility on herself with her usual courage, and allowed the two children to proceed hand in hand to the august presence of the Empress'.[14] At first this disregard of protocol did not please the Empress, but the situation was defused by the Tsar. He was amused and took a liking to the other boy – as his wife did, once she got over the shock. From this day Nikolai was allowed to play with other children.

Jane Lyon's appointment lasted seven years. She taught Nikolai his letters – in Russian as well as English – and introduced him to the literature, history and traditions of her own country, which would always fascinate him. She taught him the Lord's Prayer in Russian, so she said, and had a lasting influence on his politics. In this case, though, her influence was less helpful. As a girl of fifteen, Jane Lyon had been caught up in a popular rising in Warsaw. She saw Russians murdered on the streets and was taken prisoner with a group of about thirty women. They were held for days by the rebels without food or even the most basic facilities, until an English lord managed to persuade their captors to move them somewhere more suitable. Still they were not free, and they remained in fear of their lives for seven months until General Suvorov came to their rescue. Stories of Jane's sufferings in those months and of the cruelties she witnessed were woven through Nikolai's earliest memories and he would later say that they fired a lasting hatred of the Polish people.

He adored Jane Lyon, though, and she him. 'Her attachment to her august charge amounted to a passion,' a contemporary said, 'a fanaticism, which she retained to the end of her days.'[15] In 1802 Nikolai was handed over to a tutor, a severe man who subjected him to vicious beatings. Jane provided a refuge for him until her own position at Court became untenable. After seven years with Nikolai she was still only twenty-four and very attractive. The tutor began to pursue her. When she declined his advances he became increasingly aggressive and offensive. When she still refused he grew dangerous. In 1803 she accepted a proposal of marriage from another man and left the Court, with a gratuity of 2,000 silver roubles and an annual pension of 600.[16] Nikolai never ceased to love her and in later years he provided for her daughter and granddaughter. As a widow, Jane returned to live under his roof, in a suite of rooms in St Petersburg's Anichkov Palace where she would regularly hold tea parties for Nikolai – Tsar Nicholas I as he then was – and his family.

Jane Lyon often crossed her Russian superiors. She often annoyed Empress Maria. But her skill was unchallenged and the idea that British nurses were the best had survived the death of Catherine the Great. Paul and Maria's youngest son, Mikhail Pavlovich, was born two years into his father's reign and he was nursed by Mrs Kennedy, the former Miss Ramsbottom. She was noted for her fierce temper but Mikhail loved her and he and Nikolai regularly argued over who had the better nurse. In the next generation, Eugenia Christie became nurse to Nicholas I's older son Alexander Nikolaevich, the future Tsar Alexander II, and his sisters. She left to marry in 1830 and was given a gratuity of 2,000 roubles – the same payment Jane Lyon had received on marriage – and a higher pension than Jane's, of 900 roubles.[17]

With the passage of time the nursery establishments employed by the imperial family became smaller. Gone was the idea that each child needed its own apartment and a complete retinue of attendants: Nicholas I's children were treated as one family in a much more relaxed setting. Lady Londonderry visited them at Tsarskoe Selo in the autumn of 1836 and she described a dinner party in the Alexander Palace, at the end of which the youngest children, the little Grand Dukes Nikolai and Mikhail Nikolaevich, were brought into the room. 'They seemed very happy,' she said, 'quite at their ease rolling on the floor. Their attendants were all English. An old Scotch nurse made acquaintance with me and spoke of the whole family with enthusiastic affection. She had been with them nineteen years, said they were angels as good as they were handsome and the Empress a model to all as a mother and a wife. She concluded by declaring that they all doted on her and could not exist without her; that she kept their money, their jewels, etc. and had charge of everything.' Lady Londonderry was impressed. 'This old lady', she remarked, 'seemed quite a character.'[18]

And when the children were old enough, Nicholas I employed Englishwomen among their governesses as his grandmother had done. His youngest daughter Alexandra Nikolaevna had two English governesses, Miss Brown and Miss Higgenbottom, whom the family called 'Miss Higg'. Miss Higg became deeply attached to her charge. Alexandra Nikolaevna fell seriously ill shortly after her marriage in 1844 and during her first pregnancy, probably with tuberculosis. She 'expressed a wish to see her "Miss" again, and Miss came and sat by the bed of her "dear little girl", never again to leave her.'[19] With Miss Higgenbottom at her side, sharing the nursing with one of the maids, Alexandra gave birth to a seven-month child and slipped away during the following night, a lasting anguish to her family.

British governesses, like nurses, seem to have found their first overseas postings in Russia and their great opportunity in Catherine the Great's drive to modernise. One of the earliest Russian travel books was written by a governess, Elizabeth Justice, who went to Russia in 1734 to escape a thieving husband, and worked in the household of a prominent English merchant in St Petersburg. With the fashion for all things 'English' it was natural that others would follow and that wealthy Russian families would seek them out. By 1830, almost a century after Elizabeth Justice, the figure of the English governess was so well established in Russian society that she was celebrated in Russian fiction: Alexander Pushkin wrote a humorous story about a Miss Jackson, working for an eccentric Russian family. At around the same time a German traveller, J.G. Kohl, described the steady trail of young hopefuls, English among them, who disembarked annually on the quays of St Petersburg, 'with torn veils and ruffled head-gear. . . . Exhausted by sea-sickness, saddened by home-sickness, frightened by the bearded Russians who greet their eyes in Cronstadt, and pierced through and through by the chill breath of a St Petersburg May, they issue from their cabins, pale, timid, and slow, anxiety and white fear upon their lips, and despair in their eyes.'[20]

This is very much a man's view and perhaps a rather mischievous one. Kohl conceded that foreign governesses were highly valued in Russia and received better pay and treatment than they could hope for at home – this was the attraction that made the journey worthwhile. And those who did take the adventure were often happy to stay. But in the governess stakes the English would always have rivals. Kohl's pitiful, bedraggled newcomers included German, Swiss and French girls who had their own languages to offer and who would always compete for the best positions. It was different with nurses. By the 1830s, as Kohl himself said, the English nurse had no rivals: 'the bonnes, or nursery-maids, for the younger children in St Petersburg, must be English, who, by general consent, are pronounced better suited for the office than those of any other nation'.[21]

And so the fashion was established. A decade more, and we are back with Miss Hughes, Miss Isherwood and Kitty Strutton, and by their day British nurses and governesses were making a name for themselves in other overseas

Courts, particularly in some of the German states. Their influence, like their individual reputations, must have spread by word of mouth, by families travelling with their nurses and governesses, by contact between Courts; perhaps also by the Grand Duchesses of Russia who left their country as brides with memories of the Englishwomen who had taught and cared for them. It was the beginning.

But the story of the British royal nurse has a second beginning, and it came when the first nurse held and cared for each individual baby. Kitty Strutton took Alexander III into her arms on the day he was born. She saw him and his younger brothers and sister through from birth to adulthood and in this she was unusual; in the language of the day she was a 'permanent' nurse, whereas, in most royal households where the British practice was followed, the first nurse to care for each newborn baby was a so-called 'monthly' nurse. Her appointment began with the birth or in the weeks leading up to it and ended when the baby was settled and thriving; then she would hand over to a 'permanent' nurse like Kitty. 'Monthly' nursing was an avenue of the profession developed by women who wanted to specialise and did not want to settle in one family. A healthy baby would never have remembered its monthly nurse, though for particularly delicate babies the monthly nurse would sometimes agree to stay longer and some built up relationships with the mothers they served, returning for each new birth. The skill that set the monthly nurse apart was that she had some hospital training.

Mrs Clark, who entered the British royal household in 1840 as monthly nurse to the newborn Princess Royal, might have had a story similar to Kitty's had it not been for a romantic disaster. Five years older than Kitty, Mrs Clark became nursemaid at the age of eighteen in a well-to-do household in Hertfordshire. This was the conventional route; the nursemaid trained in service under a nurse until she was skilled enough to obtain a nurse's position in her own right. But after two years, Mrs Clark left to be married. It was a mistake. 'Her husband proved a very cruel & dissolute man, who so ill treated her, that after the birth of the first and only child, she left him.' The husband appealed for help to her former employer, Mrs Hanking, who took his side and put pressure on Mrs Clark to go back, saying that this was a wife's duty. Mrs Clark gave in. She returned to her husband but he had not changed. When she left him for the second time, four years after their wedding, she took their son right away where he could not find them.

For the next five years Mrs Clark worked as nurse to a lawyer's family in Bedford Square in London. Then, in 1837 or thereabouts, she took on the sickly child of a major and his wife in Connaught Square, but this was not a full-time position. Mrs Clark had obviously decided to specialise, perhaps because it was not in her interest to stay in one place for too long. She started working at the Lying-In Hospital in London where poorer women went to give birth. She trained on the job, presumably paying her way with her work and with whatever was left of her earnings from other appointments, once she had fed and clothed her son. Dr Locock, who was associated with the Lying-In Hospital, had ample opportunity to see her at work and he developed a high regard for her skills. He often recommended her to families with a sick child in need of care. He recommended her to the royal family too, being one of their physicians, and it is his testimonial written for Prince Albert which preserves the details of her story. 'She is very skilful and clean with children,' he wrote, 'most attentive and active in her duties – very humble minded and anxious to please, very good tempered, and indifferent to trouble or fatigue.'[22] He could have added that she was a very strong-minded woman, as she undoubtedly was, to survive the disaster in her personal life and go on to achieve so much.

But there is a mystery. The testimonial is headed 'Dr Locock concerning Mrs Roberts (Mrs Clark)', with the clear implication that the two names refer to the same person. Its date is 27 November 1840, six days after the birth of the Princess Royal. The doctor makes no further mention of Mrs Roberts; the career described in the testimonial is Mrs Clark's career, yet other documents of the 1840s do not refer to a monthly nurse named Mrs Clark working in the household. They tell only of a Mrs Roberts, who was monthly nurse to the Princess Royal in 1840 and was also present at the christening of the Princess's brother, the future King Edward VII. One reference implies that Mrs Roberts upset Prince Albert, and the testimonial itself ends, 'Dr Locock would not have ventured to name her to His Royal Highness for so important a charge, had he not felt sure that she was well adapted for it', which suggests a degree of unease about her. In the early 1840s there were arguments between the royal couple about the management of the nursery and this may have been part of them. Queen Victoria continued to think well of Mrs Roberts and she noted with some sadness in 1849 that the nurse had died.[23] On such slender evidence no one could be certain, but it seems possible that the Mrs Clark who was recommended by Dr Locock was allowed to work in the household under the name of 'Mrs Roberts' because of her family circumstances. She and her son did not want to be found, and the name of a nurse working for the royal family could easily be mentioned in print. The sudden appearance of a 'very cruel & dissolute man' demanding his rights would be in no one's interest.

Twenty years later, though, the royal family did employ a monthly nurse named Mrs Clark (sometimes spelt with a final 'e'), and she attended several notable births and travelled to Germany on demand. She is first mentioned in the spring of 1863, when the Queen's daughter Princess Alice came home for the birth of her first child. Mrs Clark arrived at Windsor on 25 March; on 4 April she attended the Princess during her labour, assisting Dr Locock, and sent for the Queen when the birth was imminent. Immediately afterwards, it was Mrs Clark who performed the duty that always attended the birth of a royal child. 'The Baby, wrapped in the velvet & ermine cloak, in which all our children had been carried,' the Queen wrote, 'was taken by Mrs Clark into the next room, where Ld Sydney, Sir G. Grey & Baron Ricci were assembled'; the nurse displayed the baby to the waiting ministers.[24] Mrs Clark also carried baby Victoria of Hesse at her christening three weeks later and was given a brooch by the Queen in recognition of her service.

Later the same year, Mrs Clark attended Princess Marie of Leiningen, and at the beginning of 1864 she was called on to take care of the most important baby in the country, the eldest son of the Prince of Wales and second in line to the throne, Prince Albert Victor. He caused great consternation by his premature appearance at Frogmore on 8 January. Hurrying from Osborne when the telegram came, the Queen found 'All in such agitation' and a house full of doctors. 'Lady Macclesfield acted as nurse,' she wrote, 'in every sense of the word. There were no clothes for the poor little boy, who was just wrapped in cotton wool. The Doctors only arrived 2 hours after & the nurse not till 1 in the morning. The child, though decidedly a 7 months one & very small, is very healthy & perfectly formed, a pretty little thing with a fine forehead & good round head, beautiful eyes & a marked nose. The Doctors assure us that if it is kept warm & takes plenty of nourishment it ought to do as well as any other child.'[25] The baby was still wrapped in cotton wool when the Queen saw him, and in the arms of the nurse Ellen Innocent, who frequently attended royal births, but Mrs Clark arrived that day to take him over. The Queen returned to the house a few days later and saw little Albert Victor, 'whom good Mrs Clark watches over most anxiously'.[26]

A premature birth like this was always a worry. A generation later, in Russia in September 1891, the life of Grand Duke Pavel's only son Dmitri, another seven-month child, was saved by the quick thinking of his sister's English nurse, Frances Fry. An accident to the mother had brought on premature labour on a country estate miles from any medical help more sophisticated than the village midwife. She delivered what appeared to be a dead baby and put it aside in a bundle of blankets to devote all her attention to the young mother, who had slipped into unconsciousness. It was Frances who saw movement in the blankets and encouraged the frail little body into life; like Albert Victor, Dmitri had to be wrapped in cotton wool and he was given special warm baths to nurse him through the first precarious weeks. In recognition of what Frances had done, the Tsar presented her with a gold and diamond brooch with two large sapphires, as did the baby's father.

At the end of 1864, Mrs Clark was on her way to Darmstadt in Germany to attend Prince Alice's second confinement, with instructions to keep the expectant grandmother fully informed. Queen Victoria urged Princess Alice to keep the nurse longer; if she did it cannot have been more than a week. Princess Elisabeth of Hesse was born on 1 November and on 13 December Mrs Clark was back in England reporting to the Queen: 'Saw good Mrs Clark, returned from Darmstadt, who gave me an excellent account of Alice, the Baby & dear little Victoria.'[27] The Princess of Wales and Princess Alice had become Mrs Clark's royal mothers. In the summer of 1865 the Queen met the nurse at Osborne Cottage with two little Wales princes. The baby, Prince George, was almost two months old so this time Mrs Clark must have agreed to stay on longer; perhaps the permanent nurse was ill or unavailable, or Mrs Clark simply liked Osborne. The family obviously valued her. We next hear of her in July 1868 at Marlborough House on the day Princess Victoria of Wales was born, and by November she was in Darmstadt again, attending Princess Alice.

This was a difficult birth. 'The time itself was very severe,' the Princess told her mother, but the child was a big, healthy boy, and for his christening a month later Mrs Clark was on hand to play her part in the ceremony.[28] It was an important day for the Hesse family. Two years earlier their country had fought on the losing side in the Austro-Prussian War, and as a result had lost much of its autonomy to Prussia. The christening of a Hessian heir was a chance to demonstrate Hesse's continuing pride and sense of identity to the Prussian representatives present. The Hesse colours of red and white were everywhere in evidence but at the vital moment all eyes turned towards the English nurse: 'When all were assembled,' one of baby Ernst Ludwig's cousins recorded in her diary, 'splendid singing resounded through the great hall. Then appeared, preceded by the Marshal of the Court, the little candidate for baptism, carried by Mrs Clarke. He wore a white silk robe. . . . The baby was very quiet during the ceremony, except that, at the most solemn moments he sneezed, quite unembarrassed.'[29]

Mrs Clark seems to have stayed in Darmstadt beyond her normal month and it was not until March 1869 that she made her report to the Queen. Twice more she returned to Darmstadt. In the autumn of 1870, when Princess Alice was nearing her time in the midst of another war, the Queen sent Mrs Clark with Dr Hofmeister, who had known Princess Alice and her siblings from childhood. This baby was another son, Prince Friedrich Wilhelm; before long he would prove to have haemophilia, though no one could recognise this at his birth. In June 1872 the same team attended the birth of Princess Alix, the future Tsaritsa of Russia. 'Kind Dr Hofmeister was most attentive,' Princess Alice told her mother, 'and of course having him was far pleasanter than not, and we owe you great thanks for having sent him. Mrs Clark has been all one could wish.'[30] After this, Mrs Clark slips from the written record.

Both Mrs Clarks chose to focus on the baby during and after birth, though their training did equip them to assist the mother and to deliver the child if necessary. In the spring of 1864, when Princess Alice was about three months into her second pregnancy and was preparing to visit England, the Queen advised her that she would not need a doctor in attendance. Mrs Clark, she said, was capable of attending women 'as a Dr entirely'.[31] There were other nurses in regular royal employment who used the title 'monthly nurse' but specialised in caring for the mother. Mrs Lilly, who attended all of the Queen's nine confinements was one such; another was her friend Ellen Innocent, whom she recommended to the Queen for the Princess Royal's first confinement in Berlin in January 1859. Ellen Innocent attended the Princess of Wales shortly after Prince Albert Victor's birth but the Princess did not like her manner and afterwards used Mrs Clark. In 1867 Ellen attended the birth of Princess May of Teck, the future Queen Mary. She returned to Berlin on several occasions, though the Princess Royal complained that she was very expensive and was also prone to illness.[32] Ellen subsequently married a Mr Womersley and from 1 January 1887 she received a Privy Purse pension of £20 a year.[33]

This group of monthly nurses – more akin to the modern midwife – occasionally used the title 'lady's nurse'. That was how another royal monthly nurse, Euphemia Johnston, first advertised her services in an Edinburgh trade directory. In 1851, soon after Euphemia qualified at the maternity hospital in Edinburgh, she did try using 'midwife' but quickly dropped it, apparently because it did not recommend her to the wealthy clients she hoped to attract. Like the first Mrs Clark, Euphemia Johnston was a strong, independent woman who used nursing to pull herself back from a personal tragedy. Born in Inveresk in Scotland in about 1824, Euphemia was happily married when her husband suddenly died, leaving her with three small daughters to support. She moved in with her aunt Euphemia Alexander, who kept the Holyrood Post Office, and managed to finance her own training. She built up a good reputation in and around Edinburgh, and when Queen Victoria asked her physician in Scotland, James Young Simpson, to recommend a nurse for Princess Helena's first confinement, it was Euphemia Johnston he named.

Euphemia attended the Princess in 1867 and for subsequent births and the Queen recommended her to friends. 'Our dear Child is recovering extremely well,' she told the Duchess of Sutherland in 1867, '& is most <u>carefully</u> cared for by that excellent nurse & kind good Woman, Mrs Johnstone. There is <u>nothing</u> like a <u>warm</u> <u>Scotch</u> heart!'[34] In 1868 Princess Helena also recommended Mrs Johnston to her friend Emily Baird, but the price of the nurse's services was a worry. The Princess made enquiries on Mrs Baird's behalf and the reply she received shows extreme tact on Euphemia's part, coupled with a boundless willingness to please. 'Y.R.H. wishes to know my lowest terms,' she wrote. 'They are twenty-five guineas and fifteen d[itt]o. But if it is any Lady Y.R.H. knows, who cannot give so much, I shall be pleased to go for ten guineas.'[35]

Euphemia established herself very quickly in royal favour and was always willing to travel on request; in 1874 she took over from Mrs Clark, attending Princess Alice in Darmstadt for her last confinement. She was also present in 1874 and 1875 when the Queen's daughter-in-law, the Duchess of Edinburgh, produced her first two children, Prince Alfred and Princess Marie. Their births are a powerful reminder of how small the nurses' world really was, though it crossed continents: their mother, the Duchess of Edinburgh, was Kitty Strutton's little 'darling', Grand Duchess Maria Alexandrovna of Russia, whose marriage to an English prince had given her old nurse such pleasure.

By the 1880s a new generation was taking over. A Mrs Paterson was found by Princess Helena for her niece, Princess Caroline Mathilde, 'Calma' of Schleswig-Holstein, and dispatched to Germany, though she did not understand the language. But Queen Victoria thought Mrs Paterson 'a nice strong comfortable person, <u>well</u> up in her profession and very kindly', and that was what mattered.[36] Princess Caroline Mathilde liked Mrs Paterson and it may have been on her recommendation, or Princess Helena's, or both, that her elder sister Kaiserin Auguste Viktoria, 'Dona', employed the nurse for her next confinement. This was the birth of a fifth son in July 1888, just weeks after the Kaiserin's husband inherited the German imperial throne.

It was a busy time for Mrs Paterson. The baby's grandmother, Kaiserin Friedrich (who, as Princess Royal, was helped into the world by the first Mrs Clark), visited in August to see the new Prince. She liked what she heard. After the visit she told Queen Victoria that she wanted Mrs Paterson for the first confinement of her other daughter-in-law, Princess Irène (one of Princess Alice's daughters, helped into the world by the second Mrs Clark).

Mrs Paterson accepted the appointment, but not before the Queen had vetted her and, liking what she saw, had made arrangements for the nurse to go on from Kiel, where Princess Irène was due to give birth in March 1889, to Darmstadt, for Irène's sister Victoria, Princess Louis of Battenberg, who was expecting a second child in the July. By the beginning of March Mrs Paterson was installed in Kiel, calming the fears of the expectant mother and helping Kaiserin Friedrich to arrange all the exciting new things in the nursery. A letter from Princess Irène to Queen Victoria captures the atmosphere: the Queen had made a counterpane for the new baby's cradle and Irène was 'so deeply touched & cannot find words enough to thank you. . . . It is too dear & kind of you darling Grandmama, also the delightfully pretty bassinet, basket – charming gowns & things belonging to it. The little cap & cloak are my delight too. . . . Mrs Paterson I find such a very nice person – one in whom one has confidence directly – she has seen the Doctor & they seem to understand each other very well & agree in everything, which is a great comfort.'[37]

Baby Waldemar was duly delivered and once Mrs Paterson was satisfied that all was well she set off for Darmstadt, where Princess Victoria was delighted with her. But she seems to have let herself down after this. Four years later, in 1893, Kaiserin Friedrich's third daughter Sophie, the Crown Princess of Greece, was expecting a second child and asked her mother if she could have Mrs Paterson. The reply was not encouraging: 'If you are positive you want to have her, I will let her know. Henry and Irène swear by her, so does Victoria Battenberg, but Dona says she drinks, and I am not able to discover whether it is true or not. She was overworked at the Schloss and kept in such terribly small rooms and was so bothered by C. that she may have taken more than was good for her, but I will find out once more before finally advising you.'[38] 'C' was probably Princess Caroline Mathilde, who had had another baby at Schloss Glücksburg in 1891, but as for the drinking . . . It would be fascinating to know how Kaiserin Friedrich broached such a delicate subject ('Excuse me – do you drink too much?'), but it seems that she did; or perhaps she was simply being tactful when she told her daughter that Mrs Paterson did not have a drink problem but was already booked around the time that the baby was due. We hear no more of Mrs Paterson in Germany, but in the summer of 1900 she attended the birth of Prince Louis of Battenberg, the future Lord Mountbatten.

The stories of Mrs Paterson and Euphemia Johnston show how much reliance was placed on British nurses in Europe by the end of the nineteenth century. There must have been women in Germany who were capable of assisting mothers and babies before, during and after a birth, but the universal perception was that British practices were the most advanced, particularly when it came to nursery hygiene. So the demand increased. A Mrs Rosa Green was well known to the royal family around the turn of the century. She attended Princess Mary, Duchess of York from 1894 onwards, for the births of Princes Edward, Albert and Henry and of Princess Mary, the first four York children, two of them future kings. Mrs Green returned in 1905 to assist the acting nurse at the birth of Prince John, the youngest child, and she was the monthly nurse at several other royal births in England. But her talents were more widely appreciated too. In 1906, 1908 and 1909 she was called to Germany to attend the Duchess of Saxe-Coburg, one of the daughters of Princess Caroline Mathilde, and in 1907 she was in Spain for the first confinement of Queen Ena. In a letter to Queen Mary the young Queen praised Mrs Green, who 'has been so kind to me all this time and was the greatest comfort during those awful 12 hours before Baby was born'.[39]

Mrs Green, Mrs Paterson and Mrs Johnston all focused their care on the mother rather than the baby. The most famous monthly nurse of the other group, who specialised in the baby's welfare, was surely Elizabeth Francklin, and her story takes us full circle, back to imperial Russia and on into the world of the permanent nurse and the care of older children.[40] Mrs Francklin may have thought of herself as a specialist, at her best with a small baby and unwilling to put down roots, but the most fixed of intentions can be overset by a sudden, unexpected emotional bond.

Like Euphemia Johnston and the first Mrs Clark, Elizabeth Francklin became a monthly nurse to escape from a difficult personal situation. In her early years she probably never imagined anything beyond marriage and children. Born at Toddington in Bedfordshire and christened in the parish church on 19 October 1834, Elizabeth Sophia Cook was the daughter of Joseph Cook, the local innkeeper, and his wife Ann. The family moved to Upton cum Chalvey in Buckinghamshire and in April 1858, at the age of twenty-three, Elizabeth married Thomas William Francklin, a grocer from Slough. They had three children, Thomas, Annie, and Walter, but the marriage was not a success. When the census was taken in 1861, three years after her wedding, Elizabeth was at home with her parents in the Red Lion Inn at Upton cum Chalvey with two-year-old Thomas and baby Annie, then just five months old. She was also pregnant, and Walter would be born before the year's end. It is possible that the census entry simply records a visit home, but the collapse of Elizabeth's marriage certainly happened before her children were old enough to understand; they never knew what became of their father and Elizabeth never spoke of him, though she continued to describe herself as 'married', not 'widowed'.

She made her own way, and in April 1871 she was nursing the newborn child of a Mrs and Mrs Lethbridge in Dover Street, Mayfair. Her own children were boarded out, Thomas with a farmer in Berkshire and Annie and Walter nearer to home with Mrs Wenham, a widow living in Mayfair; this was probably the only way their mother could manage, as anyone who employed a nurse would expect her full-time attention. Annie married in 1879, and in the spring of 1881 her mother was based in London and working in the home of Reginald Brett, the MP for Penrhyn and Falmouth. His nineteen-year-old wife Eleanor had just produced their first child, a little boy named Oliver, and Elizabeth Francklin was his monthly nurse. By this time she had an excellent reputation in London society, built on her abilities as a nurse but also on her willingness to accept slightly longer-term appointments with favoured clients, to 'bring on' a delicate baby. Her rooms were decorated with a gallery of photographs of the babies she had nursed to full health, and it was this particular skill that brought her to the attention of the royal family.

In the summer of 1882 Tsar Alexander III's wife Maria Feodorovna gave birth to her sixth child. The baby, a little girl, was undersized and frail and in such cases an English nurse was thought to offer the best hope. The Tsaritsa spoke to her sister Alexandra, Princess of Wales, and the Princess's enquiries among her London friends led her to Elizabeth Francklin. Details were sent to St Petersburg and an official invitation dispatched to London: it landed unannounced on Mrs Francklin's Fulham doormat on a bright morning, just as she finished her breakfast. (In later years she liked to describe this scene to her grandson. She was reading the newspaper, she said, over her third cup of tea, listening to the sparrows quarrelling in the trees and the distant rattle of the milk-cart. She propped up the unexpected envelope against the tea-cosy, looked at it and wondered . . .) The letter came as a complete surprise but the Tsaritsa offered very favourable terms. She also requested an immediate reply: if Mrs Francklin accepted the appointment there would be very little time to prepare.

Elizabeth Francklin had never worked overseas before. At forty-five years old and with an established reputation she had no need to impress and no desire for adventure. She was comfortable, but she still had an eye to the future. The appointment would only last a year – two at the outside – and the money the Tsaritsa offered was excellent. The savings Elizabeth could make in Russia would cushion her retirement. So she accepted, packed her trunks and set off for St Petersburg on a short-term appointment that would last for the rest of her life.

Elizabeth was accustomed to delicate infants but she formed a bond with this particular baby that proved impossible to break. She conceived a fiercely protective affection for the little Grand Duchess, who seemed at once so endearing and so vulnerable. A mother herself, she was keenly aware that as time passed she was watching precious moments in the development of someone else's child and this was an experience she had not had before. 'Yesterday as she was running about in the garden,' she told the Tsaritsa, 'she said, "I so happy Nana." I said, "Why are you so happy my darling?" and she answered me, "The sun shines. You so stupid, Nana, you don't know the sun shines, I do, and I so good and I love all the things and everybody Papa, Mama, Nicky, Georgie, Zenny, Misha, all the flowers and all the things . . .". I wish so much Your Majesty could hear all her pretty talk and see her sweet engaging ways,' Elizabeth wrote. 'She misses Your Majesty very much and says every time you go out "Poor Olga! No Papa, No Mama go to see now."'

This was probably written when Olga was two or three years old, to judge from the babyish language and the picture the letter gives of a child beginning to find her own feet: 'She is very cheerful and happy, and insists upon walking everywhere "all alone". This morning she said, "I no can ride in my little carriage any more I quite big now, just like Misha."'[41] But the theme of Olga's loneliness was one to which the nurse would return in a letter written two or three years later, in 1887, her only other surviving letter to the child's mother. 'I am thankful to be able to give Your Majesty a good account of dear Baby,' she wrote, 'she is very happy with her little friends, playing all day in the garden. She is very pleased to write this telegram every morning to send to Your Majesty and never forgets that it must be done before going out. Many times during the day she says "I like best for Papa and Mama to be at home – I like to see them."'[42]

Perceiving a need, Elizabeth Francklin stayed. Years passed and still she stayed, even when the Tsaritsa wished her a thousand miles away, because Olga refused to let her go. She had, in short, crossed the divide between nurses. No longer a monthly nurse, she had made herself permanent.

TWO

'Yesterday a Nanny Arrived . . .'

NURSES

Madam, I am so vexed about something. I have sent by Royal Messenger to your Majesty a long letter about a nurse containing all her testimonials and her photograph. She seemed so likely that I hoped she might suit – and this morning after the letter had gone I have heard from her that she is afraid of the responsibility & cannot think of undertaking it. I must apologize very much for the trouble I shall give your Majesty for I shall have to ask you if all the testimonials may be returned to me as of course she must have them back again though she is such a tiresome woman. I am only glad she has discovered her inability to go in time as it would have been worse later. I will at once set to work to hear of someone else.[1]

In 1917, after the last Tsar and his family had been removed by their captors from the Alexander Palace at Tsarskoe Selo, their home for over twenty years, representatives of the new regime began to collect the physical reminders that were left behind: not only furniture and the personal possessions of generations, but also a paper trail of documents and photographs bearing witness to their lives. Among the mass of material gathered was a small file of letters in English dating back to the 1890s. It related to the engagement of a permanent nurse for the Tsar's children and still gives an unusual insight into the way things were done and the expectations on both sides.

The story behind the file begins in 1895 when the young Tsaritsa Alexandra Feodorovna – Princess Alix of Hesse – was expecting her first child. Her grandmother Queen Victoria engaged a permanent nurse for her as royal mothers and grandmothers had done for generations, but the Queen's choices were not always in tune with the young people's wishes. Her chosen nurse arrived on 29 December when the baby was a month old, and she struck the wrong note immediately. The very next day the Tsar wrote to his brother, 'Yesterday a nanny arrived from England, whom we do not particularly like the look of – she has something hard and unpleasant in her face and looks like

a stubborn woman. In general she's going to be a lot of trouble and I am ready
to bet that things are not going to go smoothly. For instance, she has already
decided that our daughter does not have enough rooms, and that, in her
opinion, Alix pops up into the nursery too often. How do you like that? It's all
very boring, especially when the first apple turns out to be rotten.'²

The appointment was doomed from the start. When the imperial couple
visited the Queen at Balmoral with their baby in the autumn of the following
year, nurses played a large part in the conversation. Lady Lytton was in waiting
during the visit and she described a evening she spent with the young mother.
'The Empress talked to me a long time after dinner and was so nice,' she said.
'Like anyone else she has had nurse troubles and the first she had was rude and
domineering, never even bowing to the Emperor. The one she now has is
housekeeper in a Russian family and she cannot keep her, but she is nice.'³
Another nurse employed for the baby drank too much, was found in bed with
a Cossack and dismissed on the spot; hence the family's need for someone they
could rely on. In 1898 the vacancy was looming again and the Empress asked
her lady-in-waiting Princess Bariatinsky to consult Emily Loch, lady-in-waiting
to her cousin 'Thora', Princess Helena Victoria of Schleswig-Holstein, about a
new permanent nurse.

Emily made enquiries. She already knew of one nurse, who had been with
Lady Lytton and was then working as a lady's companion, 'but she is over
50 years of age & so I think that would be really too old as 30 to 35 was the
age mentioned'. But this was not the first time Emily had been sent in search of
a royal nurse, and she knew the right people to ask. By 5 December 1898 she
was ready to make her report. Unsure whether Princess Bariatinsky was still at
Court – the Princess left for family reasons in 1898 – Miss Loch wrote directly
to the Tsaritsa, whom she had known for years.

I have been very highly recommended by the wife of the Scotch Minister in
London a Miss Eager. She is a lady by birth & education about 33, very fond
of children with considerable experience with them though she has not been
as yet a <u>domestic</u> nurse. Has had some training in a hospital & is at present
engaged till Jan 1 – acting temporarily as matron in an orphanage. I enclose
her photograph which was taken some few years ago but which seems to me
a pleasant sensible face. Unfortunately she is *not* tall being only 5ft 2 or 3 –
but is strong & active & seems to me very well fitted for the position of a
responsible nurse. She has been in France & knows french which would also
be a great help in Russia & she is very desirous of filling such a situation as
offered by your Majesty. I have had a very nice letter from herself evidently

quite understanding the duties of a nurse – but saying she knows nothing of court etiquette. This I feel is an advantage in your Majesty's eyes who wishes for a simple unspoiled person. . . . Miss Eager is Irish & a protestant & very bright & pleasant in manner the minister's wife tells me.[4]

In filling in so many details, Emily Loch was obviously trying to satisfy the requirements she had been given: age was a reasonable stipulation, so were appearance and religion, but the insistence on the nurse's height is intriguing. We can only guess why it mattered so much. Because the Empress herself was tall? Because the cupboards in the nursery were a long way up? Obviously great stress had been placed on this as Emily returned to it later in her letter. 'I thought I had better write at once, for if her height or any other reason made it sure that she would not do I would write at once & tell her so & not then arrange to see her.'

But as well as answering the given requirements, Miss Loch was introducing ideas of her own, particularly the business of the '<u>lady</u> nurse'. Traditionally nurses were not ladies, in the language of the day, and their status was that of a servant. They came from a lower or lower middle-class background: the daughters of rural estate workers, perhaps, or of artisans or tradesmen from the towns, or of other servants. The idea of the 'lady nurse' would sweep royal nurseries in the next decade, but Emily Loch was claiming a very early precedent. 'I think being a lady born is also an advantage,' she said, 'as she is thoroughly accustomed to manage those who are under her & yet will fulfill all her own duties, & it might make it pleasanter also to your Majesty in the daily intercourse with her. Many years ago, I think 14, I found a <u>lady</u> nurse for Princess Calma (Duchess of Glücksburg) who has been the greatest comfort & is still with her, so I feel I am speaking from experience.'

The letter was a long, careful one, including not only the photograph mentioned but also Miss Eagar's original letters of reference. Miss Loch was staying at Windsor when she wrote it and no sooner had she entrusted it to the royal messenger and waved it on its way, than a letter arrived from Miss Eagar to say she had changed her mind, the responsibility was too much. The result we have seen: 'Madam, I am so vexed about something . . .', written two days later, on 7 December. By this time Miss Loch had returned to her search and was able to report three more nurses. Two were in their fifties, 'but I fear also besides being older than you wanted they are also not tall', and there was 'a scotchwoman who seems capable. . . . I would like to get a scotch one if possible,' Emily told the Empress, 'as I have more confidence in them than in any. I should so like to find a treasure for you dearest Madam.'[5]

Little did she know that the treasure was already within her grasp. The letters jump a stage now with no explanation of what happened in the interim. By 1 January 1899, the day Miss Eagar's temporary appointment in the orphanage ended, she had been in correspondence with Emily Loch and was preparing herself for Russia. It seems most likely that the Empress was so impressed with what she read of Miss Eagar in the first letter and its attached references that she asked Emily to apply some persuasion; given Emily's mood on 7 December it seems unlikely that she would have accepted an unsolicited change of heart from the 'tiresome woman'. Emily mentioned sending a telegram to Russia – presumably to say that Miss Eagar had agreed – then came the letter of 1 January which begins, 'Madam, I have had two most satisfactory letters from Miss Eager. She is going to some place – she has not quite decided where – to have a thorough training with babies, but she has already had considerable experience with tiny infants having nursed one through a very bad illness who is now a fine healthy child of some years old. I am going to see Miss Eager in London when she comes over from Ireland & then I will write more details to your Majesty.'

There was a special reason for the emphasis being placed on tiny babies. The imperial couple had two little girls at this time, Grand Duchesses Olga and Tatiana. Tatiana, the younger, was already eighteen months old, but the Empress was three months into her third pregnancy, with the fervent hope – doomed in the event to disappointment – that the child would be a son and an heir for Russia: no wonder Miss Eagar felt awed by the responsibility. She expected to be available by mid-February, once her course had ended, and asked when the Empress would require her.

Margaretta Alexandra Eagar (she always spelt her surname with a final 'a') came from a respectable background in the south-west of Ireland. She was born in Limerick in August 1863, the name 'Alexandra' almost certainly chosen in honour of the new Princess of Wales, whose marriage a few months earlier had made 'Alexandra' a popular name. In Margaretta's case it also recalled her grandfather, Alexander Eagar, a County Inspector of Constabulary. He had added colour to the family tree by choosing a wife from the McGillycuddys – one of the last great Gaelic clans of Ireland that still held its own extensive lands and boasted its own chieftain, 'The McGillycuddy of the Reeks'.

The Eagars were a family of high achievers – on the male side, at least. One was a colonel in the Irish Regiment who fought for Spain in the Peninsular War; he later became Governor of Manila in the Philippines. Another was a junior officer on HMS *Agamemnon* under Nelson. Margaretta's father, Francis

McGillycuddy Eagar, was Governor of Limerick Prison before his retirement in the 1880s, and afterwards a Justice of the Peace. Her elder brother Alexander was Senior Moderator of Trinity College, Dublin, later a vicar in Cornwall and a published poet and theologian. According to one source her second brother James was a licentiate of the Royal College of Surgeons in Edinburgh, and among her nephews, one became Assistant Harbour Master at Brisbane, another was a respected mining engineer and a third, Waldegrave McGillicuddy Eagar, published books on the social and economic problems of the day. He gave such distinguished service to the National Institute for the Blind that on his retirement in 1949 *The Times* declared, 'It is due to him more than to anyone else that blindness has come to be regarded in this country as a handicap to be conquered rather than an affliction to be mitigated.'[6]

On her mother's side too, there were ancestors of note. Her maternal grandfather, Francis Smollett Holden, held a Doctorate of Music from Trinity College, Dublin. He was a key figure in preserving the traditional music of Ireland and a published composer in his own right – no wonder poor Margaretta was acutely conscious of her own inability to hold a tune. But the women in the family were a different story. They were born, they married or not – that was all. On the Holden side, only Margaretta's grandmother, Sarah Anne Holden, struck out on her own. When her husband died at an early age, leaving her with five dependent children, Sarah Anne opened a finishing school in New Ross for the daughters of officers. She is said to have been a gifted linguist and musician. But on the Eagar side, in six generations Margaretta was the only woman remembered for doing anything other than existing or marrying.

Where did the spark come from that made her different? Some clues may lie in the written testimonials preserved in the Alexander Palace file. 'I have known her from childhood,' writes one correspondent, 'she is extremely well educated, a good needlewoman and an experienced housekeeper, thoroughly understands cooking and has had much experience in managing children . . . Miss Eagar is a bright, cheerful girl very active and energetic, and most conscientious about everything she undertakes.' Others returned to the same theme: 'She possesses also good <u>practical</u> knowledge of household affairs, derived from long experience at home'; 'she has good powers of observation, and has had great experience of different branches of housekeeping, and I should say that her powers of management in this respect are very good. She has been a good deal in company with children, and can easily and readily manage them.'[7]

Margaretta Eagar was one of ten children, three boys and seven girls. She was seven years old when her mother lost an eighth daughter. Sources differ as to her position in the family: she may have been the fourth child or the sixth but in either case she had ample opportunity to see what married life entailed for a woman at that time, even one 'of gentle birth'. All that emphasis on housekeeping and child management strongly suggests that she was the practical one in the family who carried the load when her mother could not. There was at least one sister older than Margaretta, but she was a lifelong invalid. It was all very well to be 'bright' and 'cheerful' when you had no choice, but as Margaretta grew older, perhaps she concluded that this life was not for her.

Fragments of her early career survive in Emily Loch's letters and in the testimonials. She spent some time in France. Whether this was for her education, for work, or just travel for its own sake is never explained, but years later she could still write fluently in French. She was eminently well qualified to be a governess – a much more conventional choice for a young woman with her background, but Margaretta does not seem to have been interested in convention. She chose to train as a nurse – in medicine, not childcare – in the Royal Hospital in Belfast; then came the temporary matron's appointment at the orphanage which preceded her move to Russia. The idea of being a permanent nurse in a family, with its overtones of 'going into service', was probably not something she had considered: it found her, and she is unlikely to have accepted such an appointment for anyone less than royalty.

The closest friend Margaretta would make in the nursery world was Elizabeth Jane 'Lilian' Wilson, who was nurse to the children of the Tsaritsa's brother, Grand Duke Ernst Ludwig of Hesse. They were close in age: Lilian was just eight months younger, being born in Thrapston in Northamptonshire on 20 April 1864. Like Margaretta, she found her position with royalty on personal recommendation, though in her case the nurses' grapevine played a part. Towards the end of 1894 the young Grand Duchess of Hesse was well into her first pregnancy when her sister-in-law Victoria, Princess Louis of Battenberg, began to make enquiries for a nurse for her. Princess Victoria asked her own children's nurse Ellen Hughes if she knew anyone in need of a position. Ellen did not, but wrote to her previous mistress, Lady William Seymour, for help.[8] Lady William Seymour seems to have been an excellent source of nurses. She had already provided Princess Victoria with Ellen, with a Mrs Jones – whom the Princess's sister Irène thought 'such a nice creature'[9] – and with a third nurse, Mary Adams, so it was probably through her good offices that Lilian Wilson found her way to Darmstadt, arriving to take up the position on her thirty-first birthday, 20 April 1895, when Princess Elisabeth of Hesse was about five weeks old.

Caring for children who were cousins, and whose parents were close, Lilian and Margaretta met on several occasions; not frequently, but when they were together it was for weeks at a time and they became friends. They were poles apart in character. Margaretta was intellectual, wanting to know the hows, whys and wherefores of everything she heard or read about and always keen to discuss politics, while Lilian was warm and placid, happy to immerse herself in the nursery and its smaller doings. But it was socially that the real difference showed, for Lilian Wilson was more typical of what people expected a nurse to be. In contrast to the Eagars with their distinguished record in the professions and their awareness of their family as a historical entity, Lilian's father Edward Wilson was an ordinary working man; a railway porter. At the age of sixteen her mother, Emma Powell, was a general servant in a grocer's shop in Twickenham. Like many girls, Emma would have gone into service in her early teens with no chance of formal education; when she married Edward at eighteen years old she could not sign her own name in the register. She died while Lilian was still a small child and Edward Wilson returned to his native London with his children and soon remarried. The Wilsons were decent people but they moved in very different circles from families like the Eagars and the Holdens. In a world where such things mattered a lot it was to Margaretta's credit that they did not matter to her at all.

Most royal nurses came from backgrounds like Lilian's. In the late 1850s, when Queen Victoria was preparing for the marriage of her eldest daughter and looking ahead to future grandchildren, she chose one of her own housemaids to go to Berlin as part of the Princess Royal's household. Georgina Hobbs agreed to this on the understanding that she would be responsible for the Princess's rooms only, that her post in the Queen's household would be kept in case her health was not up to life in Germany, and that the Princess would bring her to England once a year and provide travelling expenses.[10] The Princess married Prince Friedrich Wilhelm of Prussia on 25 January 1858. Georgina went to Berlin and her quiet, discreet ways pleased the young couple; she was 'always gentle & in good spirits', so the Princess said, and quite different in manner from the German housemaids.[11]

Georgina had a sister, Emma. She was nurse to Lady Scott's children but they had outgrown the nursery and Emma needed a new position; when the Princess Royal fell pregnant within months of the marriage the Queen snapped her up and brought her into her own household to get to know the head nurse, Mary Anne Thurston. 'I should wish Emma Hobbs to speak a good deal to Mrs Thurston and learn how every single thing was done with your children,' the Princess told her mother four months before the birth, nervously anticipating the time when she would have to preside over a nursery.[12] From the Queen's point of view, Emma was to be her eyes in Berlin and she would expect the nurse to keep in regular contact with Mrs Thurston about the baby's progress. Both mother and daughter drew comfort from Emma's glowing references. 'I have heard again such a very high character of Mrs Hobbs from Lady Leigh in whose neighbourhood L^y Scott is,' the Queen wrote shortly before the birth. 'She is so vy safe & trustworthy & has had so much charge of the Children during L^y Scott's absences, wh as you will often move about – is peculiarly valuable.'[13] On 5 November, with the day drawing ever closer, the Princess urged her mother to send Emma to Berlin before Christmas. The Queen obliged. On 18 December the Princess told her: 'I like Mrs Hobbs very much, she is just the sort of person for that place, & I am so glad she likes the arrangement of the rooms and the layette so much.'[14]

Georgina and Emma Hobbs were Londoners. Their father John Hobbs owned a wharf in the docks and there are references to both sisters speaking with Cockney accents. But that was their only similarity. While Georgina was gentle, cheerful and uncomplaining, Emma's temper was a sight to behold – from another room. 'The thing is Mrs Hobbs is not by nature inclined to submit to any authority or person whatsoever man or woman,' the Princess told her mother in 1861, 'and with all her excellent qualities wch make her so precious she has the most violent & ungovernable temper I ever saw – she always owns it – & says she cannot help it, but she is a difficult person to deal with.'[15] When Emma was not in a rage, she was often in copious floods of tears and, as so often happens in families, her sister – so willing, so gentle – seemed to have the unfailing knack of setting her off. Things were always more peaceful when they were not together. At the end of 1859 Georgina became the Princess's housekeeper but she was involved with the nursery too and at times stood in as nurse, so there were often fireworks. 'I am grieved to hear that dear Mrs Hobbs's temper is not of the best,' the Queen commented, in response to one of her daughter's letters, 'but however with a little management – I dare say you will be able to avoid any very distressing scenes. So many good servants have that defect.'[16]

The nurse was a servant. Frances Fry, who saved the premature baby of Grand Duke Pavel Alexandrovich, was the daughter of Henry Fry, a 'paper hanger' from south London. His death late in 1857 left his wife Caroline with no income and five children to support: twelve-year-old Henry, nine-year-old Caroline, twins Frances and Jane, who were seven, and four-year-old Cornelius. This forced her to make what must have been an agonising decision. She could not keep them all. Henry was almost old enough to bring in a wage and by the age of fifteen he was supporting the family as a bookbinder. It was the twins who had to go, perhaps with the thought that at least they would have each other. So, from the age of eight, Frances Fry was brought up with her twin sister in the Female Orphan Asylum in Lambeth, with over 130 other girls aged between eight and sixteen. With only two teachers on the resident staff lessons must have been basic but at least the girls did have lessons, and were prepared to make their way in the world. Frances would have been found a position when she left the orphanage. In April 1881 she was nurse to four-year-old Violet Cotton, a landowner's daughter from Birchington in Kent. Exactly nine years later she arrived in St Petersburg, to care for the infant Grand Duchess Maria Pavlovna.

Charlotte Bill, 'Lalla', one of the most famous of British royal nurses, followed a similar career path, though her family life was happier. She was born in Maidenhead in Berkshire early in 1875 and grew up with her brother and sisters in a cottage at Taplow; her father William James Bill drove a steam launch on the Thames. In 1891, aged sixteen, she became nursery maid to the Purdey family, who owned a well-established firm of London gunsmiths. Their home was in Taplow and she worked for them for four years. The Royal Household Appointments Book lists her as a nursery maid at Marlborough House from 6 July 1895, something of a curiosity as at that time Marlborough House was the London home of the Prince and Princess of Wales, and their children had long since left the nursery. It can only have been the grandchildren Lalla was employed to care for – perhaps when they came on visits, in support of their regular nurses. In the spring of 1896 she transferred to the nurseries of the Duke and Duchess of York, but she was still the nursery maid, or under-nurse, until 1 July 1900.[17]

The last document in the Alexander Palace file is a letter of 30 January 1899 in which Emily Loch explains the arrangements to be made for Margaretta's journey to St Petersburg. A Mr Ewen was dealing with the practicalities, making the bookings through Thomas Cook & Son on the understanding that the Russian Embassy would refund the money. 'Mr Ewen is so pleased at being able to do anything he can for your Majesty.' Emily outlined their plans: 'She is to start on Saturday night Feb 11 – & go by Flushing to Berlin. There he will get the Chancery servant from the Embassy to meet her & see her off 4 hours later in the train to Wirballen where he will write to the head official to ask for her to be looked after & put in to the train again.' Wirballen was the border station between Germany and Russia. The two countries used rails of a different gauge so all train journeys between them involved a complete change at Wirballen. Mr Ewen was also writing to the British Embassy in St Petersburg to ask them to send an English-speaking servant to meet Margaretta at the station and hand her safely to whoever was sent from the palace to collect her; that last part of the arrangement was in the Tsaritsa's hands. And having left London on the night of Saturday 11 February, Margaretta was due to arrive in St Petersburg at ten o'clock on the Tuesday morning – a considerable improvement on the seven weeks the Dimsdales had taken to make the same journey.[18]

This seems to have been the pattern for conveying nurses to their place of work. The Palace Archives in Madrid have the original documents relating to Eugenie Doherty's journey to Spain at the end of October 1911, when she went out as nurse to the Prince of the Asturias. Mr George Butcher of Clock House, Kensington Palace, made all the arrangements, probably at the request of the Queen of Spain's mother, Princess Beatrice, who lived in the palace. (Some years before, a George Butcher had been valet to Princess Beatrice's late husband and this may have been the same man.) He received the invoice from Thomas Cook's ('General Railway & Steamship Agents, Foreign Bankers &c') with a covering letter: 'Referring to your telephonic instructions of the 31st ulto, and your letter regarding Mrs Doherty's journey to Madrid, we have this morning heard from Paris that everything went off alright there, and we now beg to enclose an account for the ticket, money, and expenses, amounting to £16:4:4. Kindly favour us with a cheque as arranged. . . .' The invoice explains how the sum was reached: Mrs (actually Miss) Doherty was given a first-class ticket from London to Madrid via Boulogne for £9 7s 11d and a sleeping berth was booked for her from Paris to Irun for £1 8s 5d. A 'Special man in Paris' cost 5s (25p today); presumably he was the equivalent of Margaretta's Chancery servant in Berlin. Three shillings more were spent on telegrams and Eugenie Doherty received £5 spending money. George Butcher paid the account, then submitted the documents to Madrid and was duly reimbursed.[19]

But even the most careful plans could go awry. Emily Loch and Mr Ewen seemed to have thought of everything. They even gave Margaretta a telegram to send to the Tsaritsa's chancellor at the border if she had any problems. It should all have been straightforward but Margaretta would later describe the nerve-racking experience her journey became. Someone in the Berlin Embassy had decided that a palace employee travelling to St Petersburg was an opportunity not to be missed. The Chancery servant greeted Margaretta in Berlin as promised but, instead of simply looking after her during her wait on the station and transferring her and her luggage to the connecting train, he presented her with 'an immense white linen bag, tied round with red tape and sealed with several great seals'.[20] A letter from the ambassador instructed her to guard the bag and not to allow it to be searched at the border. It was to be handed intact to the embassy messenger who would meet her at the station in St Petersburg and she was given the appropriate documents to show to customs officials. The bag even had its own passport.

For a woman alone in a foreign country whose language she did not understand, this was a daunting commission. The bag became a looming presence on Margaretta's journey; too big to ignore, too important to put down, it seemed to take on a life of its own. But worse was to follow. Margaretta was expecting a servant from the Tsaritsa to meet her at Wirballen (though this does not seem to have been part of the original plan, which she may have misunderstood). Finding no one, she presented herself to the station staff and sent off her emergency telegram. Customs officials refrained from touching the dreaded bag, but they examined Margaretta's own luggage, and 'Oh! What an examination it was! Everything I possessed was turned out of my trunks, and they even put their hands into my boots and gloves. I then had to pay sixpence for the examination of each trunk.'[21]

Unable to fathom the layout of the Russian train, Margaretta then settled herself into a second-class carriage with some helpful Russian ladies, who had bought tea and a sandwich for her when the cumbersome bag made it impossible for her to enter the station restaurant. But the guard would not allow her to travel second class on a first-class ticket so he moved her on, into the 'solitary grandeur' of a first-class carriage with the bag. There was no one to help her and nervousness almost overwhelmed her. At St Petersburg there was no waiting embassy servant to collect the bag as promised, but the Tsaritsa did not let her down. One of the Court ladies was waiting with a carriage, probably Maria Feodorovna Gueringer, a Russian colonel's widow, who handled the Tsaritsa's business affairs and dealt with everything relating to the nursery; in time she would become a good friend to Margaretta. A meal was waiting at the palace, after which Margaretta was shown to her room to rest but she dared not be parted from the wretched bag; eventually the servants assumed that she was insane and left her to it. She had just gone to sleep when the embassy messenger finally appeared to relieve her of her troublesome charge. Shortly after she was shown to the Tsaritsa's rooms: 'I thought her then,' she said, 'and think her now, the handsomest woman I have ever seen.'[22]

The respect was mutual. Emily Loch's prediction that the Tsaritsa would find it more pleasant to deal with a 'lady' nurse did prove far-sighted and the two women quickly developed a good working relationship. Through a combination of her own decisions and the chance that drew her to Emily Loch's attention, Margaretta had found quite independently a version of the structured career path that a number of young women were beginning to follow, which in time would transform the nursery world. By 1899 when she left for Russia, over 400 hopefuls – all of them 'ladies' – had already passed through the doors of the first training college for children's nurses.

The idea of the 'lady nurse' as a qualified professional, quite separate from the traditional nursery-trained servant, grew from the educational work of Emily Lord, who opened an infant school at Norland Place in London in 1876. Miss Lord was inspired and energised by the theories of the German Friedrich Froebel, founder of the 'kindergarten' movement, who advocated a gentler system of education designed to develop the natural abilities of the very young. His ideas were practised at Norland Place and in 1879 the school was commended by the Froebel Society of Great Britain. A decade later, Miss Lord was training her own teachers.

But she was not content to stop there. Miss Lord's experience of the children raised by traditional nurses made her question the whole system. She came to believe in an idea very similar to the one Emily Loch had urged on the Tsaritsa; that it would be better for children and more pleasant for their parents if their nurses were more refined and better educated – more like themselves, in fact. In modern terms it sounds uncomfortably elitist but it was an honest reflection of the world she knew, with its sharp divisions between the social classes. From where Emily Lord was standing, parents who entrusted their babies and small children to women they would not be willing to mix with themselves were failing to value their children. She also saw an opening for young women from professional backgrounds – like Margaretta Eagar, or the unnamed 'lady nurse' of Glücksburg – who needed to earn a living and were not academic enough to be governesses, or did not want to be. A training course leading to a professional qualification in children's nursing was her answer. To bring it into being she called on two of her Norland Place teachers: Isabel Sharman, who provided a counterweight of calm practicality to set against her own boundless enthusiasm, and Mildred Hastings, a quietly reliable soul who would long outlive Miss Lord and Miss Sharman to become the memory and the chronicler of their new venture – and its heart.

The project was ambitious and it needed support. Miss Lord invited key figures from the world of education to discuss her intentions and she encouraged press interest in their meetings. A spate of articles began to appear in the summer of 1892. They gave the idea a mixed reception: 'Why should these young women be content to remain as servants after all this priming,' commented one writer in the *St James's Gazette*, missing the point entirely.[23] But others were supportive, and in September 1892 the first five probationers began their training in a suite of rooms at the Norland Place School. This suite had been Miss Lord's home until, in 1891, she married a retired tea merchant named Walter Ward, much to her friends' astonishment, and moved out. In doing so she unwittingly provided a convenient first premises for her college and a name: the Norland Institute. Students were offered a course lasting approximately eight months and including classroom work, practical skills and three months in a maternity or children's hospital, all designed for young women who had the means to pay. The course and the selection procedures were experimental at first and about a third of the early students dropped out, but the majority completed. By the time Margaretta went to Russia in 1899 they were poised to make their mark in the nurseries of the world – particularly, as it happened, in royal nurseries

The first Norlander to find employment with royalty joined the institute as part of the second intake of students in January 1893. Helen Caroline Ken Spence, nurse no. 10, was eighteen years old when she entered Norland. A master mariner's daughter from Newcastle, she had a school education and very little experience with children to offer the institute; her only qualification was a first aid certificate. But she stayed the course and caught the eye of Norland's first royal employer. As a young bride, the Princess Royal had been nervous about the prospect of presiding over a nursery: so nervous, that she appealed to her mother to let Emma Hobbs glean as many tips as possible from her own former nurse. By 1893, forty-five years and eight children later, Kaiserin Friedrich, as she then was, was confident, assured, and fascinated by all things concerning the nursery and the treatment of young children. She was a keen supporter of the kindergarten movement in Germany and a very active patron of the Pestalozzi-Froebel house in Berlin, where children attended the kindergarten and young women teachers were trained in the new methods, some travelling all the way from Britain. Kaiserin Friedrich was in England in the spring of 1893 and she applied to Norland within months of its opening for a nurse for her daughter Sophie, Crown Princess of Greece, whose second child was due in the summer. Helen Ken Spence was chosen to go out to Greece as '2nd to a lady nurse'. It was her first job and she earned £20 a year. No clue remains as to how long she stayed with the Crown Princess, but when the institute celebrated its twentieth anniversary in 1913 an article in the *Norland Quarterly* noted that 'for several years our nurses worked in the nursery of Her Royal Highness, and through her influence we have had introductions to many Royal households'.[24] In 1902 Norlander Catherine Welsh Salmond, 'Gertie', a farmer's daughter from Scotland, took over the Crown Princess's nursery and she would stay for three years.

That same year, 1902, Beatrice Todd, the daughter of a clerk in the Ecclesiastical Commissions Office, found a place with Kaiserin Friedrich's daughter-in-law Irène, Princess Heinrich of Prussia, at Kiel. Beatrice was rather unusual among Norlanders because she had worked as a governess before starting her training; she was also a Froebel-trained teacher, which would have won the Kaiserin's wholehearted approval. The reputation of the institute was spreading rapidly through Court and aristocratic circles in Europe. In April 1900 nurse no. 113, Kate Fox, was chosen by the Marquise de Talleyrand for her daughter Princess Ruspoli, who had two small sons and was expecting a third. The family lived a nomadic existence, sometimes in Monaco, sometimes Italy or Switzerland; Kate enjoyed the sightseeing but found it all 'a little tiring, more especially on account of the luggage, which, when one has no house in which to leave things, accumulates, and is very costly.'[25]

Kate left the Ruspolis in 1903 and happened to be available when Princess Nicholas of Greece, sister-in-law to the Crown Princess, approached Norland for a nurse for her infant daughter Olga. At only a few weeks old, the baby was not thriving as she should. No one was willing to go out to Greece on a permanent posting that summer so Miss Sharman appealed to Kate, who agreed to go on a temporary basis to give the family more time to find someone permanent. 'However, in spite of the difficulties of *very* primitive conditions in the King's Palace where we lived for the first few months,' Kate would later recall, 'the difficulties of language and managing Greek servants, the baby Princess so quickly bound herself into my heart, and the charming manner in which her parents treated me, added to the fact that there was soon to be another baby . . . made me decide to stay permanently.'[26] It was the start of one of the great nurse/royal family partnerships.

Kate seems to have used her younger sister Jessie as a guinea pig before deciding on nursing. Jessie Fox entered Norland in December 1893; on 30 October in the following year Kate wrote to Miss Sharman, 'I am thinking of following my sister's example and being trained as a Norland nurse, have you a vacancy for a resident probationer at Christmas? and if so, will you please send me the necessary forms to fill in. We are all very glad that Jessie is getting on so well, and is so happy in her work.'[27] The Fox sisters were born in Middlesex and grew up in Kingsbridge in Devon, though by the 1890s their home was in Surrey. Both described their father Charles Fox as a 'gentleman' in the Norland register: census records identify him as a newspaper publisher. As little girls the sisters were taught by a governess and later both attended private schools. Jessie was also to work for Princess Nicholas on occasion. 'I came out to help my sister with the babies; and after I had been here for ten days, my sister left for her holiday', she wrote in 1906. 'Now she has returned, and we are looking forward to spending a few months together.'[28] In 1907 the nursery acquired a Norland probationer to work under Kate; her name was Grace Gibb.

By this time there were Norlanders working for Princess Max of Baden in Karlsruhe (Beatrice Halls), for the young Duchess of Saxe-Coburg (Marie Odgers), and for Kaiserin Friedrich's youngest daughter Margarete, Princess Friedrich Karl of Hesse. She employed Katherine Robb and her sister, the daughters of a surgeon in the Indian Medical Service. Katherine sent a postcard of the Hesse family's home, Schloss Friedrichshof, to Mildred Hastings; 'September 20th 1905'; it reads, 'My sister and I arrived here on Wednesday evening. In three weeks we all return to Frankfurt for the Winter. This is a charming place and the Princes are sweet little boys.'[29] With six 'sweet little boys', two very close in age and two pairs of twins, Princess Margarete needed a lot of nurses. She certainly employed one other Norlander, Florence Newman, and several others who were not Norland-trained.

Victoria Melita, Grand Duchess Kirill of Russia, lived in Coburg with her husband from the autumn of 1905 because their marriage was not sanctioned by the Tsar. She would have heard of Norland from her sister-in-law Princess Nicholas and from the young Duchess of Saxe-Coburg, her cousin's wife. In February 1907 she employed Marian Burgess, one of twins who trained at Norland, for her new baby. When 'Burgie' came down with influenza another Norlander, Irene Collenette, a native of Guernsey, stepped in until 'Burgie' was well enough to return; 'she is still disinfecting herself,' Princess Nicholas remarked to Kate Fox in November.[30] Nurse Irene went on afterwards to Grand Duchess Kirill's sister Beatrice, Princess Alfonso of Orléans-Borbón. The Grand Duchess of Mecklenburg-Schwerin employed the first of her two Norlanders, Constance Sadler, in 1910; another Norland nurse, Lilian Duncan, travelled all the way to India, to the nurseries of the Maharani of Indore. The list was growing all the time and these young royal mothers were not content simply to employ their nurses from Norland, they came to identify with the institute itself, to know its leading personnel and to take a close interest in its doings.

King Edward VII's funeral in 1910 brought a number of Norland employers to England. Remembering events for the *Norland Quarterly* at Mrs Ward's request two decades later, Mildred Hastings tried to list the royal visitors Norland had received that year, at the institute itself, then based at no. 10,

Pembridge Square in London, and at 'Fieldhouse' in Bognor, the seaside holiday home used by Norlanders and 'their' children. 'H.R.H. Princess Max of Baden and H.R.H. the Grand Duchess of Mecklenburg-Schwerin [who were sisters], attended by a lady-in-waiting, came to see the Institute', Mildred wrote. 'Princess Max had heard much about it from her Norlander, Nurse Beatrice Halls, and the Grand Duchess from Nurse Constance Sadler. . . . The two little Princes, sons of the Infanta Beatrice of Spain, visited the Institute twice with Nurse Irene Collenette, and on the second occasion they accompanied the Infanta Beatrice, who went all over the houses. The two Princesses, daughters of the Grand Duchess Kirill of Russia (a sister of the Infanta Beatrice) came to see us, in company with Nurse Marion Burgess; and on more than one occasion Nurse Kate Fox escorted the Princesses Olga . . . Elizabeth and Marina, daughters of the Grand Duchess Nicholas of Greece, to the Institute; all these five little Princesses stayed at Fieldhouse.'[31]

She did well to remember so many, but there were still some she missed. The *Quarterly* of Christmas 1910 noted that Princess Nicholas herself had been to Pembridge Square, and it preserved a delightful comment relating to the Infanta Beatrice whose visit seems, after all, not to have taken place that year – perhaps Mildred was remembering another time; 'Owing to spring cleaning, we were not able to receive a visit from H.R.H Princess Alfonso of Orléans-Borbón, but we hope that we shall have that honour on some future occasion.' Royalty or not, a good nurse knew her priorities! Another 1910 visitor was the Grand Duchess of Hesse, who 'came to see the Institute and Nurseries, and not only graciously expressed her interest in all she saw, but allowed the two little princes to visit the nurseries'. This was not Princess Margarete of the six 'sweet little boys'; she had married into another branch of the Hesse family. It was Grand Duchess Eleonore of Hesse, the second wife of Grand Duke Ernst Ludwig, Lilian Wilson's former employer (and as if to underline how very complicated royal relationships could be, his first wife was Princess Victoria Melita, Grand Duchess Kirill, whose daughters visited the institute and stayed at 'Fieldhouse'). Lilian Wilson had remained with the Grand Duke after his divorce and cared for the elder of the 'two little princes' of his second marriage. When she left in 1908, her place was taken by Norlander Elizabeth 'Lilian' Eadie, a bank manager's daughter from Devonshire.

But not all of Norland's royal contacts were so successful. In June 1910 Mrs Ward was proud to announce an invitation from Crown Princess Cecilie of Prussia for a nurse for her sons Wilhelm and Louis Ferdinand, then aged three and two. A few months later she had to admit, 'We sent Nurse Amy Wood. The honour, however, was of a brief duration. We are glad to say that no blame was attached to her dismissal, and we fully appreciated the difficulties attending the introduction of a fully qualified Norland nurse into the Royal German nursery. We are confident that had it been otherwise, Her Imperial Highness would have had loyal, faithful and loving service.'[32]

The attention paid to Norland by Europe's royal mothers contained a strong element of professional interest. The fields of childcare, education, and women's employment had been the province of royal ladies for generations and the work begun at Norland had a bearing on all three spheres. The idea was taken up very quickly in other places. Kaiserin Friedrich's younger sister Helena, Princess Christian of Schleswig-Holstein, was a prime mover in the establishment of the second British training college for nursery nurses, the Princess Christian College, which opened in Manchester in 1901. This grew from the discussions of the Gentlewomen's Employment Association which was founded in 1891 with the Princess as its patron – and it may have been no coincidence that Emily Loch was so taken with the idea of the 'lady' nurse: her spells of duty as a lady-in-waiting were spent under Princess Christian's roof with her unmarried daughter, Princess Helena Victoria.

Not content simply to give her name to the new college, Princess Christian also made various stipulations about its guiding principles and organisation. While Emily Lord came to nursery nurse training from an educational background and focused on teaching and the needs of the child, Princess Christian had a special interest in hospital nursing and wanted to make a clear separation between the two forms of nurse. To prevent students of the new college from confusing their training with that of hospital nurses and thinking themselves trained in areas they were not, she had physiology and hygiene omitted from the nursery course in favour of general lectures on 'Rules of Health'. She asked that nurses be taught to avoid the various 'soothing' remedies that were still common, often based on gin or laudanum; and that they be warned not to hit children on the head, 'Above all things the nurse should be forbidden to punish children herself.'[33] This was a ruling far ahead of its time and it would have made life difficult for nurses left alone with children for long periods. Norlanders did not smack children, or were not supposed to, but they did apply gentler forms of control. A child raised in the nurseries of Pembridge Square remembered disapproval being the usual punishment, with standing in the corner for more serious offences or jam deprivation at tea time.[34]

At Princess Christian's the royal connection was present from the start. The Tsaritsa was fascinated by her aunt's new endeavour and decided to set up something similar herself in the park at Tsarskoe Selo, where she could keep a close eye on its progress. On 10 June 1904 she wrote to Gretchen Fabrice, who had been governess to Princess Helena's daughters and was her own first lady-in-waiting, 'My school which I am building outdoors here at my expense will soon come under a roof; I hope it will be habitable by November. Here nurses will be trained; I will select them from the girls at my "patriotic schools".' She explained that she planned to have a nursery on the site; to establish fruit and vegetable gardens and teach nutrition and cooking. Nothing like it existed in Russia and she would import teachers from London and Stockholm, perhaps also Dresden.[35] She applied to Princess Christian's for suggested rules. When Kate Fox visited Russia with the Nicholas children in the summer of 1905, 'the Empress sent one of her ladies-in-waiting to ask me about our Institute. Since then Her Majesty has started a similar kind of thing,' Kate told her fellow Norlanders, 'but I understand it is not at all a success.'[36] The Tsaritsa persisted, though, and was constantly seeking advice and making improvements. In later years Norlander Lilian Eadie was helpful both to her and to the Grand Duchess of Hesse, who started a similar venture.

Many royal ladies found inspiration in the nursing colleges. In 1911 Princess Christian's younger sister set up the Princess Louise Nursery College in Edinburgh, a much smaller, more informal establishment which placed great emphasis on cookery. In the summer of 1908 the Crown Princess of Sweden sent the principal of a Swedish training home to Princess Christian's for a fortnight, 'to increase her knowledge and experience and to understand English methods'.[37] Kaiserin Auguste Viktoria (Princess Christian's niece) sent a German doctor, the newly appointed director of an institution aimed at reducing the high rate of infant mortality. Then, in 1909, Princess George of Greece became Vice-President of the Princess Christian College. Her son Peter was born in 1908 and her daughter Eugenie in 1910; they may well have had a Princess Christian nurse. Curiously, Nurse Violet Mary Croisdale is mentioned in the college magazine as working for Princess George in 1930, long after the children had grown up and before the appearance of any grandchildren. Violet left the college in 1912 and there are references to her working abroad from 1913 onwards.

Nurse no. 9, Elizabeth Alix St John, entered the nursery of Queen (formerly Crown Princess) Sophie of Greece in April 1913, with the birth of Princess Katherine. Elizabeth St John was born in Finchampstead in Berkshire in the autumn of 1869 with a twin brother, Edward; two younger brothers followed. Their father died when they were still very young but unlike the Fry twins, forced to fend for themselves in the Lambeth Female Orphan Asylum, the St John children's widowed mother was financially secure, with sufficient income from land to pay her family's way. Elizabeth left Princess Christian's in February 1902 and was abroad from about 1907. She worked for the Greek royal family until the end of the First World War and in 1921, Princess Katherine's elder sister Helen called her back to nurse her own baby son, Prince Michael of Romania: by the 1920s and '30s Princess Christian nurses had begun to vie with Norlanders (in the nicest possible way) for vacancies in royal nurseries.

But with traditional nurses, independent 'lady' nurses and college-educated nurses all working for the same group of people, how did they get on? Margaretta Eagar and Lilian Wilson were social opposites and yet friends; Emma and Georgina Hobbs were sisters who could hardly be left alone together. In large nurseries friction was a common theme and rigid hierarchies were devised to keep it in check. When the Princess Royal took on a second nurse in Berlin in 1862 to help Emma Hobbs with her rapidly growing family – the birth of a third child was then imminent – her mother was quick to offer advice. 'I hope dear, that your second nurse is not equal to Mrs Hobbs? We never had a second nurse, but only a head nursery maid, capable to act as a nurse, and I hope you will not attempt the contrary or you will entirely fail. Dear Papa always directed our nursery and I believe none was ever better; I therefore should be sorry, if you went upon another system.'[38] This appears not to have had the desired effect and a week later the Queen returned to her theme; 'I hope you will take care that Mrs Hobbs is quite the head nurse', she wrote, 'else it won't go on! That every one will tell you, who has ever had a nursery.'[39] In 1868, with a fifth child on the way in Berlin and another nurse installed she tried once again, with an almost audible sigh of resignation: 'I hope the new person in the nursery will suit but you should not call her Nurse. Two nurses never will do. Dear Papa, the Baron and Sir James as well as Lady Caroline will tell you and can tell you that never can answer. I mention them as I know that my experience and advice never goes for much with you, dear child.'[40]

The Queen may very well have given the same advice to her granddaughter the Tsaritsa. In her nursery from 1899 to 1905 Margaretta Eagar was nurse and the rest of the staff answered to her. Given previous experience of unwanted Cossacks in the nursery Margaretta was most particular on one point. 'The maids in the nursery used always to tell me if any man paid them attentions,' she wrote, 'and just for all the world like an anxious mother, I used to make enquiries about his character, temper, position in life, and whether the would-be suitor could give his wife a home of her own. If satisfied on these points I made no objection, but allowed the wooing to continue, but I would never hear of allowing any of them to go and live in the country with the husband's relations, and be treated as a beast of burden.'[41] There was harmony in the nursery and the Tsar approved; 'all runs smoothly between nurse and the other girls,' he told his mother in the autumn of 1900, 'it is real paradise in comparison with the dismal past.'[42]

The only problems Margaretta experienced came from another source. The Tsaritsa's old nurse Mary Ann Orchard had followed her to Russia. She was long past actual nursing but they gave her an honorary right to supervise the nursery. Margaretta rarely mentioned her in her memoirs but there is one very telling little glimpse. One day, she said, the children were enjoying a noisy game, 'and old Mrs O, who had brought up the Tsaritsa, came into the room. She began to rebuke me for letting them romp, and declared that their mother had never made a noise in all her life. And I said, "We have all heard so often that the Tsaritsa was a perfect angel when she was a child, but she has only given me human children to look after." Olga was listening, and rushed across the room, threw her arms round me, and exclaimed earnestly – "I won't be a *human* child, I'll be an angel child too." She was greatly comforted when I told her I preferred her as she was.'[43]

The advent of the professional 'lady' nurse into a world where the traditional servant nurse had held sway for generations offered obvious potential for conflict. This is apparent in the pages of the *Norland Quarterly* where contributors often returned to questions of how Norlanders should be identified and treated, and how they were to treat traditional nurses. Norlanders were supposed to be known as 'Nurse —', with their own name, while Princess Christian nurses preferred 'Miss —'. There was some debate about this in the *Quarterly* in 1928 and Irene Collenette, who then considered herself 'a very old Norlander', remarked, 'My testimonial book says: "The Norland Nurses are called 'Nurse', adding, if preferred, the Christian or surname." I think that is as it should be and I have always insisted on that title myself.'[44] 'Nana' or 'Nanny' were firmly ruled out, though in practice the nurse's title depended on the family. Lilian Eadie was always 'Nursie' to the Hesse princes and Kate Fox ended up as 'Nurnie' to the Nicholas children and 'Foxie' to their parents. But the distinction between nurses was a very sensitive point. The professionals considered themselves better, understandably, as they had invested time and money in their training and were expected to conform to a very high standard. They resisted any suggestion that they were servants and were hurt to be treated as such. But on a human level most were profoundly aware of how unattractive it was to adopt a superior attitude. In the summer of 1904 May Palmer, who would later work for the Princess of Thurn and Taxis, wrote to the *Quarterly* condemning the 'I am a Lady Nurse, and I don't speak to common nurses' attitude she had noticed in some of her colleagues.[45]

In Greece in the early 1900s the royal family employed a mixed community of nurses whose relationships are captured in vivid detail in the letters Princess Nicholas sent to Kate Fox whenever they were separated. Lively, chatty – utterly biased towards her own point of view and her own children – they evoke the atmosphere of the nurses' world and the friendships and tensions played out between them, which precisely mirrored the feelings of the mothers they served. At the start of the correspondence, the King and Queen of the Hellenes had five grown-up sons in Greece: Crown Prince Constantine, Princes George, Nicholas, Andrew and Christopher. They were close – and close to their only surviving sister Marie, Grand Duchess Georgi Mikhailovich of Russia – it was their wives who introduced a note of tension. Princess Nicholas, born a Grand Duchess of Russia, and Princess Andrew, Princess Alice of Battenberg, found it hard to get beyond a rather brittle cordiality. It is always said that Princess Nicholas was too proud of her imperial lineage to accept a sister-in-law born into a morganatic family, with no rights of succession, but there is no sense of this in the letters. Rather, Princess Alice was someone Princess Nicholas simply did not understand and could not warm to and, on a very human level, both young mothers were constantly on watch to see that their children received a fair share of the King and Queen's attention.

This was the real rivalry, and the nurses were in it with them. The three Nicholas children, Olga, Elizabeth and Marina, were nursed by Kate Fox until 1913, with other Norlanders as back-up, then, after 1913, by another Norlander, Margaret Alison. It was ironic, perhaps, that against these 'lady' nurses was set Emily Roose, the traditional nurse Princess Alice employed for all five of her children: her elder daughters, Margarita and Theodora, who were close in age to Elizabeth and Marina, then Cecile, Sophie and Philip (HRH Prince Philip, Duke of Edinburgh), who was born on Corfu in 1921. Emily was two years younger than Kate Fox. She came from Plymouth and her father was a boot maker. In 1901 she was nurse to the children of Commander Herbert Savory, RN in Kensington and this may be the link that took her to Greece: Princess Alice's father, Prince Louis of Battenberg, was in charge of Naval Intelligence at the Admiralty when his daughter first needed a nurse, and he and his wife may well have known Commander Savory. On the fringes of the argument were the nurses of the other family groups: 'Gertie' Salmond and Elizabeth St John for the Crown Prince's family, Nana Bell for Princess Marie's.

The rivalry between mothers and nurses began with a niggling attention to detail on both sides. In the summer of 1909 when the two Princesses and their children were staying with the King and Queen at Tatoi and Kate Fox was on leave, Princess Nicholas told her, 'The children have got the good nurseries with the big balcony & Roosie is where we were last time – P^cess Alice told me that you told Roosie that you wanted to have these nurseries! is that true? . . . Roosie proposed that they should all drive together in case there is no second carriage & that they should also have tea together. The children are delighted to have their little cousins to play with. The King seemed very pleased to see our children.'⁴⁶ The following spring Kate and the children were with their Russian grandmother when Princess Nicholas visited Corfu: 'Margarita and Dolla [Theodora] received us at the palace & of course were made much of being the only children; how I wish ours were there!'⁴⁷ And a few days later, 'Margarita & Dolla are very much made of here; they go every day in the yacht while we are having lunch there & play about all the afternoon; I heard one of the gentlemen telling P^cess Alice that he had never seen such dear children – Roosie must be having a grand time; she went there to church on Sunday & in the evening went to a performance given by the sailors to which we all went.'⁴⁸

Emily Roose was loved by Princess Alice's family but Princess Nicholas harboured dark suspicions of her: that she was not so careful with the children as Kate, that she put too much energy into her social life. In the spring of 1914, after Kate had gone back to England and Margaret Alison had taken over, Emily had a serious illness coinciding with Princess Alice's fourth pregnancy and a new nurse was brought in to assist her, a young Norlander named Gladys Metzger. After this the trouble really began. 'It will interest you to know,' Princess Nicholas told Kate in the early weeks of 1915, 'that P^cess Alice's little nurse (the Norland probationer), is very unhappy & wants to leave – Roosie is horrid to her & makes life unbearable.' We can almost hear Kate Fox pulling the strings of this one, tutting at the idea of a Norland nurse being placed under a traditional nanny; 'Do you remember', Princess Nicholas wrote, 'you told me you thought it would never do, when I told you that P^cess Alice had engaged a Norlander as under nurse to Roosie. She is such a nice girl, lady-like & always bright & cheerful & ready to work & do all she can, but R gives her practically all the work to do – she used to go out night after night & let that poor girl sit up till goodness knows what hour.'⁴⁹

Poor Gladys had inadvertently stirred a hornets' nest by crying on Margaret Alison's shoulder. Margaret told Princess Nicholas, then they weighed in on Gladys's side, advising her first to write to Miss Sharman at Norland, then to hand in her notice, which she finally did in April. Princess Alice must have realised the part Princess Nicholas and her nurses had played in the affair and Gladys's announcement produced one of those emotional scenes in which old resentments are brought to the surface and people say more than they mean, or can easily retract when tempers cool. Princess Nicholas spared no details when she described it all to Kate: 'You <u>can't think</u> what P^cess Alice told her . . . Nurse Marg was horrified. She said that . . . you & I used to do nothing but scold the children from morning till night & that there were only two people in Athens who knew how to manage children & that was herself & Roosie!!!'[50] This is only one side of the story, of course, and Princess Alice must have felt just as hurt, just as outraged. But the atmosphere was now thoroughly soured and as far as Princess Nicholas was concerned the family had split into two camps; herself and Margaret Alison against Princess Alice and the conniving Roosie.

In March Princess Nicholas told Kate that the housekeeper had gone over to Roosie's side. By the autumn she was convinced that Elizabeth St John had joined the enemy camp. 'The jealousy of the other nurses for our children continues to be the same,' she told Kate. 'Nurse Margaret tells me many curious little incidents; Roosie & St John are very friendly & always sit out together & leave Nurse M out. Baby Catherine has got a little house at Phaeleron where they have tea; the other day it was very windy & cold & St John asked Roosie & her babies to have tea with her, but not a word was said to our children who had to have their tea out on the beach in the wind . . . it reminds me so of the old days & all you used to tell me.'[51] It was petty and trivial but outside pressure would soon bring about a complete reversal of feeling. In 1917 the Greek royal family was forced into exile. The years that followed were painful enough to eclipse all other bitterness, so that when Princess Nicholas met Emily Roose and the children again in the early weeks of 1920 it was as if the old tensions had never been; 'To me Roosie is a part of the old days, the only one remaining of those far-off baby-days,' the Princess told Kate, 'Her hair is quite grey now.' Later that year she would write without a trace of irony, 'It was so nice to see Roosy again. She told me, she had written to you and said that your handwriting brought back the happy old days of long ago.'[52]

THREE

'A Lady-like Form of Suicide'

GOVERNESSES

I felt that a new life, quite unknown, was opening before me, and its very brilliancy, to one who had always lived in retirement, was startling. My future pupils came forward to meet me: the elder, a blooming girl of sixteen, fresh as a rose, but more womanly in appearance than I had expected . . . the younger, a pretty child of eleven, more shy than her sister. The rooms, plainly furnished in bright chintz, looked comfortable and homelike. After a few minutes of general conversation, the door suddenly opened, and the Duchess came in quickly; a tall, graceful figure, very commanding in appearance, the court lady from head to foot, very beautiful, and most elegantly dressed. Being very near-sighted, she drew close to me with half-shut eyes and peered down at me, very much as if she were trying to find a fly on the carpet; but in the conversation that followed, when we had resumed our seats, her manner was most courteous, and even a little embarrassed. . . .[1]

The 'fly on the carpet' was Anna Bicknell, being interviewed by the Duchesse de Tascher de la Pagerie, wife of the Grand Master of the Household to the Empress Eugénie, at the Tuileries in 1856. The Duchesse needed a governess for her daughters, Eugénie and Hortense, and Anna had been recommended to her by relatives. Anna tells us nothing of where she herself came from, beyond hinting that her father's background was military. She gives no indication of what she did before arriving in Paris, but it seems that she fitted the requirements of the Duchesse, who wanted 'a gentlewoman, accustomed to good society, conscientious and reliable, who would be capable of entirely filling her place by her daughters, and who would constantly be their friend and guide.'[2] The only reservation the Duchesse had was that Anna seemed very young, but the other applicants did not appeal to her as much. So Anna was chosen and lived at the Tuileries for nine years, a modest, clear-eyed observer in the midst of an extravagant fantasy.

The qualities the Duchesse had recognised in Anna – gentility and pleasant manners in company which would set her daughters a good example – were the qualities royal and noble houses had looked for in their governesses for generations. A few years later the Queen of Hanover, wanting someone to supervise her own two daughters, twelve-year-old Frederica and ten-year-old Mary, approached their previous governess Margaret Collins for advice. Margaret had left the family to marry a German nobleman. When asked to recommend someone 'young, well bred, soft and not seeking her own amusement', she thought of her cousin Pauline Harriet Stewart, from Hillhead in Scotland, always known as 'Hartie'. Hartie was chosen and arrived in Hanover in February 1860. With a cousin already in place to show her her duties it was a painless beginning for her and the Hanover family welcomed her as one of their own.[3]

If the young ladies of the Norland Institute and Princess Christian's had been born half a century earlier, they may well have found themselves in a similar position to Hartie or to Anna or, worse, may have languished in far less grand houses, longing for admission to the upper levels of society where a governess had her best hope of being treated well. For generations, being a governess was the only respectable work open to women from professional backgrounds when circumstances forced them to earn a living, but the very name carried a stigma. Most governesses led a miserable existence, whether at home or overseas. In her 1866 novel *Wives and Daughters*, Mrs Gaskell called the governess trade in Russia 'a lady-like form of suicide'. Governesses were valuable but they were not valued: when the Brontës described the treatment meted out to Jane Eyre and Agnes Grey they were writing about what they themselves had suffered. At her own level of society the governess was despised because she was equal or superior to her employers in every respect but one: they had money and she did not. Her presence was a constant reminder of what could happen to them if the money ran out.

But aristocratic and royal employers were different. When May T found herself unable to sleep for excitement on her first night in the castle of Count Badeni, the Austrian Governor of Poland, she turned to her diary. 'The Count is delightful', she wrote, 'and they have all treated me as an honoured guest; there is not a touch, trace, or hint of the "You are a paid companion, and do not forget it" attitude. It just shows that the higher one goes, the more considerate the treatment. In a family such as this is, to be good enough to be with them and teach them, one is as good as they themselves are.'[4] And happy as she was during her time with the Badenis, May's ambitions reached higher yet. On 28 April 1895 she announced to her mother: 'You will be pleased to hear that I am appointed English governess to the Archduchess Elizabeth Marie, the only child of the late Archduke Rudolph, and granddaughter to the Emperor of Austria. I am delighted, as I always told you I meant to be in a Royal Family.'[5]

May is an enigma. She published her memoirs anonymously while including several photographs of herself in the book. She even told her readers her height, five foot ten – 'it is such a blessing to be tall!', she said.[6] That her Christian name was May is apparent only from a facsimile letter in the book to 'Dear May' written by the little Archduchess, and the initial 'T' (or possibly a reversed 'F') for her surname appears on another facsimile. Otherwise she remains a puzzle. Much of her book is taken up with letters to her mother, whom she addressed as 'My dearest Ver'. She had brothers, whom she did not name, and she mentioned two sisters: Lily, who became engaged in the early summer of 1896, and another, identified only as 'A'.

May was a fervent Roman Catholic, conversant with Church politics at the highest level and fired with a sense of vocation. She seemed to have a knack of forming instant friendships with influential people – the Hungarian Countess Karolyi, for example, who met her during a retreat in a Viennese convent and promptly asked her to stay for several months. In the same way she became close to Madame Merry del Val, whose husband was the Spanish Ambassador in Rome. May stayed at the embassy and in the spring of 1896 the couple's son, Monseigneur Merry del Val, who was private secretary to Pope Leo XIII and a rising star within the Catholic hierarchy, secured a private audience for May with the Pope himself. The Pope was very elderly and frail at that time and individual papal audiences were rare, yet May knelt at his feet and discussed the position of her pupil's mother Archduchess Stephanie at the Austrian Court – but with all this, May's sister 'A' was Protestant. When she mentioned the Russian Church to May in a letter, May's reply – perhaps slightly tongue-in-cheek – changed 'Church' to 'Schism' and added, 'The word "Church", I understand, you claim for your own little heresy, but there is a limit to such charity. Ever your affectionate sister . . .'[7] But who was May? The final clue, the dedication of her book to 'my best loved pupil Ursula Chaloner' leads nowhere. Ursula was the daughter of the 1st Baron Gisborough, but surviving members of the family have no record of the name of her governess.

In some respects Ethel Howard is as enigmatic, though she did at least leave her name and a fragment of her story. The youngest child but one in a large and close family, Ethel showed none of the ladylike skills of her sisters but she was clever, so her father – who must have been a teacher, or perhaps a clergyman – educated her as he would a boy, drumming mathematics and the classics into her head in the hope that she would go to university. In the 1880s this was a very unusual ambition for the parent of a daughter but in the event it was Ethel who rebelled. Finding her unwilling to go on studying, her father steered her towards teaching instead. She began to offer private coaching and her second pupil was Prince Sitiphorn, a nephew of the King of Siam; this suggests that her family must have been well connected.

The next stage of Ethel's career was decided behind her back. In 1895 Kaiserin Auguste Viktoria approached her former governess Miss Walker, principal of the Royal School in Bath, for advice on a governess for her elder sons. Miss Walker was a family friend of the Howards and recommended Ethel, without consulting her. The first Ethel knew about it was a letter in a crested envelope from Berlin offering her the position: she thought it was a joke and ignored it. Then she received an indignant note from Miss Walker, passing on complaints from the German Mistress of the Robes. The Kaiserin was very keen to have Ethel because she was young enough to cope with five active boys; 'They liked the governess to play games with the Princes and join in the fun generally,' Ethel said, 'and not to mind any little harmless boyish pranks.'[8] So when Ethel tried to decline on the grounds that she had little French and no music, it was made perfectly clear to her that 'no' was the wrong answer. Having no choice, she duly set out for Berlin in December 1895, though 'my courage failed me and I actually jumped out of the railway carriage, exclaiming, "No, I can't go so far from home, not for any Emperor!" My mother, whom I worshipped,' she said, 'gently pushed me in again; and so, amid blinding tears, I set forth to my new life.'[9]

Ethel was one of a long line of English governesses at the Berlin Court that seems to have started in 1870 in the family of the Crown Princess of Prussia (the Princess Royal, later Kaiserin Friedrich). The first governess to her children was a German, Sophie, Baroness von Dobeneck, who started work in the spring of 1861. Her role was like Anna Bicknell's, to supervise every aspect of the children's lives rather than to teach them, and the Crown Princess was not happy with her. She complained to her mother that the Baroness,

> never left the children for one minute all day and directed their lessons which she understood nothing about – and did a great deal of harm. I cannot and will not abandon all right of interfering with the children's education, and must reserve to myself to judge of what they are to learn and who is to teach them and also of making remarks to the governess who has charge of them. It is very difficult here as the princesses were given up hand and foot to a countess or a baroness who had the unlimited control over everything – lessons, meals, dress, walks and all answerable to the sovereign whoever he might be. This is the predicament here.[10]

Sophie Dobeneck had left to be married in the summer of 1866, shortly before this letter was written. For a few years the Crown Princess was content to leave the teaching to her eldest son's tutor and the French teacher, Octavie Darcourt, and to do the supervising herself, but as her second daughter, Princess Victoria, approached schoolroom age she was persuaded to try something new. She had misgivings about this but her elder daughter Charlotte, who was six, seemed too disruptive to share lessons with a younger child. 'I forget whether I told you that we have engaged an English governess for this autumn called Miss Byng,' the Crown Princess told her mother. 'I wish we could have done with Mlle Darcourt alone, as it causes us a deal of extra expense and trouble, but everyone was *d'accord* that it would not be good to put another child with Charlotte on account of the peculiar difficulties in her education. . . . So I gave way, at first against my will but now I think they are right. When we return to Berlin next November (if we are all alive) Vicky will go to Miss Byng. Having an English governess saves my having English masters and mistresses who are very difficult to get here – and with whom we have had a deal of trouble. The children must be able to talk and write good English.'[11]

The choice was far better than she knew. Augusta Maria Byng turned out to be a natural teacher who succeeded in winning over even the difficult Princess Charlotte; in one letter of 1874 the then teenaged Princess signed herself, 'Your most affectionate & dutiful & most obedient & most naughty little friend Charlotte.'[12] The Prussian royal children obeyed Augusta, teased her, played with her and adored her; they called her 'Spin' or 'Minny'. Princess Victoria remembered how her little brother Waldemar, who was not even born when Augusta started working for the family, paid their governess what seemed to him to be the highest possible tribute: 'One afternoon when we were seated in the schoolroom he spent some minutes gazing intently at . . . Miss Byng. Then he said very suddenly and seriously: "Minnie! You've got a face like a horse." Miss Byng was terribly upset,' the Princess said, 'but poor Waldemar really meant it as a compliment, since he adored horses above all other creatures.'[13] It is the only glimpse that remains of Augusta Byng's appearance.

Augusta's teaching gift seems to have been something of a family trait. Born in Staines, to the west of London, in about 1829, she came from a prosperous family: officially her father William Bateman Byng described himself as 'gentleman' but he was also a scientist, civil engineer and public benefactor, credited with establishing the gas works at Staines and Egham. It may not sound very inspiring today, but in the 1830s gaslight was hailed as a miracle and when Augusta was a little girl, her father's public lectures, 'On the process of extracting gas from coal, for the purposes of illumination', were like the performances of a magician, drawing large and excited audiences. The *Windsor and Eton Express* described how William Byng would outline the composition of coal and the general properties of gases in simple terms, then give practical demonstrations with the aid of beautifully constructed models, to loud cheering from his audience. 'When Mr Byng . . . lectures upon the subject of coal gas, we listen with unabated faith – we feel perfectly satisfied of the reality of his facts, and the testimony of his experience.'[14] Was this what fired his daughter with the ambition to teach? She had no need to earn a living; William Byng was a wealthy man, owning houses in Kent and Suffolk as well as in Staines, and his daughter's career was established long before he died. But it seems fair to guess that a man so committed to the idea of public education would have demonstrated his scientific toys to his children too and he must have been an inspiring teacher; in adult life his son Henry followed his engineering footsteps while Augusta went on to hold smaller audiences spellbound with her own special brand of magic.

In August 1881 Augusta was suddenly forced to retire through illness and a replacement had to be found. In the spring of that same year a governess named Marianne Elizabeth Green was working at Sutton House in York, teaching the three teenaged daughters of Georgiana Liddell, a widow, whose late husband's family had associations with the Court. Whether this was how the Crown Princess found Marianne is never stated, but by the beginning of September the governess was preparing to go to Berlin and the Crown Princess asked Augusta to take on one last commission on her behalf. 'It is most kind of you dearest Minny to say you will see Miss Green', she wrote. 'I hope you will tell her all you can think of. She has been highly recommended to me – and will I trust get the little people on with their lessons – and be able to keep them in order for the winter.'[15]

The two governesses met as promised on the very day this letter was written and Augusta reported back straight away. 'Many thanks for your dear letter of the 11th,' the Crown Princess replied a few days later. 'It is such a comfort to have a few lines from you now and then, but you <u>must</u> <u>not</u> tire yourself or do more than you feel <u>quite</u> <u>fit</u> for! It is most kind of you to see Miss Green! I am afraid the children will not make it easy for her at first, they are so loyal to their own Minny & so fond of her that any one else [who] attempts to take even a part of her duties – they will not readily accept – but I hope this difficulty can be got over! . . . I am very glad you liked her, on the whole; I too thought her pleasing.'[16] In October Marianne Green arrived in Berlin on a temporary appointment that would last for the next eight years.

It is apparent that both the Crown Princess and Augusta did have reservations about Marianne at first, though in many ways she was the classic governess and her references were impeccable. A clergyman's daughter from Nayland in Suffolk, Marianne had been to Germany before and her grasp of the language was good. She was thirty-four, eighteen years younger than Augusta, but was not so warm or so immediately sympathetic a person on first meeting. It would have been hard for anyone to follow a governess as popular as Augusta Byng and Marianne took time to establish her own place within the family. 'Miss Green is very nice,' Princess Victoria commented in a letter to Augusta after Marianne's first few weeks in Berlin, 'but I can not get very fond of her yet'.[17] Later letters would send greetings from Miss Green, or mention briefly something she had done or said: in time she did gain affectionate respect from the Princesses, but not the playful, confident love they continued to feel for Augusta Byng.

Marianne Green belonged to a new wave of academic governesses whose approach was more serious and their manner more brusque and unemotional; this must in part have been a defence mechanism in a society which saw something mannish and unnatural in an educated woman. One of the Crown Princess's letters suggests that Marianne had formal qualifications; these probably came from Queen's College in London, which began to issue 'Certificates of Qualification for Governesses' from the time of its foundation in 1848. The college was set up under the auspices of the Governesses' Benevolent Institution, founded under royal patronage five years earlier to raise the status of governesses and so to improve female education in general.[18] Some of the foremost names in Victorian women's education were students of Queen's in the early years: Dorothea Beale, headmistress of the Cheltenham Ladies' College, for example, and her colleague Frances Buss, of whom schoolgirls would later chant:

> Miss Buss and Miss Beale Cupid's darts do not feel
> How different from us, Miss Beale and Miss Buss

This echoed the feeling (quite natural to schoolgirls) that too much education would rob a girl of her chances of marriage. Higher education was still the province of men. The Crown Princess made a telling remark in 1887 when her sister-in-law was looking for a governess: 'Miss Green,' she said, 'is as learned & clever as a man.'[19]

Another reservation, apart from Marianne Green's manner, concerned her political views. Augusta Byng said as much when she reported on their meeting to the Crown Princess, comparing Miss Green to a governess at the Berlin Court whom they both knew well. 'As to Miss Green's politics – and their being the same as Miss Jackson's,' the Crown Princess said in reply, 'I regret it but it does not matter! I am tolerant, I hope, as becomes a true Liberal.'

The Miss Jackson they referred to was ten years older than Marianne Green and cast in the same, no-nonsense mould. A woman of very forthright opinions,

Margaret Hardcastle Jackson is said to have walked out of a position with the Herbert family because her employer converted to Catholicism. She was a strong person and she needed her strength, working in the household of Prince Friedrich Karl of Prussia; his brutality to his family was renowned. A shock wave had swept the European Courts in 1858 when his immediate response to the birth of a third daughter instead of the son he craved was to strike his wife so hard on the head that her hearing was damaged for life. He was the Crown Prince's cousin and the Crown Princess felt great sympathy for his wife and encouraged his youngest daughter, Princess Luise Margarete, to mix with her own children. In July 1877 she told Queen Victoria, 'We take little Louise of Fritz Carl's with us to Ostend, she is so pleased, poor child, she is by far the nicest most sensible and nice of Marianne's girls, the only one who is intimate with our children . . . and quite brought up by an excellent English governess, a Miss Jackson, whose sister is governess to the Duchess of Buccleuch's daughters.'[20] 'Little Louise' was approaching seventeen at this time, and by the end of the year Margaret Jackson had moved on to the Hesse family.

It was Margaret's advanced approach to the teaching of girls which secured her the position in Darmstadt. The Crown Princess's younger sister Princess Alice, Hereditary Grand Duchess of Hesse, had five daughters by 1877, the eldest of whom, Princesses Victoria and Elisabeth, were then in their early teens. Their mother had very progressive views on their education which so far had been undertaken by a succession of governesses. 'You say rightly, what a fault it is of parents to bring up their daughters with the main object of marrying them,' she had commented to Queen Victoria a few years earlier. 'I want to strive to bring up the girls without seeking this as the sole object for their future – to feel they can fill up their lives so well otherwise.'[21] Margaret Jackson was a woman after her own heart. Both wanted the Princesses to grow into independent young women, capable of thinking for themselves and aware of the world around them. Margaret Jackson discussed politics with even the youngest child and she taught them about the conditions in which other people lived. She maintained a consistently high-minded tone in the schoolroom, forbidding gossip and training the girls to discuss abstract subjects intelligently.

Similar things are said of another English governess, Julie Douglas, who worked in the family of Prince Georg Viktor of Waldeck from the late 1860s, teaching Princesses Pauline, Marie, Emma and Helene. The small Court at Arolsen, a few miles to the west of Kassel, was not so important as Berlin or Darmstadt but the Prince and Princess were an intelligent, highly literate couple, keenly interested in the arts and sciences and all things of the mind and very ambitious for their children. One of their granddaughters would later write, 'Apart from their schooling by different tutors and governesses, the children also attended courses and did a great deal of independent reading. All were marked by this education and benefited from it later on. Meeting any one of them, one was invariably struck by their culture and general knowledge. The daughters had widely different talents; one was distinguished by erudition and a gift for science, another had a clear mind and great practical sense combined with a lively imagination.'[22]

The religious tone of the Waldeck household was also high, with strict morality and a sense of duty instilled into every child by the local pastor. Like Margaret Jackson, Julie Douglas gave a practical slant to this morality by teaching the Princesses about unemployment and the living conditions of the poorest working people and she encouraged them to join in with their mother's charitable projects. Julie was a gifted storyteller, who could hold her charges enthralled while at the same time introducing them to the lives of people so far removed from their own small world, both geographically and socially, that otherwise they could never have imagined their existence. Princess Emma, who went on to become Queen Regent of the Netherlands, recalled the lively mealtimes of her childhood when she and her sisters and Julie Douglas would sit down at table with the rest of their family and attendants; seldom less than fourteen people and each one expected to play a part in the conversation, whatever it might be.

All this learning and high-mindedness for girls, including princesses, was viewed with a degree of unease in a society which still expected little more of its women than to look decorative and chat politely over the teacups, to manage the servants, play piano duets and turn out some delicate handiwork in between pregnancies. For many families it was still enough to employ a traditional governess like Anna Bicknell, 'a gentlewoman, accustomed to good society, conscientious and reliable', who could set a refined example to her charges. May T appears not to have had any formal qualifications and to have done more supervising than teaching. Miss Walker, one the other hand, who recommended Ethel Howard for her position in Berlin, was almost certainly college-trained as she went on to be a headmistress, and Ethel was coached by her father, but there was never the same social divide between governesses as there was between college- and service-trained nurses. For a long time the two approaches coexisted amicably, though the idea of employing a qualified governess steadily gained ground. When the Duchess of Connaught (Miss Jackson's old pupil, 'Little Louise') asked the Crown Princess in 1887 to help her find a governess for her two daughters, she expressed a wish for the traditional qualities; someone ladylike, with a good command of languages and music. 'If you will let me continue my search,' the Crown Princess told her, 'I have no doubt that we could find some one! – I would advise her having passed her Governess examination or else, it is really <u>no use</u>.'[23]

Marianne Green was in Berlin long enough to see the Crown Princess's daughters outgrow the schoolroom. She saw the accession of their father Crown Prince Friedrich and his brief, tragic reign as Kaiser: he was suffering from cancer of the throat when his father died and survived him for only a few months. The same events were witnessed by the first English governess of the new generation, Ada Leslie, who joined the household of the Crown Prince and Princess's eldest son, the future Kaiser Wilhelm II, in November 1886. This was the family Ethel Howard would work for later, but in Ada's day there were only three boys – she saw the fourth one born – and the eldest was four years old when she arrived in Berlin.

At first sight, it is not immediately obvious whether Ada was a nurse or a governess: the only evidence of her time with the German imperial family is in the letters she sent to her cousin Mary Anne Galsworthy, 'Pollie', still kept by Pollie's descendants. They never mention her job title, which Pollie presumably knew. Ada began her working life as a nurse and her background was similar to other traditional nurses – Charlotte Bill, say, the Hobbs sisters or Millicent Crofts; like Millicent, Ada was a printer's daughter. She was born in Islington in the early spring of 1861, the second child of William and Sarah Leslie. They had a large family, with at least six daughters apart from Ada and two sons and, unlike the Crofts, the family did not employ a house servant. By 1881 Ada had left home and was working as a nurse in the household of John Riley, a shipowner who lived in Lambeth. In 1883 she found a position in India with a colonel and his family, as nurse to two small girls. 'Mother does not like me going at all,' she told Pollie, 'still it's only the idea – because you know I have been away from home so much.'[24]

In Berlin too, Ada was associated with the nursery because the children were so young. 'My duties are light and pleasant', she wrote to Pollie soon after her arrival. 'I think I told you there are three German nurses and there are two footmen who wait on the children's rooms and there are two carriages for their special use. The young Princes drive out every afternoon. I go with them as a rule every alternate day. It's great fun driving out with them.'[25] But she was not employed as a nurse. Gradually, through the letters, it emerges that Ada had achieved something very unusual when she took up her position at Court: her status had been raised from nurse to governess; servant to lady. This is apparent from her descriptions of the Court functions she attended, to which a nurse would not have been admitted. It is confirmed by the fact that in 1888 she was poached by the children's grandmother Kaiserin Friedrich (formerly the Crown Princess), to serve as lady-in-waiting, initially to herself but always with the intention that Ada would go to Greece with her daughter Princess Sophie when she married the following autumn. As lady-in-waiting to the Crown Princess of Greece, Ada visited and was accepted at several of the European Courts: her story demonstrates that though the society of the day was deeply divided, a woman with enough ability and confidence could still find her way across the gulf.

Unfortunately there is nothing to show how Ada made the all-important change. Appointments to the future Kaiser's family had never been smooth. In 1882, when the eldest Prince was born, the young parents caused terrible upset by ignoring his grandmother, the Crown Princess, and asking her sister Helena, Princess Christian, to find an English nurse for them; they then compounded the offence by dismissing this nurse and appointing a German in her place. From then on the nursery was staffed by Germans. But by 1886, with little Prince Wilhelm fast approaching schoolroom age, they must have decided that an English presence was necessary. They would not have advertised the position. They may have approached somebody like Miss Walker, who later found Ethel Howard for them, but it is also possible that Princess Christian and her daughters were involved in Ada's appointment. Ada was certainly in contact with them in 1891 when she wanted to find a position for her younger sister Josephine, then working as a lady's companion. 'Do you know I hope that Josephine will go to Berlin next June?' Ada told Pollie. 'You know perhaps that Princess Christian's second daughter is engaged to be married. She is going to marry a young German Prince and of course new people are being found to make up a new household. She is very nice, so I thought it would be rather a good thing to get Jo there as one of the dressers.'[26]

When Ada left Berlin in 1888 the vacancy was filled by a Miss Atkinson, an excellent linguist under whose guidance the Princes made up all the ground they had lost in not having an English nurse, and English took over as their first language. Ethel Howard encountered her briefly on arriving in Berlin in December 1895; Miss Atkinson had resigned due to ill health but stayed on long enough to meet Ethel at the station and explain her duties to her. A complete breakdown in health would also cause Ethel's resignation in 1898; the family did not appoint an English governess for some time after that. When they did, the governess did not stay long: succumbing to 'Cupid's dart' – it may have been rare for a governess, but it was possible – she left in a romantic flutter in August 1902 to prepare for her wedding, scarcely pausing to tell her successor anything but that white kid gloves were essential at all times and that everything else would become obvious to her.

This was not a reassuring beginning for Anne Topham, the daughter of a prosperous tenant farmer from Mackworth in Derbyshire, but at thirty-eight she was much older and more experienced than her immediate predecessors and she had travelled independently in Germany before. She swallowed her anxieties and coped – a task made all the more difficult for her by the fact that her immediate superior, the German 'Ober-Gouvernante', was ill and in quarantine, so she had two sets of duties to perform with no one to tell her what they were. Her feelings towards the departing English governess were neither warm nor friendly; 'to this day I bear her somewhat of a grudge,' she said.[27]

Anne's pupil was the seventh and youngest child and the only daughter in the Kaiser's family, Princess Viktoria Luise, and Anne saw her through to confirmation. This was an important rite of passage for a girl, marking her transition from child to young lady and her freedom from the schoolroom. Anne would later earn her living from writing about her experiences at the Kaiser's Court and in Germany generally, but she left no clue as to how she was chosen for the post.

It may be that she had met someone on her first visit to Germany who became her link to the Court. This is certainly what happened for the last of the Berlin governesses, Lilian Brimble. Lilian had spent three years in Germany in the early 1900s and she became friendly with two German countesses; it was on the invitation of one of them that she returned to Germany in 1911. The Crown Princess – Lilian's other friend was one of her ladies-in-waiting – interviewed her for the post of governess to Princes Wilhelm and Louis Ferdinand, eldest of her four sons. Lilian was appointed and stayed with the family until July 1914. She was on home leave when the First World War began: 'Early in August the Crown Princess cabled me to the effect that she would be glad if I could return immediately, but quite understood if it were impossible,' she wrote, 'it seemed wiser to wait and see how matters would develop before taking any definite steps to return. Two days later England declared war on Germany and Austria, so of course I never went back.'[28]

Within Europe, personal recommendation was the norm. A royal lady who needed an English governess for her children would usually start by asking around her family and ladies or by consulting someone she trusted: her own former governess, perhaps, or an English governess working for another royal family whom she had met and liked. Application to someone at the English Court, like Princess Christian and her daughters, could also produce results. Some royal ladies would then interview applicants themselves while others left this to their senior lady-in-waiting; in cases like May T and Ethel Howard the appointment seemed to go on trust alone, with no interview considered necessary. A governess may be ambitious to work at Court – as May was – but the only route was to prove herself in the job and attract the eye of the right people. Beyond Europe, however, where English governesses were just as much in demand, a woman could make the opportunities for herself.

This certainly happened in the case of Maria Graham, a naval officer's widow and inveterate traveller and diarist, whose husband died of fever off Cape Horn in April 1822. She lived in Chile for a while before setting out again, entering the Bay of Rio de Janeiro on board Admiral Lord Cochrane's flagship on 13 March 1823. Her intention was to sail for home but while in Brazil she requested an audience with the newly crowned Empress Leopoldina, an Austrian Archduchess by birth, whose elder sister Marie Louise had been Napoleon's Empress. Leopoldina was gentle, shy, fiercely intellectual and very much alone in Brazil, where the rather more earthy husband whom she adored to distraction was cohabiting openly with his mistress. Leopoldina took an immediate liking to Maria, who became ill soon after her arrival and was forced to stay longer in Rio than she intended. She was invited to the San Cristovao Palace several times and was struck by the intelligence of the imperial couple's eldest child, four-year-old Dona Maria da Glória. Maria told a Brazilian friend that she would like to educate the little girl. The next thing she knew, the Empress had taken up the idea and asked her to apply to the Emperor for the role of governess. 'I remained marvelling at the chance that had brought me into a situation so unlike anything I had ever contemplated,' Maria noted in her diary.[29]

She wrote the application, as commanded, and by 16 October 1823 had been officially appointed governess, with leave to go to England for a full year first, to wind up her affairs following the death of her husband and to collect anything she needed for her new life. But soon after her arrival in England the year was cut to six months, then representatives of the Brazilian government arrived urging her to sail for Rio at once. Friends were very sceptical about her future. The novelist Maria Edgeworth, whose cautionary tales for children and manuals for parents and teachers would have been familiar in most school-rooms, offered some hard-headed advice: 'be clear before you take the weight of labour and responsibility . . . that there is a solid well-secured remuneration balancing the weight,' she told Maria. 'Whatever you agree for, put in writing, for verbal agreements, though mighty pleasant and made with a smile on the face and flattery on the lips, at Court or Drawing Room, are after all precarious tenures.'[30] Miss Edgeworth had clearly been around. But Maria Graham, unwilling to disappoint the gentle Empress, gathered up her globes, her storybooks (specially translated into Portuguese, the language of the Brazilian Court) and all the schoolroom equipment she had bought and set off for Brazil less than two months after she had left, to take up the appointment she herself created.

The most famous English royal governess of all, Anna Leonowens, was, like Maria Graham, a widow, forced to make her own way in the world. Representations of Anna have sung and danced across stages and cinema screens for decades in the musical *The King and I*; the true story is less romantic and more complex. In her later writings, Anna claimed to have been born in Wales in 1834, the daughter of an army officer – officers' families, like clergy families, had always been a good source of respectable governesses. Anna said that her father was posted to India when she was six years old and her mother went with him, leaving her and an older sister behind for their education; that her father was killed on the north-west frontier, and she sailed to India at the age of fifteen only to find her mother remarried to a man she did not like. To escape her stepfather's plan to marry her to a man twice her age, she said, she left on an extended tour of the Middle East with a clergyman and his wife, returning two years later with the confidence to elope with the husband of her choice, a young officer named Thomas Leonowens. It was a happy marriage which lasted until Thomas suffered a stroke and died, while hunting tigers in Singapore.

This was not quite true. Anna was really born in Ahmadnagar in India, on 6 November 1831, and her background was certainly not that of the typical governess, or one that would have been acceptable in Europe. Her father Thomas Edwards, who died before her birth, was no officer but a cabinet maker from London who volunteered for the Bombay Infantry in 1824 and rose to the rank of sergeant. It is said, though without conclusive proof, that his wife Mary Anne was partly Indian; when he died leaving her penniless, six months pregnant and with one small daughter, she had no option but to remarry. In January 1832, when Anna was two months old, Mary Anne became the wife of Patrick Donohoe, a corporal in the engineers.

Some accounts of Anna's childhood would have it that she was an 'army rat', brought up in the squalid setting of a communal barracks and exposed to the daily lives of the men, but the truth was probably not so grim. Patrick Donohoe was seconded to the public works department and worked his way through a series of respectable postings in Deesa, Aden and Poona, always taking his growing family. Anna is most likely to have received her education in the garrison schools. In about 1849, during her family's time in Aden, she did embark on a long tour of the Middle East, as she said, with the resident chaplain, the Reverend George Percy Badger. A recognised expert in oriental studies and perceptive critic of colonialism, Badger must have noticed how bright the seventeen-year-old was and he began to teach Anna about the cultures, religions and languages of the East, firing the interest that would last for the rest of her life. But the rather gleeful speculation in several books about what else the clergyman might have been doing with a teenage girl turns out to be unfounded; his wife Maria was in the party, just as Anna said.[31]

On her return, on Christmas Day 1849, Anna married Thomas Owens, a clerk from the commissary general's office at Bombay whom she is thought to have met three or four years earlier. It was no elopement; Anna's stepfather and sister were at the wedding, but there seems no reason to doubt her word that she and Thomas were happy. Somewhere around the middle of 1852 they began to use the surname 'Leonowens' and they went to Perth in Western Australia, where Anna opened a school for 'young ladies'. Her first two children had died in infancy but in 1854 she gave birth to a daughter, Avis, and in 1856 to Louis, her only son. In February 1857 the family left for Singapore, then for Penang where Thomas became a hotel keeper. He died in 1859 and Anna, left penniless with two small children, returned to Singapore where she opened another school. She had been teaching there some three years when King Maha Mongkut, Rama IV, applied to his consul in Singapore and to William Adamson, manager of the Singapore branch of the Borneo Company, to find an English teacher for his children. Both men recommended Anna. 'At first it was with much reluctance that I consented to entertain the project,' she said, 'but, strange as it may seem, the more I reflected upon it the more feasible it appeared, until at length I began to look forward, even with a glow of enthusiasm, toward the new and untried field I was about to enter.'[32]

Like Ada Leslie, Anna Leonowens had managed to cross the social divides that dominated her part of the world on the strength of her own ability and personality. One other royal governess achieved a similar leap and, like Anna, appears to have embroidered the truth about her background in order to help her on her way. No discredit to her in this: though her story was to end unhappily, Miss E. Saxton Winter – Saxton Elizabeth Winter as her parents named her – was one of the best and most inventive royal governesses of her generation and she held one of the most responsible positions in Europe for ten successful years.

In the autumn of 1878 King Willem III of the Netherlands visited the Waldeck family at Arolsen and took a fancy to Julie Douglas's former pupil, Princess Emma, who was then nineteen. Most girls of Emma's age would have turned away from a sixty-one-year-old widower with a notorious temper and a hopelessly divided family. The match was viewed with considerable surprise and not a few raised eyebrows around the European Courts, but Emma was a clear-headed girl with a realistic understanding of what she was taking on.

Soon after the engagement she told Miss Smith, her old English nurse, 'I seek my happiness dearest Nanny in making the king happy and my future people. My task is a very difficult but a very high one, and if God grants me his help, I hope that I will be able to fulfil it.'[33]

Against all expectations the marriage was happy and Emma gave the King one child, a little girl. At that time the King had a son surviving from his first marriage, but Prince Alexander was almost completely estranged from his father and in 1884 he died, leaving three-year-old Princess Wilhelmina the only heir. To be her governess really would be a prestige appointment, with responsibility for an only child and future reigning queen. As the time drew near, Queen Emma consulted Julie Douglas, who had married the Reverend Peter Acland after leaving the Waldeck family, and asked for her help in finding the right person – but let Miss Winter take up the story: 'It was in the early autumn of 1885,' she said, 'that I was introduced by a mutual friend to the lady who had been entrusted by Her Majesty Queen Emma of Holland with the task of finding an English governess for the young Princess Wilhelmina, then a child of a little more than five years of age. I had always hoped, with the extravagant enthusiasm of youth, that Fate would be kind and provide me with some serious work in life. . . . But never, in my wildest fancies had I pictured myself as the trainer of a Royal child. After many doubtful misgivings I accepted the post, and on January 1st, 1886, I was officially nominated by His Majesty King Willem III, as English governess to his only child.'

Miss Winter was thirty years old at this time and in Holland it was believed – is believed to this day – that her father was an army officer. In fact he was a butcher, from Portland in Dorset. Saxton Winter may have created a new life history for herself, as Anna Leonowens did, or may simply have allowed someone else's misapprehension to pass uncorrected, but her true story makes her achievement all the more impressive. Her father Richard Winter was quite prosperous, for a butcher. The son of an innkeeper, he married Bernice White in the parish church of Melcombe Regis in July 1845. By 1861 their family was complete with five children: two sons, Robert and Richard, and three daughters, Saxton, Nancy and Bernice, for whom the parents were able to employ a teenage nursemaid. They also had one live-in servant and a butchery apprentice.

Their lives were blown apart when Richard Winter died, probably in the spring of 1863, and what happened next is a mystery. Robert, the eldest child, was seventeen and was probably already working. He became a carpenter and by 1871 was a married man. If Bernice could not afford to keep up the home and look after the four younger children herself, her normal recourse would have been first to family, then, if they were not able to help, to the relieving officer of the parish union, who administered poor relief under a Board of Guardians. From 1834 onwards this usually meant the workhouse, though in some districts widows with dependent children were given financial help at home. Often one or more of the children would be placed in the local orphanage – like Frances Fry and her twin sister Jane when their father died. The extraordinary thing about the Winter children is how widely they were scattered. By April 1871, ten-year-old Bernice was in the Female Orphan Asylum in Beddington in Surrey; Nancy, who was thirteen, was in the British Orphan Asylum in Upton cum Chalvey in Buckinghamshire (where Elizabeth Francklin's parents kept the local inn). Saxton, at fifteen, was a pupil in the Royal Asylum of St Anne's Society on Streatham Hill in London – a charity school set up in 1829 in a handsome, three-storeyed Georgian mansion to provide care and education for poor children. Richard, at eighteen, was working as a draper's clerk for a large business in central London, while their mother had left her native Dorset far behind and was matron of the hospital at Saffron Walden in Essex.

Whatever had happened, it must have been traumatic for the whole family, but it proved to be the foundation of Saxton's career. The St Anne's school had just under 200 pupils from all over the country of both sexes, ranging in age from seven to sixteen years, and a full complement of trained teachers and domestic staff. It offered a much more academic education than ordinary orphanages; most of their girl pupils were prepared for a life in service. While no hint remains to explain why Saxton was singled out for St Anne's, it seems likely that the selection was based on ability. She was clever, and benefited from a better education than she might have received if her family had stayed together. Her brother Richard may also have been at St Anne's: he too was well educated and in time became an ordained priest in the Church of England.

Saxton would have finished at the school in 1872, when she was sixteen. She may have joined her mother in Saffron Walden, as her younger sisters did when their time came. Nancy worked as a masseuse in the hospital and later inherited the matron's position, while Bernice became a milliner. But Saxton's sights were set much higher. Her first recorded governess position was a very good one, at Blithe Court in Newnham, Gloucestershire, working for the family of a solicitor, Augustus Henry Maule. She had three pupils, Lilian, Hugh and Monica, and they must have been fond of her: she remained in contact with the family for the rest of her life and in the 1930s Hugh became her executor. Saxton was with the Maule family in 1881 and it was probably from their home that she left to be governess to Princess Wilhelmina, who would later describe her as 'a strong personality, sincere and open . . . afraid of nobody. She was a "bold woman". She had all the virtues that characterize the

English nation and that it fosters in its children. These virtues form the backbone of the British nation,' Wilhelmina remembered, 'a fact often emphasized by Miss Winter.'[34]

It was fortunate that the British nation, in its capacity of governess, seemed to get on very well on the whole with the governesses of other nations, usually Swiss, French or German, who shared their responsibility for the children. Miss Winter stood alone for most of her years as governess to Princess Wilhelmina and shared the teaching with tutors, but this was rare in royal circles, where the children needed to be fluent in several languages.

Occasionally there was friction between governesses. Anne Topham described the difficulties she had with the first 'Ober-Gouvernante' under whom she had to work in Berlin, Fraülein von Thadden, who seemed to her to exercise an unhealthy influence over Princess Viktoria Luise, then about nine or ten years old. 'I found myself out of sympathy with von Thadden's methods,' Anne said. She described how, visiting her pupil to say goodnight at times when the Kaiserin was away, she would find the little girl crying into her pillow. 'I found out later that it was an axiom of Fraülein von Thadden's educational methods always at bed-time to work on a child's conscience. . . . The small disobediences and omissions of the child's life were made to appear enormous wickednesses, and the woman's strange travesty of piety was utilised to its full extent to give her power over the mind of the child.'[35] Then there would be sudden and arbitrary bans on things the little girl enjoyed doing – like riding, which Anne saw as a vital release of energy. It was a difficult situation, relieved only when the 'Ober-Gouvernante' had to leave for an operation and was afterwards pronounced unfit for the work, much to her annoyance.

For the most part, though, relationships between governesses were good. Relationships between governesses and nurses, on the other hand, were absolutely dreadful. Any idea that two British women working in the same household overseas should have been natural allies pales in the face of the evidence: far from cooperating, competing plans for the children set them against each other from the start. 'It used to hurt me very much that my only compatriot living within the Palace precincts should prove such an enemy,' Ethel Howard said, in describing her many battles with the children's nurse.[36] Mrs Matcham was appointed to the Berlin nursery in Miss Atkinson's time, when the fifth child, Prince Oskar, was a baby, and to say that Ethel and Mrs Matcham did not get on very well is an understatement. They hated one another on sight. 'If I drove with the Princes, she resented it,' Ethel said, 'in fact, whatever I did she resented. It was astonishing what power one in her position possessed, chiefly on account of her having the Kaiserin's maternal ear. She feared no one, and ruled the lackeys with a rod of iron, trying hard to annex me as nursery governess under her thumb. When I arrived, she tried to arrange that I should be given . . . the same status as nurse that she herself possessed. That she did not succeed was due to the governors, who naturally wished to give me my rightful position as a lady of the Court, provided on all public occasions I was kept in the background and not seen with the Princes.'[37]

Ethel believed that the children were coddled and cosseted too much and tried to introduce a little mess and mischief into their lives. She may have had a point: when Ada Leslie was with the Princes five years earlier, she told her cousin how snow had to be brought up to the playroom in a bucket for the children to play with indoors, snowballing anyone who came within reach. Ethel's fingers itched to gain control of the youngest boy Prince Joachim, a pampered little doll of five years old at the time of her arrival in Berlin, whose long blond ringlets had only just been cut away. Joachim was the pet of both his mother and Mrs Matcham. 'If I left him alone for a minute, he would scream and go on screaming till someone came,' Ethel said. 'When I would find him like this and tell him there was nothing to be afraid of, the old English nurse would arrive on the scene and resent my presence, generally managing to insinuate that it was I who had upset the child.'[38] Ethel described how one day, when the boys were playing in the garden, 'little Prince Joachim began to scream because he had some mud on his hands. His brothers took care to rub them well in the earth,' she said, 'in which drastic form of correction I assisted: his attitude seemed so unnatural in a child, and I wanted to teach him a more normal, boyish view of dirt!'[39] We can well imagine what Mrs Matcham thought of that.

Getting small princes dirty does seem to have been something English governesses liked to do. Lilian Brimble described some of her adventures with water and mud in the next generation, when she and the Crown Prince's elder sons would go mad in the garden, 'and we were looked at askance and with haughty disdain by the nursery party, who would promenade by, immaculately clad, just as we were in the thick of some delightful but watery game'.[40] Even larger princes came under the spell. One story she told described how, on a Sunday afternoon in May, she and her two Princes and their tutor casually began to divert a little stream in the park, digging with their hands and creating a waterfall on some marble steps, with a complete disregard for her own white muslin dress and the children's pristine white sailor suits. The diggings became more and more ambitious. Prince August Wilhelm, the children's uncle, came by and could not resist joining in, stripping off his jacket and waistcoat, and eventually his socks and shoes as well (it must have revived fond memories of boyhood games with Ethel). Then the dam they had made gave way and the greater part of a flower bed began to slide down the steps. 'By this time,' Lilian said, 'we were all past praying for', the boys soaked and filthy – 'but they had spent a gloriously happy afternoon' – and their uncle in such a state that he had to go back with them and wash in the nursery bathroom. The nurses, needless to say, were horrified, having had to drag two miserable smaller Princes past the diggings, flatly refusing to let them join in.[41]

But even when governesses were more ladylike there was a natural clash of interests. For the nurse, having exercised complete authority over the children's lives from the cradle, it was hard to give them up. In May 1861 the Princess Royal told her mother how Emma Hobbs reacted to the imminent arrival of her children's first governess; 'I foresee civil war,' she said, 'as Mrs Hobbs is frantic about it and in floods of tears from morning till night. I have made my mind up to every sort of storm.'[42] In response, Queen Victoria was most insistent once again on the importance of maintaining a clear hierarchy within the nursery so that everyone knew their place and she was probably right, to a point. But the rivalries that took place between nursery and schoolroom, nurse and governess – usually over very trivial issues – were an inevitable part of the system and it was probably just as well that palaces were large enough to allow ample space to each of the warring camps.

Anne Topham knew Mrs Matcham in Berlin several years after Ethel and the nurse had locked horns and she gained a rather different perspective. In her time there were no children left in the nursery and Mrs Matcham was ready to bow to the inevitable. Anne wrote,

> She has been thirteen years in the service of the Empress, has brought up the younger children from birth, watched by them together with their mother many nights when they were ill, and practically saved the life of Prince Joachim . . . by her constant and faithful care of his delicate infancy. But one by one her nurslings have been taken from her, not without a certain fierce opposition on her part. . . . It is not good for children to be, as they frequently are even in less illustrious circles, the centre of warring elements; so at last the inevitable happened, and with much reluctance 'Nanna's' dismissal to England, of course with an ample pension, was finally decided upon.

Anne provided comfort for the nurse in her last weeks at Court, and felt she had been 'a very efficient safety-valve for her emotions, which poured over me in a constant flood'.[43] In the struggle between governess and nurse, the governess was ultimately bound to win.

FOUR

'A Little World of its Own'

NURSERIES AND SCHOOLROOMS

The imperial palaces of St Petersburg are gradually coming back into their own, restored and refurbished for the pleasure of tourists and local people alike. But some parts of them are never likely to see the light of day; funds are limited and the administrative offices have to be housed somewhere. The nurseries on the upper floor of the Vladimir Palace on the city's Neva Embankment were once a byword for spaciousness and luxury. The palace itself was purpose-built in the late 1860s in anticipation of the day when Grand Duke Vladimir, the Tsar's second surviving son, would marry and have a family. Today the long, dark corridors of the nursery floor are drab and forbidding. The rooms where the children played and bathed and slept – and where their nurses slept too, in beds next to theirs or, later, in an adjacent room, well within hearing – are today offices or are used for storing the things no visitor wants to see: paint tins and workmen's benches, tools and cleaning rags.

But reminders of the past are everywhere: a narrow spiral staircase in wrought iron at the far end of the old nursery corridor was once used by the children to climb to the palace chapel. A glass panel set in the floor of a small box room gives a private view of the magnificent golden staircase below. The palace's first generation of children would have seen that staircase under construction. Their children, on visits to their grandmother, could have peered down and watched her visitors come and go from this secret vantage point, unseen and unsuspected, above the jewelled and glamorous adult heads. Most evocative of all, the alcove where the children's bath once stood retains its exquisitely painted panels of coloured tiles, with flowers and birds set against a brightly coloured background – turquoise on the dark side, brilliant yellow on the side facing the window, to catch and reflect the light. The designs are not childish, but the children must have loved their colour and detail.

The stories those rooms could tell . . . Grand Duke Kirill, one of the palace's first children, recalled from exile,

I remember two things, one was its gas-lit passages; interminable they seemed to us and cavernous! Gas at that time was something of a novelty, and even now I remember the interest which it aroused in us. The other memory I have is that of the Carcelle oil lamps, which were wound up like clocks by special lampmen.

It was in our nursery at the Vladimir Palace that I remember several visits from Grandpapa. This must have been two years before his murder. One occasion stands out clearly in my memory of early childhood days in connection with him. He had given us what might best be described as a wooden 'hill' – a kind of slanting platform from which we used to slide down on a carpet one after the other, like little icebergs sliding down into the sea. Grandpapa on these occasions would stand at the window watching and enjoying our performance with nurse Milly next to him encouraging us. I remember too the dolls he gave us. They were little stuffed soldiers, dressed in the various uniforms of the Guards.[1]

'Grandpapa' was Tsar Alexander II, who was assassinated in the streets of his capital in March 1881. Kirill remembered looking down from his nursery window and seeing the street lamps far below shrouded in black on the day of the funeral. 'Milly', Kirill's nurse Millicent Crofts, was the first Englishwoman to live and work in the Vladimir Palace nurseries. Kate Fox worked there too a generation later, when her little Greek princesses went to Russia on visits to their grandparents. 'Everything is exquisite,' she told her father. 'My nurseries consist of eight beautifully furnished rooms; dining-room, two saloon ante-rooms, night nursery, dressing-room, bathroom and so on. . . . There must be a regular army of servants here; it is a huge place. . . . We are such a distance from the Grand Duchess's rooms that when I take the children along to their mother I have to wait for them. It is too far to go again to fetch them.'[2] These early visits were exciting times for Kate but she would also endure the worst moments of her career in the luxurious nursery suite of the Vladimir Palace.

For the children, the nursery was a safe, private world, cut off from the rest of the house. Frances Fry's elder charge Maria Pavlovna recalled how she and her brother Dmitri 'lived with our nurses and attendants in a series of rooms on the second floor. This nursery suite, the domain of our infancy, was entirely isolated from the rest of the palace. It was a little world of its own, a world ruled by our English nurse, Nannie Fry, and her assistant, Lizzie Grove. . . . Few persons were permitted to visit us. When there was company we were not allowed downstairs. Various members of the imperial family paid occasional dutiful calls to our nursery. They would watch us play, exchange a few remarks with Nannie Fry, and rapidly depart.'³

Sometimes Maria and Dmitri were taken to play with the Tsar's little girls in the Alexander Palace at Tsarskoe Selo, where Margaretta Eagar held sway.

Their nursery apartments occupied an entire wing on the second floor of the Alexander Palace,' Maria said. 'These rooms, light and spacious, were hung with flowered cretonne and furnished throughout with polished lemonwood. The effect was luxurious, yet peaceful and comfortable. Through the windows you could see the palace gardens and guardhouses and a little beyond, through the grille of a high iron gate, a street corner. The Emperor's daughters were governed as we were, by an English head nurse assisted by innumerable Russian nurses and chambermaids, and their nursery staff was uniformed as ours was, all in white, with small nurse-caps of white tulle. With this exception: two of their Russian nurses were peasants and wore the magnificent native peasant costumes.⁴

The Victorian period saw a huge expansion in decorative items designed for the nursery – wallpapers, furniture and furnishings – and in ideas about making rooms more suitable for children's use. Margaretta's memoirs show how child-centred the Alexander Palace nurseries were, and how much thought had gone into their design. 'The walls of all the new rooms are painted in oil with beautifully executed friezes of the same flowers as appear in the chintz,' she wrote, 'interspaced with golden butterflies or birds. The bathroom has sea-gulls painted on the frieze. At the end of this suite is the play-room. It is all yellow and green, like a bunch of daffodils, and has a frieze of peacocks strutting about amidst greenery. The carpet is a pale sage green, unpatterned. Over each window is a panel, in painted poker work, each representing some scene in animal or bird life.'⁵

In the Winter Palace Margaretta lived and worked in nurseries which held an unusual position, on the ground floor beneath the Tsaritsa's rooms. The custom of putting nurseries on an upper floor was almost universal; it is said to derive from an old superstition that if a baby is to rise in the world it must be taken upstairs at birth. Generations of children had grown up in the Winter Palace but each successive family altered the apartments to suit their needs. In the 1890s the children had a 'mountain' – we would call it a slide – just as the Vladimir children did, in a room upholstered entirely in red, which was used for their dancing lessons. The next room in the suite was decorated in yellow brocade and housed their toys; next came the day nursery, overlooking the palace gardens and, beyond them, the quay and the Neva river. 'It is very sunny and bright, and is furnished in blue. A plain velvet pile blue carpet covers the floor. The walls are covered with cornflower patterned chintz. Very sweet and charming it is. From this two bedrooms are entered. Both are upholstered with pink and green chintz, and have plain velvet pile carpets in green.'[6]

Not all nurseries were so palatial and most royal parents wanted their children to live as simply as possible. But few royal nurseries were as small as the ones in York Cottage where Charlotte Bill brought up the children of George V and Queen Mary. 'Lalla' found it a terrible squash, particularly when a new baby arrived and brought its own retinue of monthly nurse and wet nurse into the already cramped quarters. The Duke of Windsor, the oldest of her royal charges, recalled a conversation he had with her years later about the York Cottage day nursery. 'There was very little room for toys in it,' she said. 'You had only one small-sized rocking-horse. Perhaps it was a good thing your sister didn't go for dolls. They would have cluttered the place up terribly.'[7]

But small or large, all royal nurseries were protected, ordered worlds into which each successive child would be brought within a few weeks of birth. Wet nurses had been employed by royalty from time immemorial and in some countries they were publicly honoured. To others they were a necessary evil, their only qualification being a ready supply of milk. 'We have got a pretty, nice little Irish nurse born on the same day as you and who has three children – one born the same day as William,' Queen Victoria told her elder daughter in 1863, shortly after the birth of Princess Alice's oldest child. 'She had hardly any clothes and we are dressing her and had to wash her! She is just the right nurse – very dark and thin and plenty of milk.'[8] The Queen had definite views about wet nurses. For her fourth son, Prince Leopold, born in 1853, she insisted on sending to the Highlands for a nurse, so strong was her faith in all things Scottish. A Mrs Mackintosh duly arrived at Buckingham Palace swathed in her plaid shawl and understanding barely a word of English. But the baby failed to thrive and screamed incessantly. After a month, the doctor realised that Mrs Mackintosh's milk was the problem; he brought in another wet nurse and the baby suckled and slept peacefully.

Usually the wet nurse was married, but some were single mothers; it happened, then as now, but then it was considered shameful. A generation later, when the health of Prince Leopold's infant son was causing concern, the Queen wrote expressing concern for the nurse who was feeding him who was, quite clearly, an unmarried mother. Victoria was not troubled by this; on the contrary, she showed great sensitivity towards the woman's position. 'The Nurse must not be changed for some time,' she said, '& I am thankful this had not been done or I sh^d feel terribly unhappy ab^t it. Let her be called <u>Mrs</u> Nichols (her own name) & wear a gold ring, & no one need be the wiser. If people in the House inquired ab^t the Husband the answer might be one did not know but that her own family was respectable w^h is quite true.'9

The idea of breastfeeding slowly gained ground among royal mothers. Crown Princess Victoria and Princess Alice both fed their younger children, much to their mother's disgust, and in October 1874, when their brother Prince Alfred's first child was born, the Queen told the Crown Princess that the young mother, 'nurses the child, which will enchant you. As long as she remains at home – and does not publish the fact to the world – by taking the baby everywhere and can do it well – which they say she does now – I have nothing to say (beyond my unfortunately – from my very earliest childhood – totally insurmountable disgust for the process).'10 In Spain in 1907 Queen Ena announced her intention to breastfeed her first child, contrary to custom. Ordinary people thoroughly approved the plan, though the aristocracy were disdainful; in the event it had to be abandoned because the royal doctors were paid commission for finding wet nurses and they were not willing to lose the money.11

In Russia in 1895 a wet nurse was brought in for Tsar Nicholas II's eldest child but her role was only secondary, helping a first-time mother learn how to feed her own baby. Royal fathers in the Russian imperial family were always more involved in the nursery than their English counterparts, and the business of feeding the new baby turned into a rather jolly circus in which everyone took part. A day after the birth the Tsar's sister noted in her diary that the Tsaritsa had started to practise on the nurse's baby. 'Alix started feeding herself,' she said. 'During dinner the wet-nurse's son started *to take her breast*, and we all took turns to go in and watch the spectacle! The wet-nurse stood next to her, looking very satisfied!' The proud father was there too and wrote, 'The first attempt at breast-feeding took place, and ended up with Alix successfully feeding the son of the wet nurse, while the latter gave milk to Olga! Very funny!'12

An old account preserved among Kate Fox's papers from Ray Barton, a children's outfitter and babygoods supplier in Mayfair, gives a fascinating picture of the amount of preparation that went on in the nursery when a new baby was expected. It has no date but probably relates to the spring of 1904 and the birth of Princess Nicholas of Greece's second daughter Elizabeth, the first royal birth Kate had to oversee. Barton's submitted an estimate of £66 8s for a formidable list of items: '6 Vests 1st size, 6 Vests 2nd size, 12 Night

Gowns, 12 Day Gowns [listed in three groups of four, against which someone has written 'Long or short?'], 4 Long Slips, Varied, 4 Night Long Flannels Bound Silk, 4 Night Long Flannels scollop bottom only . . . 2 Dz Turkish Squares oversewn . . . 2 Dz Harrington Squares [these were presumably the nappies] . . . 2 Flannel Aprons, 2 Macintosh Aprons [for the nurse] . . . 2 Large Turkish Bath Towels, 4 Small Turkish Towels . . . Length Flannel for Binders'. There are twenty-six items on the list altogether, most of them wanted in multiples, ending with '8 prs Wool Shoes 2/-'.

The shop's formal estimate, with prices, is then followed by a second, rougher list on an attached sheet in the same handwriting. Items needed for the birth itself or for the mother, 'Lady's Belts, Accouchement Sheets', are crossed out with the comment 'your things will not be got here'. There is mention of a crown and initials being embroidered on some the items; then the cot, bassinet basket and bedding are listed, without prices, and alongside the list someone else has added an increasingly frantic discussion of details: 'Where would the bath, scales, enamel bowls, glass jars etc. be got? I expect you have already ordered the things. The crown could be put on the dresses, pillow-cases, sheets, towels, nightgowns, handkerchiefs. Are any simple bibs necessary? if so of course it can be put on them too – Please add anything you think not sufficient!'[13] And even with shopping lists as long as this, a certain amount of borrowing still went on. In 1914 Princess Alice, Princess Nicholas's sister-in-law, was expecting her fourth child. 'Pss Alice is getting on it is her last month & she is pretty big – I wonder if it will be a boy,' Princess Nicholas told Kate Fox, 'she asked again for the basket & the bath.'[14]

Older children had to be told something about an impending birth and the information they were given became more detailed as the nineteenth century gave way to the twentieth. 'You can't go on explaining to biggish & specially very clever & sharp children, that babies are found under cabbage leaves etc. there comes a moment when this theory doesn't convince them,' Princess Nicholas remarked to Kate. She had explained in answer to her daughters' questions about Princess Alice (they were eleven, ten and seven years old at the time) that women put on weight before a new baby came because of all the milk the baby needed. But she also found that children had their own ways of knowing what was going on: 'they told me the other day that Pavlo said he thought Pcess Alice was going to have a baby because they had sent for a new nurse'.[15]

When the baby arrived, reactions in the nursery could be vary enormously. On the day Prince Maurice of Teck, the third child of Prince and Princess Alexander of Teck was born, Nurse Kemence told the children's mother how

four-year-old May and two-year-old Rupert had taken the news: 'Your little
Princess May I shall never forget telling her,' she wrote, 'she turned very red
and laughed and cryed together the tears ran down her face then she turned her
face in my lap . . . the sweet boy takes not the slightest notice . . . I am longing
to know all the particulars'.[16]

The flannel binders mentioned in Barton's estimate were the last vestige in
English nursery practice of the traditional swaddling bands which were still used
on the Continent decades later. In August 1926 Naomi Rowles, 'Rowley', who
worked in Zywiec in Poland with the grandchildren of Archduke Karl Stefan of
Austria-Hungary, told her fellow nurses, 'The Poles have some very stuffy ideas
about babies. They put the poor mites into uninteresting vests, and then into a
tight padded bag, and there you are! There are no fluffs and frills about the
Polish babe. Also fresh air is considered highly dangerous for it, and it very
often does not take its first walk abroad until it is six months old. And how
boring to be tied up in a bag so that it can't kick!'[17] Confining babies in this way
was always anathema to the English. When Queen Victoria asked her children's
nurse, Mary Anne Thurston, to send patterns for baby clothes to Emma Hobbs
in Berlin in 1858, her daughter wrote to thank her: 'They are too pretty,' she
said, 'and so well made, I think it will do the people here good to imitate them,
they will learn at least what a child ought to look like, and perhaps leave off
stuffing the poor little things into cushions and tying them up.'[18]

But even in the nursery, fashions changed. When, nine years later, the Crown
Princess saw a photograph of her nephew Prince Christian Victor wearing a bib
she was quick to object. 'He has got one of those German things around his
neck "– a dribbling bib". I am sure someone from Germany has made Lenchen
a present of it,' she told her mother. 'It belongs to the swaddling clothes and
baby-binder and the rest of the antediluvian apparatus the poor little Germans
are stuffed into, shortly after their appearance into this vale of tears, which
always shocks my English principles!!'[19] This time Queen Victoria did not
agree. 'As for the "bib", which horrified you so,' she replied, 'you are quite
old-fashioned in thinking it antediluvian for, for the last six or seven years,
every English child wears one.'[20]

Occasionally English nurses were even willing to concede that the
Continental nursery had some ideas worth copying. Irene Collenette wrote to
the *Norland Quarterly* from Coburg in October 1910 to praise a little wonder
called the 'Wickeltisch', which was proving invaluable in dressing baby Prince
Alvaro of Orléans-Borbón – far more practical, she said, than the English
method of balancing the baby on your knee. It was a table,

. . . made like a chest of drawers, with a flat top with sides on the back and two sides. Both the top and sides are padded with soft mattresses, so that the baby can roll about and kick without hurting himself, and the sides prevent him falling off; even my very lively baby of six months is still quite safe on it, and likes to lie on it; he will often lie quite good on his wickeltisch when he will not lie anywhere else. Just below the level of the table on each side is a ledge which slides in and out; on one I keep my puff boxes etc., on the other I put the clothes ready to hand, when I dress my baby. The drawers in the table are used for baby's clothes etc., so that everything needed for the baby is at hand.[21]

A generation later, from her retirement in South Africa, Emily Roose looked back with fondness on the years when she had been responsible for bathing and changing babies. The third of 'her' little girls, Princess Cecile, was expecting her first child in the summer of 1931. Kate Fox had written to Nana Bell about it (the old Greek nursery circle still active years after all the children had grown and flown). Nana Bell was working in South America but wrote to Roosie to ask if the Princess needed a nurse: she would gladly go to Germany for her. The news that Cecile was to employ a German nurse, from the training college set up by her mother-in-law the Grand Duchess of Hesse with advice from her Norlander Lilian Eadie, provoked a little flood of nanny-ish reminiscence: 'I am glad you are having a young German nurse excellent, from the Grand Duchess Schools,' Roosie told the Princess. 'All the up to date methods which are splendid – I used to use for you all Taylors Cimolite Powder it is the very best – I know Miss Edie used it for your husband when a baby & Savory & Moore cold Cream soap, but your nurse may know a German kind just as good – nearly all nurses have their pet powder & soap. When I think of you & your Baby I go back to when you were born & how wonderful the birth of a baby is! to come so perfect, & Oh! the joy & reward for any pains.'[22]

For English nurses working in Courts outside Europe, though, the local methods of dealing with a small baby seemed anything but admirable and they could be positively hair-raising. At the Khedival Court in Egypt in the 1870s the normal practice was to wash a newborn baby in wine and then bandage it tightly for forty days – presumably the wine acted as a form of antiseptic and it may have been cleaner than the available water, but to the English minds the idea appalled. Governess Ellen Chennells described the coming of an experienced English nurse who refused to wait the requisite forty days. She took over the baby at once, peeled off the bandages 'and holding it over a cold bath, sponged it well from head to foot. Some of the old harem nurses looked on all the while,' she said, 'frowning much at the innovation, and auguring the direst effects to the child. . . . They were evidently astonished at his vitality, and argued that he must be a wonderfully strong infant not to succumb to such treatment.'[23]

Once the infant was past its first few months the appropriate food became a live issue for debate between nurses. In 1899 Kate Fox's sister Jessie wrote to the *Norland Quarterly* to recommend an interesting discovery – 'the Shredded Wheat Biscuit'. 'We obtain it from Harrod's Stores,' she said, 'but doubtless any grocer could procure it. I break up a biscuit and pour over it boiling milk: the result is a very good porridge, which my baby likes well. It is also a very good remedy for constipation.'[24] Kate, on the other hand, swore by 'Mellin's Food' a powdered milk 'for infants and invalids'. 'Some nurses may like to know that Mellin's Food may be added to Bovril without materially affecting the taste', she wrote. 'I found it very useful a few weeks ago when my baby was ill, and I could not get him to take the necessary amount of nourishment.'[25] Later she would call on a bewildering range of food supplements for her growing Princesses, particularly when they went through the fads and ailments of their teens: 'Scott's Emulsion' (based on cod liver oil); 'Savory and Moore's' when they refused their pudding (Savory and Moore was the royal pharmacy in Belgravia, and produced the first commercial baby food); 'Maizina' (a fine cornflour used for making sweet custards and blancmanges), and good, reliable 'Robinson's Groats'.[26] She must have been famous for this in the Greek royal family; in 1921 Princess Margarita, the eldest of Roosie's four Princesses, wrote; 'I can't tell you how I have missed you & long for our nice long talks to-gether like in the "old days"! – I wish you would come & make me some "Savory & Moore" sometimes, I'm sure I need it, don't you think so?!'[27]

All nurses had their stock of basic remedies. For stomach aches Kate reached for the Eno's fruit salts or the castor oil. She and Princess Nicholas were convinced that Marian Burgess's charges – the children of the Princess's brother Grand Duke Kirill – were overfed and over-fussed, that 'Burgie' had too little say in the management of them and their grandmother too much. In 1910 Princess Nicholas was staying with the family when the eldest child was very sick: 'she kept on eating everything when she came to tea – a thing I would never allow one of our children to do'. The Princess suggested castor oil, 'as you always give it to the children when they are upset. . . . I said we had a special castor oil which was almost tasteless,' she told Kate, 'so she asked me where one can get it, so please give me the address in your next letter.'[28]

The appearance, growth and loss of teeth could cause trauma in the nursery. In 1867 Nurse Smith reported to the Princess of Waldeck on the condition of her baby son and received the reply, 'It is so nice that Fritz can go out again, & as his health is much better I do not dread the breaking through of the last tooth; but when this is really there, we shall then cry Victory!'[29] When the younger of the Kirill children began teething it caused a major panic as Burgie and the doctor both thought she had measles and a specialist had to be called in to reassure them. Nurse Smith was away in 1866 when Helene, the fifth of her little Waldeck princesses, had to have a tooth removed, but one of the older children made sure she knew all about it: 'Before it came out she allways cried at the meals', Princess Sophie wrote, 'because it hurt her to bite with it, but later she was quite brave and let D. Beneke pull it out and she did not cry then, only think.'[30] Baby teeth were often set into jewellery as a keepsake for mothers and nurses.

Illness in children was treated on doctors' orders and sometimes the remedies were grim. When the Crown Princess of Prussia's six-month-old son Heinrich developed bronchitis in 1863, the doctor gave him 'a double dose' of emetic. 'He was sick six times from which he remained perfectly exhausted', his mother wrote. 'One felt so helpless watching the dear child, who lay on Mrs Hobbs's lap, so changed and pale – though in such a burning heat, fetching breath 100 times in one minute; a hot bath, mustard poultice, hot oil etc. were all applied without the possibility of putting him into a perspiration.'[31] Miraculously, he lived. Emma Hobbs had more than her fair share of this kind of thing with the eldest child, the future Kaiser Wilhelm II, who suffered from a birth injury to his neck that left him with a weak and undersized arm and a number of lesser disabilities. Emma was the one who applied the compresses and salt baths, poultices and ointments, tight binding and massage, and supported her little charge through electrical treatment and the severing of an over-tightened muscle. She had to assist when his arm was placed into the body of a freshly slaughtered hare twice a week, though goodness knows what she, as an English nurse, made of that. It sounds more like magic than medicine.

The choice, purchase and maintenance of the children's clothes was also part of the nurse's responsibility. Another gem in Kate Fox's papers is an old account of 15 June 1903 which she must have inherited with the nursery – it narrowly pre-dates her arrival in Greece and relates again to items ordered from Athens for a new baby, Princess Olga, over the five months leading up to the birth (£181 13s 1d's worth, including shipping and customs charges). It is written on the magnificently headed paper of 'M.E. Penson, Juvenile Outfitter' of

3, Mount Street, London. Above the coats of arms and official accreditations to 'Her Late Majesty Queen Victoria' and 'H.M. The Queen of Italy', M.E. Penson boasts no less than fourteen royal ladies as customers: the Empresses of Russia and Germany, the Dowager Duchess of Saxe-Coburg-Gotha and her daughters the Crown Princess of Romania and the Hereditary Princess of Hohenlohe-Langenburg, the Duchess of Albany; and so it goes on, conjuring up a wealth of images of the little royalties of Europe dressed all alike in their white lace and broderie anglaise dresses with sashes and shoulder ribbons, broad-brimmed straw hats, caped coats and bonnets and neat white sailor suits.[32]

Kate and Princess Nicholas derived immense pleasure in shopping for the children and they exchanged notes on the things they bought. In the late autumn of 1905 the Princess was in London and teamed up for a shopping spree with Nurse Catherine 'Gertie' Salmond, who had been several years in Greece with the Crown Princess's family and was then between jobs. 'She is going to Germany', the Princess wrote, 'to the Grand Duchess Constantine's sister Schaumburg-Lippe. I think she misses Pavlo and the baby dreadfully she told me – but she couldn't stand staying there any longer.' They had a wonderful time. 'I got a very smart dress for Olga & two half smart ones – three slips for both – pink blue & white – two lovely white silk coats & hats to match – a pink dressing gown for Baby & slippers – night gowns & drawers for Olga – all marked with a Crown. The slips are too adorable – in Liberty satine, & I got sashes for Olga's smart dress – it really is lovely – all real lace & of course very expensive but then it will last for ever as the lace can always be used. I also got the gloves – lined silk ones for the smart coats & woollen for every day. . . . I got the lace to let out the petticoats & also some battiste as it is better & less expensive here.'[33] It must have been like dressing dolls.

With the children fed and clothed the biggest responsibility shared by nurses and governesses was their constant supervision and the creative management of their time. Small children needed to be watched for their safety, occupied for their happiness and well-being; the older ones, and particularly the girls, needed the same things for other reasons too. Teenage princesses had the same emotions as any other girls their age and they were vulnerable. In England in 1863 seventeen-year-old Princess Helena developed a crush on the German librarian at Court and the Queen moved very swiftly to send him away. She seemed to feel that he had encouraged the situation and she was not angry with her daughter; on the contrary she understood and was sympathetic. She was not annoyed with Helena's governess either, though Sarah Hildyard felt very much to blame. The protection of girls was never taken lightly. There was a case in the late 1890s when a teenage Duchess of Mecklenburg became pregnant by one of the footmen. It was discussed in whispers over the teacups for many years and the parents were generally held responsible, not for failing to enlighten their daughter about sex – no Victorian parent would have done that – but for failing to have her adequately supervised.

All days had to be planned with activities appropriate to the child's age and, as the English were renowned for their love of fresh air, walks and outdoor games were important to the routine. In the spring of 1868 the Crown Princess told her mother she had arranged a secluded corner of the garden of the Neues Palais in Potsdam 'where the children can play and run about without being stared at like so many wild beasts'.[34] 'I have made several improvements,' she said, in a later letter, 'such as having a swing, a see-saw and a giant strides put up for little and big children, also arranged a crocket ground. It sounds very grand but the place is small.'[35] (A giant's stride was a tall wooden pole with heavy ropes attached to the top, maypole fashion, each with a large knot close to the end on which a child could sit and, building up enough momentum round the pole, be lifted off the ground. 'Crocket' is assumed to mean croquet rather than cricket, but who knows?)

The Crown Princess told her mother she planned to have a summer house for the children. In Russia in the 1830s the children of Tsar Nicholas I had a playhouse on an island in one of the lakes of the Alexander Park which became known as 'the Children's Island'. Visitors wishing to see the heir to the throne would be taken to watch him at play, in the house itself or in the nearby miniature fortress, as his tutors advised against too early an introduction to the formality of the Court. The playhouse was enjoyed for decades and in time the children were hardly aware of how old it was. Nicholas's great-granddaughter Maria Pavlovna thought it a relic of her father's childhood: 'Burberry and syringia bushes grew all over the small veranda and stretched their branches across the windows,' she said. 'Toy railway tracks, with tunnels and posts, were set in front of the house, and a little farther along, my uncles had amused themselves, as children, by building a fortress of red bricks with a small bridge in the middle.'[36] Her father's generation had their own miniature cottage in the garden of the Farm Palace at Peterhof: a painting of 1858 shows a nurse, surely Kitty Strutton, walking towards it clutching the hand of her little Grand Duchess.

Outdoor playhouses were universally popular. Queen Victoria's children had the Swiss Cottage at Osborne and their own fortress. In the Netherlands in the

1890s, Princess Wilhelmina had a Swiss chalet at Het Loo with several rooms, a balcony, well-kept gardens, vegetable plots, hothouses, chickens, pigeons, rabbits, bees; also a swing, see-saw, jumping-board and a giant's stride. Her miniature fire engine (with hose) was very handy for making mud pies, despite the mess involved. Saxton Winter and the Princess worked in the vegetable beds together and it was a Sunday morning treat in autumn to choose the best carrots, wash them, and take them to the stables to feed the horses. Grand Duke Ernst Ludwig of Hesse commissioned an artist friend to create a fairy-tale cottage for his daughter Elisabeth, in the year after he and her mother were divorced. Lilian Wilson, Margaretta Eagar and Lilian Eadie all shepherded their charges to the small front door, though adults were never allowed inside. The children must have loved it.

Not to be outdone, Kaiser Wilhelm II commissioned the 'Bauernhaus' as a Christmas present for his daughter Viktoria Luise, and it was built in the children's garden at the Neues Palais that his mother the Crown Princess had arranged. From the beginning it served as the setting for the little Princess's adventures in preparing food. 'As I was the only lady in the Palace having the faintest theoretical or practical idea of the art of cooking,' Anne Topham remembered, 'I was chosen to guide the children in their first attempts. . . . The stoutest heart might have quailed, the best cook in the world might have trembled, at the enterprise I had undertaken.' In the event, she succeeded, after a fashion, in organising six excited children into producing a tea of pancakes, bread and butter and chocolate cake to be served to the Kaiser and Kaiserin on doll's plates.[37] It was all part of the job.

Feeding the ducks or the birds was a good way to amuse the children too, though for the nurse it was not without problems. In June 1907 Lilian Wilson told the Grand Duchess of Hesse about the time she was having with baby Georg Donatus, the Hereditary Grand Duke, who was then just seven months old 'and getting such a rascal'. They had been out feeding the chickens, she said; it was better than feeding birds because when she tried that, 'he is most anxious to give the worms himself. Yesterday I only turned my head to get the lid, & when I turned round he had got a handful and began kicking & crowing for joy. I had such a work to loose them, because the more I tried, the tighter he held them, it was so funny.'[38]

In the city, drives and walks outside remained part of the children's day, despite the attention they attracted. Some nurses positively revelled in this. Grand Duke Pavel's children had a carriage attached to their service with its own distinctive retinue. No one on the quays of St Petersburg would have doubted that the children inside belonged to the imperial family and Frances

Fry could not resist the attention. Her charge Maria Pavlovna described the scene. They 'always drove with a footman,' she said, 'sitting beside the enormous bearded coachman. Over his livery the footman wore a long scarlet coat with a cape and a bicorn hat; Nannie Fry would stop the carriage at the quay and alighting with us would have the footman follow us as we walked slowly along the sidewalk. It pleased her to have people turn around to stare at this procession, to see the soldiers and officers salute. Often at the end of the walk we would return to the carriage, surrounded by a crowd.'[39]

The toys of royal children could be fabulous, though by the late nineteenth century extravagances like the silver clockwork boats that Elizabeth Dimsdale had wondered over in the 1780s existed in memory only. A careful nurse would put away the most valuable and breakable toys, to be brought out as treats, and would allow simpler toys for every day. The American journalist Kellogg Durland, visiting Spain in 1910, was amazed by the favourite toys of the three-year-old Prince of the Asturias and his brother.

> One day I was in the nursery playroom at the Alcazar and I took occasion to examine the toys of the Royal children. What was my surprise to find a great assortment of little tin mechanical toys such as one sees exhibited all along Fourteenth street or Twenty-third street – toys that cost about ten cents each. The things that are wound up with a key and then rush about in circles. There were boxing men, and little go-carts drawn by monkeys and donkeys and a great assortment of similar devices. Of course, they have many grand toys, gifts from sovereigns, potentates and ambassadors, but so far neither of the Princes has exhibited any particular predilection for these expensive toys. The simple ten-cent things afford them as much pleasure as anything.[40]

In 1914 Princess Marina of Greece adored her 'Kewpie' – 'one of those funny pink celluloid dolls with funny big round eyes & stretched fingers & a fat tummy', her mother explained to Kate Fox. The little girl wasted no time in wheedling favours out of Kate. She slipped a card into one of her mother's letters: 'Please Nurnie will you crochet for me in wool a coat, a bonnet, and dress, to fit my kewpie he is 5½ inches high. I send you love and many kisses Marina.'[41]

Many princesses had dolls and loved them, but for one they became especially important. Taking over responsibility for Princess Wilhelmina when the child was only five, Saxton Winter fully agreed with Queen Emma that classroom lessons were not appropriate. She used the little girl's extensive doll collection as a teaching medium, and later remembered:

The Queen attached great importance to the manner in which her child played with her dolls . . . The so-called 'children' were always spoken of by their proper names; they had a large establishment of their own furnished with every possible convenience, and on such a scale that the 'grown-ups' who happened to be in charge of them could, without discomfort, move about and use the prettily-proportioned furniture. The little family consisted of boys and girls of all sizes and a baby in long clothes. The care of them occupied a great proportion of each day, as they were put to bed and got up, taken out for drives or walks, played games, listened to stories, and had their regular meals with as much seriousness as though they were really expected to consume what was placed before them.

The dolls were taken outdoors too: they 'joined in' when Wilhelmina played at cowboys with her governess and built campfires, baking potatoes which always remained hard inside – though they were still eaten with great glee. When Saxton went home on leave she was expected to take one of the dolls, 'Suzanne', with her, writing letters to Wilhelmina as if they had come from the doll. This game could become embarrassing. 'Suzanne' was expected to have her photograph taken and sent home, 'but the photographer to whom I took her looked at me with such commiserating pity when I insisted upon having her taken in various positions that I strongly suspected that he believed me crazy, and only acceded to my request as the safest means of pacifying a harmless lunatic!'[42]

Becoming Queen at the age of ten, Wilhelmina was not willing to give up her dolls and at least one had to accompany her on the official travels that were increasingly part of her life, with its own trunk of clothes, toys, chairs, and a specially constructed folding bed, all in the care of the Queen's footman. Later still, she insisted that the dolls must have a governess and an extra-large doll was made especially for her, but the effort of fastening the rows and rows of hooks and eyes on its perfectly fashioned Parisian underwear very soon palled and Saxton Winter was told to look after it. In time the doll was found wanting and dismissed and a succession of new 'governess' dolls took over – for a child Queen, this was probably a very good way of punishing your governess.

When Princess Nicholas and Gertie Salmond went shopping for the Nicholas children in London, they were not only looking for clothes. 'I got the Kinder-Garten toys for Olga & also some real toys for both,' the Princess told Kate Fox, '& heaps of picture-books – also a scrap-book for Olga.'[43] The nineteenth century almost invented children's literature, and advancements in printing technology made books brighter and more appealing than ever before. One of the classics, *Little Arthur's History of England*, was written by Maria Graham some years after her adventures as a royal governess in Brazil. The book, published by Murray in 1835, would have been used by almost every English nurse and governess. It was still in print a hundred years later, with updated chapters for the reigns of kings Maria could not even have imagined, and by that time it had sold over 800,000 copies.

Reading with children was always popular. 'Miss Winter read to me often,' Queen Wilhelmina remembered, 'in a dramatic style which I enjoyed very much.'[44] Anne Topham's readings met with a mixed reception. Her attempt to entertain Viktoria Luise with *The Fifth Form at St Dominic's* during a long train ride had to compete with constant interruptions from Prince Joachim in the corridor, trying to provoke his sister, but when she read him *Treasure Island* for his twice-weekly English lesson, both he and his tutor sat spellbound. Once, '*Treasure Island* was sorely interrupted by Princess May of Glücksburg playing on the accordion in the room next to us,' Anne remembered. 'Prince Joachim and Graf Blumenthal both rushed in to her, threatening all sorts of things if she didn't stop!'[45] When Joachim entered cadet school at thirteen years old, Anne was asked to give a weekly English lesson to his whole class – with a policeman's wife as her chaperone. She read from Conan Doyle, and 'I never had a class that hung so much on my words. As they all spoke with a very bad accent,' she remembered, 'I read to them myself, so that they could hear English, and then we discussed the story and the meaning of obscure words and phrases.'[46]

May T found that *What Katy Did* appealed most to her young Archduchess and asked her mother to send 'any simple children's stories, amusing if possible, but not with much imagination'.[47] Emily Roose read *Pollyanna* with her little Greek Princesses and Ethel Howard chose *Eric, or Little by Little* and other novels by Dean Farrar, though she did check carefully beforehand 'in order to eliminate words or episodes which did not seem suitable'.[48] On her second overseas posting in Japan, she favoured Kipling's *Jungle Book* for Prince Shimadzu and his brothers. When Kate Fox was caring for the Ruspoli princes she asked fellow Norlanders to recommend 'good books for boys, not adventures, but rather pathetic stories with a softening influence', which sounds desperately dull, but the possible effect of reading matter on young minds was taken very seriously.[49] In Queen Victoria's family in 1863 one French governess was dismissed for giving the younger Princesses novels which their mother thought unsuitable. The Queen was unusually broad-minded about Sunday though, which in most households required a literature all of its own, with the softening and pathetic very much to the fore. In an 1846 memorandum on the education of her children she stressed that their Sundays were 'to be happy Play Days, by w^h I mean that as the Children (with the exception of the short religious ones) do naturally not any lessons on that day, they may jump & run & play with their Toys & one another; I consider this an essential thing with Children,' she noted, 'that they sh^d regard Sunday as a Festive Day'.[50]

Most nurses started the children on basic reading and writing lessons quite normally in the course of supervising their activities. Margaretta Eagar began teaching the eldest of her charges, Grand Duchess Olga, at four years old, 'because she was always putting her fingers on a word in a paper and asking what it was, and she would then look for the same word again. I taught her the multiplication table. At five the Empress thought it too bad that she was able to read English, but not Russian, and thereupon got her a master.'[51] Lalla Bill set particular store by memory games, knowing how important it was for royalty to recognise and remember the people who were introduced to them. Mary Anne Thurston taught Queen Victoria's younger children to write, and wrote letters at their dictation, and half a century later, when the Grand Duke and Duchess of Hesse were away, Lilian Eadie did the same thing, encouraging the little Princes to enclose letters with her written reports, even when all they could do was scribble. The older they grew, the fuller the letters became (though often 'Nursie's' guiding hand and inspiration were obvious). 'Good morning Mama and Papa', ran one typical offering in October 1913. 'We are very sad without you, but made a sponge roll and some scones, we looked just like cooks.'[52]

The governess normally joined in or took over completely when a child was between five and seven years old. Some taught only English and their own particular skills: music, perhaps, or photography, or some form of art or craft. Some never taught at all, but were expected to supervise all the lessons the children took with other teachers. From Hanover in the 1860s, Pauline 'Hartie' Stewart told her mother, 'I find it most interesting to be at the Princesses lessons. . . . I am going to ask the Queen always to let me take their lessons of history and physics with them.'[53] But her contemporary Anna Bicknell was not so much interested as exhausted:

. . . from the moment when I was awakened in the morning till a late hour at night,' she said, 'there was not an interval of time to breathe. The two girls being of different ages, the professors, classes, lectures, etc., were also totally different; so my days were spent in rushing out with one, and then rushing back to take the other somewhere else; on foot, in all weathers, which the Duchess considered necessary for the health of my pupils; but, as I had two, the fatigue was doubled. During these lectures, etc., I had to take notes incessantly, and to prepare the work for them. Often I was obliged to dress in ten minutes for a large dinner-party, because some professor had prolonged his lesson to the very last moment. . . . In the evening there were dancing lessons three times a week. . . . As to my private correspondence, I was obliged to write necessary letters often very late at night, to the great anger of the Duchess, who rightly declared that I was wearing myself out; but I had no other resource.[54]

As the children grew older, lessons consumed an increasingly large part of the day and the schoolroom took over from the nursery. Royal schoolrooms were meant to imitate ordinary classrooms, though the illusion could be less than convincing. Princess Viktoria Luise spent her days in 'a rather dull, stately apartment, with oil paintings of Prussian Queens and Electresses of Brandenburg decorating the walls'. It had two blackboards, a school desk and its own footman to lay out the exercise and textbooks, dusters and chalk.[55] In 1895 a special laboratory was set up for Queen Wilhelmina's science lessons. It was very plain and businesslike, with a 'long deal table, intersected with upright pipes, burners and appliances, such as are always seen in scientific laboratories, plate-glass screens, behind which experiments were to be made, shelves and cupboards filled with all manner of vials, basins and glasses.' It had its own electric battery and electric telegraph too. 'It always seemed to me an immense pity,' Saxton Winter said, 'that the Queen and I should be the only persons who had the pleasure of listening to these delightful lectures and witnessing the many experiments.'[56]

Some schoolrooms also had gymnastic equipment. Saxton described the Prussian Princes' room after a visit she made in the 1890s: 'huge in size, very lofty, and fitted with almost as many appliances for muscular development as a recognised gymnasium'.[57] Archduchess Elisabeth Marie, 'Erzsi', had a swing in her schoolroom: she persuaded May T to try it one day and they were just throwing themselves into the exercise with vigour when the Emperor walked in. His granddaughter forgot May, who was left helplessly swinging and spinning round in her frantic attempts to stop. Then Erzsi remembered and grabbed the rope; a very red and flustered May scrambled down, 'and with my knees trembling, I managed a curtsy, a curtsy the like of which had never been seen at the Austrian Court. . . . The Emperor looked at me, bowed gravely, but with twinkling eyes, and remarked dryly, "It is a little late, madam, for the curtsy", then strode through the room, his shoulders shaking with laughter.'[58]

Nursery and schoolroom discipline for the children seems to have been fairly mild and there were few really cruel English governesses and nurses working for royalty. Children grew up in a very different atmosphere then, with clear boundaries which they knew not to cross, but for the most part the system seems to have worked amicably. Many of the stories of ill-treatment that do exist fall apart on closer examination. Annie Pitcaithley, a widow from Banff in Scotland who was nurse to Queen Victoria's Edinburgh grandchildren in the 1880s, kept two leather straps in the nursery 'as a warning to the unruly' but she never used them.[59]

Withdrawal of treats was a common punishment. From Kranichstein in 1875 a chastened Princess Victoria of Hesse assured her mother Princess Alice, 'I was better yesterday and not so idle and today also but the day is not past yet, I thought it would please you, to see that I <u>will</u> work. Miss Graves has told me that I am not going to the maneuver when the others go; but shall stay at home, what I deserve, at first when she told me I felt so unhappy and said something as if it was too great a punishment, so she thought I did not really see how very base and mean I was, but I think she sees it now, that I really do. . . .'[60] Princess Alice might have wondered if that little 'but the day is not past yet' slipped into the apology was quite as reassuring as it might have been.

Margaretta Eagar described the precocious calculations of her little charge Grand Duchess Anastasia and her own methods of control. Anastasia was always the most unruly of the last Tsar's children: 'At an age when most children are mere babies', Margaretta wrote, 'she could sit down and count the cost of any action she wished to perform, and take the punishment "like a soldier", as she said herself. I told her one day that if she climbed on the table and jumped off she would be punished. She deliberated for a few moments. Then she climbed on the table, but I took her off and tied her into a chair. She looked at me in surprise and said, "I don't like this at all." I mentioned that children were not intended to like punishments. She was very downcast and sad, and said, "It's better to climb on the table and jump off, and get a little slap, than not to climb and jump; but it's better not to climb and jump than to be tied in a chair."'[61]

The harshest discipline was always applied to boys. Most princes were expected to see themselves as soldiers from a very early age and all a nurse or governess could do was try to mitigate the effects of this. According to Anne Topham, the Prussian Princes' nurse Mrs Matcham and their mother Kaiserin Auguste Viktoria were in complete agreement 'that an inexperienced young officer is no person to be entrusted with the superintendence of a young child's physical and mental needs', and they did their combined best to subvert the system.[62] Ethel Howard was told that it was her duty to report any of the boys' misdeeds to their male governors but she tried wherever possible to ignore this; 'the wrongdoing was treated so severely that I often let things pass with a gentle reprimand from my own lips, hoping to save them from such stern military ideas of punishment.'[63]

The most firmly established stories of nursery ill-treatment come from York Cottage in the days before the appointment of Charlotte Bill. The Duke of Windsor described in his memoirs how his nurse would pinch and twist his arm before taking him in to see his parents. 'The sobbing and howling this treatment invariably evoked understandably puzzled, worried, and finally annoyed them,' he said. 'It would result in my being peremptorily removed from the room before further embarrassment was inflicted upon them.'[64] Sir John Wheeler Bennett, who wrote the official biography of King George VI, added the claim that the same nurse damaged the future King's digestion for life by bottle-feeding him in a badly sprung pram and the combined effect of these two charges have reverberated down the years, to the general discredit not so much of the nurse, but of the royal parents, who are held to have been distant and neglectful for allowing such treatment to continue.

Queen Mary's biographer, James Pope-Hennessey, identified the abusive nurse as Elizabeth Peters – not by naming her, but by saying that she was the family's first nurse and that the ill-treatment lasted for three years; Elizabeth Peters nursed Prince Edward of York, the future Duke, from the summer of 1894, when he was born, until April 1897. She is said to have had a nervous breakdown, finally alerting her employers to the fact that she had had no leave for three years: in fact, household records show that Elizabeth Peters left to be married. But the contradictions do not end there. Children treated as badly in babyhood as the eldest York princes are supposed to have been treated would have become withdrawn and unhappy. It was a pronounced change in the character of his eldest grandson which alerted the Kaiser to a similar situation in Berlin a decade later. Yet in February 1897, two months before Elizabeth Peters left, Kaiserin Friedrich was staying at Osborne and described the York children to her daughter as a happy and well-balanced pair of toddlers: 'The eldest, David, is such a little love,' she said, 'and talks so plainly and is so forward. I think he is very intelligent, he has a lovely complexion and such fair hair with dark blue eyes. He is a fascinating little child. The second is so bright and jolly and good-tempered and not a bit shy, not a pretty child exactly, though he has delightful little natural curls over his head, and the merriest of smiles. The little ones live quite close to me in the tower rooms, so I have a good opportunity of seeing them.'[65] She was a perceptive woman who adored babies and she would never have missed signs of cruelty in the nursery.

A further confusing element in the story is the part played by Lalla Bill. It is usually said that she rescued the children from the ill-treatment, either by reporting it herself or by being on the spot when it was discovered. She is supposed to have said something of the kind to the writer Ursula Bloom, who described how Lalla just happened to be visiting her sister who worked in the York Cottage kitchen when the Duchess of York saw a nurse slap her eldest son and dismissed her on the spot. 'When I first came, David flinched if spoken to quickly, so I knew that he had had trouble with that other nurse,' she quotes Lalla as saying.[66] Yet, as we have seen, Lalla arrived in the spring of 1896, crossing over from the nursery of Marlborough House while Elizabeth Peters still had a year to go as head nurse; both women would likely have been present at Osborne House with the two very happy children the Kaiserin described.

It is possible that the unnamed head nurse who replaced Elizabeth Peters was the real villain of the story, if Pope-Hennessey was right in his overall presentation of what happened. By coincidence or not, her tenure of the office did last three years, from 1897 until 1900, when Lalla Bill took over. But if she was the one, the children would have been older and we would have to accept that Lalla Bill was in the nursery and did nothing for three years. On balance it seems more likely that there never was any long-term cruelty in the nursery at York Cottage. The Duke of Windsor felt very bitter towards his family when his memoirs were written and he was describing a time he could not possibly have remembered. Perhaps something happened once or twice and was seen and the nurse dismissed. Even the feeding-bottle story does not stand up to examination.[67] Midwives say that bottle-feeding in a pram could not do permanent damage to a baby's digestion, and in fact this continued to be the accepted practice at York Cottage. Princess Nicholas met the children in November 1905 and told Kate Fox they were 'very nice bright & merry children & looking much stronger & healthier than I expected. The baby [Prince John] is a fine child for four months, but not at all pretty – pink & fat & smiles so sweetly when you speak to him! They feed him on a bottle & he was sucking it the other day half asleep in his pram which I thought rather funny.'[68]

The nurses' perspective on an often maligned royal couple is fresh and different. George V and Queen Mary were both very shy and found it hard to communicate with their children as they grew older, particularly the King. But the will was there, and as a young father even the famously gruff King knew how to unbend. 'I saw the sweet children yesterday evening & said goodbye to them,' he told his wife in the summer of 1896, 'I was quite low at leaving them, I undressed, washed, dried & put to bed David all by myself, I think it rather amused him, Peters said I did it really well.'[69]

And as for Queen Mary, so famous for her dislike of babies: half a century later the young King and Queen of Yugoslavia had a revealing encounter with her at Marlborough House when they took their baby son to see her. Queen Mary took the baby on her lap and played with him, questioning his nurse Nannie Howe on his weight, his diet and the details of his daily life. 'She and nannie were in complete agreement over the routine of bringing up a child, and later Aunt May [Queen Mary] told us we were very fortunate to have Nannie Howe,' the Queen of Yugoslavia remembered, 'and that she greatly approved of her. "It's so important that a child should be in charge of a reliable, sensible nannie," she said, "*and* one who believes in letting the parents be with their own baby as much as possible. I have no time for these young people who tell me that, unless they are in the nursery at a certain time, they must not see their baby because it disturbs its routine! A child can be seen by its parents at *any* time, and all the time, and the more frequently the better. Dear me, why do you suppose nature provided parents if this were not so! . . . don't you lose touch with this baby," she admonished us gravely. "If you do, the time will come when you will never forgive yourselves."'[70]

But that was in the 1940s. Fifty years earlier duty had often taken Queen Mary away from her children and something of this may have been in her mind when she spoke to the young parents – she wrote similar things to her own children. In her day and before, nurses and governesses had shouldered the entire responsibility for young children and older girls, with very little time to themselves. Until the late nineteenth century most nurses even slept in the same room as the children with only a curtain for privacy, if that. Those working overseas could, in theory, expect a period of home leave each year and the right to attend one church service a week without the children. In 1902 Jessie Fox wrote to the *Norland Quarterly* appealing for greater consideration. 'Many nurses work for eleven months with hardly an hour free except the service on Sunday,' she said. 'I think that in almost all cases the nurse could and should get far more time off duty, but this is a matter which each nurse and employer must decide together. But many mothers have their children with them for varying times, and if occasionally they would decide to keep the little ones with them for a definite time and tell the nurse to take that time for herself, it would be a great boon. In almost all cases the time without the children is spent in rushing to get some job of needlework done, and this I think should not be the case.'[71]

Others disagreed. In 1908 Beatrice Todd, who had been nurse to Princess Heinrich of Prussia's three boys, wrote to the *Quarterly* to put the opposite view. 'Why cannot Norland nurses *claim* an afternoon or evening off a week, like the old-fashioned Nana, or a day a month like the up-to-date maids? The answer is simple – we can*not* be spared! We are such very important people in the household that scarcely anyone can take our place! . . . Cannot we find joy in the thought that we are a necessity? If the mother cannot take charge of our children while we are "off duty", *who* is there, in most cases, whom we could or would trust them to?'[72]

Payment for a lifestyle which demanded total commitment of self was extremely modest. Governesses did reasonably well – Sarah Hildyard, for example, was paid £200 a year as a starting salary in 1846 – but nurses?[73] In May 1868 Queen Victoria wrote to her eldest daughter for help in finding a new position for Ann Pullman, who was due to leave her own nurseries because she was no longer needed. 'She gets a pension, but not enough, she says, to live upon,' the Queen remarked, 'and as she is a young person still, she is right to work on. There are so many people abroad who like to have English nurses that I mention her to you, for she really is a very good nurse – clean and tidy, and with good taste for dressing children. . . . She had £40 here. In Germany and Russia English nurses are in great requisition and I thought, dear, you could help me.'[74] The Crown Princess replied to Lady Caroline Barrington, the Superintendent of the Royal Nurseries, 'my cousin Alexandrina (Princess William of Mecklenburg-Schwerin) has just sent me word she will engage her from the 1st Jan 1869 as Head nurse for £30 – I have my doubts about whether it will answer but I did as I was bid'.[75] Ann Pullman was not prepared to go to Germany for lower pay so a place was found for her as Linen Room Assistant at Buckingham Palace.

Three decades later, the Prince of Wales's Household Appointment Book shows that Lalla Bill received £21 a year as a nursery maid. In 1900, as head nurse, she was paid £35 and the figure rose steadily, reaching £70 a year in 1913. To modern eyes the comparison between this and the salaries paid to other members of the Household is quite shocking. In 1902 Lalla was on £45 a year. The nursery footman Frederick Finch may have come under her authority but his pay was £72; the hall porter, the carpenter and the electrician were all on £90 and the children's tutor Mr Hansell received £300.[76] There is no question of the royal family failing to value Lalla Bill, or of their having been particularly bad employers. They took care of her welfare for the rest of her life. The simple fact is that at that time nobody thought that a woman's work was worth as much as a man's in hard cash. Even the trained nurses of Norland had a starting salary in the early years of only £20–£30 and from this they provided their own uniform.

The idea of uniform for nurses seems to have developed gradually from the 1870s. Before this, nurses wore their own, plain dresses with a bonnet or cap. An apron was a practical addition with children around and, though white was not the most practical colour, it did at least show that it was clean, and it gave a general impression of freshness to the nursery. By the 1880s the white dress and cap and white starched apron were coming into general use on the Continent as the English nurse's uniform. But not everywhere. Baroness de Stoeckl, who was lady-in-waiting to Grand Duchess Georgi Mikhailovich of Russia and was later close to Princess Marina, Duchess of Kent, described the sensation her daughter's nurse caused in Paris in 1892: 'the English nurse, all in white, once again created a riot,' she remembered. 'People used to follow her saying, "She has lost her skirt; she is in her petticoat."'[77]

The training colleges introduced their own distinctive versions of a style which had by then become universal. Both Norland and Princess Christian's favoured dresses in shades of brown (more practical than white and never liable to be confused with a petticoat). Over this the nurses wore bibbed aprons; Norlanders had plain cotton ones for 2s each or linen with openwork insertions for 5s. They wore bonnets indoors and out, and had smart capes for outdoor wear. It was estimated in 1902 that a Norland nurse would have spent around £30 on uniform in her first three years. After this she became a 'Private Nurse', receiving her own salary (which would previously have been paid to the college) and wearing her own clothes, subject, of course, to the wishes of her employer and providing she dressed 'in a neat, suitable and becoming manner, avoiding a flashy or showy style as unsuitable' – very much, in fact, like a governess.[78] In 1902 a badge was brought in, specially designed and awarded to nurses who completed three years with one family. It was especially prized.

Private lives were a luxury most nurses had to do without, keeping contact with friends and family mainly through letters and during their rare periods of leave. Even for governesses the commitment of time was vast: Anne Topham described how she would get up at 5 a.m. and go riding in summer, just to be alone. 'I can close my eyes and see it all again, feel the flap of the black stork's wing that once sailed close to my head, frightened from his morning drink, and see the dew-gummed branches in the green depths of the forest and the ferns in the crevices of the rocks that trembled at our passing.'[79] The single status of many nurses and governesses aroused curiosity in societies where women were expected to marry. A peasant woman once offered to arrange a marriage for Margaretta Eagar, but she felt obliged to decline; 'I should have been rather a disturbing element in the cabin.'[80]

The personal cost of a life spent caring for other people's children is brought home in a revealing comment Ethel Howard made in recalling her appointment with the Shimadzu princes: 'Often when my work was finished I would go upstairs and look at the children as they slept, and it helped me in my loneliness, for the evenings were very solitary. They looked so sweet with their closely-cropped heads of hair, in little pink and white pyjamas which I had made for them. I could often have taken the tiny one up in my arms. From the very first day of my arrival, however, I adhered to the Japanese custom of never kissing them. The Japanese never kiss each other, they merely bow, and it seemed wiser not to introduce such foreign customs lest they might be misunderstood.'[81] For Ethel, as for others, it could be a very lonely existence.

FIVE

'A War Dance on a Wet Afternoon'

THE CHILDREN

Castle Pelisor, Sinaia, Roumania

Dear Nurses

We have lived in Roumania about four years. Our small charge Michael, the son of the Crown Prince and Princess, was four years old on October 25th. He is a very jolly little boy, most amusing and full of energy; very good to look at, with golden hair and blue eyes, and resembles his grandmother the Queen, both in looks and ways. He speaks English – as do all his relations among themselves – but knows several Roumanian words. For three summers we have taken him to the seaside in France; this year we were also two months in England. Sea air is necessary for him. . . . We have very nice nurseries built for Michael, the special joys being a little nursery kitchen, and a very big corridor opening on to a balcony.

Best wishes to you all,

E. Alix St John and A. Stainton.[1]

With H.R.H. Princess Mafalda of Hesse, Villa Savoia, Rome

Dear Nurses

Some of you may like to hear about my present post. My partnership with Miss St John came to an end in July 1926, as our Michael was getting too big for two Nurses. Through the kindness of his mother I came, after a fortnight in England, to her cousins, the Prince and Princess Philip of Hesse. The baby, Maurice, was just half-an-hour old when I arrived, and I took charge of him the next day. His mother is the second daughter of the King of Italy, and was staying for the event with her parents at Racconigi, near Turin.

When Maurice was six weeks old we went to the other grandparents in Germany, near Frankfurt-on-Main. We came to Rome for the winter to Maurice's own home, which is a very pretty little house with a beautiful garden, in the park of the Villa Savoia where Their Majesties live. It is like living in the country. I push my pram up hill and down dale with rabbits for company!

In the spring, to my great joy, we had a three days' visit from Michael and Miss St John. They both loved my little Maurice, who of course is exceptionally charming! He is the most advanced baby I have had: could walk at thirteen months, and is beginning to say 'Nan-nan' and other small words. He is very pretty, with fair hair and big dark eyes.

We have been travelling all the summer. We were in North Germany for two months. Maurice got on splendidly, though the weather was fairly bad. We brought back a German maid to help me, and for the babies to get used to the language. We are now back again in Rome, waiting for the arrival of Baby Two.

With best wishes to you all,
A. Stainton.[2]

When Elizabeth St John and Anne Stainton wrote these letters to their college magazine in the 1920s they knew their fellow Princess Christian nurses would be especially interested in their news because the children they looked after were royal. A further glimpse of little Prince Maurice and 'Baby Two' appeared in the Norland Quarterly a few years later, when Norlander Doris Clarke visited her friend Alice Smyth, who had taken over from Anne Stainton as their nurse. 'Last year, while in Italy', Doris wrote, 'I had a most exciting visit to a Princess Christian friend who is looking after H.R.H. Princess Mafalda of Hesse's little boys. She was staying at Pisa and the Queen most kindly said that I might be invited to the palace. I was delighted to find Miss Smyth looking so happy with her two wee Princes; they are both very fair with lovely red cheeks. They gave me a doll to take to bed "in case Nanny's sister might be lonely"! They were all so kind and it was like a fairy tale to shake hands with a Queen and Princes and Princesses.'[3]

People wanted to know about royal children but this public interest, well intentioned though it was, could impose a strain on the children and on those responsible for them. What was a child to make of the cheering crowds, and how would his nurse or governess explain them? Lady Lyttelton voiced these thoughts in 1842 when Queen Victoria's children were small. She was Superintendent of the Royal Nurseries and had just accompanied the Princess Royal and Prince of Wales to Walmer in Kent with their parents. Even the nursery party had to pass through huge, cheering crowds pressing in around them, with the church bells pealing, bunting and flower garlands in the streets and cannons firing in celebration. 'The children will grow up under the strangest delusions as to what travelling means, and the usual condition of the people in England', she wrote. 'They must suppose one always finds them shouting and grinning and squeezing, surrounded by banners and garlands. "Where's the Prince? Show him! Turn him this way! Bless his little face! What a pretty boy! How like his father!" was screamed at us incessantly; and once, as I was overheard to say to Mrs Sly, "Hold up the Prince of Wales", I was complemented with "Well done! That's right, old girl!" At one place, where we had got out and were returning to the carriage . . . a great fat lady, very smartly dressed, caught hold of the Prince of Wales, and, almost dragging him out of Mrs Sly's arms, gave him the loudest kiss. . . . Mrs Sly has not yet cooled down, her rage was such at being taken by surprise.'[4]

In later generations the camera added to the pressure. Lilian Brimble described how one summer, at the seaside resort of Heiligendamm, she was standing talking to the chamberlain in the garden when she noticed that Prince Louis Ferdinand, 'Lulu', was walking in circles round them. When she asked why, 'he said, "Because of that photographer man", and we found that amongst a gathering of onlookers on the other side of some adjacent railings a man with a camera had been vainly trying to "Snap" the small scion of royalty, but was always frustrated by his subject's careful dodging. It did look funny,' she said, 'and often when we were driving Prince Lulu would suddenly disappear with alarming celerity to the floor when he saw a camera levelled at the Royal carriage.'[5] Even when there were no cameras people were a constant nuisance, 'and would follow us in a long procession as we returned from the shore, getting closer and closer till we had traversed the small piece of the woods which skirted the private part of the grounds, making audible remarks upon the children. . . .' Once, she said, the older boy, Prince Wilhelm, had been out with his footman and, on hearing two of these admirers refer to him adoringly as 'the little Prince', 'he turned with a scarlet face . . . declaring, "The little Prince is Lulu, and he is at home. This is the *big* one."'[6]

Adoration could almost smother an only child, even from courtiers who should have known better. Anna Bicknell described the difficulties faced by Miss Shaw, who was nurse to the little Prince Imperial in Paris in the late 1850s. Never was a child so admired. He was, said Anna, 'surrounded by adulation and obsequiousness to a degree which would have ruined most children', and she gave Miss Shaw much of the credit for his growing into a very likeable boy.[7] Anna described how the State Governess would invite members of the Court to watch the Prince at breakfast. Miss Shaw 'had no easy task in defending the child from the too exuberant endearments of the young ladies present, and energetically protested in English that they were "worrying him and frightening him". . . . When the nurse had extricated the little Prince from his too numerous admirers', Anna wrote, 'he stood in the circle, silent and evidently shy, a pale, grave child, with large, earnest, blue eyes and brown curls, in a very simple white frock.' Anna had stood back from the clucking and cooing ladies, feeling rather repelled by it all, and perhaps for this reason she caught the little boy's eye. Encouraged by Miss Shaw he ran to her, clutching a rose which he refused to hand to any other lady, though they all pressed forward to take it. He gave it to Anna: 'I have kept the faded leaves of that rose,' she said, 'withered liked the budding hopes which then surrounded that little royal head.'[8]

Some aspects of public attention could be very distressing for a child. Margaretta Eagar described how peasants in the Russian part of Poland would kneel in the road at the approach of the imperial carriages. She found it quite disturbing herself: 'I never got used to it,' she recalled, 'nor ever overcame the feeling of horror mixed with pity that I experienced on seeing this done for the first time.' It was worse for the children, though, as they grew old enough to notice and ask questions. 'The little Grand Duchess Olga,' Margaretta said, 'who is very sensitive, used to look at them with tears in her eyes and beg of me to tell them not to do it.'[9]

There seemed to be an edge of reverence in the way people regarded the Tsar's children which was more akin to the attitudes English governesses would meet in the Middle or Far East. Margaretta described how one officer of the guard at Peterhof ran over to talk to the children as they were getting into their carriage. They chatted to him happily and one produced a toy from her pocket and gave him it, seeing nothing but friendliness on his part. In fact, as he explained to Margaretta, 'he was in trouble, and seeing the children coming out, thought that if he could reach the carriage in time to bow to the children he would find a way out of his troubles'. The officer was using the little girls as a sort of talisman, and he went away confident that because he had seen them, and had even received a gift from them and kissed their hands, his problems would be solved.[10]

If you were the child, this overwhelming attention could lead to a deep confusion about who and what you were. If people were always admiring you, did it mean that you had to be good all the time – or could you do just what you wanted – and wouldn't it, after all, be more fun to be ordinary, whatever ordinary was? Finding themselves, for once, without their admirers and walking on the public side of the railings at Heiligendamm, Princes Wilhelm and Louis Ferdinand told Lilian Brimble with some pride, 'Now we are people.'[11] Margaretta never ceased to be surprised by the little Grand Duchess Olga's very regal interpretations of the stories she was told. Even Bible stories: 'She was angry with King David because he killed Goliath, and said, "David was much younger and smaller, and poor Goliath never expected him to throw stones at him." Fairy tales too; "Jack the Giant Killer" gave her no pleasure,' Margaretta remembered, 'it upset her idea that might was right.'[12] And as for the *Alice* books, Olga was appalled by the behaviour of the Red and White Queens: "No queens," she said, "would be so rude."' The thing that intrigued her most was that Alice shared a train carriage with complete strangers; this was so far from her own experience that she found it almost impossible to understand.[13]

The Archduchess Elisabeth Marie, 'Erzsi', May T's pupil, grew up in a peculiar atmosphere, with the intense attention that surrounded any royal child tinged by a streak of morbidity on the part of her admirers. Her father Crown Prince Rudolf had been found dead with his mistress in his hunting lodge at Mayerling when she was five years old. The sensation refused to die down and his only child existed on its fringes, a negligible figure in that she was not a boy and could not take her father's place as the Emperor's heir, yet still the Emperor's granddaughter. The Court ladies around her competed for her attention and when May first met her she was a child at sea; very young for her age, eager to be liked but volatile and unpredictable. 'She is of the same family as poor Marie Antoinette,' May told her mother, 'and in this little Austrian Archduchess one sees displayed characteristics similar to those ascribed to that ill-fated Queen. I never understood Marie Antoinette so well before.'[14]

May described one typical incident when Erzsi, who was then thirteen, had a bad cold and was proving difficult to entertain. As a treat May allowed her to visit her own rooms and do whatever she liked, a promise she would quickly regret. First, the Archduchess used May's oil paints to decorate all the mirrors and lampshades in the room. Then she went into the kitchen, rolled up her sleeves, melted some chocolate and ate it. She next cooked some sausages she had found and ate them too, then, finding a tin of flour, 'she suddenly dived into it with both hands, and shrieking with laughter, before I could stop her, pelted me until I was completely powdered white'. She emptied the rest of the tin out of the window over the sentries in the courtyard. It was too much for May, who looked at the devastation around her and, losing her control in the presence of royalty, exclaimed, '"You are a dirty little thing!" At that all the fun fled from her eyes. She drew herself up, looking ridiculously Royal, despite the smudges of chocolate on her pretty cheeks and nose, and the flour all over her frock. "I am not a thing, I am an Archduchess," she replied. Taking the cue instantly, I made a deep curtsy, and responded: "I regret my *faux pas*, Imperial Highness. I shall not forget again."'

'After that,' May said, 'relations seemed strained, and she dawdled about with a very bored manner. Then as she was about to leave, I made another curtsy, and said "*Au revoir*, Imperial Highness." She looked at me for a second and tears rushed into her sweet eyes, then she flew across the *salon*, and flinging her bare arms – her sleeves were still rolled up – around my neck, hugged me close, crying: "No, no, I am not a *dirty* little thing, but a *dear little thing*!"'[15]

At heart they were all just children. Lilian Brimble often found herself having to explain to her little Princes exactly what princes were. The idea that the sons of a king or a prince were princes too came as a revelation to Louis Ferdinand. He gazed up at his governess, 'with amazement in his brown eyes asking "Then would my children be princes? I thought they'd be just *ordinary* people."' This comment did make Lilian swallow rather hard to keep back the laughter. 'My mind,' she said, 'being full of vivid recollections of a half-bottle of toilet lotion which he had consumed that morning, to say nothing of a grand explosion in the bath room, caused by his connecting the electric light under an empty kettle; of a cut on his knee, made with a supposedly poisoned Indian knife, which he had annexed from its place on the wall downstairs, I murmured feelingly that I didn't think his children would be at all ordinary if they resembled their papa.'[16]

In the roll-call of royal children brought up by British nurses and governesses, Louis Ferdinand was one of the great characters. When Lilian took over as 'Director and Head of the Crown Princely Children's Department', he was a skinny little boy with big brown eyes and a striking crest of hair standing upright along the top of his head, Mohican-style, which the family called his 'kakadu' (cockatoo). Today the effect would be fashionable and would take a good deal of hair gel to achieve; on him it was natural and the despair of successive nurses who had tried to brush the hair into a smooth round curl. His first meeting with Lilian was not promising. Aged not quite four, he drew himself up to his full height and said, 'I do not want you to stay here with us, and if you do, I shall call in a forester and have you shot on the spot.'[17] 'I can see him even now,' Lilian wrote, 'sitting up in his bed with its rose-pink blanket, his funny little night-shirt tied at the neck with a pink bow, looking up at me with angry tears in his brown eyes, and his "kakadu" on end, threatening me with all kinds of dire things. . . . Queer, funny little Prince Lulu, with his quick temper and volatile disposition, his ready wit and extraordinary character. He certainly succeeded in creeping right into my heart and staying there for all time, though at first I thought him a perfectly detestable little boy.'[18]

Margaretta Eagar was commissioned to describe her former charges for the *Girl's Own Paper and Woman's Magazine* in 1909. A series of articles by Kellogg Durland on the life of the Tsaritsa, which made use of the reminiscences in Magaretta's 1906 book and of interviews with her, raised a clamour for more information about the imperial children. The second of Margaretta's articles appeared under a terse note from the magazine's editor: 'Our readers seem insatiable in their desire for details of the Tsaritsa and her little girls, judging by the number of requests for "more" that reach me continually. We are glad these articles on the Russian Royal Family have been so much appreciated, but they must now come to a close to make room in the near future for some articles on other little Princesses, which will prove quite as fascinating.'[19]

The children Margaretta described for the magazine were real little girls, appealing and appalling by turns. Grand Duchess Olga, whom she nursed between the ages of three and nine years, was very conscious of her position as the eldest in the family and inclined to be imperious. She could be difficult to manage; she was, on the other hand, very perceptive towards other people. One anecdote Margaretta told concerned a beautiful doll, given to the children's cousin Elisabeth of Hesse when the Russians were visiting Darmstadt. All the children played with the doll and admired it; then, when bedtime came, Elisabeth presented it to her cousins on impulse and ran from the room in tears. It was a delicate situation. 'I mentioned that it was not necessary to keep everything that was given to them,' Margaretta remembered, 'and Olga said, "I should like to talk to Tatiana."' The two had a whispered conversation, then Olga put the doll on a chair between their beds. The next morning she gave it back to her cousin, thanking her for lending it to them. In answer to Elisabeth's protests, Olga said that the doll had been a gift to her, which she should not give away. 'The other child said nothing, but her face showed her delight at recovering her treasure.'[20] For a child of seven, it was a mature way of dealing with the problem.

Olga was intelligent and full of questions. 'She wakened me one night after midnight,' Margaretta remarked, 'to know how the water came upstairs into the bathroom.'[21] Tatiana was quite different, a much gentler child, always anxious to do the right thing and, in the words of her nurse, 'always a most attractive little personage'.[22] Margaretta described Tatiana's attitude to entertaining, a skill all royal children had to learn. 'She was perhaps two and a half years old when I took her to her first party. We were met at the top of the staircase by the children we had come to see and their governess. A few days after we had a children's party, and Tatiana was frantically anxious to be dressed and ready. She would hardly stand still to have her sash tied. I told her she really must not be so excited, and she said reproachfully, "When we went to Marie's house she and Dmitri were waiting for us at the head of the stairs, and I know it must be right for us to wait for them."' Margaretta recalled that while Olga and Maria would content themselves with amusing one or two visitors at their parties, Tatiana would copy the adult hostesses she had seen and try to look after everyone.[23]

If Margaretta had a favourite among the Tsar's daughters it was Tatiana or Maria, perhaps both. Maria Nikolaevna was the first child she had nursed from birth, and the little girl's placidity and sweet nature were a winning combination. Maria adored her father, Margaretta said, and was forever trying to escape from the nursery to find him. 'Of all the children she is the Emperor's favourite. When we were in the Crimea when she was a year and four months old, she toddled round the balcony one day to where he was eating his breakfast. I quickly came after her, and the Emperor looked smilingly at me and asked me to put a chair for her. "It touches me," he said, "to see so much affection. . . ."'[24] But there was also a quickness of mind about Maria. 'She used to look out in the streets for people whom she used to call afterwards "My friends", and was very sorrowful if I did not always recognise them. "You know," she would say, "the lady in Peterhoff who wore the green hat? I saw her today in the Nevsky." She never confused anyone,' Margaretta remembered, 'she had the true "royal memory" for faces.'[25]

Margaretta nursed the youngest daughter, Anastasia, to the age of three and found her very difficult. Almost all of her Anastasia stories spoke of calculated and precocious mischief: Anastasia jumping off tables, Anastasia slapping her sister's face and refusing to apologise. When Margaretta had the three older girls making gifts for their grandmother's name day and learning poems to recite, Anastasia refused to join in. She said that she would pick flowers; then, finding that she was to be taken to her grandmother's by carriage, she grabbed a toy from the toy cupboard to give. The Dowager Tsaritsa forgave the lack of a handmade present but when the little girl tried to wriggle out of her negligence by reciting a poem she had learned for her mother a few weeks before, her grandmother was hurt and, though she accepted the tears and the proffered apology, she denied Anastasia the sweets that her older sisters were enjoying.

This mixture of naughtiness and defiance was characteristic. Margaretta told Durland about a day when she took the children out to collect apples to bake for tea. Anastasia secretly kept some apples for herself. She produced one and started to eat it later, but Margaretta took it from her. In those days it was

Nurse who decided what children ate and when, but Anastasia was unabashed, calmly producing a second apple and saying, 'If you take this apple away from me, I will scream and then the people will all think you are wicked to me.' Once back in the nursery she was put to bed while the others had their baked apples. She would not apologise. Nor would she promise to leave the apples alone if the nursery party went back to the orchard, and, though the others pleaded with her, Margaretta would not return to the orchard without Anastasia's promise: the stand-off between them lasted a full week before the little girl gave way.[26]

With the six sons of the Kaiser in her charge, all between the ages of five and thirteen, Ethel Howard prepared for her arrival in Berlin by writing out their names, ages and dates of birth; still it took some time to sort out who was who. Her memoirs bring them vividly back to life. Wilhelm, the eldest (the father of Lilian Brimble's little Princes), was Crown Prince, though he was not allowed to use the title until he was eighteen. In adult life he became a notorious womaniser and something of that charm must have clung to him even in boyhood. 'He is small built, but good looking,' Ethel noted in her diary, 'such a lovely complexion, and such delicious laughing eyes, and he *can* give such a wink.' Looking back, she would realise that he had been a disruptive influence, teasing and distracting his younger brothers until she was forced to take him to task. They developed a private code: when she said 'T', he was to stop teasing and back away. She said it so often that it became her nickname for him.[27]

Eitel Friedrich, the second son, was a fat, placid boy, very gentle, very good-natured and supremely uninterested in everything except the army. His brother Adalbert was trouble: 'all heart and naughtiness', in Ethel's first assessment. 'Very rough and affectionate, but more like any other schoolboy. Up to lots of mischief, with no feeling for others. Greedy and a bit troublesome.'[28] August Wilhelm, 'Au-wi', was a puzzle. At first he seemed shallow, 'a silly little person. . . . I *never* saw a boy laugh more. He rolls on the ground at the least thing.'[29] Yet she was to discover that Au-wi was the artist in the family, a sensitive, creative boy: 'he will ever remain in my mind as the teller of fairy tales and legends, and the reciter of poems. Many a time did that young Prince lift my mind from its petty cares and thoughts to spiritual and natural beauties. He was talented beyond the ordinary,' Ethel said, 'and if he does not eventually produce some great literary or artistic work I shall be much surprised.'[30] He did not. It was a tragic irony that August Wilhelm, the Prince who stood out in Ethel's memory as possessed by a spark of true creativity and imagination, was later to be the Prince seduced by Nazism to a greater extent than all his brothers. But at the time Ethel was writing, that was still a horror beyond imagining.

Her heart went out most to Prince Oskar, brother number five. 'He is *sweet*,' she remarked, 'the best looking of them all, except for the Crown Prince. I should say that out-and-out he has the most character. He enjoys a joke, but he is thoughtful. *Very* proud (so are they all), very sensitive, and a very deep nature. One who would take a long time to like you, and if he did so he would not forget you.'[31] The sixth son was the pampered and over-fussed little Joachim, 'Pykie', who screamed on the slightest excuse and was terrified of dirt. He should have come under Ethel's care but Mrs Matcham did everything she could to hold on to him.

Life with the others was never dull. They put vinegar, salt and sugar in her soda water. Once, Adalbert staged a fall off his bicycle in an isolated part of the park and pretended to be unconscious, allowing Ethel to struggle to carry him; 'My arms were breaking,' she said, 'and at last I felt I must drop him, or he would fall from my weakening hold. Imagine my state of mind, then, when he suddenly flung himself away from me, and danced in front of me, shouting with glee at my distress!'[32] On another occasion, the Crown Prince caught some live frogs and wrapped them into the carefully folded serviette in front of Ethel's place on the dining table. When she touched it and jumped back with a shriek, frogs exploded all over the table to be chased by five laughing boys.

Persecuting your governess with wildlife was an effective trick and many royal youngsters tried it. On discovering that Saxton Winter had a particular horror of beetles, Princess Wilhelmina, who 'was inordinately fond of teasing and always full of mischief . . . immediately conceived the idea of surreptitiously filling my pockets with these sleeping insects, and then waited with suppressed excitement for the moment of their awakening! It would be difficult to say which suffered the more,' Miss Winter said, 'I, from dismayed horror, or the poor insects, from such strange imprisonment.'[33]

When parents were away for any length of time, it fell to the nurse or governess to keep them informed about their offspring. For three weeks in the summer of 1907, Lilian Wilson had sole charge of the Hereditary Grand Duke of Hesse while his parents were in England. Baby Georg Donatus – Lilian called him 'Georgie' – was seven months old. 'Georgie is looking simply lovely,' she wrote to his mother on 28 June, 'so bonny and so happy, as lively as ever. I do not think you will see much difference in him, he does not seem to me to have got any fatter, but he is trying very hard to talk, I believe he soon will.' Even then, she followed what would become the accepted practice in the Hesse nursery, adding a 'message' from the baby on the end of her letter, in reality just a scribble. 'I hope the accompanying letter will please Your Royal Highness, we had to stop the writing very quickly as the writer wanted to eat the pencil.'[34]

In the spring of 1908 Georgie's parents went to Moscow and Lilian took him to stay with his aunt and uncle, Princess Irène and Prince Heinrich of Prussia, at Hemmelmarck on the north German coast. Their journey was not without its element of drama: 'It was a most horrible surprise to find on arriving in the Castle that our supply of food for the journey had remained in the train,' Lilian reported; 'it was too bad, and such a surprise, as on leaving the Coupée with the bag, Möller said, "I have only to put in the three bottles, and there we are quite ready"; it appears he could not get through at once, and then forgot it, he was very miserable poor man. . . .' Fortunately Georgie had not gone hungry: 'We were able to get very good bouillon in the Schloss, and we got a bottle of "kinder-milch" at once, and happily we had got some food by us, but that was the merest good luck, the tin was almost empty, and not to lose the food, enough for 3 times, I put it in a piece of paper intending to use it on arriving in Kiel, not thinking of any emergency but oh! so very thankful it was there.'[35]

This seems to have been Georgie's first long journey and the panic about the food had not affected him; Lilian was amused by the way he took over at Hemmelmarck: 'Everybody is delighted with him here, he is so sweet to them, just as tho' he had known them all his life.'[36] His uncle took him out in the mail cart and he spent time with his aunt every morning and evening. His nurse was almost bursting with pride: 'this evening he made 3 conquests, when I took him over,' she told the Grand Duchess on 13 April, 'the Duchess of Glücksburg with her daughter was there and soon after that Prince Adalbert came in, after about half an hour I went to fetch him, they were all playing together and the Duchess told me she found him perfectly charming, and Prince A said, "if that had been ours he would have been screaming long ago", I am sure he meant the little crown Prince [Wilhelm, the elder of Lilian Brimble's charges]. Baby said so sweetly good-Bye to them all – even offering a kiss to the Duchess, told them all he was a "Hesh", saluted & bowed, so that altogether my feelings rather resembled those of a Peacock.'[37]

By 17 April they were back in Darmstadt, having travelled down with Prince Heinrich and Princess Irène, on their way to visit Irène's sister Victoria at Heiligenberg. Lilian had already been charged with buying Easter eggs for the Heiligenberg cousins on the Grand Duchess's behalf and she took it upon herself to add Princess Irène's son Waldemar to the list as he had not been expected. On Good Friday she took photos of Georgie for his mother. 'Your Royal Highness will see he has on another hat, it was so very hot the days before that his hats were all too wintry and the Panama I am sorry to say, is too small, so there was nothing to do but get him one, and that is all I could get.' It was a sailor hat: 'everyone was so enchanted when he made his appearance,' Lilian said, and, seeing that his little nephew's hat ribbon was plain, Prince Heinrich telegraphed for a specially embroidered one with the title 'S.M.S Hessen' (presumably, as Admiral of the German Fleet, he knew who to ask). It was ready the next day.[38]

After Easter, Lilian and Georgie returned to Kiel with Princess Irène. The nurse had felt a niggling concern about the toddler's left leg for some time, because it did not appear to be quite straight. On her own authority she called in a specialist who advised massage, mineral baths, and keeping the little boy off his feet as much as possible. 'I have bought a sort of chair perambulator,' she told the Grand Duchess, 'I think I spoke to you about the sort of thing last year. I saw it hanging up in a shop and I went in and got it. We have it in the rooms and Baby likes it very much.'[39] The treatment must have worked as there was no further concern about Georgie's leg and he grew to over six feet five inches tall.

At the end of 1908, with the birth of Georgie's little brother Ludwig, Lilian Eadie took over as nurse. Her first separation from the Grand Duchess came the following summer, in August 1909, when the Grand Ducal couple were away and she and the boys went to Hemmelmarck. Unlike Lilian Wilson who wrote in a very relaxed way to the Grand Duchess, Lilian Eadie was more formal to start with, sending only brief notes – Georgie missed Mama and Papa, Baby's tooth was through, they had been to the sea and so on. As her confidence grew, so her messages became longer. In June 1911, when the Grand Ducal couple were about to leave for King George V's coronation, she took the boys to Hemmelmarck again. 'As soon as the train started from Langen,' she told the Grand Duchess, 'it was funny how Georgie's face changed and Lu sat quite quiet, I don't think they quite realised until then, that you were to be left behind, Georgie cried a little.' Her letter continued as from the little boy himself: 'Dear Mama and Papa, I did not roll out of my bed. I like the pigs very much and so does Lu. It is so nice here, but I wish you were here too, we made a big castle this morning. Auntie Irene gave us boats and lots of sand toys, water can and two pails.'[40]

This became Lilian Eadie's style of passing on news. The handwriting was hers, but she must have sat with the children beside her, encouraging them to think of things to say, and they added pencilled kisses, '++oo' and their own very wobbly signatures. (At about this time that 'Georgie' began to sign himself 'Don' and this gradually took over as his name within the family.) Most of the children's days were spent on the beach, warmly wrapped in 'knickers and jerseys' against the unseasonable cold. They played with the donkeys, watched the storks, and – great excitement – their uncle took them to the Schloss at Kiel to watch a naval review. 'When the Kaiser came, the canons were so loud, they banged against the windows, but the Kaiser did not come at all he stayed in the middle of the water. . . . We can see all the ships and steamers out of our windows.'[41] After a few weeks of this, though Georgie was still longing for home, Lu was no longer sure. 'Georgie counts the days off on his fingers, he is pleased to come back to Wolfsgarten, but Lu says he is a sailor, and wants Papa and Mama to come and live here.'[42]

The letters Princess Nicholas of Greece sent to Kate Fox from her travels around Europe gave a detailed commentary on the royal children she met and their nurses. In November 1905 on a visit to England she encountered King Edward VII's two-year-old grandson, Prince Alexander of Denmark, whose father had been elected to the new throne of Norway only days before, transforming the little boy's prospects. 'What did you say to Princess Maud – becoming a Queen & the little boy Crown Prince!' Princess Nicholas asked Kate. 'He is called Olaff now – everybody speaks of nothing else here & that little baby is considered as something superhuman because he said "God bless you" to the King of Denmark when he left!'[43]

It was a pity she had nothing to say about Olav's nurse as a degree of mystery attaches to her (or them). Years later, for his biographer Jo Benkow, King Olav recalled his beloved English nurse Annie Butler, who became a keen suffragette. When she involved herself in demonstrations in England, he said, someone – he thought it was his grandfather, King Edward VII – insisted on her dismissal, to his own lasting sorrow. But the story is not as straightforward as it sounds. The published diary of Halldis Bomhoff, Olav's first teacher, mentions Annie's departure on 25 February 1911 and describes how, two days later, 'both of us were a little dismal. Prince Olav was silent and thoughtful . . . and he wore an expression as if he were swallowing his tears. I understood that it was Annie he longed for. . . . She was a charming person.'[44] But King Edward VII was long dead by that time and, in any case, the diary suggests that Miss Butler was back again, perhaps briefly, in August 1911. In September 1937 she returned to the family to help King Olav's children with their English. It seems possible that there was another earlier nurse dismissed for her politics but whatever the truth, a suffragette nurse is an appealing idea.

Princess Nicholas's less than admiring reaction to little Olav may indicate a touch of envy. His father was her husband's cousin and, like Prince Nicholas, was a younger son with no particular prospects until his sudden election as King of Norway. This must have made many younger sons and their wives sit up and wonder. Anne Topham met little Olav a year later when his parents visited Potsdam and she was enchanted by him; he was, she said, 'an amusing, quaint, old-fashioned child who charmed everybody, especially the Emperor, with whom he chatted in a confidential fearless manner, treating His Majesty as a friend and companion and inviting him to help in building his house of bricks'.[45]

In the autumn of 1911 Princess Nicholas reported on the Italian royal children and their nurse Miss Brompton. 'The children are nice, the oldest girl very pretty,' she told Kate, 'they wore sailor things but not pretty – I saw the English nurse from far, she looked nice, but it must be difficult for her because the youngest child who is three is the favourite and very spoilt, they let her eat everything at the tea table!'[46] This was obviously the chief crime in the nursery of the Nicholas children; their mother returns to it so often in her remarks on other people's children. Kate Fox once gave a delightful glimpse of her children's table manners in a letter to the Norland Quarterly: 'I must tell you of a very funny saying of one of my little charges. I was reproving her eldest sister for not asking nicely for something at tea, when little Princess Elizabeth, aged three, said, in a most virtuous tone, "I don't ak (ask) like that", then there was an interval, during which I thought she was going to complete her lesson. She, however, ended with "I take it!"'[47]

But the children the Princess returned to most often in her letters were her brother Kirill's family, who were nursed by Kate's friend Marian Burgess, then by fellow Norlander Irene Collenette. A strong degree of friendly rivalry existed between the two nurseries. The oldest of the Kirill children, Marie, was a year younger than Princess Marina and according to Princess Nicholas, 'as far as beauty goes, she is not to be mentioned in the same breath as our babies!'[48] Kate must have written about Marie in the summer of 1909, a few weeks after the birth of the second daughter, Kira. Princess Nicholas replied, 'Of course they think little Marie the most lovely child in the world, but it must have been difficult for you to keep back from saying that our children are far lovelier. She must be very spoilt from all you say – it is a good thing she has got a little sister as too much attention was being paid her & that can't be good, fancy singing to her for her to go to sleep!! I would like to see you doing that to one of our children!'[49] Meeting them again in November 1913, Princess Nicholas thought the Kirill girls, 'much improved in manners & grown of course, but their faces are much the same, Kira is a sweet little thing'.[50]

Two wars and a revolution would pass before the two families were reunited, events that took their toll on the children as much as the parents. 'I never would have recognised little Marie,' Princess Nicholas told Kate in the summer of 1920; 'she is as tall as I & very fat – looks at least 18 – one would never believe she is two months younger than Marina. Kira is prettier but also too plump – she is about as tall as Marina – I never saw children eat as these do, between meals, they are allowed to stuff on sweets, cakes & c. Marie looks grumpy & dissatisfied, wants to be amused & does nothing all day – it is very sad & I can't understand her mother who is so clever & reasonable in everything, being able to spoil her children as she does!' The only member of the family with no cause to regret the past was the Kirills' son Vladimir, born in Finland in August 1917. 'The little boy is sweet & has got a fascinating smile,' Princess Nicholas told Kate, 'some people think him so like me, but I don't see it – he is very fair, curly fair hair, blue eyes & rather pale, except when out of doors or playing – He is a friendly little chap & not shy, but I'm afraid he is also being spoilt & allowed to do what he likes – I hope Nurse Colenette will be allowed to take him in hand; just now he has got a Swedish hospital nurse who doesn't seem to know how to manage him a bit!'[51]

Kate Fox wrote to Princess Nicholas almost every day when they were apart. Two letters survive from the autumn of 1921, long letters written over several days when Kate and the three Princesses were staying at Mon Repos on Corfu with Princess Alice and Prince Andrew and their family. They capture a languid month of warm autumn days when the cousins, Princesses Margarita, Theodora, Cecile and Sophie, Olga, Elizabeth and Marina, lazed in the sun, brushing their hair and dreaming, while their nurses Kate and Roosie, old enemies brought together by time and experience, did their mending, drinking tea and talking quietly over the old days. On the mainland, Greece was at war. Prince Andrew had been openly critical of the conduct of the campaign and must have been beset by worries, but Kate only noticed that he seemed stiff and unfriendly: the island was immune to the tensions of the world outside.

Four months earlier, Princess Alice had given birth to her fifth child, a boy, and he was the centre of everyone's attention. His sisters and cousins competed to hold him, as girls will. 'The baby is perfectly adorable and Vuttut [Princess Elizabeth] is very keen on him,' Kate told Princess Nicholas, 'she nurses him very nicely, and is quite as anxious to have him as Olga is, Olga was left in charge yesterday & was very pleased, he is a long suffering baby, with all these girls round him every minute he is awake.'[52]

Biographies of HRH Prince Philip, Duke of Edinburgh usually begin with his family's hurried escape from Corfu on board a British warship at the end of

1922. This was the outcome of the crisis that was brewing while Kate was at
Mon Repos: it almost led to Prince Andrew's execution. Prince Philip grew up
in exile but Kate's letters bring back a fragment of the lost period of his life
when he was, albeit briefly, the youngest Prince in a reigning family. While
Kate dosed the girls with their Savory and Moore's and their Scott's Emulsion
and fussed over their ailments, and struggled to keep them usefully occupied,
Roosie worried about the imminent arrival of her bugbear, the governess –
much more of a problem to her by this time than Kate was – and Princess Alice
was busy preparing the house for her son's christening, which was planned for
Sunday 6 November. It was to be a truly royal occasion, with a full
complement of guests.

For the nurses it was an immense pleasure just to manage a baby again.
Kate's last experience had been with Princess Alexandra, daughter of the short-
lived King Alexander and his wife Madame Manos, but then she was allowed
do little more than hold the baby; at Mon Repos she had a free hand. 'We
haven't done anything to-day,' she wrote on Tuesday 24 October, 'but I had
Philip most of the time after tea, while Olga was knitting & Roosie mending
some gloves of her own, he really is a darling.'[53] Always a keen photographer,
Kate asked the Princess to send her some films to record the baby with 'our
children'.[54] But despite her new-found friendship with Roosie, Kate was still
rather nonplussed to be asked to help with the baby during the christening
service: 'Roosie said she would rather have me, I can't help wondering how
much is sincere, & am careful what I say.'[55]

She need not have worried. The day dawned rather cool and wet and at
eleven o'clock in the morning the party set out in three cars: Prince Andrew
with Olga (who was to be godmother) and his two elder daughters in the first;
the governess in the second with the four younger girls, Kate and Roosie in the
third with the baby. Crowds had lined the streets, straining for a glimpse of
him; the red carpet was out at the church and a band was playing, while civic
dignitaries in full ceremonial dress lined up to take their part in the ceremony.
As godmother, eighteen-year-old Olga had to stand beside the font between the
Mayor and the chairman of the municipal council and to recite part of the
liturgy. 'I felt myself blushing down to my knees almost,' she told her mother.
Kate and Roosie undressed the baby (in an Orthodox christening the infant is
immersed in the font) and draped a towel over the Mayor ready to take him;
when it was done, the nurses dressed him again in his long white lace robe and
handed him to Olga who carried him three times round the font, then returned
to her place, where the Mayor and the council chairman each held a corner of
the christening robe while prayers were said. Olga told her mother she felt

rather like a bride but the baby was quiet, fascinated by the candles and the glittering robes of the priests. They emerged to be greeted by cheering crowds and returned to Mon Repos for a large reception; far too large and too overwhelming for an infant. The Prince stayed to be admired only for a few minutes before Roosie carried him away to the nursery.[56]

Written reports for mothers often described the children's occupations and amusements. That autumn on Corfu, Princess Marina devised a play with her seven-year-old cousin Sophie. Kate was rather dismissive; 'I don't stop it,' she said, 'for if it is silly it is also harmless, & they might be doing something worse if it wasn't that.' It kept the girls busy, and while Kate sat out on the porch with Olga learning to knit and Elizabeth doing her embroidery, Marina was 'making wings etc.', and 'sewing some "pearls" on pink silk for this play'.[57]

Dressing up was always popular, though royal children could usually find enough exciting costumes in the house without having to make them. The Hesse children of the 1870s – Georgie and Lu's father and aunts – were fond of devising their own plays. The eldest sister, Victoria, recalled one of their early governesses, Emma Kitz, nobly ignoring her own sick headache (she was rather prone to those) to play King Arthur for the children, seated regally on a bench with a wreath around her neck, clutching her aching head while they danced noisily round her. Noise, it seems, was an essential element of the game. One of Emma's successors, Louisa Graves, opened a letter to their mother with the immortal words, 'Madam, The Psses & Prince Ernie are quite well they are at present executing a war dance as it is a wet afternoon, the effect of which Your Royal Highness may see in my writing.'[58]

Nurse Kemence captured a typical nursery Sunday in one of her letters to Princess Alexander of Teck in 1911, which suggests that Queen Victoria's ideas about Sunday being a festive day for the children had long since been discarded: 'It is a lovely day we went to church this morning but with Prince Rupert I was afraid to stay long when I found Prince Christian and family there,' she wrote, 'they were both so good but we did not stay long enough to get fidgety, went to children's service in the afternoon and very good, sang hymns after tea so finished Sunday.'[59]

On the Continent, St Nicholas's Day in early December was widely celebrated as a curtain-raiser to Christmas, when the Saint himself (or someone dressed rather like him), would visit the house, rewarding good children and punishing bad ones. A few weeks after Nurse Kemence's nursery Sunday, Lilian Eadie wrote to the Grand Duchess of Hesse describing St Nicholas's Day with

Georgie and Lu at Lich, the Grand Duchess's childhood home. 'The children have asked me to write . . . and also to tell you "Nikolaus" came to visit them last evening,' she said, 'it was really quite as good as a play to see them, they were very pleased but also a little bit frightened, and when "Nikolaus" pointed at them and asked if they could sing something, Georgie managed a verse of "Heilige Nacht" and Lu his favourite "Mit dem Pfiel und Bogen" it was a bit shaky. Every evening the children sing with the others when the candles are lighted.'[60]

For royal children Christmas itself was often celebrated in front of the whole Court, but some enjoyed simpler family Christmases. From her retirement in South Africa in the 1930s Emily Roose looked back on her last years with Prince Andrew's family, telling Princess Cecile: 'It is strange to think of Xmas in this heat 100 in shade. My thoughts go back to our last happy Xmas altogether at St Cloud & the 7 stockings I crept around the quiet house putting one on each bed your 2 cousins enjoyed the fun of having a stocking – I remember tieing the tops of stockings with old ribbons, & the first thing Philip said – look Nana father Xmas has taken your ribbon! It was funny how you all had such pleasure out of the Christmas stocking.'[61]

British women who ventured beyond Europe had to work with children brought up in cultures completely unlike their own. When Emmeline Lott first met His Highness the Grand Pacha Ibrahim, son of the Khedive of Egypt, in the harem of the Ghezire Palace in Cairo, 'he set up a most hideous shriek' and buried his head in his mother's lap.[62] Emmeline may well have felt like doing the same; her nerves were not up to harem life and her five-year-old charge was a demon. 'Child as he was,' she said, 'his word was law and nobody dared disobey him.'[63] If the gardeners displeased little Ibrahim, he could order his eunuchs to whip them and they would do it, not stopping until he gave the word – or until his governess reined him in. He was waited on by slave children to whom he could be as cruel as the mood took him. Once, Emmeline said, one of these little slaves annoyed him and he grabbed her, pinching her arms and biting them until he drew blood, 'after which he put his fingers into the poor little creature's mouth and tore both sides of it, until the blood streamed down her chin like water'. The governess was not having this. 'I scolded him well for such brutality, when His Highness burst into tears, and walked away into another apartment.'[64]

Incidents like this underlined the difficulty of Emmeline's position. In Brazil, Maria Graham had found herself in charge of a pupil who tyrannised slave children, but the little Infanta's mother fully supported Maria's view that such behaviour 'made a great number of people very unhappy'.[65] When Ibrahim's mother saw his tears she made the injured child apologise to him, laughing off Emmeline's protests. She and Ibrahim's Ethiopian nurse did punish him when it suited by pinching him or sticking pins into his hand; Emmeline refused to do this because she felt it only taught him to be cruel. She did despair but she also persisted and managed to establish a reasonable relationship with Ibrahim: after all, he was just a five-year-old behaving as the people around him expected. Forbidden to teach him from books, Emmeline entered into his games and 'found that he possessed excellent abilities, dull and heavy-looking boy as he appeared to be'. In time she could even describe him as 'a merry little boy' and she was sure that if she could only have had him to herself, 'away from all the disgusting manners of the ladies of the Harem and the slaves', she could have made a gentleman of him.[66]

Six years after Emmeline left the Khedive's family another governess, Ellen Chennells, encountered Ibrahim. She only noted that he was clever: her charge was his sister Zeyneb, a delicate girl a year older than her brother. 'She was rather short in stature,' Ellen remembered, 'but her face was pretty – regular features, soft brown eyes (which she had a trick of screwing up), and long eyelashes.' In her own family, though, Zeyneb was considered plain and constant ill health had made her rather backward. Ellen found her 'painfully conscious of her own deficiencies. Gentle and timid to a fault, she was of a character that required great encouragement.'[67] Perhaps with a brother like Ibrahim this was understandable. In Ellen's day both Ibrahim and Zeyneb were taken out of the harem for their lessons to a house where their tutors were living. They made the journey separately and each was accompanied by one of the slave children Emmeline had known. For Zeyneb this was an Armenian girl named Kopsès, a real beauty, who excelled her gentle little mistress in everything except rank. Ellen found Kopsès a pleasure to teach, yet understood the peculiar sensitivities of her position: 'It would have been a false kindness to cultivate her powers according to their capability,' she said, 'at the risk of exciting ill-feeling on the part of the Princess, on whom she was wholly dependent.'[68]

Ethel Howard went to Japan at the start of 1901 to take full responsibility for the daily lives of fourteen-year-old Prince Tadashige Shimadzu and his four younger brothers, in an educational experiment more challenging than any other English governess is likely to have experienced. Tadashige grew up under the old feudal code of Japan. Constantly accompanied by male retainers who did everything for him, he was considered so exalted a person in his native Satsuma province that no one could even look at his face. He was orphaned at the age of twelve and, after he had spent two years in a school in Tokyo, the guardians who had charge of his family installed him and his brothers in a Western-style house and engaged Ethel to prepare them for life in the modern world. For Tadashige especially, it must have been a strange journey. Ethel found him remote and unapproachable at first; all expression of emotion had been trained out of him. When she asked him to do things for her his brothers were shocked, and attendants who came straight from his province to pay their respects would still lie prostrate on the ground before him. 'All this needed to be changed gradually,' Ethel said, 'and how was I to do it without lessening his greatness or wounding their susceptibilities?'[69]

But a strong connection grew between Ethel and the Prince, who did not seem like a boy at all. Tadashige exercised an imperceptible authority over the many male attendants who filled the house. Without him, the experiment could never have proceeded, but he did everything Ethel asked of him in silent obedience. When he left for the naval college at Etajima she felt lost, 'like a ship without a rudder, for though in a sense I had been entrusted with his education, yet he had taken most of the responsibilities off my shoulders. . . . It was hard to feel that he was to go entirely out of my life, not to be allowed to write to me, and perhaps not even to come back in the holidays. And there were some who whispered sadder things in my ears, telling me that the sons of the nobility have not deep enough affections in their natures to remember a foreigner like myself', but this last predication proved too gloomy.[70] Tadashige did write, and in time Ethel would find him 'one of the best and truest friends that life has yet given me'.[71]

With his cooperation, working with the younger brothers was comparatively easy. Ethel found Tomijiro, at nine, 'so clever a child that I have never met his equal'.[72] The guardians removed him from her care very soon as they felt he needed individual attention. Junnosuke, 'Zun', was thin and delicate but full of energy, with a bubbling sense of humour that emerged under Ethel's new regime, which encouraged the boys to express their feelings. Akinoshin, 'Arkey', was much more quiet and reserved, the strongest of the brothers, and Yonosuke, 'Tiny', Ethel found 'quite an irresistible little person, very delicate, but full of fun, nothing escaped his notice'.[73] He was terrified of her at first and had to be held in the room by one of the elderly attendants, howling and screaming; later, he came to return her affection. All the boys were quick and observant, learning from Ethel customs that were completely foreign to the world into which they were born. When they first saw Ethel kiss a friend they roared with laughter, and 'afterwards asked why she had licked me!'[74] Then, not long after, Ethel was reading aloud to the boys when little Yonosuke grabbed her hand and kissed it. Usually a silent child, he surprised her one day by saying 'Pargum' after accidentally slamming a door. Later he invented degrees of apology; 'big pargum' or 'little pargum', depending on what he had done.[75]

All children copy the adults around them, and royal children's games must always have included imitations of the ceremonial that surrounded them at Court. Once, Ethel saw the Emperor's son, who would one day reign as Emperor Hirohito. 'I remember him seated on a chair,' Ethel said, 'a very small person! – having a pair of European button-boots put on him, and much enjoying the treat of the new boots and the excitement of the endless buttons. . . . Suddenly he caught sight of me, and upon my making the bow which was expected of me the little Crown Prince, in the midst of his childish glee, voluntarily put up his small hand to his cap, and saluted with much dignity.'[76] This baby salute by little princes was a universal gesture. In 1910 Kellogg Durland was allowed to meet the Spanish Infantes, Alfonso, Prince of the Asturias, who was three, and his brother, two-year-old Jaime. Passing them afterwards in their carriage he lifted his hat, and instantly 'two little hands were raised to their right temples, elbows out, eyes front – all with military precision. No soldier could have given a truer salute,' he said. 'It was so charming, so unexpected, that I laughed outright.'[77]

A precocious awareness of all things military went with the gesture. When Alexandra Coombs, governess to the daughters of Grand Duchess Georgi Mikhailovich, helped the little Tsesarevich Alexei on with his coat and pushed his broad sailor collar to the inside she was taken aback to be told, 'Don't you know that the Emperor has made a New Order? We sailors must always wear our collars outside out coats.'[78] 'We sailors . . .' The little boy also enjoyed mimicking the military bands he so often heard and he would whistle the national anthems of his visitors' attendants: 'God Save the King' in a compliment to Nana Bell and the 'Marseillaise' for the French governess.[79]

Sometimes the imitations were more ambitious. In the summer of 1892 the child Queen Wilhelmina went on a state visit to Potsdam. Because of her age she was exempted from official functions and while her mother took on the public appearances, she and Saxton Winter spent most of their days with the Kaiser's elder sons. At first the Princes were a little in awe of the fact that their visitor was a Queen, even though she was not much older than they were. Then they decided that they must hold a military review. Wilhelmina was given a commanding position in the centre of the playroom from which to take the salute while the boys and Saxton marched past her, each representing a whole regiment at a time. Then Saxton was told she must be the cavalry, which involved 'continuous prancing, kicking, snorting, pirouetting in fantastic evolutions. . . . It was considered treason if one did not strain every effort to faithfully depict an accomplished rider or an excited steed.' Finally Wilhelmina could stand it no longer: 'she suddenly fled from her Staff without any warning of her intentions, and seizing hold of a helmet and sword, joined the wild romp. That pleased the imperial soldiers tremendously, and no soldiers ever worked harder to do themselves credit than we did that afternoon,' Saxton Winter remembered. It would have been a good deal easier for her to attend the adult review, but she had had more fun with the children.[80]

'It was like a fairy tale . . .' Doris Clarke had said, describing her visit to the royal palace in Italy. The nurses and governesses who worked for royalty knew that royal children had the same potential for mess, mayhem and destruction as other children, as well as the same appeal, but because their charges were royal there would always be an added dimension. It was the thought of what the children might become; the thought that, in being close to them you were somehow touching history. Lilian Brimble expressed it perfectly in recalling an early morning paper chase with young Prince Wilhelm: 'Once, as we were dashing along through the bracken in an opening in the forest,' she said, 'I glanced down at the little figure running beside me, his blue eyes alight with eagerness, cheeks pink with excitement . . . how queer it was to think that in all probability, in years to come, that selfsame little blue-trousered, white Jersey-clad boy would be reigning over every inch of land on which his feet trod that day. He caught my glance, and smiled back at me with an ecstatic "Isn't it nice, darling?" and we just touched hands and nodded, and went gaily on; while I thought what a charm the unconsciousness of childhood has.'[81]

SIX

'The King Came Up to Tea'

BEING PART OF THE FAMILY

We stood politely while our lunch got colder and colder and the Crown Prince acted the buffoon, seizing a spoonful of potato purée and smearing it all over the boys' heads, or pouring asparagus sauce on their hair, laughing immoderately meanwhile. Often he would pour their cups of cocoa over them, or a glass of water down their back, or rub the whipped cream from a sweet dish all over their faces, Prince Lulu being nearly always the victim on account of his getting so easily irate, though once Prince Wilhelm had to stand with open mouth while his father poured a ladleful of soup into it through a funnel which chanced to be in the room. Can you wonder we found such jokes not in the least amusing, merely very disgusting, and of course the boys had to go and be washed and brushed and generally polished before they could come back to luncheon or their supper again.[1]

Relating to your children's family was not always easy for a nurse or governess in royal service, as Lilian Brimble discovered. Few royal fathers would have been as annoying as Wilhelm, Crown Prince of Prussia – but then, Ethel Howard who had known him as a boy and had given him the nickname 'T' for his teasing could have told Lilian that this had always been his way. At least it had been possible for Ethel to control him. As a man he played his tricks when he wanted, to the admiring giggles (or the screaming frustration) of his four young sons and the suppressed fury of the women who were paid to look after them – and to teach them not to follow their father's example. The Crown Prince liked disrupting bedtime too, bursting in just as the boys were settled and starting a fight between them and his dogs, as 'the beds got unmade and in the greatest disorder, the room like a bear garden, and the boys shrieking and rushing wildly about. . . . The final act usually consisted in the Crown Prince seizing one of the bedroom jugs from the wash stand and emptying its contents over Prince Lulu in bed. . . . As soon as he had made his son and the bed thoroughly wet and miserable, out he would go with his dogs, with a guffaw of amusement, leaving order to be restored.'[2]

The Crown Prince's taste for risqué music-hall songs made life even more difficult, as it amused him to teach the songs to his children, who had no idea what they were singing about. And 'it became not a comedy, but a tragedy,' Lilian said, 'when the five-year-old Prince Hubertus suddenly lifted up his small voice in the Belle Vue Park and gave a spirited rendering of "And that, the maidens love so dearly", followed by other equally edifying ditties, in spite of frantic attempts on the part of his overwhelmed and flustered nurse to make him be quiet'. Unfortunately the audience on that occasion included the little boy's grandmother, the Kaiserin, not a woman known for her broadmindedness. She was shocked to the very core of her being to hear such words ringing from the lips of her little grandson – and in a public place, too. She asked who had taught him the songs and the nursery held its breath, sighing thankfully when he said that it was 'Papa'.[3]

Even the children noticed 'Papa's' fondness for the ladies, which might have become a problem once they were old enough to understand. 'It did not seem to matter whether they were ladies or not,' Lilian said, 'his tastes being very catholic in that direction.'[4] She described the adoring collection of nursery maids who used to gather outside the family's villa in Danzig, hoping to see him pass. The crowds on the beach that were such a nuisance to her and the children seemed to give positive pleasure to their father. Lilian described how he would stretch out in the sun in his red bathing drawers with a handkerchief tied over his head waiting for a crowd to gather. When enough people were watching he would go for a bathe – dragging along his unfortunate adjutants, whether they wanted to join him or not. The sightseers would then undress and follow the royal example and at such times the nursery party tried to steer well clear. 'The results were sometimes so appalling,' Lilian said, 'they fairly took my breath away.'[5]

There were other practical jokers among the princes of Europe but none to quite the same extent. Grand Duke Mikhail Alexandrovich, Tsar Nicholas II's younger brother, had a mischievous streak. His stepdaughter Natalia, 'Tata' Mamontov, described how he teamed up with her English governess Edith Rata to play a trick on the great singer Chaliapin. Miss Rata had been in hospital with typhoid and in the course of the illness she had lost most of her hair. She wore a wig but, on learning that the hair underneath was not growing back very well, the Grand Duke persuaded her to let him shave it off, which she did, while the rest of the household stood around and enjoyed the joke. 'It really suited her,' Tata remembered, 'she had a very nice round head, and being a big woman she very successfully went to some fancy-dress party dressed as a man and carried it off.' The Grand Duke's family were living in Cannes that winter and Chaliapin often visited from Monte Carlo where he was working. Over coffee one morning, as the singer's back was turned, the Grand Duke signalled to Edith Rata to remove her wig. She took it off quickly and slipped it under a cushion. 'A few seconds later Chaliapin turned to her with some remark and was confronted with a completely bald head with the faintest black down just beginning to show. He remained completely speechless for a moment and then pulled himself together, gave a gulp, and went on with his remark, to be greeted with a roar of laughter.'[6]

Sometimes involvement with the family's pleasures could almost overwhelm the delicate feelings of a single lady. In Harrogate during the First World War the Grand Duke's cousin Marie, Grand Duchess Georgi Mikhailovich of Russia, gave a fancy-dress party for her birthday and persuaded her daughters' governess Alexandra Coombs to join in, covered in cotton wool 'snow' to represent winter. Her lady-in-waiting's brother Billy Barron, who was serving as an officer in the British army, dressed as a woman and the party was swinging along nicely when suddenly the lights dimmed and went out. Panic ensued, because this was the warning signal for a German air raid. Billy Barron's costume had suddenly become an embarrassment. His sister described how he rushed round the room 'trying to find somebody to help him get out of the tight pair of stays; he could only find the governess who was very prudish; she refused; he implored her and kept saying, "I shall be shot at dawn, if the Germans find me masquerading as a woman." He appealed to her Christianity and, at last, with tightly closed eyes, she cut the laces and the stays fell in two separate parts on the floor. He flew to his room, washed off all traces of his womanly beauty, and reappeared a British Officer.' What happened to poor Alexandra Coombs we are not told, but at that point the 'all-clear' sounded.[7]

Nellie Ryan enjoyed an interesting relationship with Archduke Karl Stefan of Austria-Hungary, in whose household she worked for several years from the late 1890s. He was not a practical joker but he was something of a tease and life was never dull with him around. Discovering quite soon after her arrival at Court that Nellie had a flair for arranging furniture, he summoned her to his private study one day and she arrived to find his entire family – he had six children – looking rather flushed and exhausted. He announced that they had just rearranged the entire room: '"As you have such wonderful ideas on alterations, and readjustments," he said with a very amused look at me, "tell me if it is an improvement."' Nellie had never seen the room before so this was something of a challenge but, finding herself surrounded by expectant faces, she had a quick look round, pronounced it almost perfect, and then found something that might, just, look better in an alcove. 'Instantly there was a chorus of delight from all; something else to move – oh, the fascination of it all! It did one good to see them.'[8]

The Archduke returned the favour the next day, turning up uninvited in Nellie's sitting-room with some English novels and announcing that he did not like the way the room was arranged: 'And, before I had recovered from my amusement and astonishment, he had picked up one or two Persian rugs from the beautiful polished oak floor, and opening the door flung them out into the corridor. He then proceeded to push the bigger pieces of furniture from the corners of the room all into the centre, and before I could protest, or make myself understood, the entire contents of the room were standing huddled up in the centre of the room, looking exactly like a store-room in a furniture shop.' By this time Nellie was in fits of laughter. She could no longer see the Archduke behind all the furniture. Then his wife, the Archduchess Maria Teresa arrived, bemused by the sight of Nellie's carpets in the corridor, and she was just laughing at her husband's impetuosity when the Court chamberlain came by looking for the Archduke. The two men hurried off together on business of some sort and Nellie was left to restore her room to a semblance of order.[9]

A gifted, clever man with many interests and a streak of quicksilver in his being, the Archduke was forever organising his family and household into new ventures. There were times when he liked to work alone but they were few; for the most part he wanted everyone to be involved together and he relished noise and commotion. In the Schloss at Zywiec in Poland there were days at a time when the rain was so heavy that no one could go out, and the Archduke would organise his family and household in lively indoor games. 'Railways' was a favourite, and playing it archducal style involved a giant toy train set – steam driven – with all the associated paraphernalia of track and stations and signal boxes. Each person would be given his or her own position and job to do. 'The greatest joy was if a collision took place, or if anything caught fire,' Nellie said. 'I think to a stranger looking in to see the Archduke sitting or lying full length on the ground, most serious and attentive to his particular duty, with various ladies and gentlemen, as well as the eager young Archdukes and Archduchesses, the scene would be most unexpected and enlightening.'[10]

Working within a royal family was about being like one of the family – without ever quite forgetting that you were not. It was about playing with your employer's train set if he wanted you to, or washing his mashed potato out of his children's hair; about seeing him and all his relatives as they really were when the crowds were not looking and yet not being flustered or awkward about this yourself, but accepting it as normal. So if the Prince wanted to bath his own baby, a good nurse would just hand him the towel.[11] If the Tsar and Tsaritsa of Russia wanted to sit in the playpen with their firstborn like any other excited young parents, the nurse would smile, enjoy the sight privately and get on with her work.[12] If the King chose to disrupt a carefully planned timetable, the governess would sigh resignedly and note it down in her schoolroom diary – as Annie Dutton, English teacher to King Alfonso XIII of Spain's children, had to do on more than one occasion: 'March 1927: Friday 18th. Don Gonzalo absent playing chess with the King. . . . Monday 21st. Don Gonzalo absent playing chess with HM. the King. . . . Friday 25th. Don Gonzalo absent playing chess with the King.' Don Gonzalo was the King's youngest son, aged thirteen at this time. How his absences felt to his brother Don Juan, patiently enduring lessons on 'Wireless telegraphy . . . Spelling – Verb to "Buy" . . . Reading on "War" in Royal Reader Vol. VI & explication of same . . . General Geography', while Gonzalo was off playing chess with their father we are not told.

But the King was the King, and if he chose to drop in for tea it was up to the governess not to be overawed, and therefore embarrassing to His Majesty, yet at the same time not to be too familiar. 'H.M. the King came up to tea with us,' Annie Dutton recorded in her notebook for 1919, 'and although he told us he had already had his – still there was nothing that made one feel so hungry as seeing other people eat & not do so too – he therefore took a second tea with us & talked very interestingly about the Strikes all over Spain especially in Andalucia and Cataluñia comparing the latter to Ireland & its relations with England & he told Don Javier Vales Failde that it was precisely the Irish R.C. Clergy who were the Revolutionists.' Two weeks before, Annie had played host to the King's mother, Queen Maria Cristina, and found her, 'most interesting she called me apart to tell me how much she laughed on hearing the Infantas say the litany after the Rosary. On the 11th,' Annie continued, 'H.M. the King came during the lesson and heard the Infantas recite – He afterwards congratulated me as he called it upon "the Girls' Performance".'[13]

In employment terms, the nurses' and governesses' world had fewer rules than our own. Everyone understood, broadly, what a nurse did or what being a governess was all about, but the day-to-day reality was that you fitted in as the individual family wanted you to and if you had particular talents you could expect them to be used, even if this went beyond the normal range of a nurse or a governess's duties. There were many nurses who gave classroom lessons. During the months she spent on Corfu with Princess Nicholas of Greece's daughters, Kate Fox gave regular lessons to Princess Marina. In one letter she reported to Princess Nicholas, 'she really is getting something of English history into her head, I am giving her lessons each day on one reign, & sent her this morning to write out the principal persons in the reign of Henry 8th that way she will exercise her memory & get some necessary knowledge into her head, she hadn't an idea who Wolsey was, & said Henry 7th reigned after Henry 8th, but now I don't think she will ever forget Wolsey any more, nor when he lived.'[14]

It was rare for a governess to undertake the physical care of children but it was not unknown. Duchess Cecilie of Mecklenburg-Schwerin wrote of her own governess Lucie King, 'At the very beginning of our acquaintance she won my heart by nursing me lovingly through an illness, and a relationship which can only be described as friendship was soon established between us.'[15] In November 1872 the Crown Princess of Prussia wrote to Augusta Byng from Bex in Switzerland with particular concern about the health of her four-year-old son Waldemar: 'Many affectionate thanks for your kind and charming letter of the 17th. Thank God all the news you give me of my beloved ones is good; though Waldie's being hoarse fidgets me. I hope you will <u>only</u> keep him shut up indoors if it is pouring with wet or if the wind is unusually cold, sharp or high, and use your discretion about letting him go out, as it will never do to deprive him of air. His throat and chest ought to be rubbed <u>every</u> <u>morning</u> & night with a rough towel dipped into <u>cold</u> water and completely wrung out, then with a dry towel, and lastly with a piece of red flannel, <u>nothing</u> is so strengthening and such a preventative against colds & sore throats, I have had this treatment introduced for both William <u>and</u> <u>Henry</u>!'[16]

This was not the only occasion when Augusta was asked to nurse the children through illness, or at least to supervise the nursing and make sure it was done in the way the Crown Princess wanted. An undated note tells her, 'I think Vicky had better not leave the schoolroom all day and not get into a draught as she has such a heavy cold. She had better have a mustard and linseed poultice on just before she goes to bed at 11 and again tonight. Waldemar had better not go near her – or he is sure to catch her cold.'[17] It makes for a telling comparison between Augusta and her successor Marianne Green. They held the same position but while Augusta took on a motherly role in the family, with nursing care as one of her duties, Marianne's brisk and academic approach inclined her more towards secretarial work for the children's parents.

In December 1961 *The Times* carried an article about a book belonging to Marianne Green which turned up on a bargain barrow outside a second-hand bookshop. It was *Friedrich, Crown Prince and Emperor*, a biography of the children's father who died of cancer of the throat in 1888, commissioned by his widow and written by Rennell Rodd, a young diplomat from the Berlin Embassy. The book was inscribed, 'To dear Miss Green, a token of grateful affection – in memory of the time of deep affliction and bitter sorrow, 1888, Nov. 21 – Windsor Castle Victoria Empress Frederick.' Marianne Green's marginal notes, written at intervals throughout the book, give a revealing picture of the role she created for herself within the imperial family. Beneath the foreword of the book she added, 'I read the M.S. of this book through to H.M. the Empress Frederick and "revised" it under her instructions.' Before his illness took hold the Crown Prince had given a speech at the opening of the English Church in Berlin. Alongside the detailed report of his words in the book Marianne noted, 'This speech, as it appears here, was written by me from some notes dictated to me by the Crown Princess. The Crown Prince copied them out in his own hand-writing as he said he would be able to read it better, if he wrote it himself. After the ceremony was over, he happened to pass close by me, & he said in his usual kind way: "How do you think *our* speech went?"'[18]

Playing the English-speaking secretary was quite common for British governesses overseas; their language skills were always in demand. They were also figures of trust. After all, if you could leave your child in someone's care, other things would surely be safe in her hands as well. Queen Emma of the Netherlands liked to entrust her jewellery to Saxton Winter when they travelled on official visits. The results could be comical – in retrospect, at least. On the state visit to Potsdam in 1892, Saxton Winter was carrying Queen Emma's most valuable jewels in a small, plain handbag. Their train was delayed and when they reached the palace the evening meal was about to be served. Queen Wilhelmina was considered too young for a formal dinner so the royal families ate in private, away from the visiting suite and officials of the Kaiser's Court. But Saxton Winter, ushered straight into the courtiers' dining-room, had no time to make arrangements for the jewels and no chance to speak to Queen Emma. She dared not let go, 'but my bag was evidently distasteful to the orderly mind of my stiffly-stayed and uniformed neighbour. In fact, so persistent was he in his offers to relieve me of its care that, had I been of a suspicious turn of mind, I might have thought him possessed of a knowledge of its contents and an irresistible desire to purloin them. To end discussion of the matter I resorted to a practical demonstration and sat on the bag, which still further mystified my cavalier and gave me intense discomfort.'[19] It was the price of being thought trustworthy.

Sometimes, it was the intimate knowledge which both governesses and nurses possessed of the families they worked for that was tapped into. In 1898 Queen Victoria relied on May T to keep her informed privately of the condition of her cousin's daughter, Crown Princess Stephanie of Austria, who had influenza and for a time seemed close to death. But such contact was more commonly used by royal parents wanting marriage partners for their children. When the Queen surveyed the single princes and princesses of Europe with her offspring in mind she always valued what the nurses had to tell her. The

Princess Royal wrote to her in 1860 to recommend Princess Alexandra of Denmark for the Prince of Wales, remarking, 'I know her nurse who tells me that she is strong in health and has never ailed', and the Queen came straight back with the question, 'Who is her nurse?'[20] It turned out that the nurse was a friend of Emma Hobbs who had worked for ten years in the family of the future King Christian IX of Denmark. In 1860 she was in Berlin, nursing in the far less congenial household of Prince Friedrich Karl (who attacked his wife for giving birth to a daughter). Each day the two nurses took their charges out walking and Emma was able to find out everything the Queen wanted to know. She reported the other nurse's account of Alexandra, 'that she is the sweetest girl who ever lived,' the Princess Royal told her mother, 'and full of life and spirits. She says she has always been as strong and healthy as possible and has a very good constitution. That she has never ailed anything in her life except having the measles.'[21]

Eighteen years later it was a governess who provided a similar service to the Queen when Luise Margarete, Prince Friedrich Karl's youngest daughter, was suggested as a bride for Prince Arthur. The Queen approached her daughter Alice, Grand Duchess of Hesse, this time, knowing that Luise Margarete's former governess 'Madgie' Jackson had just moved on to work for the Hesse family. 'I have spoken to Miss Jackson as you wished,' Alice told her mother, 'she has put down her opinion & she has put even <u>less</u> than she could say in her [Luise Margarete's] favour – if she chose – being anxious to be most impartial. . . . Miss Jackson says she has serious tastes & tries to cultivate them by reading by herself – she is in correspondence with Miss Jackson to whom she is much attached & I am sure she could have no better friend, so straight & true & loving.'[22]

Miss Jackson's own report offered a very favourable assessment of Luise Margarete's character and did not shy away from the problems between Prince Friedrich Karl and his wife which had overshadowed her former pupil's childhood. 'Her tact & judgement have been perhaps all the more fostered by the very difficult Home Life,' she wrote, 'and in self-control and decision she is in no sense wanting – The very shortcomings of her Parents seem only to have served as examples to avoid and at the same time, nothing can be more touching than her natural reverence and tenderness towards her mother. . . . In tastes, P^{cess} Louise is very simple and dislikes great ceremonials, being never happier than when Drawing & having someone read – or reading alone. In disposition she is both gentle and affectionate, without being in the least weak – on the contrary she has much decision of character.'[23] Luise Margarete and Prince Arthur were married on 13 March 1879; by that time Miss Jackson had

had several long conversations with Prince Arthur as well, while staying in England with the Hesse family, and it would surely have pleased her to think that her report had played some part in her pupil's future happiness.

In royal circles the children's grandparents could often be more important than the parents, and nurses and governesses had to be aware of their feelings and wishes. Princess Alice died within a year of Madgie Jackson's appointment and this left the governess with more authority than she would otherwise have had, sharing day-to-day responsibility for Princesses Victoria, Elisabeth, Irène and Alix with their nurse Mary Ann Orchard and with Baroness Wilhelmine von Grancy, one of the senior ladies-in-waiting. The Queen relied on Madgie to keep her informed about her grandchildren's lives but, though she trusted her in this as she had trusted her on Luise Margarete, the relationship between them was never easy. In 1881 the Queen complained to the children's father, Grand Duke Ludwig of Hesse, about something Madgie had said or done. Princess Victoria, who was very close to her governess, replied on her father's behalf, 'I am so sorry you are so very much vexed with Miss Jackson whom in spite of her hastiness I sincerely like and respect but Papa has told me you have written to him about her & that he will settle all himself with you.'[24]

The matter passed, but the Queen did not forgive. In March 1887, with only Irène and Alix (the future Tsaritsa of Russia) left in the palace and Irène already engaged to be married, she began to push for Madgie Jackson's dismissal, saying that Alix 'must not be left to Miss Jackson alone, with her bad health, hard ways & crabbed, bad temper. It wld ruin Alicky. Some one must be found for her, younger, softer, brighter, else her life all alone will be utterly miserable.'[25] This was unfair to Madgie and the family knew it, but the Queen had to be approached with care. Princess Victoria replied that, although of course it would be nice for her youngest sister to have 'some one fresher & younger' the time was not yet right and 'Papa also would prefer no change'. Princess Alix was due to be confirmed in the following year. It would make a more natural end to Madgie Jackson's appointment and, as Princess Victoria reminded the Queen, 'in spite of her various faults we all owe her a debt of gratitude, as she has really tried to do her best & has shown us real affection & devotion, in spite of her unfortunate outward manner'.[26]

The mistake was in assuming, as the Queen appeared to assume, that a brusque and unemotional manner implied an unnatural lack of emotion. Madgie Jackson had become deeply attached to all four Princesses, particularly Alix, who was only six years old when her mother died. Madgie called the little girl 'My Poppet Queen number III' and a warm, affectionate correspondence between Alix and her 'Darling Madgie' lasted almost to the end of both their lives. But the Queen, who liked talking to nurses and valued their opinions, seems to have felt ill at ease with governesses. This was odd, because her own governess, Baroness Lehzen, was a key figure in her early life. It may be that she shared the general prejudice in England against educated women; the words 'an English governess' seem to have stirred unpleasant feelings in her. When her daughter-in-law the Duchess of Albany – who, as Helene of Waldeck, was one of Julie Douglas's pupils – was looking for a governess for her own children in 1890, she submitted her choice to the Queen. The reaction was tight-lipped: 'The Queen returns Miss Pott's letter. Honestly speaking she does not particularly admire it. The feeling of dread of <u>little</u> Children . . . does not promise very well. Governesses accustomed to older Children, especially English Governesses, seldom suit as well as those who have been in the habit of bringing up little Children. The Queen wishes the Duchess w^{ld} engage her for a <u>year</u> <u>on</u> <u>trial</u>.'[27]

Jane Potts had served several aristocratic families before becoming 'finishing' governess to the Duchess's younger sister, Princess Elisabeth of Waldeck. The Duchess engaged her and she joined the family at Birkhall that September. 'Charlie was directly friends and brought his Robinson Crusoe to show,' the Duchess told Sir Robert Collins, the Comptroller of her Household; 'Alice was a little shy. After luncheon Alice knitted and could at first not comprehend that Miss Potts could help her as well as I. I had a long talk with her; she entered very nicely into everything; & certainly it is a relief to have to deal with a woman who knows all about it & will help one, instead of having to be trained first.'[28] So far so good, but there was still the introduction to the Queen to be faced. Jane Potts had been only two days with the family when the Duchess was able to report, 'Yesterday being a wet day the Queen came to tea & to see Miss Potts, the moment she left the room the Queen turned to me with "What a nice person she looks, not at all like an English governess, those I know, were not at all like that, she looks something better" (I felt inclined to say: "I told you so!"),' the Duchess said, 'but kept to myself. You can imagine how delighted I am after all the growls I turned a deaf ear to. Lets hope this first impression will last! Children have quite taken to her, they still appeal too much to me, but that will come gradually – Miss Potts has a very nice quiet way to remind Charlie that he is at dinner & in the land of the living.'[29]

And so began another successful appointment. The overwhelming impression left by their nurses and governesses is that royalty were, on the whole, very good employers. It was demanding work and the financial rewards were not great; ''tis more glory than gold one earns by serving Royalty,' May T remarked.[30] But in terms of consideration, kindness and simple human respect, both nurses and governesses seem to have been looked after very well. It shows in the details –

remembrance of birthdays, for example, and anniversaries. When Madgie Jackson had been ten years with the Hesse family they presented her with a bracelet of miniatures of Princess Alice and all her children. At Easter in 1908, Lilian Wilson wrote to thank Grand Duchess Eleonore of Hesse 'for the lovely little egg you so kindly sent me, it is a perfect little gem and has been tremendously admired'. The Tsaritsa, who had known Lilian years before when she nursed the only child of the Grand Duke's previous marriage, remembered her too: 'Her Majesty the Empress also sent me one might I please ask Your Royal Highness to thank her very much for me'; and Lilian was overwhelmed by the family's realisation that for her, that particular Easter had an extra significance. 'Your Royal Highness will you please accept my very grateful thanks for your kind remembrance of my Birthday,' her letter continued, 'I cannot tell you what a pleasure it gave me, and I got it this morning too, besides being my birthday it was also the 13th anniversary of my coming to Darmstadt, it made the whole day different that you thought of me.'[31]

These were not isolated examples. In 1901 Margaretta Eagar was staying at Fredensborg in Denmark with the Tsar and his family. Queen Alexandra called on her one day to tell her that King Edward VII was on his way to visit the nursery, 'and asked me to make the children look very nice. I showed her the dresses I had prepared for them,' Margaretta wrote, 'and she admired them very much.' The King made a point of speaking to Margaretta often during the visit, calling her 'My Irish subject'. When the family party broke up, Queen Alexandra gave Margaretta a signed photograph of herself and the King with their grandchildren. Three years later, when the Tsar's family was finally able to celebrate the birth of a little Tsesarevich, the King sent Margaretta a personal gift to mark the occasion, 'a brooch, in green enamel, because I am Irish. They say he never forgets anything,' she said, 'and I know he never forgets to be kind.'[32]

When Kate Fox took her little Greek Princesses to the English seaside for three summers running she received long visits from Prince Nicholas's brother, Prince Christopher of Greece, and their cousin, King Edward VII's daughter Princess Victoria. They wanted to see the children, of course, but they were very friendly to Kate as well. Princess Victoria was taken ill at Bognor in June 1910 and had reason to be glad that Kate was there. 'Poor P[cess] Victoria!' Princess Nicholas wrote. 'I do hope she is all right now. How nice that you were able to look after her; I am sure you will always remain friends now.'[33] Princess Victoria gave Kate a brooch as a 'thank you' and at the beginning of July she sent some photographs taken at Bognor, writing 'how grateful I am & shall always be to you for all your kindness to me during those days when

I was so seedy'.[34] They would meet again afterwards on several occasions. In 1915 and 1916 Kate worked in the Salvation Army Mothers' Hospital in Clapton Road, Hackney, improving her nursing qualifications, and Princess Victoria arranged a special visit to the hospital while she was there.

In 1869 Emma Hobbs left Berlin to be married to one Jesse Skinner, much to the Crown Princess of Prussia's amazement. 'I did not know whether to laugh or cry,' she told Queen Victoria. 'She will be a great loss to me and I fear impossible to replace. She has rendered us very valuable services, and I am much attached to her, and grateful for her devotion to the children. The parting with her will be a pang to me and to her too, I am sure. But she seems very happy and her prospects are very fair so I hope it will all be for the best. Will you let me say a kind word to her from you?'[35] For someone who had served her daughter and grandchildren so well, the Queen was anxious to give more than a kind word. She offered a wedding present and, after some deliberation with her daughter, gave a pair of silver candlesticks, presenting them to Emma in person nine days before the wedding, which took place on 18 October at Southborough, near Tunbridge Wells.

The goodwill stretched in the other direction too, and there was often friendly contact between royal employers and the families of their nurses and governesses. From the moment 'Hartie' Stewart joined the Hanoverian Court as governess to Princesses Frederika and Mary, the King and Queen began to send greetings and wishes to her parents in Scotland. At her first Christmas in Germany in 1861 the King sent a boar's head to her family; it must have been in a sealed container of some sort and the King assured the Stewarts that it would keep in a cool place until February if it was not opened. Hartie even passed on his recipe suggestions for the leftovers.

The King and Queen treated Hartie like a daughter. Their involvement with her family became more intense and more personal when an officer from their Court, Lieutenant Colonel Otto von Klenck, made it known that he wished to marry her. As etiquette demanded, he first asked her if he might write to her parents. Hartie felt unable to give any sort of answer without their permission but her mother took against the idea immediately. An anguished exchange of letters between mother and daughter followed, as Mrs Stewart demanded Hartie's return, questioned von Klenck's financial position and attacked him for his presumption while Hartie tried to defend him. It was the King who helped them out of the impasse by sending a long, kind but very forthright letter to Mrs Stewart in favour of the marriage: 'This, my dear Mrs Stewart, is my view of the case and I should be acting wrongly towards you and your daughter and indeed your family if I had not given my candid opinion on so serious a matter.'[36] The courtship would be a long one, but on 8 August 1865 Hartie and Otto von Klenck were married in Scotland.

This sealed the friendship between the two families. When war threatened Hanover in 1866, with Otto away at the front and Hartie in bed having just given birth to their first child, it was the Queen who went in person to collect them and bring them to safety, taking the newborn baby in her own arms while eight footmen carried Hartie, bed and all. The baby girl was christened in the palace with one of the Princesses as godmother and the Queen held her under her first Christmas tree for a traditional blessing. In the years that followed, Mrs Stewart often visited Germany, and members of the Hanover family called on her in her house in London. In 1879, she organised a tea party for Princess Frederika to meet Tennyson and hear his poems. Meanwhile, little Frederika von Klenck was often invited to stay with the family of the former Crown Prince of Hanover, then Duke of Cumberland. As a boy he had been especially fond of Hartie. One year she told her mother how they were sharing the task of rearing a baby hedgehog he had found, which they kept in her room: 'It has succeeded admirably, eats quantities of bread and milk and makes the Crown Prince and me very vain of our powers of education.'[37]

When Mary Anne Thurston became nurse to Queen Victoria's children in the spring of 1845 she was a widow in her early thirties with a daughter, who was probably boarded out somewhere or cared for by relatives. In time this daughter had two daughters of her own, Marion and May Bryan, and Queen Victoria paid for their education.[38] Mrs Thurston died in 1896, too old and frail to understand that her daughter had died only ten days before, and the Queen wrote to her own daughter about the tragedy, assuring her that she would do whatever she could for the grandchildren.[39]

Provision like this for nurses' families was not unusual. Emma Hobbs's replacement in the royal nursery in Berlin was Mary Ann Wakelin. Like Mrs Thurston, she was a widow in her early thirties when she accepted the position; she appears to have been recruited by Lady Caroline Barrington, who was then Superintendent of the British royal nurseries. When Mary Ann Wakelin went to Berlin in October 1869 she left her two children, eight-year-old Gertrude and John, who was seven, in Miss Catherine Edwards' school in Tutbury in Staffordshire. The 64-year-old schoolmistress had twenty-seven pupils to manage between the ages of three and fourteen, sixteen of them boarders (including all the very tiny ones), with two young governesses, a cook and two maids to help her keep order. In 1873 a royal messenger was sent from Berlin to collect Gertrude and John from the school and escort them to their mother. Kaiserin Augusta, the Crown Princess's mother-in-law, had recently opened a school at Charlottenburg under her patronage and Gertrude was enrolled as a pupil there. The twelve-year-old slipped naturally into a group of nine other English girls – they called themselves 'the Colony' – and she also became friendly with the Crown Princess's daughters. She continued to exchange cards and gifts with the Princesses for many years. In adult life she became governess to Sybil Coke, whose mother was lady-in-waiting to both the Duchess of Teck and her daughter Queen Mary.

The Crown Princess had thought Emma Hobbs 'impossible to replace' but Mary Ann Wakelin filled her place admirably. She was on hand to help in a real family crisis in 1879 when eleven-year-old Prince Waldemar and Augusta Byng were both down with diphtheria in the Crown Prince's palace in Berlin and, some miles away to the west, Princess Charlotte felt herself going into labour with her first baby. Her husband Prince Bernhard of Saxe-Meiningen telegraphed directly to Mary Ann Wakelin for help. She told the Crown Princess, who felt she had to be on hand for her daughter, though she was beside herself with worry for her son, whose condition was critical. 'Fancy my scare last night!!' she told Queen Victoria, '. . . I dashed off with Mrs Wakelin to the Railway Station we fetched the midwife (old Frau Haft) – & took her with us – & carried the Baby Linen wch was not quite into Baskets, and away we went on a bitter cold night! Arrived at Potsdam drove to Villa Siegnitz – & found Charlotte all right with only a trifling pain in her back – it was all a false alarm & so after staying an hour I came back leaving Mrs W & the midwife there! I was in a fine way on the road – not knowing wch I ought to do – to devote myself to Charlotte & leave my poor Waldy, or abandon Charlotte wch I could not do either with Peace of mind for Dr Grimm is not here. . . .'[40] It was an impossible situation, eased only in that she had someone she could trust, Mary Ann Wakelin, to leave in her place.

The baby, Princess Feodora, was not born for another six weeks and Mary Ann stayed with Princess Charlotte to nurse her until November 1879. But Prince Waldemar died on 27 March, the day after his mother wrote her letter to the Queen and two days after that anxious dash through the night. How relieved his mother must have been that she had gone back to him. When Mary Ann Wakelin left her service, some time in the early 1880s, the Crown Princess presented her with an extraordinary sewing machine, her own, made especially for her in 1865 by the Pollack & Schmidt company in their Hamburg factory. The whole piece was finished with silver gilt, beautifully engraved. There were imperial eagles carved on the oak treadle and the Prussian and British coats of arms worked into the cut-glass cover; even the ivory cotton reels were marked with a crown. In its own day it must have been priceless; in 1997 it sold in auction at Christie's in London for £23,500, the highest price a sewing machine had ever achieved.

The sewing machine was tangible evidence of the Crown Princess's respect for Mary Ann Wakelin and the gratitude she felt for the nurse's service. The relationship between a mother and her nurse or governess was the most personal one of all, because love for the children lay at its heart. Society expected that royal women – all women who had the means to do so – would hand the daily care and upbringing of their children to employees from the moment of birth. Some mothers were content to do so and to lead their own lives, seeing their children at prescribed moments only, washed and brushed and on their best behaviour, but for most this was not enough and the sharing of responsibility – and even more, of the children's affections – came hard. A good nurse or governess had to sense her way into the relationship, finding the stance that would be most appropriate for her particular mother, and therefore the happiest for all concerned.

If the mother was very young she would often turn to her children's nurse as she had to her own nurse, and feel quite at ease being treated as one of the children. Princess Marie of Edinburgh and Saxe-Coburg was seventeen years old in January 1893 when she was married to the Crown Prince of Romania and she knew nothing of sex or responsibility, or of anything that had to do with adult, married life. Before the year's end she had given birth to her first child and in her misery she turned to his nurse, Mary Green. 'Old Green was an antidote,' she remembered; 'she would begin by weeping with me, then with a loud sniff she would put tears aside and take repossession of her broad good-humour. Patting me on the back she would urge me to cheer up, and would launch forth on one of her endless yarns about one or other of the royal children who had been her charges. Her stories were enhanced by pantomimic play; she was most expressive, and if not orthodox, her language was certainly picturesque. At times even, I was thoroughly admonished, as though I too were but a child.'[41] A question mark hangs over Mary Green's treatment of the Romanian children, as we will see, but to Crown Princess Marie she was always the most staunch of defenders.

Equal friendships between royal mothers and nurses were comparatively rare because of the social gulf between them, but with the advent of 'lady' nurses things began to change. When Kate Fox started to work for Prince and Princess Nicholas their approach to her was quite formal. In 1905 she was 'Dear Miss Fox', though a letter written to her by the Princess in that year contains one of the most appealing instances of a royal employer taking notice of a nurse's family. Prince and Princess Nicholas accompanied King George I

of the Hellenes to England on an official visit in November 1905. For most of
the time they were at Windsor but their programme included a day in London
with a luncheon at the Guildhall. They rode in the leading carriage with
King George and Prince Arthur of Connaught, but while the crowd waved and
cheered and strained for a glimpse of the royalties, Princess Nicholas was
staring just as eagerly at them. 'Fancy,' she told Kate, 'the day we drove to the
Guild Hall I felt sure I would see your sister in the crowd & so I did!
I recognised her directly – it was just in front of Buckingham Palace when we
were driving back to the station – she stepped out of the crowd & waved her
handkerchief & I recognised her directly after her photograph – isn't it
amusing!'[42] This would have been Emma, the eldest of the Fox sisters, who
had stayed at home to look after their father. That Princess Nicholas was
interested enough to study Emma's photograph and remember it, and look out
for her in the crowd, suggests that she was not the haughty, dismissive woman
she is always said to have been. There was real warmth in her and Kate Fox
found it.

As an only daughter, with three elder brothers and a proud mother whose
ambitions for her were notorious, Princess Nicholas probably had a rather
lonely girlhood. She was always with her English governess, Mrs Saville, but
the only girl of her own age in the Russian imperial family was her cousin
Grand Duchess Olga Alexandrovna and they were poles apart in character.
Their parents, particularly their mothers, were confirmed rivals. 'Poor little
thing, I feel sorry for her,' Olga's mother once wrote, 'for she is really quite
sweet, but vain and pretty grandiose.'[43] But it may be that the quality people
perceived as undue pride in Princess Nicholas was no more than an uncertainty
about how to relate to other people once the dominating presence of her
mother was removed. Her letters to Kate are friendly, enthusiastic, quite naïve
at times, and they do betray a degree of uncertainty about the people she met
and how to understand them. She was certainly not too proud to write to Kate
Fox as a friend, confiding the most intimate details with absolute trust.

By 1907 'Dear Miss Fox' had become 'Foxie' and so she remained – to all
the Greek royal family. She kept a note from Queen Olga: 'My dear Foxie!
Thanks so much for the darling children's hair, but I am afraid you have
forgotten to put baby <u>Marina</u>'s hair into the little paper – there was nothing in
when I opened it; would you kindly send it tomorrow to Pavlovsk. With best
love, Olga.'[44] In 1910 Prince Nicholas sent her a rude postcard from the spa at
Marienbad, with a cartoon showing a bathing attendant washing mud off the
bottom of a very fat man and the message, 'These are the people we associate
with, although we see them, of course, with their clothes on! Yrs Nicholas.'[45]

But at the centre of the 'Foxie' correspondence was the friendship between Kate and the Princess. When they were apart Kate wrote daily, sometimes twice a day – reporting on the children, of course, as her job required, but on everybody and everything else as well. She knew not to overstep the mark and kept a certain formality in her letters; those that survive are addressed 'Dear Madam' and end, 'Your loving and devoted servant' or 'Your faithful and loving servant', but the content is chatty and there was no formality about the replies. 'England is too delightful for words!' the Princess told Kate in 1905. 'I wish I could always live here! . . . Oh! how I wish you were here too!'[46] In the aftermath of her father Grand Duke Vladimir's death in 1909 Princess Nicholas had gone to Russia with her husband, and her mother kept them longer than they intended: 'How could we refuse!' she wrote. 'Don't mope! I'm so sorry for you, Foxie dear, but it can't be helped.'[47] In the late autumn of 1911 when Kate and the children were at Westgate on Sea the Princess was worried because Kate had not been well: 'you never think of yourself & don't look after yourself enough'. She urged her to bring the children to London, to spend more time with their grandmother. 'Besides,' she added, 'I want to have you too and think we have been separated quite long enough!'[48] It is quite possible that Kate Fox was the first woman friend Princess Nicholas had ever known.

A royal mother and her children's governess started on a less unequal footing, and friendships between them developed more often – particularly if the mother was unhappy for some reason. The Englishwoman, coming in from outside, could supply a need no courtier could. When Maria Graham visited the San Cristovao Palace in 1823, the connection between her and the Empress Leopoldina was immediate and profound. They were both lonely. Maria was still coming to terms with the death of her husband and the Empress was faced daily by the Emperor's very public infidelity. They were intelligent women with no one at hand to share their interests, studies and researches, and the concern Maria showed for the little Infanta sealed their friendship. In the afternoons, when the inhabitants of the palace settled down for a siesta, the two women would meet in the Empress's rooms to study botany together – a shared passion – or discuss the latest books from Europe. When jealousy of their friendship among the ladies of the Court and a growing resentment against Maria put an early end to her appointment, Leopoldina was heartbroken. She helped Maria to pack and begged some of her school books so that she herself could continue her daughter's lessons. As Maria was leaving she pressed a letter into her hand. 'My very dear Friend,' it read, 'believe me I have made a very great sacrifice in separating myself from you, but my destiny has always been to be obliged to estrange myself from those persons dearest to my heart and whom

I esteem. But be persuaded that neither the frightful distance which must in a short time separate us, nor the other circumstances which I foresee shall ever weaken the lively friendship and true esteem which I vow to you. . . .'[49] The friendship endured by letter until Leopoldina's death two years later. She was just twenty-nine years old.

The Crown Princess of Prussia's initial reservations about engaging Augusta Byng were dispelled very quickly. Like the Empress Leopoldina, the Crown Princess also had reason to be unhappy – not in her marriage, which was everything she could wish, but in the Berlin Court which persisted in seeing her as an outsider. Before Augusta, the only Englishwomen in her household had been the squabbling Hobbs sisters – Emma with her dropped 'h's and fiery temper, Georgina so willing, so easy-going, and so good at pulling her sister's strings – the other nurses and the maids. Much as the Crown Princess valued them and relied on their skills, Augusta Byng introduced a more refined note. She filled the emptiness in the Crown Princess's immediate circle. In the first surviving letter, written two years into Augusta's appointment to 'My very dear and kind Spin (or Minny)', the Crown Princess expressed both her gratitude and her growing sense of life as a constant struggle. '<u>Many</u> thanks for all your kind wishes which are touching & gratifying to me! As sincere kind wishes from a person one feels sympathy, attachment, respect & gratitude for – <u>is</u> <u>always</u> soothing to a heart which cannot exist without a little affection from those around. As I grow older – difficulties, & duties without end crowd upon me – and I can only pray for strength to be guided in the right way, anxiety and troubles are indispensable it seems!'[50] When the Crown Princess was unwell Augusta nursed her as she nursed the children, and when she returned to England on leave her absence could be felt. 'I cannot say <u>how</u> much I <u>miss</u> you!' read one undated note, found among the governess's papers. 'Your kind familiar face haunts the schoolroom and <u>all</u> the little rooms on this floor.'[51]

In the summer of 1881 the Crown Princess travelled to England with her daughters and Augusta, who left them on arrival to spend time with her own family. She was due to rejoin them on the Isle of Wight but instead a letter arrived, to say that she was ill and needed time to see a doctor. 'My own dear Minny,' the Crown Princess wrote. 'Your letter has distressed me <u>much</u>. I am <u>so</u> sorry to think you should not be well during your Holidays – & <u>do so</u> wish I could make you well! I am sure the right thing to do is to have the very best advice and an eminent Doctor is sure to know of some treatment to set you right and <u>of course</u> you must give yourself all the necessary time to carry out whatever you are ordered – & to get quite well. . . . Of course <u>you</u> <u>know</u> that you will be <u>sadly</u> missed both by the children and me – you know we are never comfortable without you! The naughty chicks <u>will</u> <u>not</u> be Governed by anyone but Minny who knows so well how to manage them; & <u>I</u> feel that I have not a truer friend in the House; & you know I have not many in Germany, I cling very much to you dear Minny and for that reason I wish you to get <u>all</u> <u>right</u>, & think of <u>that</u> <u>first</u>.'[52]

But it soon became apparent that Augusta was not going to 'get all right', and she would never go back to Berlin. Her doctor sent word that she had cancer and a bewildered Crown Princess turned to her mother for comfort. 'It was a shock and blow to me I cannot describe!' she wrote. 'She is not only my dear kind devoted true & faithful friend – but quite a second mother to the children and loves them as if they were her own. She is my one principle support in their education, & I have such thorough confidence in her! She understands their characters – & knows how to manage them so well – She is such an element of peace & so steady & reliable & experienced! I shall miss her too terribly indeed I do not know how I shall get on without her!'[53] A few days later she made a comment which showed just how much reliance she had come to place on Augusta; 'How often I had made her promise that if I died she would never leave the children until they were grown up and married.'[54]

Augusta moved in with her sister and brother-in-law. A younger sister, who normally kept house for their single brother in Ipswich, joined them to help take care of her. In September the Crown Princess visited. 'I will not indulge in selfish grief over what the palaces at Potsdam & Berlin will seem to me without you!' she commented afterwards, 'you know & feel that all better than I can say!'[55] A few days later she returned to Germany, 'The 1st thing yesterday evening I went to your room, it made me <u>wretched</u>. How many a little chat & a happy quarter of an hour we had in that little corner! – Now you are in a far nicer & more comfortable room with a pretty cheerful look out, but I miss you dreadfully.'[56] She took down some of the pictures from the schoolroom to send to Augusta and from this time onwards was constantly recommending or sending small items that could make an invalid life more comfortable: special cushions, pillowcases and chairs and suggestions for 'nourishing light food'.[57] She sent regular greetings to the sisters, Julia Byng and Mrs Curtis, who kept her informed when Augusta was unable to write, and appealed to Queen Victoria to send her own doctor to Mrs Curtis's cottage in Staines.

Weeks passed and the sense of loss did not ease. The routine of royal life had always seemed empty to the Crown Princess. Now faced with the start of a new season at Court she complained, 'The horrid Court festivities begin tomorrow, trains & diadems – heat & standing – being <u>tired</u> & <u>bored</u> out of one's very Life! It is so senseless & so useless! – It does not even improve one's powers of endurance!'[58] Julia Byng wrote to the Princesses and although the news seemed encouraging, still it made their mother wretched to think that her friend was enduring so much, so far away. 'You don't know how miserable it makes me to think of you in pain dear kind Minny without being able to do anything to relieve it. I wish I could nurse you myself, I would do it so carefully & devotedly. How often you have sat by me and rubbed my head & back and feet so kindly when I was unwell, and now I cannot even return your kindness – except in thought! I am sure you are patience itself, & make it easy for all around to nurse you!'[59] This letter was written on 27 February 1882. Princesses Helena and Beatrice had visited in the last weeks and in mid-March Augusta Byng died. She left an unfinished letter to Princess Victoria, her first pupil, which her sisters forwarded.

The anguish shared by the royal family and the governess's family during the seven months of Augusta Byng's illness would not be forgotten. The Crown Princess kept in touch with Mr and Mrs Curtis, sending the occasional photograph and the news and souvenirs of her family that she would once have sent to Augusta. When she was in England in the summer of 1890 she arranged for Mrs Curtis to visit her at Windsor and the news of Mrs Curtis's sudden death a few months later, at Christmas, revived all the old feelings. She was still trying to come to terms with her own widowhood. 'Your dear & excellent wife,' she wrote to Mr Curtis, 'so sweet & so good, respected & beloved of all – who knew her! Our dear Minny's kind sister to whom she was so devoted! – How deeply grieved I am! . . . What sad grief ever increasing loneliness is – no one can know better than I do – no one can feel <u>more</u> sympathy for those in a like way bereaved! There is but one consolation, – the knowledge that when the <u>good</u> go to their rest, even their memory becomes a <u>blessing</u>, their influence & their example continue to uphold us – in all the darkness of sorrow and mourning. They <u>were</u> ours – & we continue theirs, though they know nothing of the gratitude, the Love – the bitter longing that fills our hearts!'[60] Three years later, while staying in England, she and her sister Princess Helena made a special visit to the graves of Augusta Byng and Mrs Curtis.

But as a curious footnote to what clearly was an intense, genuine friendship between two women, in which the distinctions of rank appeared to play no part, it seems worth noting that an echo of formality was retained. Though the Crown Princess's letters to Augusta Byng always concluded in terms of affection or love – 'With an affectionate kiss and much love', the last letter ran – the Princess invariably signed herself, 'V Cpss & Pss Royal', as if she were writing a business letter. It only serves to emphasise how very different their world was.

SEVEN

'Candles in Open Air'

COPING WITH DISABILITY AND THE DEATH OF CHILDREN

A small notebook bound in maroon cloth, preserved among the papers of the Hesse family, shows the bonds that were forged between a nurse and her royal employer when tragedy affected the children. At those times all traces of formality and class distinction became as nothing, and nurse and Princess were simply two women, united by a shared anxiety, love and grief. The notebook contains the souvenirs and impressions of the Crown Princess's sister Alice, Princess Louis of Hesse, collected in the terrible days that followed the death of her younger son Friedrich Wilhelm – 'Fritzie' to the family in general but to his mother almost always 'Frittie'.

Fritzie died on 29 May 1873, following a fall from his mother's bedroom window. He was two years and seven months old. As she struggled to accept what had happened, Princess Alice brought together photographs of him: one showed a painting with his birth date on the frame, another Fritzie as a little baby, . . . Fritzie laughing, . . . growing older, . . . then the last, poignant image of Fritzie on his deathbed. These she pasted into the book with handwritten verses that caught her mood: 'To my gathered Lily', . . . 'It is well with the Child', . . . ''Tis not for thee that tears I shed, thy sufferings now are o'er'. She copied down a long memorial poem which must have been specially written; another, 'A shadow', appears to have been her own composition. Some of the photographs she framed with bright scrapbook cut-outs of flowers, and she added real flowers too, pressed and sewn onto the page: 'from my sitting room that I had placed on darling Frittie's bed, Thursday May 29 1873' . . . 'roses from my writing table which sweet Frittie had wished to have on Thursday morn: I placed them on <u>his</u> bed a few hours later when our Darling was no more' . . . 'From a nosegay of wild flowers an old gentleman made for sweet Frittie & laid at his feet on the 30 of May'. The book became an intensely personal, painful record, but Alice did not make it for herself. Her dedication reads, 'For dear Orchard, In remembrance of our darling Fritzie, Alice,

Darmstadt, June 1893'.[1] '*Our* darling': the Princess compiled the book for her children's nurse.

Mary Ann Orchard was born in Dublin on 20 March 1830 and came from a large family, with at least four boys and two other girls.[2] Nothing is said of her life before 1866, when she was found by Queen Victoria to replace Elizabeth Moffatt as nurse to the Hesse children; she must either have been working for someone known to one of the Queen's ladies or she herself must have known one of the royal nurses. She may have been appointed in the summer of 1866 when the children, three-year-old Victoria, and Elizabeth who was nearly two, were sent to their grandmother in England because their country was at the point of war. Perhaps Elizabeth Moffatt took the children to England and then decided to stay: Germany was not so safe as it had been and in the next few weeks the children's home town was invaded by Prussian troops. There was even talk of cholera. The children returned home in late August after an armistice had been signed but there is no record of Elizabeth Moffatt's whereabouts until April 1871, when she was nurse to Princess Christian's children at Frogmore. By then, Mary Ann Orchard was firmly established in Hesse. 'I can't praise Orchard enough', Princess Alice told her mother in April 1867. 'Such order she keeps, and is so industrious and tidy, besides understanding so much about the management of the children's health and characters.'[3]

For Mary Ann Orchard the first three years in Darmstadt were a time to get to know her new surroundings and to consolidate her place in the family. Whoever she had worked for before, the Hesse children became 'her' children: they called her 'Orchie' and the name would stick for the rest of her life. Princess Alice's third daughter, Irène, was born during the war of 1866 and in 1868 she gave birth to her son Ernst Ludwig: for both births Queen Victoria sent the monthly nurse Mrs Clark to Darmstadt. Her presence, albeit temporary, must have offered some support with the ever-growing responsibilities of the nursery. By the end of 1869 Orchie also had an English under-nurse, Emma Bailie. There were some stressful times, when illness attacked one – or on occasion almost all – of the family, but the anxieties for Orchie really began in the autumn of 1870, with the coming of Fritzie. He had haemophilia. The fall that killed him might have killed any child, but for him there was no chance at all.

His condition must have become apparent very soon to Princess Alice, who had seen the same symptoms in her younger brother Leopold. Within the first year her letters home show particular concern for Fritzie's health and the anxieties would grow. Alice was well placed to advise Orchie on his special needs and the nurse may also have been told to speak to Mary Anne Thurston, who had brought Prince Leopold through so many crises. Specific medical treatment was provided from England by the Queen's doctors. In the spring of 1872 the Princess told her mother, 'Fritz still has constant swellings, but on Sir William's advice he is taking "stahl" and is otherwise strong and rosy. I hope and trust that he will grow out of this.'[4]

For Orchie the haemophilia would have been a constant worry as Fritzie, like Leopold, was a lively toddler, forever running into trouble. But it also meant that he needed her more, which is likely to have deepened her attachment to him; this was certainly true of other nurses who cared for disabled or particularly vulnerable children. It must have been a special agony for Orchie, as Fritzie's nurse, that after nearly three years of vigilance and care the fatal accident took place when she was not even in the room, though it happened so quickly there was nothing she could have done. Grief and regret for the little boy's fate only deepened Orchie's commitment to the family and made her all the more anxious for the remaining children. The sorrow, Princess Alice said, 'has entered into the very heart of our existence'.[5]

Weeks and months passed, and life settled into something approaching a normal pattern. For Orchie, the after-effects of Fritzie's death were particularly hard to deal with in four-year-old Ernst Ludwig, who had seen his brother fall: the simplest remark could reawaken his fear of death and he needed sensitive handling for a long time. But children are resilient and the little ones brought laughter back to the nursery. Princess Alix was too young to remember her brother and 1874 saw the birth of the seventh and last Hesse child, Marie. The two little girls became especial pets of their mother and their nurse until tragedy struck again. On 5 November 1878 fifteen-year-old Princess Victoria complained of a stiff neck. She had diphtheria. Exactly a week later, at three o'clock in the morning, Orchie woke the Princess because she was concerned about Alix; the six-year-old was in a high fever and showing unmistakable signs of the illness. The two women fumigated the nursery that day and isolated the sick children but by evening Marie was ill as well and the others soon succumbed, even their father. Only fourteen-year-old Elisabeth was unaffected by the disease.

Orchie was among those who helped the Princess to care for the patients; 'Poor Orchie – like a ghost – from one <u>child</u>'s bed to another', Alice wrote to her mother on the 15th. 'What will tomorrow bring?'[6] Her question was answered all too cruelly. Little Marie died in the early hours of the next morning and it was Orchie who performed the heartbreaking task of laying out the child's body for burial, according to Princess Alice's wishes. For days all those involved in the nursing had not stepped outside the palace, unable to leave the patients and unwilling to spread the infection. The funeral service for Marie was held privately in a downstairs room on the afternoon of Monday the 18th, attended by the Princess, her Court and the servants. When Princess Alice and Orchie finally emerged from the Neues Palais the next day, they were together. 'I mean to try & drive a little this afternoon,' the Princess told her mother. 'I shall go out with Orchie.'[7]

The death of a second child in five years was tragedy enough, but two weeks after this first outing the Princess herself came down with diphtheria and in her weakened state she could offer no resistance. She died on 14 December. For Orchie, who had shared so much with her mistress in the twelve years she had lived in Darmstadt, the effects were overwhelming. Princess Alix retained an abiding memory of the nurse, sitting alone in the nursery silently crying. Inevitably Orchie became overprotective towards the survivors. She clung particularly to Alix, adoring and idolising her, and she fussed over the others at the least sign of fragility. At fifteen years old Irène went through puberty: 'she suffers at times from headaches and a feeling of weakness & giddiness now & then that make Orchard rather fidgetty and anxious,' Princess Victoria told her grandmother in the summer of 1881. The nurse imposed a regime of early nights and no excitement on Irène and it took a determined campaign by the elder girls and their uncle Leopold to set the prisoner free. 'We have begun what Uncle calls Irène's Emancipation, but it is rather difficult at times . . .'.[8]

There was bound to come a day when the Hesse children no longer needed a nurse. Orchie had become a fixture, though, and her anxiety for the family knew no bounds. In the spring of 1892 the children's father, Grand Duke Louis of Hesse, suffered a severe stroke. He was conscious at first and in some distress and, though there were others on hand to look after him, Orchie would have her share. She was in her early sixties by then and the family looked out for her as much as she for them. Princess Irène told her grandmother that they had decided to arrange a room downstairs next to her father's for 'dear Orchie, who remains the whole day downstairs helping . . . they found that if she was upstairs she worried so dreadfully & kept running up & down those endless steps wh. might have been very injurious for her. She bears up wonderfully & it seems not to have harmed her.'[9]

But though they thought her so old and frail, Orchie still had a keen eye. When Queen Victoria visited Darmstadt a few weeks after the Grand Duke's death, she spent an hour with the nurse, questioning her on his final illness and Orchie passed on her worries for Princess Alix too. 'Dear Alicky's grief, Orchard said was terrible,' the Queen recorded in her journal that night, 'for it was a silent grief, which she locked up within her.'[10] Orchie really knew her children. But helping in the Grand Duke's final days would be the last service Mary Ann Orchard performed for the Hesse family. When Alix married the young Tsar two years later the old nurse went with her to Russia, leaving Darmstadt at last after nearly thirty years.

Few nurses shared so crushing a burden of grief and anxiety with their royal employers but many found themselves dealing with the chronic illness of at least one child, and the emotional cost to themselves was always high. Caring for haemophilic princes involved a catalogue of nurses down the years: Mary Anne Thurston and later Marjorie Chapman in England – Marjorie looked after Leopold of Battenberg, Princess Beatrice's son – also Nurse Kemence, who cared for Prince Rupert of Teck; then Orchie herself in Germany and, in Spain at least seven British women: Alice Evans, Gertrude Bunting, Mrs Conway, Eugenie and Martha Doherty, Beatrice Noon and Josephine Stainthorpe, all of whom worked in the nurseries of King Alfonso and Queen Ena, who had two haemophilic sons, their eldest, the Prince of the Asturias and their youngest, Don Gonzalo.

Little comes down to us of these seven except their names in the employment records of the Palace Archives in Madrid. The memoirs of the photographer Richard Speaight contain a brief glimpse of Alice Evans and Gertrude Bunting: two grey-uniformed figures, ushering the little Prince of the Asturias and his baby brother into Queen Ena's drawing-room to pose for the camera, as capable and as inconspicuous as good nurses were supposed to be.[11] Gertrude suffered a stroke in November 1908, not long after the photographer's visit, and she died in the Hospital del Buen Suceso in Madrid: the Court paid for her funeral and for a monument in cemetery of Our Lady of the Almudena.[12] The nurses in Spain had no easy task, with two haemophilic Princes on their hands and another rendered profoundly deaf by a mastoid infection before he had learned to speak.

The blood of a haemophilia sufferer lacks some of the normal clotting agent. This makes any minor accident a potential threat, particularly if it causes bruising, internal bleeding or bleeding from a wound in an inaccessible place; until recent years, cauterising or tight bandaging was the only treatment available. Prince Leopold nearly died in childhood after piercing the roof of his mouth with a pen nib: on several occasions Mrs Thurston had to nurse him through bleeding attacks brought on by sneezing. Acute pain in the joints was a constant problem too, and the practical difficulties involved in managing a lively little boy who suffered from the condition but was too young to understand it must have been daunting. Across the generations all the nurses coped with the same problems and any sign of illness would set the alarm bells ringing. In 1911

Nurse Kemence wrote to Leopold's daughter Alice, Princess Alexander of Teck, about her haemophilic son: 'Prince Rupert he looks a little pale he sufferd with his foot now this little cold, I don't want him to get run down.'[13]

In 1888 Princess Irène of Hesse married her cousin Heinrich of Prussia and two of their three sons were haemophilic. Their nurses at least had Orchie to turn to for advice and support, though she did tend to take over. 'Orchie is staying with me,' Irène told her grandmother in the spring of 1894, when her elder son Waldemar, 'Toddie', was five, '& so I am giving Toddie's nurse, Mrs Millington, a holiday, & she [Orchie] & Joey look after him then, which they like.'[14] (Joey was another old hand from the Darmstadt nursery, Joanne Rolestone, who had worked there as under-nurse from 1874 to 1887, was later nursery governess to Victoria of Hesse's children, and would in time become a friend and point of contact for all the nurses who cared for Princess Alice's grandchildren).

'Toddie' had haemophilia; so did his youngest brother Heinrich, who was born in January 1900. The name of Heinrich's first nurse is not recorded but Norland nurse Beatrice Todd was employed to look after him when he was two years old. (It must have caused some amusement in the nursery to have a nurse with a surname so similar to the nickname of the eldest Prince.) Little evidence remains of Beatrice's care of Heinrich, though in the albums of the Norland secretary Mildred Hastings there is a postcard sent by the nurse from the Neues Palais in Darmstadt in April 1903: 'This is where we are staying for Easter – but I have my Baby in bed with a bad cough – & I am dreading wh[ooping] c[ough].'[15] Coughing, like sneezing, could bring on a dangerous bleed. And a few years later, writing to the *Norland Quarterly* about preparing a child to face the dentist, Beatrice made a comment which surely reflected her experiences in Germany: 'while doing our best to be absolutely truthful with our charges,' she wrote, 'and being careful (so far as lies in our power) with their *first impressions* of those experiences of life which come under our control, yet we must train them to bear disappointments, to be brave over little hurts . . . even to suffer pain as patiently as they can'.[16] In Heinrich she had known a little boy who suffered a great deal of pain.

There is also a photograph of Irène's three sons in Mildred Hastings' collection which has Beatrice's handwritten inscription. In two simple words it tells us how attached Beatrice was to her little charge: 'Prince Sigismund – Prince Waldemar & My Baby – Prince Heinrich (junior) – January 1904'. '*My Baby*'. A week or so after it was taken, little Heinrich fell and bumped his head, as any child might do. He died on 26 February.

But haemophilia was far from being the only chronic illness of childhood which fell to the nurses' care. Out of a more distant past comes the figure of

Mary Barnes, disembarking from the Rhine steamer that brought her to the Schloss at Neuwied one day in 1848, 'and crossing the quadrangle with soft, noiseless tread, as gentle and calm as the evening breeze'.[17] No record remains of where Mary came from, except that she was English, or of how or why she found herself in Germany, but we do know what she looked like: 'a plain-featured elderly woman, with at times a decided squint'. In fact she was only thirty-two, and though the description does not sound very promising there was much more to Mary than her looks. The two children who watched her arrival from the Schloss window that day, Princess Elisabeth and Prince Wilhelm of Wied, quickly came to adore their new nurse for the air of tranquillity she brought with her. Mary had lost her mother at the age of ten and had afterwards brought up her younger siblings; this gave her a child's understanding of children. 'She was at her happiest as she sat, needle in hand, watching our games,' Elisabeth remembered, 'and from time to time laying down her work, the more thoroughly to enter into our merriment; we might laugh and romp to our heart's content, her calm was unruffled, her patience inexhaustible.'[18]

The Wieds were not a healthy family. The children's father had tuberculosis. Their mother suffered persistent illnesses and periods of complete immobility and she developed an obsession with unconventional healing methods. Wilhelm was considered delicate until Mary took him in hand. But these things were as nothing compared to the agonies endured by the third and last child in the family, Prince Otto, whose survival through infancy depended utterly on Mary.

Otto was born on 22 November 1850 and for some time the state of his mother's health had made everyone fear that he stood little chance: in fact, he seemed healthy at the moment of birth and all attention was focused on his mother, who was stricken by sudden paralysis. It took Mary Barnes to notice that the baby was struggling for breath and to identify the reason – a birth defect, the nature of which is never specified. The doctors agreed with her and sent straight away for a surgeon from Bonn to perform the minor operation which they thought would answer the problem.

For a generation accustomed to special-care baby units, respirators and all the paraphernalia of modern medicine, the next part of the story makes hair-raising reading. This was 1850. The use of anaesthetic was still experimental. There was no electricity, of course: gas light was only available in larger towns and the Schloss at Neuwied would have had nothing brighter than candles or oil lamps. In November the days are short. When the surgeon arrived he pronounced it too late to operate and, for Mary, 'the night that followed was a terrible one. I did not think it possible for the poor babe to last till morning' she wrote; 'it was blue in the face, as I held it, all night long, upright in my arms, to prevent it being suffocated.'

The ordeal for them both lasted well into the next morning, with the surgeon not beginning his work until eleven o'clock, after a preliminary examination. Even then the operation did not go according to plan. 'The malformation was more serious, and the operation in consequence attended with far greater difficulty, than the doctors had foreseen. It lasted so long, and left the tiny patient so exhausted, we hardly thought it would survive many seconds. His whole appearance was changed; the skin had taken on a dull yellowish hue, and the little limbs were so cold, we resorted to every possible means of restoring a little warmth. This state of utter exhaustion lasted for twenty-four hours, during which we kept moistening the lips with milk. . . .'

Unbelievably, the baby lived on through days of agony, screaming incessantly until his voice dwindled to a faint moan. On the tenth day they baptised him, expecting death, but he hung on and by the end of his second week was finally able to feed from the wet nurse. Mary never left him. 'Day and night she was at her post,' his elder sister remembered, 'indefatigable, uncomplaining, holding him in her arms for hours at a time to ease his pain and enable him to breathe with a little less difficulty, her whole thought how to bring some relief to the poor tortured little frame.' Through the winter and into the next spring the baby hardly grew and he was subject to fits of intense pain. In May the family moved to Bonn to be near the surgeon: his treatment helped, but Otto remained small, frail and pain-ridden, and every fresh stage of his development – teething, weaning – seemed to push him to the point of crisis. He neither spoke nor walked until he was two. His survival became the centre of Mary's existence; 'he was a dear, sweet child', she wrote, 'with eyes that looked at one so pitifully. . . . There was something in him quite different to all other children.' Everything that could be done was done for Otto. The family took him to London, to Paris; he endured a succession of operations and other treatments and in time showed intelligence and sensitivity far beyond his years, but he remained sickly and was never free from pain.[19]

Hardest of all for Mary was her mistress's decision that Otto was too old to be cared for by a woman. Princess Elisabeth, who describes her brother's brief life in her memoirs, does not say how old he was when this happened but he did not live to see his twelfth birthday. By the conventions of the day the Princess of Wied was acting in her son's interest: princes were always handed over to male governors or tutors at the age of six or seven, to toughen them up and give them character, but this was a boy who would never be tough, and it was agony for Mary to part with him. She accepted it – what else could she do?

– 'bravely hiding under a smiling face her own aching heart, in order to soften the pangs of separation to her beloved foster-child' and the Wieds called her back later when they knew that Otto was dying, to be with him in his final days; 'days unspeakably precious to both'.[20]

To love a child who was not your own with this intensity, and in the full knowledge that at any moment his parents could part you from him, was a dilemma faced by many nurses. Two generations away from Mary Barnes it touched the life of a more famous royal nurse, Charlotte 'Lalla' Bill, and seemed likely to end her hopes of caring single-handedly for her own special charge. The First World War was at its height in the spring of 1916 when Prince Albert wrote to his mother, Queen Mary, from the ship HMS *Collingwood* in the British 1st Battle Squadron, commenting on a change in the arrangements for his younger brother John, who suffered from epilepsy. 'I love hearing from you as you always tell me little things which go on, and which I never hear otherwise,' he said – a touching reflection of the relationship between mother and son – 'I hope Lyon is getting on all right with John, though I should not think it a very pleasant job. I do hope it will do some good and I suppose Lalla has given up her ideas of always looking after him.'[21]

For Otto of Wied the introduction of a male tutor was a matter of convention and character-building and something similar may have been happening in the case of Prince John. His elder brothers Henry and George had gone away to school at ten or eleven years but, though he had reached the same age, his epilepsy made this impractical. Lalla Bill was a clever woman, able to give lessons as well as childcare, but was this enough for a growing boy? The King and Queen had decided to appoint a tutor, a younger man than the tutor they already employed, Henry Hansell, whose responsibilities lay with John's elder brothers. In 1916 young men were hard to find but R. Cuthbert G. Lyon was an old boy of Harrow School, a lieutenant in the Royal Field Artillery and ADC on the Personal Staff, War Office, who had been invalided home from France. Lyon became John's tutor at Frogmore in May 1916; the thinking behind his appointment probably was that if he got on well with John, Lalla would no longer be needed. Prince Albert's letter certainly suggests this.

Prince John entered Lalla Bill's life at York Cottage on 12 July 1905, and it was surely she who carried him to his first public appearance, his christening, in the parish church at Sandringham. The day was 3 August and the church was bright with the flowers of summer: lilies of the valley, hollyhocks, orchids, palms and ferns. After a very wet morning the afternoon turned fine and 'at a quarter to 3 a pair-horse brougham arrived from York Cottage, and two nurses dressed in white, one of whom carried the infant Prince dressed in white with a white bonnet, alighted, and entered the church. Ten minutes later the Prince and Princess of Wales and Princess Victoria arrived. The Prince was accompanied by the Duke of Sparta. . . . The four little Princes and Princess Mary were with the Prince and Princess of Wales.' Princess Victoria took the baby from his nurse for the moment of christening, and after the ritual and the singing of Stainer's 'Sevenfold' Amen he was carried around the church so that all those present – including the regular parishioners who filled the pews – could get a good view of him.[22]

For the first few years Prince John was an apparently normal and, by all accounts, a very endearing child, with a way of responding to the world that was all his own. People treasured anecdotes about John and remembered them long after: for one aunt, it was the time he sucked his biscuit, wiped it across the floor, gave it to the dog to lick, and then handed it to his grandfather and watched it being eaten with great interest. (King Edward was, of course, quite unaware of the biscuit's previous history.) Another would recall the way the little boy muttered, as his father embraced his mother, 'she kissed Papa, *ugly* old man!' And meeting John after lunch at Frogmore one day in 1909, the Dowager Empress of Russia remarked to her son: 'George's children are very nice. . . . The little ones, George and Johnny, are both charming and amusing.'[23]

In was around this time, 1909–10, when he was four years old, that Prince John is said to have suffered his first epileptic fit. The doctors would have been consulted and there would have been great concern for John, though the idea that Lalla Bill and her little charge were hidden away from the world grew up later when people had forgotten how things really were. An examination of the Court Circulars of the day gives the true picture: whenever the royal family moved around the country to their different homes – Sandringham, Frogmore and Windsor Castle, Marlborough House, Buckingham Palace and Balmoral – John was with them. So was Lalla, of course, but the Court Circular did not notice servants. John travelled in the car with his parents, and he travelled by train. Often there would be guards of honour and cheering crowds at the stations en route and John was there, sharing as fully in the public life of his family as any royal child would have done.

In May 1910 the four-year-old watched his grandfather's funeral procession from a specially constructed stand close to the Marlborough Gate doorway of Marlborough House, with his brother Prince George, cousin Crown Prince Olav of Norway, and some little girls who probably belonged to members of the Court. They were on view to the crowd and a newspaper reporter noticed how members of the royal family in the procession acknowledged the children as they passed: 'The Queen Mother, who was greatly touched on seeing her grandchildren, smiled lovingly upon them. Queen Mary sent them a similar recognition, while their brothers and sister waved to them from their carriages. It was all so simple, so human and intimate.'[24] At the time of John's sixth birthday in July 1911 the King and Queen were on official duties in Scotland and John and Lalla Bill stayed with his aunt and godmother Alice, Princess Alexander of Teck, and her children (Nurse Kemence's charges) at Windsor. On the birthday itself, the bells of St George's Chapel and Windsor Parish Church rang in celebration. A 21-gun salute was fired in the Long Walk – how exciting must that have been for a small boy – and a few days later the Princess took John and her daughter May to the Windsor Children's Historical Pageant in the grounds of Long Walk House. 'Prince John enjoyed the performance greatly and frequently asked questions about the various characters and episodes', *The Times* reported.[25]

For Lalla it must all have been a huge responsibility. As the new King's youngest son, John would have been the object of considerable interest and if he should have a fit on such an occasion, or worse, collapse somewhere dangerous and injure himself . . . That possibility was real and, like Orchie, the nurse became fiercely protective. The daughter of one of the assistant private secretaries, who played with John as a child on family holidays at Balmoral, remembered him as 'a nice little boy' with nothing apparently unusual about him except that he was always roped to Lalla when climbing in the hills. The other children thought this 'sissy', not understanding what lay behind it.[26]

The increasing maturity of John's brothers, sister and playmates was tending to leave him behind. This was inevitable for the youngest child in the family – eleven years separated the Prince from his eldest brother – but in time people would have started to notice that John stayed with his nurse far longer than most boys. In May 1912 Prince George, who was closest to John in age, went away to St Peter's Court School at Broadstairs. John's time was spent increasingly at Sandringham and, to ensure that he would not be lonely, the Queen chose a friend for him from among the children on the estate.

Winifred Thomas was about the same age as John and had been sent from Halifax to stay with her uncle George Stratton, one of the grooms, because she had asthma and it was thought that the country air would do her good. It was probably her delicacy that recommended her as a playmate for John: that, and the fact that her aunt, Lizzie Stratton, was a friend of Mrs Bill. The Queen went to the Strattons for tea one day to meet Winifred and one of the little girl's abiding memories of the meeting was the way Queen Mary encouraged her – 'Let the child speak' – when her aunt tried to answer for her. Then Lalla

Bill and John joined the tea party and after this the little girl was invited to play with John almost every day. She helped him to work in the garden, which was one of his chief delights, and often Lalla would take them on nature walks. They went cycling and when the older princes were at Sandringham, or their cousin Crown Prince Olav, they joined in, though Winifred would later say that she and John could never catch the older boys because their bicycles were too small. George Stratton took the children out in the pony and trap and they visited local shops and exchanged little presents as children will; one of their favourite places was Playfair's sweet shop in nearby Dersingham. And when John was ill and in bed, Lalla Bill would read to them both. Neither child ever went to school. What they knew, they learned from Lalla Bill and from others on the estate.

But John and his nurse still moved around the country; more often just with his parents and sister after 1912, or with his grandmother and aunt, Victoria. At holiday times the Princes were reunited: in April 1914 the Court Circular notes that John went out riding at Windsor with his brothers Henry and George. In May, eighteen-year-old Prince Albert took him to the Houses of Parliament: 'They were shown over the House of Commons by the Speaker, and over the House of Lords by Captain Butler, the Yeoman Usher.'[27] The newspapers also published photos of John visiting the zoo.

The onset of war that summer shattered the ordinary routines of life and embroiled the older members of the royal family in new duties and responsibilities. For Lalla Bill and John things went on much as before. When he was well, John was full of life and curiosity and, like any boy, he found the idea of war exciting. Winifred remembered how thrilled he was to see Zeppelins pass over Sandringham in 1916, and his pleasure at meeting 'a real, live soldier', her father, Sergeant Frederick Thomas, who came that year on a leave visit. But John was not always well and, as he grew older, decisions about his future had to be made. Lalla was consulted on plans for him and the family took her feelings into account: this is apparent in Prince Albert's letter from HMS *Collingwood* with its reference to 'her ideas of always looking after him'. But there would still have been that sense that a boy should not always be with his nurse. The appointment of Lieutenant Lyon in May 1916 was something of an experiment. At first John found it all too exciting to focus on lessons so it was decided that Lalla should still work with him for a few hours each day. After that, things seemed to settle down very quickly and the arrangement was said to be working well. But by June it was apparent that Lyon's lessons were not right for John and in July, after little more than two months, his appointment ended.[28]

The surviving papers contain no hint of animosity or upset about Lyon's going, simply a recognition that the experiment had failed. Whether Lyon, who had been a professional soldier ever since he left Harrow and had no teaching experience, was the right person to choose is open to question. Life at Frogmore with a delicate boy and a middle-aged nurse must have seemed very restricting to him and he never went back to teaching. But John, who always seemed very normal and likeable to the children he played with, probably had a learning difficulty that showed up in the classroom, and his health was a decisive factor: in later years Lalla told a friend that his fits were increasing in frequency and severity and were becoming more distressing to witness. She said that the doctors could do nothing to halt the progress of the epilepsy and had advised that John would never reach maturity.[29] His happiness became his family's priority. For Lalla the departure of Lyon must, in a sense, have been a relief because it meant that her own plans could be followed. She would have the sole care of Prince John. By the end of 1916 the King and Queen had decided to place her and her charge in a house of their own, less cramped than the nursery quarters at York Cottage and more private, but still within walking distance on the estate.

Wood Farm was carefully arranged for John's comfort and pleasure. One of the coachmen from Windsor, Thomas Haverly, was installed in an adjoining cottage with his wife and children. He was thought to be particularly reliable and it would be his job to take the young Prince on outings into the country or to the sea, or to the big house when the family were in residence. A cook was chosen, Kate Bennett, and her niece Hilda Simpson became the live-in maid: Kate's sister Alice, who ran a boarding house at Westgate in the holiday season, gave extra domestic help at Wood Farm in the winter and other maids could be brought in from Wolferton when they were needed. As at York Cottage, an area of the garden was set aside for John and the gardeners helped him look after it; it had a special plaque saying 'Prince John's Garden'. He had his books and toys, including a pedal-car in which he was often photographed, and a ride-on train.[30] He had a bicycle and a pony. One snowy day in February 1917 Queen Mary walked across the park 'to Wood Farm in the afternoon to see Johnnie who seemed very happy there. George [the King] & Mary joined me,' she noted in her diary, '& after taking leave of J. & Lalla we motored back.'[31]

Through 1917 and 1918, the final years of the war, Wood Farm was Lalla Bill's world and her life centred on Prince John. The family visited when they were at Sandringham, or John was taken to see them – particularly his grandmother, Queen Alexandra, and his mother. At other times the family kept in touch by telephone and letter. 'My dear papa,' John wrote in May 1918, 'I'm sending you in a box some lilies out of Wolferton Woods. . . . The garden is very nice here . . . I am very busy here. Best love from your devoted son, Johnnie.'[32]

Well into the summer of 1918 John was still taking outings into the fields, but it seems likely that some time before the end – perhaps in the last weeks or days of his life – the severity of the fits reduced him to a less able state. This would certainly give a context to a callous remark made by his eldest brother: 'this poor boy had become more of an animal than anything else', the future King Edward VIII told his adored Mrs Dudley Ward when John died.[33] It was not a view Lalla Bill would have shared, or the Queen, who is known to have been hurt by her eldest son's attitude. Or Winifred Thomas, who still saw John regularly, not returning to Halifax until Christmas 1918. However serious John's condition may have been towards the end, to Winifred he was always the loving, friendly boy with whom she had shared an idyllic childhood. She treasured the mementos: she had a number of signed photographs of 'Johnnie' but one small one taken towards the end of his life, possibly the last one he gave her, she always kept in a frame on her dressing table.

Prince John died on a Saturday afternoon, 18 January 1919. It had been a lovely day; Queen Mary noted as much in her diary and described how she had spent the morning making visits around the estate. She did not mention a visit to Wood Farm but in later years both Winifred Thomas and Lalla Bill would say that she was there on that last afternoon, and left only minutes before the final seizure came. Her own account is well known: 'At 5.30 Lalla Bill telephoned to me from Wood Farm Wolferton that our poor darling little Johnnie had passed away suddenly after one of his attacks. The news gave me a great shock, tho' for the poor little boy's restless soul, death came as a great release. I broke the news to George & we motored down to Wood Farm. Found poor Lalla very resigned but heartbroken. Little Johnnie looked very peaceful lying there – Dr Manby joined us & we got home after 7.'

She visited again the next day with Queen Alexandra and the King's sisters and on Tuesday 21 January the funeral was held in the parish church at Sandringham. Like his christening, this day too was wet but, once again, the church was filled by people from the estate and the surrounding villages. The King and Queen were there, with Queen Alexandra and the King's sisters, Princess Victoria and Queen Maud of Norway; her son Crown Prince Olav joined Princess Mary, Prince Henry and Prince George. 'Canon Dalton & Dr Bowman conducted the service which was awfully sad & touching', Queen Mary noted in her diary. 'Many of our own people & the villagers were present. . . . In the afternoon I spoke to & thanked all Johnnie's servants from Wood Farm who have been so good & faithful to him.'

Most other members of the royal family left Sandringham the next morning but the Queen stayed on, visiting her son's grave in the afternoon and Wood Farm, emptied now of its life and purpose: 'Missed the dear child there very much indeed', she wrote. By the following Tuesday she was ready for the next task and, with her daughter, went back to the house, 'where we helped Lalla to choose various things belonging to little Johnnie to give to people about here. Rather a sad business touching all his belongings.'[34] Elsie Haverly, the coachman's daughter, was given John's blackboard and Winifred Thomas received several of his books with the inscription, 'In memory of our dear little Prince' in the Queen's own hand. One was *Three Jolly Sailors and Me*, a picture book which told, in rather dreadful verse, of how two children gave Nanny the slip at the seaside, were caught by the tide and rescued by fishermen, Bob and Ben:

> When Mummy got us back again,
> She cried – it did seem funny
> While Daddy talked to Bob and Ben
> And gave them lots of money.

The story must have had special echoes for Prince John and Winifred, as two children constantly accompanied by Nanny.

The day after the Queen and Lalla Bill sorted out John's belongings, they arranged the disposal of furniture from the house. Wood Farm was closed, but the nurse's loyalty to Prince John and her devoted care of him throughout his thirteen and a half years was a service the royal family would always value.

Charlotte Bill and Mary Barnes, Beatrice Todd, Mary Ann Orchard and the others looked after chronically ill or disabled children and, in so doing, formed very strong relationships with the children and with their parents, particularly when the child died in their care. The sudden death of an otherwise healthy child was a different sort of trauma but it could bring nurses equally close to their royal employers. Governesses tended to be more distanced from matters of life and death because they did not, as a rule, take on the physical care of children, but there is one story which shows that shared grief at the death of a child could not only level the differences of class and status, it could cross the widest cultural divide.

A month after the death of Otto of Wied and four years before Orchie arrived in Darmstadt, Anna Leonowens sailed into the Gulf of Siam on the steamer *Chow Phya*; it was 15 March 1862. With most of King Mongkut's sixty-seven children in her palace classroom and an unspecified number of royal wives she could hardly have been expected to know all her pupils personally, but for her as for the King one child stood out. Her Celestial Royal Highness Princess Somdetch Chowfa Chandrmondol Sobhon Baghiawati – 'Fâ-ying' – was an enchanting six-year-old when Anna arrived in Bangkok. She attached herself to the newcomer as little girls will, pleading for drawing lessons instead of the Sanskrit classes she disliked because the teacher was strict, and the King agreed. According to Anna, Fâ-ying was confident that her father would refuse her nothing.

'Never did work seem more like pleasure than it did to me as I sat with this sweet, bright little princess, day after day, at the hour when all her brothers and sisters were at their Sanskrit, drawing herself, as the humour seized her, or watching me draw; but oftener listening, her large questioning eyes fixed on my face', Anna wrote, describing the lessons that made Fâ-ying very special to her.[35] She went on to describe her earnest – and successful – attempts to convert the child to Christianity which, if true, would have been a direct breach of the terms of her contract. The King, who had previously employed American missionary wives as English teachers to his family and had dismissed them in disgust, was very specific about what he wanted from Anna: 'you will do your best endeavour for knowledge of English language, science, and literature, and not conversion to Christianity'.[36] But Anna's later accounts of her time in Siam were shamelessly slanted to appeal to Western, and particularly American sensibilities, and perhaps she never really did as she said she had done. It would be hard to imagine a chatty, confiding little girl keeping so vast a secret from her father.

The drawing lessons ended on a bright morning in May 1863 when a royal barge landed at Anna's riverside house bringing a group of excited slaves. They carried a note from the King: 'My dear Mam: Our well-beloved daughter, your favourite pupil, is attacked with cholera, and has earnest desire to see you. . . . I beg that you will favour her wish. I fear her illness is mortal. . . . She is the best beloved of my children.'[37]

Anna needed no prompting; she was in her boat at once, fretting against the slowness of the rowers, the pull of the river current, anything that impeded her progress to the palace. Still she was too late, arriving only in time to kiss the dead child's face in a room full of relatives and slaves, intoning the Buddhist chants for the dead and crying loudly. Then someone took her to the King, 'who, reading the heavy tidings in my silence, covered his face with his hands and wept passionately. . . . Bitterly he bewailed his darling, calling her by such tender, touching epithets as the lips of loving Christian mothers use. What could I say? What could I do but weep with him, and then steal quietly away.'[38]

The King issued a general proclamation, describing how he had raised Fâ-ying from infancy with his own hands and had taken her with him everywhere. And he paid tribute to Anna who, he said, 'observed that she [Fâ-ying] was more skilful than the other royal Children, she pronounced & spoke English in articulate & clever manner which pleased the schoolmistress exceedingly, so that the schoolmistress on the loss of this her beloved pupil, was in great sorrow and wept much'.[39] Not long afterwards, Anna was summoned to her schoolroom and found it decorated with flowers. Her chair was also twined with flowers and newly painted in bright red and Fâ-ying's school books were arranged in front of it, covered with roses and lilies. The King was preparing to honour the governess for the love she had shown his child. As Anna sat in the chair, seven threads were twined around her head and over the books, their ends held by seven of the King's sisters. He performed a series of rituals which she did not understand, finally placing into her hands a small silk bag: its meaning, as she discovered, was that she was now blessed with an honorary title and an estate in the interior of Siam.

The ceremony may have been very strange and in later years, from her assumed position of Western superiority, Anna was inclined to make fun of it, but the feelings that lay behind it were genuine. 'She was only aged 8 years & 20 days', the King wrote of Fâ-ying, '. . . But it is known that the nature of human lives is like the flames of candles lighted in open air without any protection.'[40] A father mourning his child; real emotion, and universal. Forty years later and in a totally different world, another royal father would learn the fragility of human life at the deathbed of an adored eight-year-old daughter and for him too, the grief would be shared with the Englishwoman he paid to care for his child.

We have come almost full circle, for this grieving father was none other than Ernst Ludwig, elder brother of little Fritzie of Hesse and one of Orchie's children. When the old nurse left Darmstadt in the autumn of 1894 to accompany Princess Alix to Russia, Ernst Ludwig was Grand Duke of Hesse in succession to his father. He had been six months married to his cousin Princess Victoria Melita of Edinburgh and Saxe-Coburg and they were expecting their first child. The permanent nurse was Lilian Wilson, who arrived in Darmstadt on her 31st birthday when baby Princess Elisabeth was just over a month old: the connection between nurse and child was immediate and absolute.

Lilian Wilson adored her little charge who seemed – like Fâ-ying, and Prince John, and Otto of Wied – to have been a very special child; perhaps this was simply the afterglow of an early death. 'I am sure she was the best child that ever lived', Margaretta Eagar wrote, remembering Elisabeth. 'Her gentleness and sweetness of disposition were a constant marvel to me. . . .'[41] Elisabeth of

Hesse was an unusually beautiful little girl with huge, soulful eyes – 'I used to wonder what those wide grey-blue eyes saw, to bring such a look of sadness to the childish face'[42] – and a mass of dark curls that needed no nurse's artifice to keep them in place. But a rather more human picture of her character comes from the writings of Meriel Buchanan, who was nine years older but played with Elisabeth in childhood. 'She was very often extremely naughty,' Meriel wrote, 'was naturally also very spoilt, had an impulsive and highly strung nature and a violent little temper. But she was so lovable, had such a fascinating way of making up for her bad humour, and so much charm and sweetness, that one could not help adoring her.'[43]

Glimpses of Elisabeth and Lilian Wilson abound, particularly in Meriel's and Margaretta's writings. Meriel's father was the British Chargé d'Affaires in Darmstadt until the autumn of 1900 and her mother befriended the young Grand Duchess Victoria Melita; the Buchanan family had the use of a house at Wolfsgarten, one of the Hesse country estates. For the first five years of Elisabeth's life Meriel spent most of her summer days with the little Princess, 'under the charge of her English nurse, Miss Wilson, a capable, fresh-faced woman in her white *piqué* dresses, possessed of endless patience and a warm, kindly heart, in spite of her occasional sharp reprimands, which were no doubt fully deserved'.[44]

In October 1903 the wedding of Princess Alice of Battenberg and Prince Andrew of Greece brought a large family party to Darmstadt, including the Tsar and Tsaritsa and their daughters, the eldest of whom was eight months younger than Elisabeth. After the celebrations, Ernst Ludwig and his sisters relaxed at Wolfsgarten with their families. It must have been pleasant for the nurses, Lilian and Margaretta – perhaps Beatrice Todd as well – to have other adults in the nursery sharing their responsibilities for a few weeks – nursing could be a lonely profession, so far from home and with only children for company. And for Margaretta it would have been an extra relief on this particular holiday because she was laid up with phlebitis for most of the time. She told Madame Gueringer on 27 October that she was just starting to move about again, adding, 'My children are very well. They are so happy to be here. Her Majesty bought them two bicycles on which they ride every day. Olga and Tatiana are taking German lessons with the Empress's old teacher. They're both making progress.'[45] The nurses spent most of their time entertaining the youngest children, while Elisabeth bicycled round the park with Olga and Tatiana and hunted mushrooms in the woods, or played in the fairytale cottage her father had given her.

In the first week of November the Russians left Darmstadt for Skierniewicz, one of the imperial family's hunting lodges in Poland, taking Ernst Ludwig and

Elisabeth. Lilian and Margaretta settled their charges into the nursery quarters; a communicating suite of bedrooms with its own dining-room attached. While the adults in the party spent their days out shooting, a carriage drawn by a pair of tame deer was available for the children's use; Margaretta also had a swing and a giant's stride set up for them, anticipating that most of their days would be spent out of doors. They were in high spirits. One evening when the day's catch of game was laid out on the lawns in front of the house, by torchlight as the custom was, Lilian roused Elisabeth from her bed and put a dressing-gown around her while Margaretta made a nest of blankets in the window seat, so that she could watch in comfort. After protests from her cousins, they too were allowed stay up a few days later, warmly wrapped against the evening air. They played a practical joke on the Tsaritsa that night with the nurses' connivance, the three elder Grand Duchesses hiding in Elisabeth's bed when their mother came to say goodnight: 'You could hear her laughter all through the house, as one by one the cousins were disclosed.'[46]

The next morning was a Sunday and Elisabeth woke complaining of a sore throat. Lilian called Margaretta, who sent for the Court doctor but also brought out a thermometer: the little girl's temperature was normal so her nurse began to dress her. Then she was sick and was put back to bed, but there seemed no cause for anxiety. Margaretta took the other children out for the day to leave the nursery in peace, returning at four o'clock in the afternoon to find Lilian much happier. Elisabeth had not been sick for some hours and was sleeping peacefully.

Piecing together the events of the next few hours is a confusing business. Margaretta described a situation in which only the Court doctor and she herself grasped how serious matters were. She remembered that the Grand Duke of Hesse and the Tsaritsa visited the sickroom at regular intervals through the evening but could find no cause for alarm, despite the doctor's insistence that Elisabeth's heart was failing. So confident were they, according to her, that they continued with a planned visit to the theatre – though the Tsaritsa did yield to the doctor's request for a specialist to be sent for from Warsaw. Once the performance was over they returned to the house, visited Elisabeth, who seemed quite bright, and went to bed, at which point 'the child speedily sank into a semi-stupor. I told Miss Wilson I could not leave her alone with her sufferer but would stay all night with her.'[47]

The hours that followed were candlelit and tense, with a mounting air of unreality. Shortly before two o'clock terrified screams from the adjoining bedroom took Margaretta rushing in to find four-year-old Maria and little Anastasia standing on their beds, saying that there was a strange man in the room. They would not be pacified, even by the Court doctor, so their nurse lit a candle and sat with them, talking quietly through their fears until both had slipped back into sleep.

At two the specialist arrived from Warsaw and at three he began to inject stimulants to improve Elisabeth's heart function, with little effect. This emerges from a letter the Tsar sent to his mother: he went on to say that the Grand Duke spent the second part of the night at his child's side, though Margaretta does not mention this. It was obvious now that events were taking the worst possible turn. At eight o'clock in the morning Ernst Ludwig went to fetch his sister, who returned with him; the Tsar followed soon after: 'When I entered her room', Nicholas wrote, 'I saw them and the nursemaid and all the Hessen people kneeling around the bed. The little girl was lying on her side and with her big eyes looking at the nursemaid's face – there was hardly any breathing to be heard – everything ended silently and imperceptibly – she died within about half an hour without the slightest suffering.' It was Monday 16 November, twenty-five years to the day since little Marie of Hesse's death from diphtheria. But even at this most dreadful moment, Grand Duke Ernst Ludwig could still find the emotional strength to consider what Lilian Wilson must be feeling. 'Poor Ernie's sorrow was at first inexpressible,' the Tsar continued, 'but he quickly got control of himself and started to comfort the dear nursemaid, who had been with his child since she was born, and who worshipped her. Then he began to feel nausea, and I persuaded him to lie down.'[48]

Margaretta and her charges were bundled off to St Petersburg within hours, for fear of infection. For Lilian, who had endured the unimaginable at her employer's side, the grief bound her to Darmstadt for ever. She stayed on with the Grand Duke though he had no more children to nurse, and in January 1904 we find her writing to an English teacher from Coburg who had sent condolences on Elisabeth's death:

Dear Mr Irwin,
I cannot tell you what a pleasure your letter gave me, that you should have remembered that little greeting of my darling little one. HRH the Grand Duke was also much touched by your letter, to whom I gave it to read, and with His Royal Highness' permission I send you this little Romanian Purse which belonged to the little Princess and which she was very proud of. I hope you will like it.[49]

Two years later, when Ernst Ludwig became a father once again with the birth of little 'Georgie', the nurse could only be Lilian Wilson.

EIGHT

'Her Only Crime'

WHEN RELATIONSHIPS WENT WRONG

How I want an hour's talk with you you can't imagine. If I had written oftener to you you would understand, but I must try and explain briefly. I have been most unhappy all this winter since leaving England, I don't know whether I ever told you that the Grand Duchess Wladimir never approved of me . . . this winter she has had me in her power and has treated me in the cruellest way possible I have borne insult on insult but would not say a word . . . in January she succeeded in separating me from the two big Princesses, and has behaved very badly to me since, but now the climax has come. . . . I feel just heartbroken, for I do not see why I should be sent away for no reason except love & devotion to my employer & her children. . . .[1]

Kate Fox had reached breaking point personally and professionally when she sent this cry of anguish to Isabel Sharman at Norland. It was April 1913. Kate had already lost control of her two elder charges, Princesses Olga and Elizabeth, to their grandmother Grand Duchess Vladimir against the express wishes of their parents. The girls remained in Russia while Kate was sent to a private clinic at Berck-Plage in the Pas de Calais with five-year-old Princess Marina. They were under the supervision of Baron Offenberg, an official from the Grand Duchess's Court, and Kate sensed what was about to happen. Against her own wishes and those of Prince and Princess Nicholas she would be forced to leave. 'I feel as if I can't bear it,' she told Miss Sharman, 'you know a little of what the children and their Mother are to me, and the thought never entered our heads that we should ever separate.'

The letter was a long, tormented one, heavy with a sense of injustice and betrayal, and it was not the only such letter that Kate penned that spring. Her father was so concerned for her that in March he sent her elder sister Emma from England to support her. Emma was normally his carer but he gave her no choice in the matter: 'Emma must not think of leaving you until you are more comfortably settled,' he told Kate. 'I know there are things here she wants to attend to, but her duty at present is to be with you. You can tell her I am taking care of myself.'[2] For six more weeks the agony was prolonged, with emotional letters and telegrams flying between Berck-Plage, St Petersburg and Greece; then, at the end of May, Kate was forced out.

Biographers of Princess Marina have always explained Kate Fox's dismissal in terms of her 'English ways', which the Grand Duchess is supposed to have disliked. Stories are told of how the two women clashed over Kate's insistence on opening the windows of the nursery suite in the lavishly overheated Vladimir Palace; and of a general sense that Kate was too strict, too dogmatic in her rule of the nursery. She is said to have hit the children. But surviving correspondence shows that these were not the reasons why the Grand Duchess was set against her. While there were certainly differences of opinion between the two women these things were only a symptom of a deeper problem. In coming so close to Princess Nicholas, Kate had touched on a vein of insecurity in the Grand Duchess's nature and had been drawn into an uneasy relationship between mother and daughter. It was one of the pitfalls of being so intimately involved in someone else's family and for Kate, as for others too, it was usually the outsider who paid the price.

During the early years of Kate's service with the Nicholas family she often stayed in Russia with the Grand Duchess and the correspondence from that time contains no hint of the trouble to come. Though Kate commented to Miss Sharman that the Grand Duchess had never approved of her, the 1913 letter was written when she felt persecuted and vulnerable: when she was struggling to reassess her experiences with the family to find some explanation of what had gone wrong. In the early years her contacts with the Grand Duchess had been unremarkable. After Grand Duke Vladimir's death in 1909, for example, the widowed Grand Duchess thought enough of Kate to have one of his tie pins made into a pretty and valuable brooch as a keepsake for her.

The first sign of tension appeared in the summer of 1910. Princess Elizabeth had an operation in a clinic in Frankfurt and afterwards Kate took her and her sisters to Field House in Bognor. Princess Nicholas left them there and went on to Russia, where she was puzzled by her mother's lack of interest in the children. Olga, Elizabeth and Marina were barely mentioned and Grand Duchess Vladimir said nothing about her granddaughter's operation, though Grand Duchess Kirill assured the Princess that she had been very upset and anxious about it. 'If I didn't speak about the children, she never would,' Princess Nicholas told Kate, 'she never asks me about them, so I have made a point of always telling her the parts of yr letters which I think might amuse or interest her. It's very strange, isn't it? & still I'm sure she is very fond of them . . . she seemed rather impressed that you write every day.'[3]

The visit passed and Princess Nicholas attached no more importance to this change in her mother's behaviour. Not until it was too late, over three years later and in the aftermath of Kate's dismissal, did she find out that something had actually happened in 1910 to cause the rift that later came between them. In April 1910 Kate and the children were invited to stay with the Grand Duchess at the Grand Hotel in Cannes and the Princess wrote to the nurse advising her how to behave in her mother's company. This was something she did when Kate travelled to royal homes without her. She wrote very freely about the royalties concerned, knowing that Kate would have an easier time if she understood the peculiarities of the people around her. She was sensible enough not to betray the confidence. So, for example, on one occasion the Princess warned Kate that it was never wise to mention Athens to her brother Grand Duke Kirill, as 'he is always disagreeable & disobliging when touching that subject'.[4] On another, she told her not to take a particular princess up on an invitation unless she was absolutely sure that it was meant. These letters survive. The letter of April 1910 does not because, quite by chance, it fell into the hands of the Grand Duchess and she read it before she realised her mistake. Her indignation is easy to imagine. Here was her daughter, a Grand Duchess of Russia by birth and a Princess of Greece, giving warnings about *her* to a servant. . . . Everything that happened afterwards happened because of this letter.

The Grand Duchess's changed attitude to her grandchildren should have been a warning. Then, in an unpredictable twist to the story, Kate Fox had an encounter in the summer of 1911 which might have alerted her to the way the Grand Duchess treated those who became too close to her children. Princess Nicholas had never forgotten her own English nurse 'Milly', Millicent Crofts, who disappeared from the scene without word or warning at Christmas in 1886. The Princess must have mentioned her to Kate; in 1910, when Kate took the children to Field House, she and Milly corresponded. She was planning to invite Milly to meet the children on her own initiative, then, at the last minute, the Princess decided that she was missing Kate and the children too much and their visit was cut short. A year later, though, during their second stay at Field House, Milly was able to join them – what she had to say shed a revealing light on a 25-year-old mystery.

'I was so interested to hear all you tell me about Milly,' Princess Nicholas remarked soon after, in a letter to Kate; 'poor soul! how she must have suffered! I remember perfectly well when she left & how I was told that she would come back & her empty bed next to mine – I was only four, like Baby is now, but I remember that day quite clearly – not of course Gatchina, but just the place in the nursery . . . where I understood that she was gone. It is all most extraordinary & to me quite incomprehensible.'⁵ Milly had left because the Grand Duchess dismissed her peremptorily after ten years' service, without even a chance to say goodbye. The charge was that she favoured Grand Duke Boris – the second of Princess Nicholas's three elder brothers – and neglected the other children. As one of those children, the Princess found the idea 'unjust and unfounded'. Grand Duke Kirill also remembered Milly with great affection. Restored to the family after a quarter of a century, Milly was enthusiastically taken up by her grown-up charges. For many years she had lived in straightened circumstances, taking care of her elderly mother. Now the three Grand Dukes provided her with a pension and Princess Nicholas wrote regularly herself and encouraged Milly's friendship with Kate. She also engineered a meeting between Milly and her mother: under the circumstances this was not a good idea. It only deepened Grand Duchess Vladimir's growing antipathy towards Kate Fox and her sense of grievance against her daughter.

It was in this context that the Grand Duchess began to find fault with Kate. She disliked the nurse, she needed reasons; niggling resentments began to fester and grow. The most important point at issue became the treatment of Princess Marina. From birth the child's left foot had been twisted slightly to one side. Doctors advised that it would need a corrective operation when she was older; until then they recommended twice-daily massages, which Kate administered with great care. Over the years the Princess consulted various specialists about the problem but otherwise it was her secret; in April 1910 it annoyed her that one of the doctors had spoken to others about Marina's foot, though she conceded that she had not told him to keep it quiet.⁶ He advised the making of a special supportive boot and by July this was in use. The family decided that Dr Calot, of the Institut St François-de-Sales at Berck-Plage, would ultimately perform the operation.

In October 1912 Kate and the children were nearing the end of their annual British holiday, this time at Westgate on Sea, when Kate suddenly had to rush Princess Marina to Berck-Plage, leaving the older girls at Westgate in the care of Millicent Crofts. There must have been some sort of accident: Marina's supportive boot was damaged and one of her legs was afterwards said to be in plaster. Princess Nicholas hurried to Berck-Plage and informed her husband by telegram, but by sheer ill luck this private drama coincided with an international crisis. On 18 October war was declared between Greece and Turkey, and there was no question of the Prince being able to leave. He sent a postcard to 'Dear Foxie' expressing his support: 'the doctor seemed to be authoritative about the admirable way baby's foot had been looked after, which is all thanks to your loving & skillful care.'[7]

The conundrum must have been what to do with the children, soon reunited at Berck-Plage. The Prince would be in the thick of the fighting, along with his father and brothers. The Princess must join the other women of the Greek royal family in support of the army medical services. Grand Duchess Vladimir was in Paris and was keen to have her granddaughters, but Princess Nicholas felt uneasy about this, particularly if it involved Kate being taken back to St Petersburg. It may be that at this point her mother simply took over. The Grand Duchess paid a handsome allowance to her daughter and son-in-law and this gave her considerable leverage over them. Princess Nicholas and Kate parted at Berck-Plage, never for a moment suspecting that eight years would pass before they could live under the same roof again.

The children joined their grandmother and Grand Duke Boris at the Hotel Continental in Paris. On 16 November the Grand Duchess, her son and little Marina arrived in London in some state, to be followed a day later by the older children, who left again for Paris on 29 November. The others followed at the beginning of December and the whole party spent two weeks in the Hotel Continental before travelling on to Munich; then Princess Nicholas asked for the children to be returned to Greece. Her mother's response was alarming. She would send Olga and Elizabeth back if the Princess wanted them but Marina was staying with her until the foot was completely cured. The Grand Duchess was outspoken in her view that this was the little girl's only chance of making a full recovery. Princess Nicholas was shocked but unwilling to separate the children from one another and from Kate, so the Grand Duchess took all three, and their nurse, on from Munich to St Petersburg.

By January Kate's daily letters to Greece were a catalogue of horrors. The Princess tried to reassure her – 'I think that you take things too much to heart & get too easily upset . . . what does it matter what others think or say, as long as you know that the Prince & I trust you & will always stick up for you' – but some sort of crash was now inevitable. Princess Nicholas could do nothing; relations between herself and her mother were too finely balanced. Even an invitation from her husband's sister Marie, Grand Duchess Georgi Mikhailovich of Russia, to have Kate and the children with her at Harax in the Crimea – freeing them from the 'wasp's nest' of St Petersburg – did not help. 'I don't dare propose it,' the Princess told Kate, 'for fear of another deadly offence!'[8]

Matters came to a head in mid-January. Princess Marina had a persistent cough and the Grand Duchess held Kate to blame for continuing to bath the child. There was an angry scene between the two women which resulted in Kate being packed off to Harax with Marina alone, while Olga and Elizabeth were held in St Petersburg under the care of a governess, Mademoiselle Perrin, and the nursery maid. They were distraught to be parted from Kate, who had cared for them all their lives: 'It broke my heart to read about the children's grief,' the Princess said, 'it must have been <u>too</u> awful, poor little angels . . . how <u>could</u> the G^d D^{chess} do such a thing! & then call me a <u>cruel</u> mother!!'[9] The Grand Duchess forbade any further communication between the girls and their nurse: this placed Mademoiselle Perrin in a quandary as she had two very unhappy children on her hands who wanted only Kate. Sensing the injustice in what she was being told to do, yet fearful of provoking further argument, she sent the children's letters to their mother for forwarding.

Anger and recrimination mounted on all sides. From the southbound train and then from Harax, Kate poured out her feelings in a series of anguished telegrams and letters to the Princess. The Grand Duchess refused to write to her daughter at all but turned on Prince Nicholas, complaining that they had 'hurt her too deeply for her to be able to speak about it'. She repeated her intention to keep Marina and said she would return the older girls after the war: 'They are now old enough to be without a real nurse under the care of their mother who nursed the poor soldiers and will have <u>learnt to take care of her own children</u>.'[10] She accused both her daughter and Kate of years of neglect. Prince Nicholas said he could hardly bear to read Kate's account of her parting from the children and he fretted against his inability to help them: as military governor of the captured town of Salonika he simply could not leave on private business. He wrote to Kate: 'I have never felt duty weigh so heavily on my shoulders as just now! . . . I never would have thought the G^d D^{ss} capable of a thing like that. She has been cruel to you, cruel to the children, and cruel to us parents.' He also said that his mother-in-law had threatened to 'withdraw her protection' from Marina if her will was crossed, 'meaning of course that she will force us to pay for everything!'[11]

Princess Nicholas sent her mother a carefully worded telegram insisting that Olga and Elizabeth should be returned to their nurse, in whom she placed absolute confidence. At the beginning of March, writing from Epirus where her ambulance trains were preparing to deal with the consequences of a major attack, and almost beside herself with worry, she wrote to tell Kate that the demand had been refused. Presumably with her mother's threat in mind, she had made enquiries and believed she had found another doctor who would perform the operation for less than the price quoted by Dr Calot.[12] On 17 March she set off by train for Vienna on her way to collect Olga and Elizabeth. But she got no further than Belgrade, where news reached her that her father-in-law, King George I of the Hellenes, had been assassinated in Salonika; she had to turn back. The Princesses arrived in Greece shortly after the King's funeral.

But the plan to place Princess Marina under the care of another doctor never materialised. The Grand Duchess kept control and in March Kate and her charge were taken by Baron Offenberg to the clinic at Berck-Plage, to prepare for the operation and the long period of recuperative treatment which would follow. The outraged grandmother, meanwhile, had named her terms. 'The G^d D^chess wants me <u>absolutely</u> to send you away,' Princess Nicholas told Kate; 'if not, it means that I love you more than her and things will never be the same again between her & me.'[13] The Princess was torn and unhappy – 'I feel quite broken by all this' – and her letter to Kate was an appeal to someone who was more friend than employee, to understand the position she was in and to take the only step that could break the deadlock.

Kate should have resigned, but her emotions were in such a ferment that she could not stand back and consider. She was certainly innocent of all the charges laid against her but, in fairness to the Grand Duchess, it has to be said that Kate Fox did not make things easy for herself or for anyone else in the situation. She was a complicated woman; exceptionally good at her job sometimes and praised wholeheartedly by some of the mothers she worked for, but this was not always the case. One of her earlier employers, the Marchioness of Ailsa, would have sympathised with Grand Duchess Vladimir. Kate suffered an emotional breakdown while working at Culzean Castle and, though the Marchioness was kind enough not to voice her reservations in Kate's testimonial book, which would be seen by future employers, she did not mince her words in a private letter to Miss Sharman. She wrote of Kate's 'perfectly childish behaviour. . . . The untidiness, and allowing her depression to come so constantly to the surface were trying but the main point was the sentimental exaggeration of baby worship to the exclusion of justice to the older child – he really required her sympathy and consideration and got very little excepting by fitful attempts to make up.'[14]

Kate may have suffered a similar breakdown while staying at Harax. Grand Duchess Marie sent a disturbing report of her behaviour there to the Princess who, faced with a fresh emotional outburst from Kate in reply to her letter, knew that there was only one way forward. 'I think a thorough, good long rest is what you want & that is what I would like you to do,' she told Kate. 'When Baby's care in Berck is over, I would like you to go home & <u>rest</u> & just do nothing; I will try & find a temporary nurse.'[15] Princess Nicholas was not imagining a permanent parting, just a breathing space. Once Marina was at home in Greece she hoped to bring Kate back too, but things had gone beyond her control. Before the end of April Dr Calot let her know that he would need Marina at Berck for up to a year. Meanwhile, she came under increasing pressure from her mother to fix a date for Kate's departure. In May the Grand Duchess lost patience and appointed a new nurse, without a word to her daughter; the first Princess Nicholas knew of this was a letter from Kate, written partly from the train and partly from England, describing the distressing circumstances in which she had been forced to hand Marina over and leave Berck-Plage. It emerged later that the pension the Grand Duchess had allowed her was given on condition that she did not communicate with the children.

In royal circles the dismissal of Kate Fox became something of a *cause célèbre*. Everyone was on the nurse's side. Grand Duchess Kirill sent her an immediate telegram of sympathy and support. Her own children's nurse Marian Burgess, 'Burgie', was, of course, a fellow Norlander and a great friend of Kate's. Once Kate was back in England the King's sister, Princess Victoria, remembering their summers at Bognor and Westgate, sent for Kate to talk about what had happened, and in October 1913 Kate received a friendly letter from the other member of the Bognor party, Prince Christopher: 'My thoughts have been constantly with you during all these horribly trying times, and if you want sympathy and friendship you have certainly got mine. Never did I think that such injustice was possible.'[16]

But in one way at least the Grand Duchess had acted very shrewdly. Her choice of the new nurse could not have been bettered, for she had gone straight back to Norland and chosen a woman whom even Kate conceded was nice and well thought-of, and who slipped into place as though she had known the family all her life. Margaret Alison was three years older than Kate but had studied later at Norland, so they had never met. The daughter of a Yorkshire cloth manufacturer, Margaret was educated at Huddersfield Girls' College and had done her hospital training in the Birmingham Orthopaedic Hospital – making her ideally suited to care for Princess Marina after the operation. Meeting her for the first time in June, on a visit to Berck-Plage, Princess Nicholas reported to Kate, 'Nurse Margaret is very nice & quiet & gentle & Baby likes her, but she is fat & not young anymore & easily gets tired.'[17] It was a mystery to her how her mother had found Margaret, who went from England to St Petersburg to be interviewed and was sent straight from there to Berck-Plage. Perhaps Miss Sharman had taken a hand in the matter. However sympathetic she may have felt towards Kate, she also had the reputation of Norland to consider and she knew the previous question marks there had been over Kate's emotional stability. Parachuting in another Norlander, with the placid, calming temperament the situation so sorely needed, was the ideal answer for all concerned. At the Princess's request Miss Sharman allowed Kate the compensation of her silver badge, even though her service with the family had been ended just short of the qualifying ten years.

Kate spent most of the summer at home in Surrey with her father. Princess Nicholas kept in touch by letter and in this way the nurse learned that Marina was happy with Margaret at Berck-Plage, where the treatment was proceeding well. It was Olga and Elizabeth who seemed to be suffering most and they never stopped asking about Kate, and comparing themselves to all the cousins around them who still had their nurses. In early October the Princess finally told them Kate would not be coming back, '& it was dreadful to see their grief, poor darlings! I would like those who have caused all this misery to have seen those tears'. Ten-year-old Olga told her, 'I always thought that if Nurnie didn't look after us any more, she would come back & live with us; Aunty Olga always had her nurse.'[18] (She meant the Tsar's sister, Grand Duchess Olga Alexandrovna, and her beloved Mrs Francklin; they had entertained Kate and the children to tea during the last miserable winter in St Petersburg.) Princess Nicholas allowed the girls to write to Kate, despite the ban. They were old enough to know that they must never mention this to 'Gammy', their grandmother.

The emotions stirred by the affair took a long time to cool. The Grand Duchess remained implacable in her opposition to Kate. She withdrew all financial support from her daughter's family for a full year to show her disapproval and in the autumn she refused to meet the Prince and Princess and their older children. Kate was depressed for a long time and the Princess tried to lift her spirits. 'I wish you would get over feeling so dreadfully miserable, & to know that I am helpless to do anything is awful, poor dear Foxie! . . . there is still such a lot of good for you to do, & then the hope of seeing us all again – you see, Milly was forgotten but you never will be – Poor dear Milly! . . . think how she suffered & still how brave she has been.'[19] But when Kate faced the inevitable and began to take on other work, it was the Princess who needed reassurance; 'how can you do it,' she wrote, 'I mean, look after other children when yr heart is aching all the time for the darlings'.[20]

At the end of 1913 Margaret Alison was at last allowed to take Princess Marina back to Greece where the family was reunited. Margaret stayed on, the Grand Duchess's insistence that the children did not need a nurse forgotten, now their nurse was not Kate Fox. They were happy enough, though Olga particularly continued to mourn the loss of Kate and always kept a photo of the nurse beside her bed. Princess Nicholas worked on various schemes to bring Kate back to Greece, all of which withered in the face of her mother's continued opposition. Kate, meanwhile, took on a series of temporary posts and had an adventurous and successful time. It was not until the summer of 1920, when the Grand Duchess and her daughter were exiled from their countries and the Grand Duchess was dying, that Kate was finally able to go back to her adored Princesses – still in secret. In January 1921, four months after the Grand Duchess's death, she returned to the family for good.

Grand Duchess Vladimir's jealous guard of her children's affections was part of her character. Her assumption that as grandmother she had the right of veto over the way her adult children ran their homes was the general expectation of her class and time. Particularly in royal and aristocratic circles, where the elder generation held the power and the purse strings and where there was a public dimension to the upbringing of children, the grandparents' word could be hard to oppose. Once the Grand Duchess had turned against Kate Fox she was able to complain that she had not been consulted in appointing her. Queen Victoria's choice of nurses and governesses for her grandchildren – Emma Hobbs, Mary Ann Orchard, and so on – was usually excellent, but sometimes things did go awry. When they did, persuading the Queen that she was wrong was a dilemma in itself.

In 1901, three months after Queen Victoria's death, the Duke of Connaught was told that Mrs Chapman, who was nurse to his children in the 1880s, was attempting to sell a letter written by his wife when the nurse left their employ. She had already sold one from the Queen for £21. He was outraged: 'We were anxious to get rid of the woman, who had been with our children for eight years,' he told Francis Knollys, King Edward VII's secretary, '& the Duchess was <u>ordered</u> by the Queen to write this farewell letter in much more familiar terms than she had ever used before & I was <u>ordered</u> to give her pensions. She had not behaved well latterly & bullied the children so we were glad to get rid of her under any conditions.'[21]

The issue sounds clear-cut, but in fact the appointment had started well and Queen Victoria never wavered in her warm regard for Susan Chapman. It was in the summer of 1881 that Susan, a gamekeeper's daughter from Geddington in Northamptonshire, first came to the Queen's notice on the recommendation of the Duchess of Roxburghe. Princess Luise Margarete, Duchess of Connaught, was midway through her first pregnancy and the monthly nurse Mrs Brotherstone had been engaged for a January birth. The Queen forwarded Susan's reference to Prince Arthur and his reaction was favourable, if a little guarded: 'She seems to have been brought up in a good school,' he said, 'Louischen supposes that she would not expect to have more than a young nurserymaid under her and would be prepared to come at the same time as Mrs Brotherstone. I see she is an unmarried person but I suppose that does not matter.' He asked if the Duchess of Roxburghe would advise his wife directly on the appropriate wages.[22] So Susan Chapman was appointed permanent nurse and in January 1882 her first charge, Princess Margaret of Connaught, was born, delivered with forceps after a long and difficult labour.

Chance gave Susan Chapman a very free rein in the early months of the baby's life. The young mother was taken ill soon after the birth and in March the Duke took her to Biarritz to recuperate. 'The dear little Princess we left in perfect health,' her lady-in-waiting told the Queen, 'Mrs Chapman is an indefatigable walker so that there is no fear of the Princess not having plenty of fresh air and exercise during the beautiful weather.'[23] In July the Duchess became pregnant again, and the following January, almost a year to the day since the birth of his sister, Prince Arthur of Connaught entered Susan Chapman's nursery, all harmonious still. The problems began eight months later when an important advance in the Duke's military career led to prolonged periods of separation between parents and children.

The Queen was adamant that this must be. A wife's place was with her husband, she said, but India, where the Duke would be stationed for the greater part of the next seven years, was no place for children. Margaret, 'Daisy', was twenty months old and her brother eight months when their parents were forced to leave them at Balmoral in the autumn of 1883. The Duke and Duchess received a steady drip-feed of news from Balmoral, Windsor and Osborne. It was the Queen's way to be critical of her children and grandchildren, particularly in writing. In January 1884 she told the Duke of Connaught how two-year-old 'Daisy' had recognised 'Mamma' in a photograph, newly sent from India. 'I am sorry to say she has a return of extraordinary ungraciousness & wilfullness,' the Queen continued, 'perhaps because she is not <u>quite the thing</u> – a little sluggishness of the liver – But good Chapman manages her so well. She is so patient and kind & yet very firm – & she can make her do things – wch is a great thing. But I think she will be *difficult*. Little Arthur on the other hand is so good-humoured & friendly. Only sometimes he gets into a passion.'[24]

These were not the details the heart craved. Later in the year Lady Elphinstone, the wife of Prince Arthur's former governor, spent two days at Windsor and sent the Duchess a long report on the children. 'You have told me more about our little ones than I have heard since I left them', came the reply.

'It was a real pleasure to hear of all their little ways. As a rule I am told nothing except that they are very well and flourishing and which of course is the chief and most important thing, but one longs to know of all they do and say and thousands of little things. . . . I do miss them quite terribly. . . .'[25] The Queen's constant praise of Susan Chapman, and injunctions to the Duchess to write nicely to the nurse, 'not in the usual stiff old-fashioned way to servants', because of the immense responsibility she carried on their behalf, cannot have helped the situation when both parents were longing to carry these responsibilities for themselves.[26]

Tensions mounted after Christmas 1886, the third the Duke and Duchess had spent away from their children. There were three little Connaughts now in Susan Chapman's care, Princess Victoria Patricia, 'Patsy', having been born in the previous spring. But they were no longer the only grandchildren living under the Queen's roof. Princess Beatrice gave birth to her first child that Christmas so, to the simple concern that 'Daisy', Arthur and 'Patsy' were growing up without their parents were added more complicated fears about the comparisons and nursery rivalries to which the children would be subject: 'We feel more than ever that our children would be much better away,' Prince Arthur remarked, 'as they must be "*de trop*".'[27] On 18 February 1887 he wrote from Aden to his sister Princess Louise, 'I have not heard much news from home and get a little exasperated when Mama enlarges on the affection of our children for 'Auntie B and Uncle Liko' – It is hard enough to be separated from the children but then to be told how fond they are of other people is a little too much. We would give anything to bring them or have them sent out to us this autumn but I fear the opposition in high quarters 'on medical grounds' will be something fearful.'[28]

He was wrong. That November the Queen finally relented and allowed the children to spend Christmas in India with their parents – presumably with Susan Chapman in tow. The elder children had to return to their grandmother in February but, reluctantly and against her better judgement, the Queen allowed 'Patsy' to remain. The two-year-old proved a constant delight to her parents and became the pet of the Bombay cantonment where the Duke was stationed, but reports of the older children back in England were not good. Princess Beatrice wrote that six-year-old Arthur was 'slow and wanting' and that both children were disobedient. In October 1889 Princess Louise was at Balmoral and did her best to assess the children's position. She reported to her brother in secret – a measure of how sensitive the matter had become – and he assured her, 'I will not show you up and no one shall know what you have written. All along I have felt that morally it was not the best thing for them to be with Mama and I was quite sure that the Battenberg children would be made no. 1.'[29]

In the spring of 1890 the Duke's command of the Bombay Army ended and he and the Duchess returned to England. For the first time in seven years they found themselves under the same roof as Susan Chapman and they did not like it. How far the nurse was at fault, and how far she paid for all that the couple had endured during the years of separation would be hard to judge. The Queen was entirely on the nurse's side, never doubting for a moment what she had said early on, that Susan Chapman 'w[ld] kill herself for the Children' – which in itself might suggest a worrying intensity in the nurse's feelings.[30] Perhaps Susan found it too hard now to share the children with their parents, whose ways were not her ways. From their standpoint though, as the Duke would say in his 1901 letter, she 'bullied the children'. In any case, it took the Connaughts only months to decide that Susan Chapman must go. Initially this was to happen in the spring of 1891. When even that began to feel like an eternity, the family set off for an autumn holiday in Germany without her and told the Queen that after their return, in November 1890, Susan's services would no longer be required.

The Queen was not pleased. 'Poor Chapman was quite composed when I saw her on the eve[ng] of the 7th,' she told the Duke, 'but she told my Annie [Annie McDonald, the Queen's dresser] that she only wished you had told her she was ultimately to go. . . . I think I had better write to her soon'.[31] She wrote to the Duchess of Roxburghe too, praising Susan and explaining the dismissal only in terms of the children's ages and the lack of nursery space in the house at Portsmouth where the family would live after their return. She suggested that the Duchess might like to take Susan Chapman on as housekeeper.[32] When no offer was forthcoming, it was the Queen who made sure that the nurse's future was secure by providing pensions – £15 a year from herself and £25, on her insistence, from the Duke of Connaught – then by offering her a job in the Linen Room at Windsor Castle, which she held until the start of 1896, retiring on an increased pension.

No clue remains to the Queen's feelings on this second retirement, but there was a little flurry of amusement in the Privy Purse Office when, in writing to acknowledge her pension in January 1896, the former nurse signed herself 'Susan'. 'How comes it that she is <u>Susan</u> now', one official noted on her papers. 'We had always known her as <u>Sarah</u>! Perhaps she was a little <u>mixed</u> when writing as I understand this is her failing!' 'Evidently', added another.[33] Then enquiries were made and the name in the household ledgers was duly changed to 'Susan'. It was the Duke in his 1901 letter who provided a translation for 'mixed'. As he told Francis Knollys, 'after a year or two she had to go for drunkenness'.[34] Bullying . . . drunkenness . . . it makes for an unappealing record. But on one charge Susan Chapman was certainly not guilty. Whoever sold her royal letters in 1901, she did not do it. She died in May 1898, having suffered a fatal stroke at the age of fifty-four, a month after burying the elderly father whose care had exhausted her strength.

Susan Chapman was not the only one of Queen Victoria's chosen nurses to become the centre of an emotional storm in the 1880s. Princess Alice, Countess of Athlone, Prince Leopold's elder child, recalled the dismissal of her first nurse Eliza Creak – a splendidly Dickensian name – 'after four years; I loved her, but she favoured me as against my delicate, nervous and tiresome baby brother. In fact, he got so on her nerves that she had to go. Grandmama Victoria was much agitated, as she had been responsible for finding her.'[35] Whether this was the story Princess Alice was told or her own rationalisation (it was his fault . . .) is impossible to tell, but it was certainly not what happened. In the summer of 1886, when Alice was three years old and little 'Charlie', Charles Edward her brother, just two, their widowed mother the Duchess of Albany sent an emotional letter to the Queen appealing for help in a difficult situation. It was fourteen sides long and explained in great detail how Eliza Creak had turned on the Duchess in the nursery in front of the children, 'saying that she was badly used, & that she had no position in the house, that <u>all</u> were unkind & never thought of her feelings, & that if I showed that I would not give her her due position, others could not do so either'.[36]

The immediate cause of the explosion was startling in its triviality: a dispute over who, mistress or nurse, should have invited two retired nurses to visit the house, Prince Leopold's faithful Mrs Thurston and the Duchess's own childhood nurse, Miss Smith. Eliza felt slighted because the Duchess had issued the invitations herself. But, as the Duchess went on to explain, this was only the climax of six months of steadily deteriorating relations between them. Once, they had been good friends – the Duchess was even inclined to blame herself for spoiling the nurse.[37] The Queen was aware of the problem; had, indeed, spoken to Eliza, but the situation had not improved and it worried the Duchess particularly that Alice, 'who takes in everything', was watching Eliza berate her mother in this way. She suspected that the little girl's mind was being turned against her and her own family in Germany.[38]

The Queen responded immediately and her daughter-in-law, acting on her advice, told the nurse that they had decided she must take some time away from the family to allow her nerves to settle. Eliza's sister Mrs Wilson, who had been a nurse before her marriage, was providing temporary cover and the

Queen suggested that the Duchess should recall Miss Smith to help her. Eliza took the news calmly at first, though the Duchess was quite certain that she would use Charlie's state of health – he was teething and rather feverish – to manipulate the situation and avoid being sent away. This much the Duchess had managed to tell the Queen in a second letter before going up to the nursery where a second and far more painful scene took place. Eliza began to cry and, as expected, to play on the baby's health 'saying she <u>would</u> not go & <u>no one</u> <u>could</u> send her away till Charlie had those teeth!' But there was more. She 'went on saying she had always done her duty to the Children, & loved them so & would do anything she could for them, for their sakes & their Father's; so I said, very gently & not for me upon which she said <u>no</u>.'³⁹

It was the most extraordinary thing for anyone to have said to a young widow whose grief for her husband was still fresh, renewed daily in the son he had never seen, for baby Charlie was born four months after his father's sudden death. But for the baby's nurse to say it. . . . Eliza's outburst was shocking but it gives a clue to the reason for her emotional state. She must have been harbouring a crush on Prince Leopold which found expression in her care of his children, particularly after his death, and which fired her resentment of his widow. She was minding them for him. The situation is not uncommon. Eliza Creak was a single woman. The Prince was attractive, very relaxed in the way he ran his home and brought his baby daughter to the fore and, in the last year of his life, bursting with happiness in his achievement of the marriage and fatherhood which, given his haemophilia, he had feared would be forever out of reach. And happiness is a very winning quality.

Even after this, though, the Duchess of Albany did not envisage a permanent dismissal. She still thought that Eliza could come back after a month, maybe longer. It was probably the Queen who saw that a complete break would be better for them both. The Duchess and her children were about to leave for Scotland. They expected Eliza Creak to join them but instead it was her replacement, Victoria Nicholls, who followed them to Birkhall, and 'came up and kissed me and seized little Charlie up in her arms and that,' Princess Alice remembered, 'was our beloved Nanna'.⁴⁰ In September the Queen told Sir Robert Collins that she would not pay Mrs Creak's expenses, though she would pay for Mrs Nicholls.⁴¹ From 1886 onwards Eliza received a pension of £15 a year and she did not see the Albanys again.

Eliza Creak was probably not the only nurse to hide feelings for her royal employer. But were such feelings ever returned? On one occasion Kaiserin Friedrich told her daughter that it was not a good idea to employ a young and pretty nurse. She probably had romantic entanglements in mind, but not necessarily with the children's father. In a Court situation there were many men who came into contact with the nurses, and any romance was undesirable in the nursery. The pretty nurse who caught the Prince's eye belongs more to romantic fiction than to history – almost. But there is one Spanish author who claims that in 1908, or thereabouts, King Alfonso XIII of Spain had an affair with his children's Irish nurse, who became pregnant, was dismissed, and later gave birth to a daughter. Others question this, while accepting that something similar did happen a few years later between the King and Beatrice Noon, who is said to have given piano lessons to the young Infantes. Beatrice became pregnant by the King and was sent to France where, in 1916, she too had a daughter. The King's friend Señor Quiñones de Léon, the former Spanish Ambassador in Paris, took charge of baby Juana Alfonsa Milán Quiñones de Léon and was responsible for her upbringing (the surname Milán, it is said, was chosen by the King from one of his own subsidiary titles).[42]

The principals in this story certainly existed: there is no personal file on Beatrice Noon in the Madrid Palace Archives today, but in the files of her contemporary, Alice Evans, Beatrice is specifically mentioned as 'Nurse in the service of His Royal Highness the Prince of the Asturias' in 1910; presumably, therefore, she was at Court for at least six years. Many nurses gave some lessons to the children and perhaps Beatrice was musical and played the piano with them. As there is documentary evidence that she was a royal nurse, it may be that the story of the unnamed nurse in 1908 and the story of Beatrice Noon the piano teacher, in fact relate to the same events.

King Alfonso and Queen Ena did not have a happy marriage and the King's affairs were legion. But the couple remained together until much later, when the King had lost his throne and both were living in exile. Separation and divorce were rare in royal circles, or at all in society in the nineteenth and early twentieth centuries, but they did happen and there were cases where the Englishwomen who cared for the children were drawn deep into the tangle of their employers' emotions.

In the spring of 1914 Hilda Maybury, the daughter of a manufacturing chemist from the Midlands, was appointed governess to Princesses Ingeborg and Altburg, the Grand Duke of Oldenburg's younger daughters, who were twelve and ten years old. Hilda was in her late thirties and had spent many years in Germany and Italy, but nothing in her previous experiences had prepared her for the state of affairs in the Grand Duke's household. The Court lady who met her at the station was quick to warn her of complications in the Grand Ducal family. The children's mother lived apart from her husband in her family home at Schwerin. 'Later on I heard many strange stories of the Grand Duchess,' Hilda wrote, 'of her many scandalous escapades with men of high and low degree, and of the dramatic manner in which the plans for elopement with one of her lovers were frustrated by the secret police. Already on that drive to the Palace I found that my eyes were opened.'[43]

From the start Hilda's duties included supervising the Princesses when they spoke to their mother on the telephone in the evening. 'The Grand Duke knows that his wife is intriguing to take Ingeborg away,' she was told, 'and we do not know how much the young Princess understands of the reasons for their separation.'[44] Hilda foresaw endless difficulties and was keen to avoid accompanying the girls on their visits to their mother, when they could never be left alone for a moment. She noticed how on their birthdays, gifts from the absent Grand Duchess came with 'hysterical appeals to the Almighty to restore her stolen children to her and reminders to the Princesses of solemn promises which she had exacted from them when they were with her'.[45] The letters and gifts would be whisked away and disposed of, but the Grand Duchess remained a looming presence in the palace, though Hilda never saw her.

But she did find herself dealing with two very confused children, 'under the impression that their mother was a kind of saint who received messages from God through a medium, and that her extreme spirituality made it impossible for her to countenance the worldly life of the Grand Duke'.[46] Hilda did not take to Princess Altburg and the feeling seems to have been mutual, but she liked Ingeborg, to her mind the more sensitive of the girls and the more disturbed by her parents' estrangement. It saddened her to find Ingeborg in tears, uncertain of whom she could trust in her father's house and beyond any reassurance.

In the event it was the First World War, not the Grand Duke's marital problems, that put paid to Hilda Maybury's career as a royal governess: the summer of 1914 was a bad time to be English in Germany. Hilda turned her back on Court life without regret and went home to write a salacious little memoir about the scandals that had swirled around her innocent head. Many, many years later, Princess Altburg would claim that the governess had been nursing an unrequited passion for the Grand Duke and had written the book as her revenge. Who knows?

Some years earlier Lilian Wilson was caught up in the marital problems of her Grand Duke and she almost came to a violent end. When Lilian knelt at the deathbed of little Elisabeth of Hesse and was comforted by Grand Duke Ernst Ludwig, one important person was missing from the scene. The child's mother, Grand Duchess Victoria Melita, had been divorced from the Grand Duke nearly two years earlier, in December 1901. They agreed that Elisabeth, who was then six years old, would spend half of each year with her mother, half with her father. On paper it was a fair arrangement for the parents but it was a lot to ask of a child, to uproot for such long periods from the home she had known all her life. In a private memoir written for his sons the Grand Duke described how he had reassured Elisabeth that her mother loved her. Her reply was telling: 'Mama says it, but you really do love me.' He recalled how once, when the time came for Elisabeth to leave him, he found her hiding under his sofa, trying to swallow her tears.[47]

It was Lilian who had the job of taking the little girl from one parent to the other, of staying with her and becoming her stability in an atmosphere of deepening bitterness. We can fairly question the Grand Duke's view of events – he was hardly impartial – but Lilian would have known exactly what went on in the palace before the breakdown of the marriage – servants did. She would have had her sympathies too, unspoken at the time but made apparent later in her continued service to the Grand Duke. The only clue to her relationship with the child's mother comes in a letter written by the grandmother, the Duchess of Coburg, describing a traumatic incident that happened shortly after the divorce.

In February 1902, Lilian and Elisabeth were staying with Grand Duchess Victoria Melita and the Duchess of Coburg in Nice. Despite all attempts to persuade her otherwise, the Grand Duchess was insisting that all her belongings must remain untouched in the marital home in Darmstadt even though she had left. Her mental state worried the Duchess, who told her elder daughter, Crown Princess Marie of Romania,

Now comes all the bitter, bitter disappointment. The evidence that she had blundered, had made mistake upon mistake and through it has never been able to have real friends who will stick to her in need. Neither amongst her suite or even her servants. . . .

She gave me a terrible fright about a week ago, as she went into a shameful fit of unbounded fury against Wilson about some letter from Darmstadt, mentioning her jewels. She began to scream in such a way that actually the whole of the servants rushed upstairs.

She slapped Wilson and tore at her hair and made a dart at a big lamp to throw it at her head. Wilson just had time to seize it and carry it out of the room. Frightened maids rushed into my room to fetch me as the saving angel and I found her crying, but the first fury over. Everybody was trembling and quite pale. . . . You know that she could have killed Wilson with the greatest ease.[48]

It makes Lilian Wilson's loyalty to the Grand Duke, and his child's feelings, very easy to understand.

The Duchess of Coburg did not have an easy time with her daughters. Two years earlier Crown Princess Marie had been in deep trouble and that crisis destroyed the career of one of the most respected of British royal governesses. In her own version of events, written for publication in the 1930s, Marie pictured herself as an innocent victim: young, beautiful, enchanting even in her little follies, whose harmless adventures were constantly misunderstood by the unyielding tyrants of the older generation. She related how the King, her husband's uncle, employed people to act as spies in her 'poor little household', reporting back on her activities, and how the process reached its climax in his choice of a governess for her five-year-old son: 'The moment I set eyes on her all hope vanished. I understood that my worst fears had been realized. The woman was just everything that could not be borne, thick-set, heavy with staring, goggle-eyes, a large, fleshy nose and repulsive mouth; she was common, with a commonness that only one of her own nationality could rightly appreciate.'[49]

The time that followed, according to Marie, was a living hell in which her son was kept from her and her every action misrepresented to the King, until she could not bear to live in her own house and took refuge in travel. The hated governess was a monster without a single human feeling. 'I will not relate all the misery of her two years' reign; it was the blackest period of my youth, engendering endless misery and grief.'[50] Marie named her enemy only as 'Miss W' but the gesture was paper-thin. Her identification of the governess as 'an Englishwoman who had brought up the Queen of Holland' could point only to one person: Saxton Elizabeth Winter.[51]

The transformation of Queen Wilhelmina's dear Miss Winter – 'I continued to love Miss Winter, and a firm friendship came into being in later years, when she was no longer my governess'[52] – into an ogre of nightmare is one of the strangest reversals imaginable. Saxton Winter had left the Netherlands in November 1896 with the gratitude and affection of the young Queen and Queen Emma. She returned to her mother in England, then, in the following year, Queen Emma contacted her with an offer of work from her cousin, Princess Marie of Wied, who wanted a governess to teach English to her teenage daughters, Luise and Elisabeth, for 100 Reichsmarks a month. From July 1897 until the following summer Miss Winter was happily installed at Neuwied – where Mary Barnes had once worked and was still remembered by the girls' father, Prince Wilhelm, one of 'her' children. In the summer of 1898 the Wieds heard that his sister Elisabeth, then Queen of Romania, was looking for a governess for the Crown Prince's eldest son: they had no hesitation in recommending Miss Winter.

So it was that Saxton Winter acquired her fateful appointment. She joined the King, Queen and Crown Princess in Vienna at the end of September and spent a day with them in the city, visiting the art exhibition at the Glaspalast and the studios of the painter Kaulbach, where the Crown Princess was sitting for her portrait. 'She is certainly exceedingly pretty,' Miss Winter told Wilhelmina, her 'most precious Queen', '& the great charm is, that there is absolutely nothing artificial about her appearance – no powder, no paint – only plenty of strong scent & jewels which could be dispensed with!'[53] That night the royal party left Vienna, finally arriving at Sinaia in Romania in the early morning after two nights and a full day on the train. The Crown Princess went off immediately to her own house and Saxton stayed with the King and Queen for an introductory visit lasting three weeks, after which King Carol told his brother, the Crown Prince's father, 'One could not make a better selection.'[54]

By the following spring Saxton was at work in the Crown Prince's household. To say that she was settled would be untrue; she was obviously very unhappy. Romanian delegates were about to leave for the Netherlands. 'I would give anything I possess to be going with them to The Hague!' she told Queen Wilhelmina, adding, 'It is so strange to feel oneself absolutely without a friend near at hand.' But against the Crown Princess's claim, 'from the first, I felt her hostility towards me, which cropped up at every turn', set this, from the governess herself: 'I generally stay with the Princess for some time after lunch and all the evenings are spent together – generally helping her with whatever she is doing or playing from time to time whist with the Prince. I foresee that my own painting will go to the wall & that my fancy works will fare very badly! Yet, here too, as I wish to gain her confidence, I suppose I had better continue as I am doing, at least for a time.'[55]

And about the child, for whose sake Miss Winter had gone to Romania, the two women's accounts could not be more different. According to Marie, 'Miss W from the first set about alienating our child from us. . . . I could never get at my own child without scenes.' But Miss Winter told Queen Wilhelmina that her time with five-year-old Prince Carol was severely restricted. There was more, too. 'The boy fills me with dismay & infinite pity,' she said; 'he gives one so completely the impression of having been cowed and bullied by a hard authority, a natural consequence of which is, that he is half afraid to speak the truth.'[56]

This calls into question the actions of the other Englishwoman in the case, the children's nurse Mary Green, preserved for posterity by the Crown Princess as 'a motherly soul who, though humble, was a real comfort . . . a figure worthy of Dickens. Broad of girth, loud-voiced and jovial. . . . Never had woman stauncher defender than I had in old Nana.'[57] A real heroine, then; but Marie was only considering her own relationship with the nurse, not her children's. If Miss Winter's assessment of Carol as a bullied child had any substance, it must have been Mary Green who did the bullying. Queen Elisabeth had no doubt that she did. Writing to a friend in the spring of 1900, when the drama had reached its climax, the Queen remarked on the good Saxton had done for little Carol, adding, 'The old nurse was in the habit of beating him with a stick! That delicate child.'[58]

In November 1899 Carol became seriously ill with typhoid. Marie was away at the time and heavily pregnant but she hurried back to Romania where, she said, Saxton Winter tried to deny her access to her son. As soon as he was recovering and there was no further danger, she left for her mother's home in Coburg where she stayed until her baby was born. With her mother's support, she refused to return until the governess was dismissed. By April 1900, she said, 'the fatal Miss W had finally been relinquished, but not without endless and painful debates'.[59]

But Marie had left a good deal out of her story which, if told, casts a very different light on the whole sorry business. In appointing Saxton Winter above her head, the King and Queen had only been using the privilege claimed by the elder generation. Marie herself would do the same in the 1920s when she did not approve of Sylvia Crowther, her Yugoslav grandchildren's nurse. But King Carol and Queen Elisabeth had extra reasons for their watchfulness. For some years Marie's behaviour had been far more damaging to the reputation of the family than the innocent flirtatiousness she herself described.

This was not entirely her fault. The Crown Princess was married young, by arrangement, and in complete ignorance. After the first disillusionment she began to discover the power her own beauty could give – and she was a real beauty. The Tsar's coronation in Moscow in 1896 allowed her and her sister Victoria Melita unaccustomed freedom and they enjoyed it to the full, coming away from the protracted celebrations happy, in love with their cousins Boris and Kirill – the sons of Grand Duchess Vladimir – and determined to enjoy themselves at every opportunity. In the autumn of 1897 Marie became pregnant by one of her lovers. There was trouble and she was dispatched to her mother's home for the winter; the fate of the child is unknown but it appears that the father, whose identity she managed to conceal, was Zizi Cantacuzino, a Romanian officer appointed to her service by the King in the summer, when her husband was seriously ill.[60]

Marie's behaviour continued to cause anxiety – to her mother, as well as the King and Queen. Despite all attempts to control her she encouraged her admirers and enjoyed the attention they paid her. As she herself said, 'I was supposed to settle down and be a good and dutiful little princess, without any imagination, tamely acquiescent to the severe King's every behest. This, alas, was not entirely my ideal, and there followed still many a year of conflict.'[61] The affair with Cantacuzino continued; for a time he acted as young Carol's gymnastics teacher and in the summer of 1899 the Crown Princess went with him to Constanza, taking his teenage cousin at the Queen's request. It seems to have been Saxton Winter who discovered what was really happening and told the King and Queen: this certainly makes Marie's blind hatred of the governess easy to understand. It also makes sense of Saxton's 'spying'. If she did find out, it was her duty to tell someone or become complicit in the affair herself.

Cantacuzino was sent away. But Marie was pregnant again and not by her husband. This is made clear in a letter written to her by her mother, who insisted on taking her to Coburg once more to give birth: 'The most important problem is to restore your reputation and to save you from this terrible situation.' When the baby, born at Coburg in January 1900, proved to be a girl the King remarked to his brother: 'It is a true stroke of luck that Missy gave birth to a daughter. A son born abroad under the given circumstances would have been a great embarrassment.'[62] For the family's sake the Crown Prince acknowledged the child and treated her as his own, but he was not the father. The King's secretary Eugeniu Buhman noted in his diary that Marie, in an angry scene with the King, claimed it was Grand Duke Boris; this may have been true or she may have been shielding Cantacuzino, who had more to fear from the King's anger.[63]

For the King and the Duchess of Coburg the priority was to hush up the whole affair and hope no one would ever know. But in royal circles the news had already spread. The Wied family knew. So did Queen Emma and the British royal family. The Duchess of Coburg claimed – and seems to have believed – that Saxton Winter was responsible for spreading the news. A portion of a draft letter she wrote to the governess survives: 'By your present behaviour in my daughter's house, you undo a whole life of honest and successful labour in Holland and your name will bear the stamp of infamy and intrigue, never to be wiped out during your whole life. . . . My daughter has greatly sinned, I have no excuses for her, but I have no words of blame strong enough for those who are paid to spy upon her . . . and who spread the scandal all over the world.'[64] Without condoning her daughter's actions, the Duchess had undertaken to sort out the mess, and the sacrifice she demanded if Marie was to return to Romania was Saxton Winter.

It no longer mattered if Miss Winter had done what the Duchess said. It seems highly unlikely that she did. She would never have written to Queen Wilhelmina about the Romanian scandal; such things were not discussed with an unmarried girl. There is no evidence that she corresponded with Queen Emma and if she had done so, the tone of their relationship was not one that would admit the passing on of juicy gossip about other princesses. Saxton Winter knew her place. The source of the stories is more likely to have been Queen Elisabeth, who was close to both the Wieds and Queen Emma and deplored the Crown Princess's behaviour; she, of course, was beyond the Duchess of Coburg's reach.

As the argument deepened the Duchess and her daughter convinced themselves of Saxton Winter's infamy. She became the scapegoat for everything that had gone wrong. Through the early months of 1900 the King resisted their demands for her dismissal – did she have some sort of hold over him, they wondered? In January 1902 an official from Romania suggested to the Duchess his own theory: 'He felt almost sure that she had some very compromising papers or letters in her hands and gave them up only after having received a big sum of money in return.'[65] The Duchess was intrigued and asked her daughter if she knew anything about this, but really there was a more simple explanation. The King wanted to keep Miss Winter because he liked her and was impressed by her work with Prince Carol. He told his brother as much and, when the dismissal became inevitable, admitted, 'I could not hold on to her. Missy, and especially her mother, who in every way is an insane and violent woman, would hear nothing of it.'[66]

The King did reserve the right to appoint Saxton Winter's successor. Anne Louisa Ffolliott, whom he chose, was not Irish as the Crown Princess believed. Her family came from Bethnal Green where she was born, eldest of the nine children of William Folliott, a fabric designer (the double 'f' spelling was adopted by Anne and her younger sister Katherine, another governess, presumably because it looked good). Like Margaret Alison at Berck-Plage, Anne Ffolliott had the calming temperament the situation needed: 'if anyone can be a comfort to everyone', the Queen wrote, 'it is certainly Miss Ffolliott, with her gentle, tender ways and deep understanding. She seems to love that child already.'[67] She proved acceptable to everyone, even little Carol, who had responded to the imminent loss of Saxton Winter with horror. 'He was in utter despair, when he heard that Miss Winter was going to leave him, he rolled on the floor, he screamed, he declared he would go with her, it was really dreadful.'[68]

The child was the most pathetic figure in the whole affair and only Queen Elisabeth seemed to think of his needs. In the midst of all the scandals, demands, accusations and recriminations, an excellent governess had been doing the job she was paid for and it showed in the changes in Carol himself and in his attachment to her. 'He is a very bright and quick child,' the Queen wrote. 'At least, he has become so, in the hands of Miss Winter. He was so terrorised before, that he never spoke and dared not express a wish!'[69] In April she, the King and the Crown Prince, took the little boy to Abbazia on the gulf of the Adriatic with the two governesses, for Miss Winter to complete the handover to her successor. Once she had gone, the Crown Princess would rejoin the family and the whole party return to Romania. For Saxton Winter it was the end of a tortuous episode in an otherwise distinguished career. Echoing almost precisely the words Kate Fox had used at the moment of her dismissal, Queen Elisabeth said of Saxton Winter, 'Her only crime was her being deeply devoted to my family, beloved by cousins, nephews, and nieces.'[70]

NINE

'Like a Poor Little Sparrow'

LIFE AT COURT

During my first few months at the Court I lived in deadly terror of committing a breach of etiquette. It seemed to me I was always doing something I ought not to do, or leaving something undone which I ought to do, or else being entirely at a loss as to what I should do. It did not seem safe to copy the ladies in everything. It was like an army – each one had her particular position assigned to her. . . . To say that I was horribly home-sick at times is to draw it mildly. I longed for the free-and-easy life of my English home, and though I knew I had been very lucky to get this appointment at the German Court, yet I sometimes felt that I simply could not bear it any longer. Apart from the intricacies of precedence and the rigid ceremonial which enveloped one's whole life, one was so restricted it almost seemed like living in a prison.[1]

Ethel Howard was both awed and frustrated by her experience of life at the German Court. It was a serious business; or at least, the inhabitants took it very seriously indeed. Believing that the grandeur of their surroundings was so overwhelming that a newcomer might be temporarily deranged, Berlin Court officials gave Ethel rooms in the visitors' wing of the palace at first to provide a gentle entry to their world. 'I was inwardly rather amused at this,' she said, but she was soon to discover that they had their reasons. The German housemaid assigned to her was also new to the palace. Ethel was not sure how to react when the woman 'suddenly began to kiss my feet very vigorously, tickling them horribly as she did so'. But English governesses were renowned for their coolness under fire: 'I thought her manner rather strange,' Ethel remembered, 'but put her action down to some curious German custom of which I was ignorant.' A few days later a different maid reported to her room, 'and I was informed that the foot-worshipper had been discharged as temporarily insane'.[2] So it did, after all, prove to be quite an introduction.

The daily life of a royal Court was played out on a scale that could not help but make a newcomer feel out of place. Anna Bicknell, on her first day at the Tuileries, found her presence required almost immediately at a family meal more imposing than anything she had ever known. 'The large, handsome dining-room, where the numerous members of the family took their seats,' she said, 'the servants, in and out of livery, the display of plate, and all the ceremony of a formal dinner party . . . made me feel more than ever like a poor little sparrow which had strayed alone into an aviary of tropical birds.'[3]

To survive in this rarefied and at times almost surreal environment, it was important to learn the ways of the Court very quickly. First, there was a correct form of greeting for everyone you might meet. For ladies, mastery of the various degrees of curtsy was all-important. 'You may well ask how I can keep up with all the grandeur,' May T told her mother soon after arriving at Laxenburg, Emperor Franz Josef's summer palace outside Vienna, in 1895. 'At first when I came here I did not know in the least what to do, so I kissed the Archduchess' hands and made my court curtsies as best it seemed to me. Not one of the ladies told me how to comport myself, nor showed me anything. However, it did all right, and everyone said, "you are so natural!" I took it all as a matter of course and as if I had been used to it all my life!!!'[4] But May was also coached by Erzsi, her pupil. 'She tries to help me and tell me what to do. She has taught me all my curtsies, and when to bow. "This for Grandpapa – this for Mamma, and this for me!" And it is very quaint to see her watch me. . . . Of course, none of the other ladies knows that she does this, and she loves the secret.'[5]

But mastering the forms of greeting – the curtsy, the bow – was only the beginning. You still had to know who the people around you were and what position they occupied in the hierarchy, and only instant recognition of each and every person could save you from some awful breach of etiquette. First came the royalties themselves, usually living in large extended families of several generations and with a constant procession of royal visitors, all of whom would be more or less related. Then there were the members of the Court and members of visiting suites – many of whom were also titled and all of whom held some form of office and had some official function to perform. In European Courts the English governess ranked on a level with the junior ladies-in-waiting and was sometimes expected to deputise for them. Below members of the Court came the servants – including the English nurse, though her intimate connection to the family tended to set her in a class apart.

The Court could be a very gossipy world. It was often plagued by intrigue and rivalries, particularly over who gained the royal ear and was seen to be in favour. Maria Graham lost the position she had made for herself in Brazil after a year because her English dress and English ways, her independence of mind and manner and the friendship shown to her by the Empress Leopoldina had so angered the Court that its members conspired against her, led by the most senior lady. Pestered constantly by grumbles against Maria, the Emperor ordered her confined to her rooms except during lessons. This Maria would not accept, and her letter of resignation, composed with the Empress's help, made it plain that she knew where the real problem lay: 'As to those Ladies who have invented so many falsehoods concerning me,' she wrote, 'I forgive them and pray Your Majesty may never find reason to have listened too eagerly to their complaints.'⁶ Maria left the palace of San Cristovao on 10 October 1824, ignoring a last-minute change of heart from His Imperial Majesty and riding to Rio in his personal carriage, the hated ladies having tried to force her to leave on foot.

Almost a century later, Hilda Maybury recorded a very scathing view of the sort of people she encountered at the Court in Oldenburg, saying that they were 'invariably of two categories – either they are stray members of some once distinguished but now decayed family, or else they are people with talent but no enterprise who have seized Royal favour as the line of least resistance, and have been content to hang on to grandeur as dependents rather than face the world on their own merits.'⁷ But Ethel Howard took a kinder view. Though she recognised the strange limitations of a life devoted entirely to precedence and dress, and to the support of a very unpredictable sovereign, she was happy to concede that in Berlin, 'one and all were exceedingly kind to me. Had it not been for them I should never have been able to grope my way through the intricate maze which the routine of the Court presented to me, ignorant as I was of its language, etiquette and customs.'⁸

In Ethel's case the word 'grope' was particularly apt. She was extremely short-sighted and this made Court life difficult for her and led to all sorts of trouble. For her the resident royalties, visiting princes and princesses, ladies in gala dress, gentlemen in uniform and liveried servants, blended into one colourful mass – and there was no question of wearing glasses. In Berlin at least, looking at royalty through glass was completely forbidden. Once, Ethel mistook the children's uncle, Duke Ernst Günther of Schleswig-Holstein, for a liveried servant who had been failing in his duty to wash the young Princes' hands before meals. There had been comments on Prince Oskar's grubby hands and Ethel was not pleased with the servant. She told him – and showed him – precisely how the washing should be done, ignoring the children's giggles, and did not discover her mistake until later, when she was summoned away to be introduced to the Duke. 'Imagine my consternation', she said, 'when this latter informed me that he needed no introduction, as I had kindly given him a very useful lesson before luncheon on the subject of hand-washing.'[9]

But this was as nothing to the moment when she failed to give proper acknowledgement to the Kaiser himself at army manoeuvres – in full view of his loyal subjects. It was Ethel's first appearance with the children at an outdoor event and she mistook the All-Highest for one of his officers who had threatened to make her laugh while on duty. She was curt, to put the offender in his place. Summoned afterwards to appear before the Mistress of the Robes, for all the world like a naughty schoolgirl, Ethel explained her problem and was told to send the Kaiser a letter of apology. In response she received a written instruction to carry lorgnettes on all State occasions.[10] This was a sensible concession – even an obvious one – but it only ensured that she would not mistake the Kaiser himself again. Etiquette was unbending and though 'the Kaiserin also allowed me to look at her through glass . . . she could not give me power to do so to all these Princes and Princesses; there would have had to be a public declaration each time'.[11] So, as far as all other royalties were concerned, Ethel was still obliged to squint, curtsy and hope for the best.

The etiquette that forbade the wearing of glasses seems absurd now, and even in the 1890s it may not have applied at Courts other than Berlin. But Court dress was a nightmare to royal governesses everywhere. White kid gloves seem to have been the first essential for ladies in Courts across Europe. May T was officially reprimanded for forgetting hers at an informal celebration in 1895. For her first Christmas in Vienna, on being told that she was allowed to choose presents to the value of about £6, she put fifteen pairs of kid gloves on her list; 'we use so enormously many white ones here,' she told her mother. (The £6 also bought eighteen white handkerchiefs!)[12] Then, to go with the gloves, you needed a whole wardrobe of costumes for particular occasions: 'For luncheon and dinner we had to have dresses with long trains, the bodices of which were tight and boned severely along every seam. How hot and uncomfortable they were!' Anne Topham remembered. 'No wonder the ladies of the Court moved with slow "dignity" and were inclined to be stout.'[13] Then there was 'walking out' dress, 'calling costume' and so on, and everything had to be replicated in black for the many occasions when mourning was required.

Nor was it wise to rely on having only one of each type of outfit. For her first formal invitation to dine with the imperial couple, Ethel Howard chose to wear her only dress with a Court train; 'the colour was eau-de-nil and it was the best and richest frock I had,' she said. 'To my dismay, I suddenly found out that the Kaiserin had selected a dress of that particular shade to wear at the dinner.' Etiquette made the wearing of Ethel's dress unthinkable and she was forced to adapt another in just a few hours of frantic needlework. She did pay tribute to the improvement this brought both to her sewing skills and to her sense of style, but it was trying on the nerves just the same.[14] For each royal birthday or visit a new silk dress was essential and any attempt to slide round the rules would surely be noticed and remarked on. Ethel thought she got away with it in her favourite silk dress until one of the children said, 'Papa calls that dress "Miss Howard's uniform".'[15] 'My letters home contained many plaintive appeals to my mother and sisters to go and buy me clothes in the London shops and to send them out at once,' she remembered. 'I spent much money on telegrams to the same effect, when the urgency of the moment required; but try as I would, I never seemed to have an appropriate dress for the occasion.'[16]

The expense of all this for a young woman from an ordinary home with only a very modest salary was crippling, but the rules were made and enforced by women who had never faced anxieties about money and had no conception of them. Anna Bicknell described the extravagant style of the French Court, particularly at Compiègne, where 'It was understood that no dress could be worn more than once; for a week's stay it was usual, therefore, to take fifteen dresses, seven of which were intended for the evening, and consequently must be of the most expensive kind.'[17] It did no good to say that you could not attend a particular event because you did not have the appropriate dress or accessory. You simply had to find it, and it must have been hard to resist the enticements of the local dress shops and fashion houses that offered free outfits in return for a recommendation. This was a common practice, but it was absolutely forbidden.

Jewellery only added to the burden. In Berlin in the 1890s brooches had to be worn during the day and necklaces or pendants in the evening: a lady could be dismissed from the dinner table for not wearing the appropriate jewels. At one Court ball Ethel wore a necklace of imitation pearls, made of Venetian glass, and happened to mentioned this to one of the officers who asked her about them. The word spread. Her next invitation card carried a handwritten instruction that pearls must be worn, and only real pearls would be acceptable. Fans also were compulsory at times. Once, stopped on her way to luncheon by the Mistress of the Robes who told her the Court had gone into mourning, Ethel rushed back to her room, threw on a black dress and hurried down with only minutes to spare. One of the ladies stopped her in the doorway, saying, 'Are you mad?' and pointing to what Ethel thought was her fan. 'I looked at my right hand,' Ethel said, 'and to my consternation, found that I was holding not my fan, but my curling tongs. . . . Was ever anything so quickly hidden out of sight, I wonder?'[18]

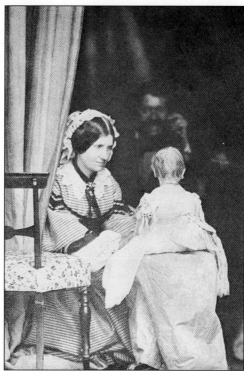

Above, left: Emma Hobbs with Princess Charlotte of Prussia, 1860. *Right:* Mary Anne Thurston coaxing Princess Beatrice, May 1858.

Below, left: The second Mrs Clark and Princess Victoria of Hesse, Windsor Castle, 20 April 1863. *Right:* Nurses Marjorie (standing) and Susan Chapman with (left to right) Princesses Margaret and Patricia of Connaught, Princes Alexander of Battenberg, Waldemar of Prussia, and Leopold of Battenberg (above), Princess Ena of Battenberg and Prince Arthur of Connaught, Balmoral, May 1890.

Above, left: Elizabeth Francklin with Grand Duchess Olga Alexandrovna of Russia, 1885/6. *Right:* Frances Fry, Grand Duchess Maria Pavlovna and Grand Duke Dmitri Pavlovich, mid-1890s.

Margaretta Eagar (behind, left), Mary Ann Orchard (in black) and a nursery maid with Grand Duchesses Olga, Tatiana and Maria of Russia, 1900.

Above, left: Margaretta Eagar with her four little Grand Duchesses (left to right) Tatiana, Anastasia, Olga and Maria, at Livadia in 1902. *Right:* Their cousin Princess Elisabeth of Hesse and her father Grand Duke Ernst Ludwig, 1903.

Below, left: Lilian Wilson with 'Georgie', the Hereditary Grand Duke Georg Donatus of Hesse, 1908. *Right:* Norlander Lilian Eadie holding 'Lu', Prince Ludwig of Hesse, 1909.

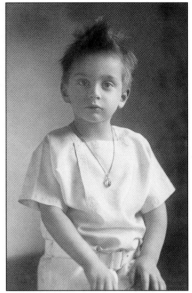

Above, left: 'Georgie' and 'Lu' of Hesse outside the playhouse at Wolfsgarten, built for their sister Elisabeth. *Right:* Lilian Brimble's little Prince 'Lulu', Louis Ferdinand of Prussia.

Elizabeth St John and Anne Stainton's children, Prince Michael of Romania (*below, right*), and Princes Moritz and Heinrich of Hesse-Cassel (*left*), 1927.

Below, left: 'Georgie' and 'Lu' with their toys.

Above, left: Charlotte 'Lalla' Bill (sitting) and a nursery maid with Princess Mary and Prince Henry of York, 1902. *Right:* Norlander Beatrice Halls, in uniform, and Prince Berthold of Baden, 1908.

Miss Brompton (right) and another lady with the Italian royal children (left to right) Princess Mafalda, Princess Jolanda, Prince Umberto, 1906.

Above: Saxton Winter. *Right:* Her pupil, Queen Wilhelmina of the Netherlands in 1892.

Below, left: 'Erzsi', Archduchess Elisabeth Marie of Austria, *c.* 1892. *Right:* Erzsi's governess, May T.

Nellie Ryan's Archduke, Karl Stefan of Austria, his wife Archduchess Maria Theresa and their children (left to right) Renata, Leo Karl, Wilhelm, Eleonora, Karl Albrecht and Mechtildis, 1895.

Below, left: The sons of Kaiser Wilhelm II: from the top, left to right, Princes Wilhelm, Joachim and Eitel Friedrich, Adalbert, Oskar and August Wilhelm, 1895. *Right:* Ada Leslie, governess to the three eldest Princes from 1886–7/8.

Above, left: Mary Ann Orchard holding Princess Alix of Hesse, 1873/4. *Right:* Prince Friedrich Wilhelm, 'Fritzie', of Hesse, with his sisters Victoria (left) and Elisabeth, April 1873.

'Fritzie's' deathbed, from the album his mother Princess Alice made for Mary Ann Orchard, with the verse in her own handwriting, May 1873.

Above, left: Lalla Bill's first royal charges, Princes Edward and Albert and Princess Mary of York, 1899. *Right:* Lalla Bill and Prince John, *c.* 1912.

Below, left: Prince's John's playmate, Winifred Thomas, with her father Frederick Thomas at the time of his visit to Sandringham, *c.* 1916. *Right:* One of the last signed photographs Prince John gave Winifred, 1918.

Above, left: Beatrice Todd's photograph of Princes Sigismund, Waldemar and Heinrich of Prussia, January 1904. *Right:* Beatrice herself (still wearing her Norland badge) in retirement with her nephew Jack and a friend.

Below, left: Eliza Creak and Princess Alice of Albany, March 1884. *Right:* Helene, Duchess of Albany with her children Alice and Charles Edward, 'Charlie', *c.* 1889.

Above, left: The children of King Alfonso XIII and Queen Ena of Spain: (left to right) Don Juan, Don Jaime, Infanta Maria Cristina, Alfonso, Prince of the Asturias, Don Gonzalo, Infanta Beatriz, in about 1919, when Annie Dutton became their English teacher. *Right*: Norlander Irene Collenette and Prince Alvaro of Orleans-Borbón at the Rosenau, Coburg, September 1913.

Below, left: Crown Princess Marie of Romania, her son Carol and daughter Elizaveta, *c.* 1897. *Right*: The Crown Princess's beloved 'Nana' Green with Elizaveta (right) and the next daughter, Marie, *c.* 1902.

Above, left: Kate Fox with Princesses Olga and Elizabeth of Greece, 1904. *Right:* Emily Roose and Princesses Margarita and Theodora of Greece, 1906.

Below, left: Marian Burgess's charges, Princess Marie (right) and Kira of Russia, 1912. *Right:* Margaret Alison (in Norland uniform) with Princesses Olga, Marina and Elizabeth, *c.* 1916.

Above, left: Marian Burgess and Prince Vladimir Kirillovich of Russia in Finland in the summer of 1920. *Right:* Irene Collenette with Prince Vladimir.

'Emily and her 4 Babys, St Moritz, Sep. 10th, 1917': Emily Roose, 'Roosie', with, from the left, Princesses Margarita, Sophie, Cecile and Theodora.

Above, left: Prince Tadashige Shimadzu as a child. *Right:* Tadashige as Ethel Howard knew him (centre) and his brothers (left to right) Akinoshin, Tomijiro, Junnosuke and Yonosuke.

Below, left: Khedive Ismael Pacha of Egypt with his son, Emmeline Lott's pupil the Grand Pacha Ibrahim. *Right:* Ellen Chennells' pupil Princess Zeyneb, the Khedive's daughter.

Above, left: Anna Leonowens in later life. *Right:* Norland nurse Anne Chermside.

Rosalind Ramirez and King Faisal II of Iraq on Naval Hospital Beach, Alexandria, September 1944.

Above: Kathleen Wanstall's photograph of the Princess of Stolberg-Wernigerode with her children, Ludwig Christian and Anne-Marie, 1913. *Right:* 'Old May' Hull in a bath chair given to her by Queen Victoria, 1887.

Below, left: Lalla Bill aged 76 in September 1951, from Queen Mary's album. *Right:* Summer 1947: Kate Fox in retirement with her two grown-up Princesses, Elizabeth of Toerring-Jettenbach (centre right) and Marina, Duchess of Kent; also Princess Alexandra and Prince Michael of Kent.

There was sometimes an intrusiveness to the rules that added insult to the financial strain they imposed. Hilda Maybury recalled being told to wear her hair in a particular style, 'high above the forehead and neatly brushed back over a pad', because the Grand Duke of Oldenburg's grown-up daughter was expected on a visit and 'it would be incorrect for me to have a coiffure dissimilar to hers in any way'.[19] And Ethel – who seems to have suffered more from the oppressive attentions of her Court than anyone – was taken to task by the Kaiserin at their first meeting simply for looking too young. In her early twenties and with a taste for separates – coat, skirt and blouse – and for the sailor hats and boaters that were fashionable then for active young women, Ethel was forced to model herself on the more staid Court ladies, wearing one-piece dresses and bonnets to add to her age: 'my greatest bugbear from beginning to end,' she said, 'was that of dress.'[20]

But Berlin was renowned for the number and scope of its rules and the humourless way in which they were enforced. Princesses came under as fierce a discipline there as governesses for what they wore, where they went and what they did. Edith Keen, who was employed as a governess-companion to the Kaiserin's teenage niece, Princess Margarete of Prussia, in 1909, described how the Princess was reprimanded in writing by the Kaiser for riding without a groom, and for attending a ball without an approved chaperone. And Ethel gained a vivid insight into the discipline required of royalty when she was deputed to attend on a visiting Princess at the opening of a bazaar. The duty done, they climbed into their carriage and drove away and all the while the Princess smiled and waved to the crowds. For some minutes Ethel had no idea that anything was wrong; then she noticed a bloodstain spreading over the carriage mat. The Princess's fingers were trapped in the door. She must have been in agony but she had somehow suppressed her pain for fear of disrupting the event.

So perhaps it should not be too great a surprise that very high standards were also expected of the young women who worked at the Court. This was a world where reputation mattered. On social outings in their free time, particularly at night, most young governesses were expected to have an approved chaperone. Nellie Ryan, in the household of Archduke Karl Stefan, found herself in a difficult situation one night at his summer residence of Podjavori, on Lussin island in the Adriatic. She had been out to a ball at the local hotel and her chaperone left her at the gate, beyond which only members of the Court were allowed. Normally there would have been several courtiers returning through the park but this night Nellie found herself with one companion only – a young Polish officer who attended one of the archdukes.

That in itself would have been compromising if anyone had seen them, but when they reached the side door giving access to her part of the building Nellie found that she had also lost her key.

It was after three in the morning. The only bell was at the main entrance and to ring it would create an uproar and almost certainly rouse the family. Nellie decided to return to the hotel and hope that the night porter would find some way to help her. But she needed to be on her own and the officer would not leave her. They retraced their steps through the park together and had almost reached the gate when they heard someone coming: 'Thinking, I suppose, to shield me,' Nellie remembered, 'my companion caught hold of my arm and drew me behind some projecting rocks, saying it was perhaps wiser to let the oncomers pass without seeing us. But alas, it was too late! As the figures of the two men reached our temporary hiding-place, the well-known voice of the chaplain called out: "Whoever is in hiding, I am afraid you were seen."'

Nellie's career at Court might have ended that night. The chaplain was a humourless man who was likely to interpret the incident in the worst possible way. But she was fortunate in his companion. The Archduke's Lord Chamberlain, Admiral Count Chorinsky, was both quick-thinking and gallant and had saved her from other tricky situations in the past. Whatever he thought he had stumbled into this time – whether, indeed, more had been going on than Nellie Ryan admitted in her later memoirs, which make no secret of her fondness for the Polish officer – the Count took control immediately. Before Nellie had a chance to speak he had sent the officer away to his quarters and was explaining to the chaplain that he himself had told her to wait by the gate so that he could escort her home. He put the couple's clumsy attempt to hide down to an English practical joke and, as the chaplain left them on reaching his own door, called out 'You mustn't give me away . . . for keeping the Miss waiting about so long.'

It was only now, when they were alone, that the Count demanded an explanation. Nellie was almost in tears as she told him, and the missing key turned out to be as much of a problem to him as it was to her. The Count lived in a separate house. He was willing to give Nellie shelter but if she was not in her room when the household awoke a scandal could not be averted. It was his valet who came to the rescue with a pass key he sometimes used in the course of his duties. The door was opened, Nellie escaped to her room, and nothing was ever said on the matter again. But she had had a very close call.[21]

All Court ladies faced rules about where they could go, even in their free time, and who they could go with. Margaretta Eagar, in St Petersburg, had always to be accompanied by a policeman when going about in the city and it was said by other governesses there that she was not allowed to join the women's club that met at the English Church. Even modes of transport came under restriction. Ethel Howard was entitled to use a carriage only when she was on duty. She relished these working drives, with the children or on official errands, for the sense of power they gave her: the city traffic had to clear a path for royal carriages and those who failed to move out of the way quickly were subject to on-the-spot fines. But in her free time no carriage was permitted and, as public transport was also forbidden, she had no option but to walk. This could be a very public business. Ethel found the smart shops on Berlin's Unter-den-Linden 'too fascinating for words', but she did not dare to go shopping there often, 'as I would meet so many officers that I knew, and it much embarrassed me to be so constantly saluted. I seemed to be kept under lock and key'.[22]

Sometimes the rules had more to do with the safety of the Court than the reputation of its members. The restrictions placed on Margaretta's movements were probably designed as much for the imperial family's protection as for her own. There was always a fear that members of the Court might, in innocent conversation, betray some detail that would be useful to a terrorist. All the surviving accounts suggest that the women employed to work with royal children – particularly the English ones overseas – were recognised in the street and regarded with curiosity. Articles were written about them in newspapers; much of this was innocent and done simply to satisfy public interest. Ethel described how the editors of society journals 'tempted one to give anecdotes and details of Court life'.[23] But it was as well to be careful. Her parents warned her before she left England that she must not give details about the Court in letters home, as mail was liable to be opened and censored. Ethel believed the warnings, but May T, responding to a similar caution from her mother, was far more bullish: 'it is simply *absurd* to say anyone would *dare* open our letters,' she said. 'Why, we are the first people in the country and far above all police, etc. You do not know what a position this is, or you would never believe this nonsense told you about opening letters.'[24]

And gaining access to palaces could pose all manner of problems, even for the residents. At Podjavori Nellie Ryan was allowed outside with a key, but that was a holiday villa where life was more relaxed. In the grander palaces of Europe the entrance doors were guarded night and day and access given only to those who could show the appropriate pass. Anna Bicknell described the fierce discipline governing entry to the Tuileries, where the gates were closed at midnight; 'any one returning after that hour was noted by the officer in command, and reported the next morning'. Very early in her service she went outside – with permission – to an evening party and was brought back shortly after the fateful hour. She was reported to her employer who took her to task for her lateness the next morning. He was amused, not angry, but she had learned her lesson just the same: 'There was . . . so much trouble and ceremony attending the opening of the gates, after any such Cinderella mishap, that I soon gave up all evening parties.'[25]

In Berlin all members of the Court carried a colour-coded pass – the *einlasskarte* – which alerted the guards both to the status of the bearer and the buildings to which he or she might be admitted. These were vital documents. Anne Topham would have found herself in a police cell on one occasion if she had not had her *einlasskarte* in her purse. It happened at a time of civil unrest from left-wing groups, whose activities Anne thought far less alarming than the reaction of the Berlin police. 'They panicked', she said, 'and smote unoffending citizens on the heads with their truncheons.' So it was not pleasant to find a policeman seizing her by the arm one day as she returned from a shopping trip – presumably because she was crossing the square in front of the palace laden with packages. She produced her *einlasskarte*: 'the policeman let go and apologized when I showed it. I told him he was a fool, and he apologized more humbly than before.'[26]

But sometimes even the *einlasskarte* was not enough. Lilian Brimble was carrying hers one night when she returned to Berlin's Marmor Palais from a visit to the theatre. She brandished it for the sentries on the gate and for the first sentry beside the building, but by the time she reached her own entrance, the pass had slipped to the bottom of her bag, 'and the sentry had to hold my fan and wisp of a handkerchief while I extricated the little green card and held it out for his inspection'. He nodded her on and continued his rounds, but when he came back she was still outside, standing on the steps, having failed completely in her attempts to rouse someone to open the door. So she grabbed the sentry. 'I made him come round with me to the playroom windows,' she said, 'and told him to knock on the pane with his gun.' This proved something of a shock to the nursery attendant who was waiting up for Lilian, but at least it got her in, and the sentry 'seemed quite glad to have had a little variety in his monotonous round'.[27]

In Russia, the most security conscious of monarchies, the sentries often proved an impenetrable barrier even for those who had every right to pass them by. Margaretta Eagar had constant problems with sentries, made worse because she spoke no Russian. Even arrangements made by the Tsaritsa could fall foul of these men and their orders. One Cossack refused to let her through to the Great Palace at Peterhof in the summer of 1899, though she was expected there to assist at the christening of the infant Grand Duchess Maria. Thinking that perhaps her carriage had gone as far as was permitted, she climbed out and tried to pass by on foot, 'But no! he lowered his bayonet and blocked the way. There I stood in my white dress in the road, with the assembled crowd gazing at me.' She was rescued from her predicament by an officer she recognised who spoke French, and understood her explanation. He took her past the guard and into the palace church – but after the long ceremony the guards would not allow her out again. She had no choice but to make her way through the State rooms of the palace, an apparently endless succession of glittering halls where she lost herself completely, missed her carriage, and did not finally find her way back to the imperial villa in the Alexandria Park until some seven hours after she left, by which time she was very hot, very tired and very hungry.

Sometimes even members of the imperial family encountered the same difficulty. Once the Tsaritsa asked Margaretta to slip into the family's private chapel by a side door during a service, in case the children became restless. The guard on the side door would not let her through, but as she tried to reason with him one of the Grand Dukes came by and recognised her. He told the sentry to let her pass. The sentry refused. The Grand Duke told the sentry who he was: the reply must have come as a something of a shock to such privileged ears. 'I don't care if you are the Emperor himself.' The man said he had been ordered into the position by his corporal, 'and without his permission I shall not allow anyone to pass through this door.' And that was his final word, so there was nothing for it but to fetch the corporal.[28]

Security at this level was bound to be frustrating. Anna Bicknell described how every movement of every inhabitant of the Tuileries was watched not only by sentries but by plain-clothed detectives who stood in every corridor, gathered in groups in doorways, and even followed members of the Court outside: 'The ladies of the palace were often surprised to receive bows in the street from unknown persons, who also would spring forward to help them in any difficulty; on such occasions the rule was to receive their advances most graciously. They were not men whom it would have been prudent to offend.'[29] But there were good reasons to be vigilant. The nineteenth century saw a steady rise in political violence and royal families were a prominent target; many nurses and governesses gained experience of this. Anna was in the Tuileries one January night in 1858 when Felice Orsini threw three bombs under the Emperor's carriage outside the Opera. The imperial couple were unhurt but 10 people died and 156 were injured by the blast, which sent a shock wave through Paris. A few days later, Anna was asked to interpret a letter written in English to the Empress: it contained a warning of further assassination attempts in the cause of Italian independence.

The high profile of royalty also attracted all manner of damaged and dangerous individuals. In England in the 1840s Prince Albert took overall charge of the security of his children's nurseries and kept the most important key in his own hands. 'The last thing we did before bedtime was to visit the access to the children's apartments,' Lady Lyttelton told her daughter, 'to satisfy ourselves that all was safe. And the various turns and locks and guardrooms, and the various intense precautions, suggesting the most hideous dangers, which I fear are not altogether imaginary, made one shudder! . . . Threatening letters of the most horrid kind (probably written by mad people), aimed directly at *the children*, are frequently received.'[30]

A generation later, the Crown Princess's nurseries in Berlin seemed particularly prone to upsetting intrusions. In the spring of 1868, when Emma Hobbs was head nurse, a man broke into the nursery during the night, 'flung some of the nursery-maid's clothes about, had a scuffle with one of the footmen who prevented his getting into Ditta's room. Vicky woke in a great fright at the noise – it was between twelve and one – and screamed at the top of her voice', the Crown Princess told her mother.[31] And just two years after this, the under-nurse Catherine Anne Hawes had to deal with something even more threatening – and terrifying – when she was driving out with the children and a man grabbed the reins of the carriage, forcing it to stop. He jumped in 'and sat down on Mrs Hawes's lap. The children were soon got out', the Crown Princess wrote, 'but the man would not leave the carriage and bit the footman's hand. However he was soon marched off in safety. . . . Of course the poor nurses were horribly frightened.'[32]

So life at Court could pose real physical danger. Both Lilian Brimble and the mysterious 'Miss B.', who wrote an anonymous account of her service in the household of a German prince, had the experience of a suspect parcel bomb arriving in the nursery addressed to one of the children. In both cases the parcel proved harmless – Lilian described how she had handed hers to a footman with strict instructions that he was to have a bucket of water handy when he examined it. 'The man returned with a face from which he vainly tried to banish all trace of expression,' she said, 'and gravely handed me a square pink box, from which a shock-headed golliwog Jack-in-the-Box sprang out as I opened it' – but the story might have had a very different ending.[33]

The life could be dangerous; it was difficult and demanding, frustrating too – why did anyone want to do it? The answer is that service at Court provided an opportunity for women from very ordinary backgrounds to experience a lifestyle and inhabit a world which otherwise they could only have dreamed of, or read about in those very same society journals that came to them for insights and anecdotes when they rubbed shoulders with the great. Like Ethel Howard, sweeping down the Berlin streets in the royal carriage while other people were hustled out of the way, or May T proudly telling her mother, 'I have been given an apartment in the Palace in Vienna, the first English woman who has received this honour! . . . I have only one large room, an antechamber and small kitchen – really a very poor apartment; but the honour is great, as we live with the Emperor in the same Palace'; if you worked for royalty you felt that you *were* somebody, and were generally treated with more respect, as nurse or governess, than you could have expected in ordinary life.[34]

Several British women must have enjoyed the experience of visiting their own country with their foreign employers and staying at Windsor, Balmoral or Osborne as a guest of Queen Victoria. That really was something to write home about. Ada Leslie had the experience twice: first, in 1887 for the Queen's Jubilee, then again in the following November, travelling with the recently widowed Kaiserin Friedrich. She wrote to her cousin from Windsor Castle:

You will, of course, have seen by the newspapers days ago that we have arrived in England. . . . It was my first voyage in the 'Victoria and Albert'. Last year I crossed in the royal yacht 'Osborne', the latter is smaller than the former, else it's much the same. Both are perfectly fitted according to the newest ideas. . . . Here we are very comfortably lodged only we found the rooms in the castle very small after the great barrack-like German castles, but these are in many ways much more comfortable. You cannot imagine how pleased I am to be able to sit beside an English fire again after being accustomed to the closed stoves in Germany. I have already been over many royal apartments & staterooms here and have arrived at the conclusion that although the Germans are very rich in castles & royal palaces yet there is nothing in the whole Empire to compare with Windsor Castle. We go to Osborne with the Queen & Royal family for Christmas, & in January, it's said, on a visit to the Prince & Princess of Wales at Sandringham.[35]

A month later she was writing from Osborne where the fresh air, the sea and the good weather had quite taken away the sense that Christmas was near, 'save that there is a great commotion & feeling of Christmas in the house'. She was pleased to report on Queen Victoria, 'so good & nice but so short. Her Majesty's photographs always give one the idea that she is very much taller than she really is', she said and, despite her new-found dignity as a lady-in-waiting, she was able to take a professional interest in the royal grandchildren. 'One of my greatest pleasures in Windsor was, & here is, visiting the Nurseries, the little Prince Alexander & the Princess Victoria of Battenberg are the sweetest little things you can imagine. The little Prince is two & the little Princess rather more than a year. If I possibly can I will get you a photograph of them' – which gives an idea of how much freedom was allowed to the visiting ladies.[36]

In the spring of 1895 Saxton Winter accompanied the two Queens of the Netherlands to Windsor. Queen Wilhelmina was then in her early teens; was it genuine curiosity or simply tact that made her reply, when Queen Victoria asked if there was anything she would particularly like, that she wanted to hear the bagpipes? Whichever it was, the Queen must have been highly delighted and wasted no time in arranging for the pipers of the Scots Guards to play 'their most patriotic airs and marches' under the window. According to Saxton Winter, Wilhelmina 'was evidently much impressed with the weirdness of the performance, and though she expressed herself as being delighted, I never quite made out whether the originality of the instruments or the quaintness of their sounds pleased her more'. The young Queen did make one other request. She was curious to know what the Court function known as a 'Drawing-Room' was all about. One was due to be held during the visit and, though etiquette made it impossible for the young Queen and her mother to attend, Queen Victoria satisfied their curiosity by allowing them, and Miss Winter, to watch unobserved from the slightly opened doorway of the private apartments with some of the younger Princesses.[37]

Functions like 'Drawing-Rooms' and celebrations of all kinds were an integral part of the routine of royal Courts. Some focused on milestones in the life of the resident royal family: the christenings and birthdays, weddings, anniversaries and funerals. A new birth always created great excitement. 'I expect you saw the announcement of the birth of another Prince in the newspaper,' Ada Leslie told her cousin in the spring of 1887. 'It gave great satisfaction throughout the country and here the town was gaily decorated on January 29th – only two days after the Prince's birthday. A salute of 71 guns was fired at midday and do you know that a German Prince's income commences from the day of his birth? A great pity it's not so with all children, is it not?'[38] The gun salute was a traditional way of alerting the public to a royal birth, with a much longer salute for a prince: 'when the cannon from the Lustgarten near by thundered forth their salutes, the enthusiasm of the populace knew no bounds,' Lilian Brimble noted in describing the birth of the Crown Prince's fourth son, Prince Friedrich, a generation later. 'The whole

"Platz" in front of the Kronprinzen Palais was thronged with a dense mass of people, and all day long a steady stream of representative persons came to inscribe their names in the visitor's book.'[39]

Royal christenings could be spectacular events, attended by an exotic mix of visitors to the Court. For Margaretta at Peterhof – having once found her way past the Cossack sentry – the christening of Maria Nikolaevna was a carnival of colour, with the younger Court ladies in their 'scarlet velvet trains embroidered in gold, with petticoats of white satin', the elder in green and gold; the Roman Catholic Cardinal 'with his red hat and soutane', the Lutheran prelate 'wearing a black gown with white ruffles' – both contrasting with the gold-robed Orthodox priests, though these she did not mention – and the diplomatic representatives including the Chinese Ambassador's wife, who 'wore a gorgeous blue-figured silk Kimono, and had a little round blue cap on her head, a red flower over one ear and a white one over the other'. The baby was carried into the palace church on a cloth-of-gold pillow, 'in the full glory of her lace robes lined with pink silk'. In Berlin, the infant Prince Friedrich wore 'the celebrated Hohenzollern baptismal train of silver brocade, 20ft long and very heavy, on which is embroidered the names, and dates of their birth, of each Hohenzollern child of the reigning house'.[40]

Royal birthdays and name-days were always the occasion for great jollity, with flowers being presented by everyone to everyone else, gifts and various types of party and special event, depending on the age and importance of the person. Nellie Ryan described the ceremonies for the birthday of Archduchess Maria Teresa at Podjavori. These began in the morning after Mass, when everyone gathered in the entrance hall, 'carrying small nosegays, and all arrayed in the regulation white kid gloves; then we proceeded in procession to the boudoir of Her Imperial Highness, and offered our congratulations'. First the six children went to their mother in procession to give their flowers and presents – which were usually home-made – and then recited verses, 'each one in a different language'. Then the ladies and gentlemen came forward and, having dealt with the serious business of the day, the rest 'was given over to festivities, a special dinner, and possibly an evening dance'.[41]

In Berlin before the First World War the Kaiser's birthday was one of the highlights of the winter season, 'kept with zeal and earnestness from early morning until night'. The celebrations began very similarly to those at Podjavori, though on a much larger scale, but as the day progressed the events became grander, culminating in special theatrical performances by the very best artists and for invited guests only – including the English governess. Anne Topham described the scene she witnessed one year from her very privileged vantage point in the stage-box. 'The whole house was decorated with wreaths of flowers, and the . . . stalls were filled with the gentlemen of the diplomatic corps, ambassadors and envoys from the remotest parts of the world: Chinese mandarins in yellow silk robes, wearing peacock feathers in their caps, Turks and Egyptians in red fezzes, mingled with the uniforms of every existing army in the world.'[42] Even Court officials might be barred from the occasion if the Kaiser chose not to invite them. One year the birthday concert was held in the palace and Anne described the extraordinary sight of two people, a man followed by a very fat woman, crawling along the floor of the minstrel's gallery. Her first thought was an assassination attempt, but the size and awkwardness of the woman was reassuring. 'She did not look to be of the stuff of which conspirators are made.' Nonetheless, Anne alerted Countess Stolberg, one of the Kaiserin's ladies, who recognised the couple as the wife and son of a palace official. The Countess was outraged, but there was no need for her to act. The Kaiser had also seen and made sure that the son was punished, the mother disgraced, and the father almost lost his job.[43]

May T had her first encounter with the Habsburg Court four years before she was employed there, while she was still teaching Wanda Badeni, the daughter of the Governor of Austrian Poland. The occasion was a royal wedding, of the Archduchess Louise of the Tuscan branch of the Habsburg family and the Crown Prince of Saxony, and the Badenis had permission to stand in the corridor of the Hofburg to watch the procession. 'It was a brilliant sight,' May recorded in her diary, 'the grand corridor of the Hofburg, all a-glitter with crystal chandeliers, the men in gorgeous uniforms and diamond-studded orders, the splendid gowns of the ladies, each with pages to carry her train. It was a scene which I shall always remember, but the thing that impressed me most deeply was that amid all this splendour, all this magnificence, no one, from the Emperor and bride down to the ladies-in-waiting of the Royal suite, looked happy.'[44] She was right. The marriage was an arrangement only and it ended in one of royal Europe's most celebrated scandals, when the bride ran away with her lover.

In October 1889 Ada Leslie, in her new capacity as lady-in-waiting, was on hand to help when a much happier royal wedding was almost blighted by one of those organisational setbacks that can happen to anyone. Princess Sophie of Prussia's veil, which was ordered and probably designed by her mother Kaiserin Friedrich and handmade by a team of 200 German girls – it took them four months – went missing the night before the ceremony. Sending her cousin Pollie one of the official wedding photographs a few months later, Ada takes up the story: 'It somehow got packed into the wrong box', she wrote; 'there was one great big zinc lined box for all the wedding garments packed by the assistants of the dressmaker who had made the wedding dress. When this was opened the night before the wedding, no veil was to be found. The Princess had to be ready the next morning at nine o'clock & the Empress commanded that no one in the palace, beyond the members of her own suite should be told as the Greeks are a very superstitious people. So we made up another veil out of some tulle we had with us & the newspaper correspondent who had travelled with us, received a quiet hint not to say anything about the matter, so scarcely anybody knew. The Princess herself was very glad as she had always wished to wear quite a plain one. I persuaded her to be photographed in the lace one afterwards.'[45] *I persuaded her . . .* that was quite something to be able say, as you showed your family the royal wedding photograph.

Royal weddings in Berlin were celebrated in the evening and the festivities always included a famous ritual, the Torch Dance, in which the bride and groom and their guests processed around one of the great halls of the palace to the light of flaming torches. Anne Topham was invited back to Berlin in May 1913, some four years after her appointment ended, to attend the wedding of her pupil, Princess Viktoria Luise. She watched what would prove to be the last ever Torch Dance from the gallery of the Weissersaal of the Berlin Palace. The band of the Imperial Guard was playing

slow, stately marches . . . old-world tunes that were an echo of past times. The royal ladies were seated with their multicoloured trains spread out in front of them, while rows of red-clad pages stood behind their chairs waiting to advance when the time arrived. From the side entrance of the Saal, stepping in time to the music, came Prince von Fürstenburg, the Marshal of the Court, carrying his wand of office and preceded by a double row of twenty-four pages who bore large torches. In rhythm, they moved once around the room. When the Marshal stopped and bowed to the bride and the bridegroom, the couple at once descended from the slightly raised platform where they sat, and hand in hand, preceded by the torch bearers and with four ladies carrying the bride's train, they moved around the hall in time to the music.

The dance developed slowly, to its own graceful rhythm. Once the couple had made a circuit of the hall they drew in their parents, the bride walking between the two fathers, the groom and mothers following, and so, turn by turn, guests were brought into the dance, the elder and more important first, then the younger, until all had made their circuit and, at a signal from the

Kaiser, the torchbearers left the Weissersaal, followed by the couple and their guests in slow procession. The music and light faded with them and all was left in darkness. 'I cannot express its wonderful fascination,' Anne said, 'its mixture of poetry and romance. There was a lulling monotony of sound, the flicker and smoke of the torches, the dignified movement of the dancers. . . . It had a fairy-tale quality, an aspect of Cinderella.'[46]

There often was an other-worldly aspect to the great ceremonies at Court. Margaretta Eagar described the sight of her Empress, the Tsaritsa Alexandra, dressed for the celebration of the New Year in the Winter Palace. The Tsaritsa wore the Russian Court costume that was designed by the Tsar's great-grandfather from historic Russian folk dress and was worn nowhere else in the world: 'very magnificent she looked in her court dress of white satin with its long train of brocade,' Margaretta wrote, 'seven chains of diamonds round her neck, a girdle of the same sparkling gems round her waist, the ends falling to the hem of her dress. On her head she wore the kokoshnik, the crescent-shaped head-dress, in white brocade, lavishly decorated with large single stone diamonds. A rich lace veil depended from it and hung at the back almost to her knees.' At the height of the Russian winter the halls of the palace were transformed into an exotic garden for the first ball of the season, with 'groups of palms, flowering lilacs and laburnums . . . appearing out of grassy beds in which grew crocuses, daffodils, and other flowering bulbs. Walks covered with carpets to imitate sand ran through the rooms in various directions; electric lamps hung in the trees and tables were set out under their shade.'[47]

The season that began with New Year lasted until Lent, when the balls and parties ended and a more sombre mood descended in preparation for Easter. In Catholic Austria, Holy Week was observed with great solemnity by the Emperor Franz Josef, who spent several hours each day in the Royal Chapel, attended by members of his family and Court, all wearing mourning black until the day itself. On her first Maundy Thursday in the Hofburg, May T noticed twelve old men in black cloaks being led into eight o'clock Mass. She was told 'that these were the twelve selected for the ceremony known as the "Washing of the Feet"'. After breakfast the men were seated in the banqueting hall where the Emperor, 'carrying a golden jug, and attended by Archdukes carrying a golden basin and fine towels, goes to each old man in turn. The Archduke places the basin under the feet of the old man while the Emperor pours the water from the ewer over them. Then another Archduke dries the feet with the towels.' The procession moved to each man in turn while prayers were read, then, when this first ceremony ended, the Emperor served each man with a plate of food to be taken home, and with money.[48] Finally, on the evening of

Easter Saturday, the entire Court assembled in gala dress for the Resurrection service, which began in complete darkness in the Lady Chapel, to the voice of a lone priest reciting prayers, and exploded into a festival of light, colour and music.

Saxton Winter attended the Orthodox Easter services during her troubled appointment at the Romanian Court and described them for Queen Wilhelmina. It was something for which her Protestant background had not prepared her; 'such a curious mixture of solemn ceremony and uncivilized barbarism'. On the evening of Good Friday, the Crown Princess invited her to a service at which they carried lighted candles and walked in procession three times round the outside of the church, '& if the candles kept alight it was a great sign of approaching good luck. Mine was blown out twice so were I superstitious I might be rather uneasy for the future!' The midnight service of Easter Saturday was an altogether more formal affair with the King 'in full state accompanied by a mounted escort & military band. Gentlemen in gala uniforms, ladies in light, elegant morning gowns & bonnets.' Miss Winter described the sumptuous gold and jewelled vestments of the clergy, the procession and the service, which began with prayers outside the church, leading to a moment of climax when, 'The Archbishop then said aloud "Christ is risen" and everyone answered "Yes, he is risen". A rocket was sent up, 101 canon shots fired, the band played, and the procession reformed and entered the church again. Here all was done with the most gorgeous pomp imaginable.'[49]

The following afternoon was given over to an Easter Egg hunt for the royal children; a tradition followed in Courts across Europe. 'The great event of Easter Sunday,' Ethel Howard remembered, 'was the children's egg hunt, instituted by the old Grand Duchess of Baden, and held in the grounds of the Bellevue Palace. Chocolate eggs, sugar eggs, little animals stuffed full of sweets were hidden under the various bushes and trees, and there would be a huge gathering of children belonging to the numerous members of the Royal Family.'[50] Anne Topham was often a spectator at these Easter Egg hunts. Sometimes, she said, the Kaiser insisted on hiding the eggs himself, 'but once he and his adjutants made an unfortunate choice of the porcelain stoves . . . the chocolate eggs melted away under the influence of the heat and betrayed their presence by long, brown stalactites dripping to the floor below'.[51]

Anne found the hunts rather stiff affairs; 'the children were overawed and probably over-admonished before coming as to their behaviour'. But one year, she said, the atmosphere was transformed by a little Prince of Saxe-Altenburg, who arrived, 'clad in a most immaculate white sailor suit and white linen cap, but in his earnest pursuit of eggs he thrust himself into the heart of the thickest and sootiest bushes, conscientiously penetrated the most tangled thorny shrubs, and explored the coke-cellar of the greenhouse, and emerged at last with his face covered with black smears and the dazzling whiteness of his garments seriously diminished'. He then produced a pair of goggles – the sort that drivers wore in those very early days of motorised transport – put them on 'with an aspect of the greatest joy', beamed at the Kaiser and the assembled children and led a mad chase around the bushes.[52]

Eggs were a traditional gift. On Easter Monday in the Winter Palace a ceremony was held in which the Tsar and Tsaritsa personally greeted about 5,000 men of the Imperial Guards regiments, the Tsar exchanging the Easter greeting and kissing each man in turn, the Tsaritsa receiving a hard-boiled egg from each and presenting a porcelain one. 'It is very wearisome', Margaretta remarked, but for the imperial couple it was only the tail-end of a procedure which began the previous day with an Easter kiss for each of the men and women of the household.[53] In Russia even some of the small presentation eggs were made by Fabergé. In Berlin the Kaiserin presented each of her ladies with an egg of Berlin china. 'These eggs had a little cork stopper at one end,' Ethel Howard said, 'and were intended to be used as scent bottles. I believe the size of the eggs was in proportion to the status of the recipient.'[54]

But nothing could compare with the magnificence of a Christmas at Court, the climax of the social calendar and of the family festivals of the royal year, which was celebrated with gusto – and generosity – in royal households large and small. Preparations could begin as early as October with presents being brought in – practical items intended for distribution to local charities. By November Court ladies would be called on to sort these items, a major task in itself. For her first Christmas in Berlin Ethel Howard found herself sorting men's socks from boys' with one of the young Princes as her assistant. It took them two hours. The Kaiserin took a very personal interest in this work and even before her husband succeeded to the throne she was active in bringing Christmas to people outside the palace. In 1887 Ada Leslie told her cousin how her mistress, then Princess Auguste Viktoria, and the ladies worked to make clothes for 150 poor children. These were given out at a party on 23 December. 'It was arranged in a splendid large marble corridor and to make it more interesting for them, they were – by the Princess's wish allowed to come in at the Grand Entrance, which is used as a rule on State occasions only. It was beautiful to see the children's pleasure and such presents they had! Fancy each girl getting a change of under linen, a warm petticoat, a nice dress – not made charity fashion, but trimmed with velvet etc. – and as well shawls and comfortable hoods, such as the girls here wear and three or four books and a big basket of oranges and nuts. The boys were served accordingly.'[55]

Courtiers and members of the household were generally invited to select their own presents to a given value but in Russia at the turn of the last century, the Tsaritsa preferred to chose the gifts herself. According to Margaretta, the Tsaritsa also liked to decorate the trees with her own hands – there were eight in the Tsarskoe Selo palace at that time and the children's tree 'was fixed into a musical box which played the German Christmas hymn, and turned round and round'.[56] The small Court of Archduke Karl Stefan at Zywiec had one giant tree 'reaching up to the lofty ceiling, which was one mass of glittering lights, and hung with beautiful gifts', with present tables arranged around it, one for each member of the family and household.

Across Europe the celebrations began sometime in the afternoon or early evening of Christmas Eve with carols – in the chapel at Zywiec these were sung by everyone around the crib, but in Berlin the singing was a family affair. For the Christmas of 1886 Ada Leslie described how the little Princes – then aged four, three and two – 'had to solemnly wish their father a Happy Xmas and then sing some Christmas songs, all the ladies and gentlemen of the Court were present'.[57] By Ethel Howard's time the family had grown: Ada's three Princes were eleven, ten and nine years old then and there were three smaller brothers to sing with them, and a little sister. They sang carols to the whole Court in the afternoon and helped their mother distribute presents to the servants; then, in the evening, came another informal carol service for the Court, a beautiful, domestic set-piece in the Kaiser's writing-room with the children gathered in a group around their parents. They sang carols and took turns to read parts of the Christmas story to the assembled Court, then begged their parents to lead the whole company into dinner, knowing that after the feasting would come the trees.

And the Christmas display at Berlin made the eight trees of Tsarskoe Selo look positively niggardly. A forest of Christmas trees was arranged in the Muchselsaal of the Berlin Schloss – a room which was in itself a tourist attraction, even then, its walls 'made of beautiful shells, in patterns of fishes and dolphins and roses, and so on, but really graceful designs' (this is Lilian Brimble writing), 'not horrid crude patterns, while the pillars and lower part of the walls were entirely composed of semi-precious stones – crystal, onyx, jasper, lapis lazuli, agate, cornelian and lovely fat lumps of amber, with every kind of quartz'.[58] But with Christmas trees – one for each member of the imperial family (graded by size to denote the age and importance of the person) and one large one for the ladies and gentlemen, 'lit by a thousand candles' (this is Ethel), 'the green of the foliage glistening with hoar-frost and threads of silver, an angel with outspread wings surmounting each', and the lights reflecting on the semi-precious stones – the effect was breathtaking.[59] 'Really Val', Lilian wrote, 'it looked like a fairy forest, each tree glittering and sparkling with silver, and flashing back the countless blaze of lights . . . it really seemed as if we had strayed by chance into some fairy palace.'[60]

But for Ethel the one thing that stood out, that made her first Berlin Christmas one of the most memorable experiences of her working life, was the revelation that even to a royal Court, that most trying, frustrating, restricting and intrusive of places, which caused her so much heartache, even there the warmth of Christmas could penetrate. The youngest child but one in a large and close-knit family, Ethel was finding her first Christmas away from home quite a trial, though she tried to hide it. She was more touched than she could say to find that, for once, etiquette was set aside. Ignoring all precedence the Kaiser called her forward first and directed her attention to a large table laden with presents – all for her. 'I learned subsequently that not only Their Majesties, but all the ladies and some of the gentlemen in the Court, had combined with true warm-heartedness to extend an extra welcome to me – a stranger in their midst. . . . And thus ended such a Christmas as I can never forget,' she said.[61]

TEN

'Alone at Night without a Revolver'

SOME TRAVELLERS' TALES

Well, kind reader; there I was, totally unacquainted with either the Turkish or Arabic tongues; unaccustomed to the filthy manners, barbarous customs, and disgusting habits of all around me; deprived of every comfort by which I had always been surrounded, shut out from all rational society; hurried here and there, in the heat of a scorching African sun, at a moment's notice; absolutely living upon nothing else but dry bread and a little pigeon or mutton, barely sufficient to keep body and soul together . . . stung almost to death with mosquitos, tormented with flies, and surrounded with beings who were breeders of vermin; a daily witness of manners the most repugnant, nay, revolting to the delicacy of a European female.[1]

Poor Emmeline Lott, struggling through her two-year appointment as governess to His Highness the Grand Pacha Ibrahim in Egypt, had neither the adventurous spirit nor the flexibility of mind essential to a good traveller. She was a Victorian lady through and through; every aspect of life in the Khedive Ismael Pacha's harem was an affront to her senses. But she had courage, and simply to take a position overseas in the days before the aeroplane, the telephone and the computer, when the only link with home was by letter and a letter could take weeks to arrive, if it arrived at all, needed courage in plenty. You had to make your way alone to any part of the globe, without even understanding the language. You had to adapt to whatever conditions you found there.

The only support system that existed for these lone women travellers was the scattered network of British communities and official representatives in other countries: the earliest recorded nurses and governesses who worked overseas, in the eighteenth century, would have left home armed with letters of introduction to these people. For example, in April 1800 Dr Rogerson, who gave hospitality to Baron and Baroness Dimsdale on their visit to Catherine the Great's Court, wrote a letter for a travelling English governess to take to his colleague Dr Charles Brown, Physician in Ordinary to the Court of King Frederick William II of Prussia in Berlin. 'I learn just now that the Countess Tolstoy sets out to day or to morrow to visit her Mother the Princess of Holstein Beck in Berlin. A countrywoman of ours, Miss Emery, who will have the honour of delivering you this letter, accompanies her Daughter as Governess. I recommend her to the Civilities of you and your house. She is liked and has been connected while here with some of the most respectable families of our Countrymen and it is at their desire that I beg that you and Mrs Brown will favour her with your countenance and counsel.'[2] This is the way things were done in the early days.

Travel was an arduous business then and it could be dangerous. The Dimsdales took seven weeks to reach St Petersburg in 1781, travelling by horse-drawn carriage over poorly sanded roads which sometimes took them so close to the sea that they ran the risk of drowning. There is no record of Miss Emery's adventures on the same road; she flits briefly across the stage and is gone and, with her, her fellow governesses and nurses in the age of the horse and the sailing ship. Only Maria Graham left a detailed account of her travels in the early 1800s and Maria was different: she came from a naval family and travel was in her blood. But Miss Higgenbottom and Eugenia Christie, Helen Pinkerton and Mrs Kennedy in Russia, Catherine Strutton as well; Mary Barnes in Germany, and the unnamed nurse of Prince Christian of Schleswig-Holstein, who left him with the one abiding memory of her grief on learning that, far away in England her King, William IV, had died – of these women's experiences on the road or at sea, nothing now remains. For most the upheaval of leaving home was so vast that they settled where their work took them and never returned.

By the mid-nineteenth century railway networks were spreading across Europe and beyond. Trains were much faster and more convenient but nobody seemed to like them much. The first, and universal complaint was the unbearable heat. One of the ladies in the party Queen Victoria sent to Russia in 1874 for the marriage of her son Prince Alfred, Duke of Edinburgh found the experience of Continental train travel so appalling that she swore she would marry the first man who asked rather than face the return journey. Her companions seized on the idea with glee. 'I can tell you how we shouted and how great an occupation it was ever after, to look out for the coming "man"', Lady Augusta Stanley said, in a letter home.[3] Remembering the State visit she made to Potsdam with the two Queens of the Netherlands in 1892, Saxton Winter described how their party had been cooped up for hours in a train on a hot, airless day at the height of summer. 'Long before the destination was reached', she wrote, 'one and all were suffering acutely from protracted inaction in a stifling atmosphere and choking dust.'[4] And Jane Potts, leaving Berlin at the end of her appointment with Queen Emma's sister the Duchess of Albany in January 1901, gave a report on her journey which showed that, in a quarter of a century, very little had changed. 'The carriage was so hot', she wrote, 'I thought we were going to be really cooked. We all looked like lobsters.'[5]

German trains in particular were renowned for the unevenness of the track. 'One was hurled backwards and forwards and jolted and jerked with every form of movement known to science,' Anne Topham recalled. 'Sometimes we seemed to be moving over rippled granite, and then a horizontal spasm mixed up with weird scrunchings seized the whole train, which appeared to be having some kind of hysterical fit.' Anne found it impossible to dress and undress on an overnight journey, even on the Kaiser's luxurious train. 'Brush and comb, hairpins, all went sliding away on the floor,' she said, 'after washing in a basin in which a miniature tempest of soap-tipped wavecrests was raging, I renounced the adventure of undressing and lay down uncomfortably in most of my clothes to wait for morning.'[6] Saxton Winter would have sympathised. The train to Potsdam was so late that her entire party was obliged to change into formal dress while still in motion, to be ready for the official reception committee on the station – including the imperial couple. 'What an exhausting process it is to dress for a State occasion in the narrow compartment of a railway carriage,' Saxton said, 'travelling at the rate of fifty miles an hour with a plentiful supply of tunnels and innumerable curves!'[7]

And even when you had borne the jolting and jerking and the suffocating heat, there was still the unexpected to contend with. In the spring of 1892 Ada Leslie accompanied the Greek royal family to Denmark for the golden wedding of the King's parents, King Christian IX and Queen Louise. The initial stage of that journey proved hazardous, with violent storms in the Mediterranean which damaged their escort ship and so exhausted the royalties that they took their first day on land, in Venice, just to recover from the ordeal. They were wiser in this than Ada, who couldn't resist the chance to explore. After all, it was Venice. 'In the first church I visited,' she told her cousin Pollie, 'I met two English ladies who could speak Italian & who had made out a delightful plan for the morning. They very kindly invited me to accompany them, which I gladly did.'

Ada expected to catch up on sleep in the special train that would take the royal party overnight to Munich, but she was disappointed: 'Just as I was enjoying my first sleep, the train came to a sudden stoppage,' she said, 'because the King's sleeping car was on fire – there was a delay of an hour or more before we could go on. The next night was shortened by the stupid engine-driver bringing us to the Baltic Sea at half-past 4 o'clock instead of 8 o'clock in the morning. Imagine on a cold raining morning, to have to go on the yacht at 5 o'clock!!!!' The party finally reached Copenhagen in the early evening after their gruelling journey and threw themselves headlong into a week of celebrations with royal cousins from across Europe. It was exhausting but Ada still made time for her own agenda; 'I want to rush about & see as much as possible,' she said, in the brief time she had left in Copenhagen after the festivities ended.[8]

A few months after Ada's adventures, in the autumn of 1892, May T suffered the full gamut of horrors on her journey across Europe to take up her appointment with the Badeni family: railway employees whose German was unintelligible, so that 'it was as much as I could do to obtain a cup of coffee and get half my change back'; uneven tracks – 'I was thoroughly worn out with the bumping and pounding I had endured', and always the overpowering heat. 'How hot it had been in that railway carriage I well remember,' she recalled, 'and I, acting on the illusion of most English people of twenty years ago that it would be cold in Poland, had travelled in a thick cloth costume.' Then, as a final insult, she was waiting for a connecting train at Cracow when she realised that her luggage was missing from the pile on the station platform.[9] It arrived at her destination only three weeks later than she did.

But poor Ethel Howard had the worst experience. On her way to Berlin to take up her first appointment in 1895, bewildered, homesick, and almost consumed with nerves – far too distracted to notice heat or jolting, or even the passing scenery – she found herself sharing a compartment on the train with a young woman in an emotional state more desperate even than her own. They began talking and the woman told Ethel that she had been summoned back to Berlin by telegram because her mother was dying. 'As the night wore on,' Ethel said, 'she became more and more distraught, and it was a horrible moment when she suddenly flung open the carriage door, crying, "hold me, hold me, or I shall jump out!" I duly held her, and managed to soothe her, but was grateful for the morning light and Berlin at last.'[10]

Sea travel could be equally fraught with problems. When Anne Topham arrived at Homburg-vor-der-Höhe in 1902 to start her work as governess to the Kaiser's daughter she felt thoroughly drained and depressed. 'A stormy, eight-hour night passage on the North Sea, during which one is tossed on the waves in a state of acute seasickness, and a long train journey through stifling heat, affect anyone's spiritual bouyancy,' she said.[11] Chloroform was thought to be the best preventative for seasickness but, misused, it could be worse than the disease. For the most part, you simply coped with the unpleasantness and longed for it to pass. And if you were a good sailor, it was almost inevitable that your companions would not be. May T found herself in a very delicate situation on a pleasure cruise to Lussin – the island where Nellie Ryan spent most of her working summers. A sudden violent wind made the ship pitch and roll so badly that Countess Badeni was overcome by seasickness and terror. She clung to May, refusing to let go and predicting their imminent drowning. This posed the governess with something of a dilemma. While she had no choice but to pacify the Countess, from the corner of her eye she could see her teenage pupil Wanda – evidently a much better sailor than her mother – taking advantage of the situation and 'desporting herself on the bridge' with a handsome member of the crew. Fortunately for all concerned (except Wanda) the storm was a very short one.[12]

Fellow passengers could be a trial. Even when they were not committing suicide or being sick, their behaviour was not always what you might wish. In the summer of 1865, in a letter to her mother, the Crown Princess of Prussia described a journey she had shared with her own old nurse Marianne Hull, known in the family as 'May', who could always be relied on to give temporary cover in the nurseries of 'her' grown-up children. The two women were taking the four little Prussians, ranging in age from five years to ten months, on a sea crossing to the Isle of Föhr off the north German coast. The Crown Princess told her mother,

Fancy our horror on finding the packet . . . so crowded that there were not seats enough for us, we were crammed on two benches on deck – with the children and all – with more than sixty other passengers who kept eating and drinking and smoking nasty cigars. There was such a smell of melted butter – it was horrible. So we sat for four hours. The children almost drove us wild – they would not sit still one minute, but kept slipping and fidgetting about for everlasting. Henry, who cries and grumbles more than any other child I ever came near, screamed and roared the whole time and was not to be pacified by coaxing or threatening, slapped May's face and shouted 'No, no' to everything that was said. You never saw such a business . . . thank God no one was sick – what that would have been I cannot think of; there was nothing in the shape of a basin on the ship![13]

And even the most palatial of vessels could be put at risk by one headstrong woman. Around the turn of the last century Archduke Karl Stefan commissioned a new yacht, the *Watūrūs*, from the shipyards at Leith. Once it had completed its sea trials he hurried to Scotland to collect it while his family and household, including Nellie Ryan, made their way north to meet him and the yacht at Kiel. They planned to cruise the northern coasts as far as the Gulf of Finland. 'A chorus of delight and admiration came from all,' said Nellie, 'as we wended our way over the spacious decks, on which two most comfortable and splendidly furnished deck-houses were provided for wet weather. Down a broad staircase we reached an elegant dining-saloon, upholstered in dark green leather, with walls of oak panelling, leading out of which were two light and airy drawing-rooms, with dainty chintzes. Quaint but comfortable seats were let into the wall, piled with soft cushions, and there was everything that money could buy.'

The *Watūrūs* was the Archduke's new toy and he was fiercely protective of it and very strict about behaviour on board. He would not even allow trunks to be carried down the stairs – presumably for fear of bumping his new woodwork – so his disgruntled family and staff were forced to unpack on deck. He also forbade the opening of portholes when the yacht was in motion, but Nellie . . . The English were noted for their love of fresh air and Nellie found the atmosphere on board unbearably stuffy. So she opened the porthole in her cabin, taking care, of course, to close it securely when she went outside. Or perhaps not. One evening she was sitting on deck admiring the rough sea – she prided herself on being an excellent sailor – when Count Chorinsky, her hero of the lost key incident at Podjavori, disturbed her pleasure with the words, 'the ship is sinking, your cabin is already under water, and the waves are pouring in your window! His Imperial Highness is filled with wrath and indignation, and you are requested to proceed at once to your cabin.'

The devastation that met her below was alarming. All the luxurious new fittings, the velvet carpet, the bedding from her cabin, were piled in a sodden heap in the corridor while sailors on their hands and knees attempted to mop up the water, 'and my pretty room was a scene of desolation'.[14] She had not latched the porthole securely and the force of the waves had pushed it open. She expected to be in real trouble this time but Nellie, like Ethel Howard in Berlin, seemed to have a talent for creating chaos which her employers accepted with amused resignation, putting it down to an unfortunate tendency of the English. Beyond a few teasing remarks on the need for safety measures at sea, the Archduke said no more about it.

And sometimes the sun shone, the flags flew, and travelling with royalty was exciting enough to make up for any discomforts and dangers. For Ada Leslie, her first sight of Greece in October 1899 was pure magic. She told her cousin,

The weather was quite glorious, like a golden July day, when we went on board the King of Greece's yacht at a place called Calamity & steamed up the Gulf of Piraeus . . . between two long lines of Austrian, Spanish, Russian, Danish, German & English ships & not one of each but many. There were for instance 4 Austrian, 6 German etc. They were all beautifully dressed with flags, all had their yards manned by sailors in 'spick and span Turn-out' & as we passed, each banged away its royal salute of 121 guns – such a deafening noise as I had never heard in my life before. And sometimes there would be so much smoke & even flashes of flame from the mouth of some big gun, that one felt some damage must have been done – but after smoke & report had died away, instead of cries of pain, one heard half a dozen different National Anthems & the word 'Hurrah' called out in as many different tongues. . . . It was a sight that I shall long remember.

This was the welcome for a royal bride, Sophie, Princess of Prussia, soon to be Crown Princess of Greece, from the combined Mediterranean fleets of the European powers. For Ada Leslie, a printer's daughter from Islington, it was quite an experience and she enjoyed recounting the details for her cousin at home in England. From Piraeus, the royal party travelled on by train to Athens – 'The reception was much, much grander than I had expected it to be' – and celebrated the wedding in the royal palace. Then the newly-weds and their Household, including Ada, moved into the Crown Prince's palace, set on a splendid vantage point with views over the whole of Athens, '& not of modern Athens only, but also the ruins of the ancient city. These ruins are marvellous,' Ada said, '& I think it will be long before I am tired of Athens so long as I am free to wander up to the Acropolis as often as I like.'[15]

Just as in Venice, Ada determined to see as much as possible when she went to Copenhagen. Travelling with and for royalty opened a whole new world of opportunities for her and she seized them with relish. On her way to Berlin for her first royal appointment, she broke her journey in Antwerp to visit the cathedral. From there she toured all the sights in the city connected with the painter Rubens – in one day. She left the next morning and stopped again in Cologne a few hours later. Cologne Cathedral had been completed only six years before after 600 years in the making: 'Do you know,' she said, 'it's been one of my daydreams for years, to see this wonderful cathedral?' She found that by moonlight 'the view was so beautiful from my bedroom window, that I could scarcely persuade myself to go to bed'.[16]

It was one of the great bonuses of overseas service, to see things which, before, you could only read about. Saxton Winter and the Dutch royal party broke their journey to Berlin in 1892 so that the little Queen could see the cathedral at Strasbourg. They made the visit incognito: royalty often did this because it saved all the fuss that etiquette demanded if their identities were known and their visits announced beforehand. Usually, from courtesy, people respected the incognito even if they knew perfectly well who the visitor was. But sometimes they did not know, and the results could be amusing. On the visit to Strasbourg Cathedral, Wilhelmina was keen to climb the tower, so Miss Winter and some of the other more active members of the party made their way with her to the gate. They tried to buy a full-priced entrance ticket for the Queen, though she was obviously a child, because paying half-price for her seemed unfair to other visitors; 'such concessions were never taken advantage of for the Queen'. But the confusion this caused was immense because the elderly custodian on the gate had no idea of who they were. He insisted; they insisted. Finally he gave way, but all his sympathy went to Wilhelmina. 'Poor child,' he said (rather too loudly), 'she cannot understand French.' This gave the Dutch party ample opportunity to tease the 'poor', and by this time very indignant child, who spoke French quite as well as he did.[17]

In royal service you were constantly on the move from winter to summer residence, holiday villa to relative's palace to hotel; private visit, State visit . . . Norland nurse Doris Hincks, writing for the Institute's magazine about her year with the Yugoslav royal family, showed that as late as 1930 this lifestyle was still very much in force.

When it was decided that I should come out to Jugo-Slavia in January I was met with startling tales of wolves, bears, brigands and snowed up trains! So far, I have met with none of these adventures, but I have seen some lovely country.

I had a very good journey out, travelling through France, Switzerland and Italy, on the Simplon–Orient express. . . . On arriving at Belgrade, it was delightful to find that our nurseries were a little thatched cottage in the garden of a new palace which had been built on a hill outside the town. . . . By April, Belgrade was becoming very hot, and at the end of the month we left for Split on the Dalmatian coast. This was my first experience of a Royal train and I certainly found it comfortable travelling. The journey was to take 24 hours, and we boarded the train complete with all equipment and servants and guard. The saloons are luxurious and have all necessities. We took 2 cots for the two little ones and life went on just as usual. Nothing delighted the little groups, who waited on stations of railway banks, more than to see the children being bathed. Prince Tomislav certainly enjoyed the audience! . . . At the end of May we moved to Bled to Her Majesty's house on the side of the lake. Bled is very beautiful. It is near the Austrian and Italian borders with high mountains round. We arrived at the time of orchids, gentians, lilies and campanulas, and many lovely flowers which I had never seen before.

By July, it was getting very hot, so it was decided to go to a shooting lodge in Bosnia. This meant a night's journey by train and then 4½ hours motoring. We found ourselves very high on the borders of the Forest, and we lived in a picturesque little wooden house. The forests of pines and beeches were wonderful, I have never seen such trees, but it was tragic to find great stretches of shattered trees, old trenches, dug-outs and gun positions, relics of the late war.

One day I was lucky enough to motor into Serajevo, about 2 hours run. It is a most interesting old town. Here the Moslem influence is very strong, and in Bosnia it is a common sight to see veiled women and red fez on the men. Yugoslavia is an interesting country; the types of people and the costumes alone are a study – so varied are they.[18]

This was a pattern of life generations of British women at foreign Courts had known. During her time with Crown Princess Sophie, Ada Leslie travelled widely, revisiting Berlin and the German spa towns of Homburg-vor-der-Höhe and Wiesbaden. In 1890 she enjoyed a brief visit to Russia with her employers: 'The Russians treated us most kindly & I had a great desire to go again.'[19] Then to Denmark for the golden wedding, and in between there were seasonal moves from one part of Greece to another: the islands, the cities, the mountains. It could be annoying to have to uproot quite so often on someone else's whim. Writing from the island of Poros in 1890, Ada complained that she had left Athens 'in such an absurd hurry that I had no time to think of ink. There's no reason why we should have had so little time to pack,' she told her cousin, 'as the Prince and Princess are here for pleasure only. But it's always the same, whatever royalties do, they must do in a hurry.'[20] She found Poros in spring very beautiful, though, 'and the weather intensely hot, a cloudless sky and a burning sun, but there is much less dust than in Athens and the mountains are much greener. . . . But the great charm of all,' she said, 'is the beautiful flowers which grow quite wild, the gigantic palm trees and the great straggling aloes that grow all over the mountains.'[21]

For Ada, though, these natural beauties soon palled. When the summer heat became unbearable the Greek royal family liked to leave Athens for four or five months, to relax at Tatoi in the mountains. The isolation of Tatoi made it a paradise for them. Kate Fox's employer Prince Nicholas recalled the estate as 'a memory of sunshine and beautiful nature that brings a warmth to my heart even in my saddest moments'.[22] His brother Christopher saluted Tatoi as 'the one place where we could live a real home life and forget, for a short time, that we were not supposed to be ordinary human beings'.[23] But even before her first visit there Ada had misgivings. 'It will be dull and lonely,' she told her cousin, 'not a creature to be seen beyond the members of the Household and the servants.'[24] She was right. She hated the place. The pace of life was slow and there was no society to be had. Postal deliveries came only twice a week, brought by a man on horseback. 'If I should die here,' Ada wrote in the spring of 1893, 'I have begged my friends to have the word Tatoi inscribed on my tombstone.'[25]

Ada needed people around her and she hungered for Athens where there were people in plenty. 'There is military music,' she said to her cousin, 'gaily dressed crowds everywhere in the evenings, soldiers and the queer foreign gaily dressed folks who seem to belong to nowhere in the world but Athens.' Nearby Phalerum on the coast boasted an open-air theatre too, which she much enjoyed, and the seaside. But though Ada liked the sea, she refused to do more than paddle in it: 'it's great fun,' she remarked, 'though there are so many fishes, that I am quite nervous, they come so close . . . it's so nasty to have such dabby-flabby wet things come against one. The Princess teases me so much because I can't swim.'[26] Margaretta Eagar would have made better use of this opportunity. She longed for a swim on her first visit to the Crimea and, having no 'bathing-dress', she sent one of the under-nurses into Yalta to buy her a ready-made costume or some material to make one. All that came back was the shopkeeper's scorn: 'Bathing-dress, indeed! French fashions! Tell her to go and bathe in her skin as her grandmother did before her' – an indelicate suggestion which Margaretta declined to follow.[27]

Margaretta became the most widely travelled of the nurses and governesses who worked at the Russian Court, benefiting both from improved communications and from a pattern of marriages over the years which had linked the imperial family ever more tightly into the royal families of Europe. In Jane Lyon's day, at the end of the eighteenth century, the family remained in Russia for the most part, dividing its time between the great city palaces of St Petersburg in winter, the country estates at Tsarskoe Selo and Pavlovsk in spring, Peterhof on the Gulf of Finland in summer, Gatchina for the autumn hunts and distant Moscow for the great ceremonies of State. In Catherine Strutton's time visits to the Crimea and to Tsaritsa Maria Alexandrovna's family home in Darmstadt were added to the annual round: the Crimea alone meant a 1,400-mile journey which could take up to six days even at the end of the nineteenth century, when the railway had reached as far as Sevastopol, the main city on the peninsula. A panorama of varied scenery rolled past the train windows and in some remote communities whole populations turned out on the station platform to welcome the train, to pick up news and to sell their fish, fruit, bread and cakes (as they do to this day).

On 29 October 1888 Tsar Alexander III and his family were on their way home from the Crimea on the imperial train near Borki, not far from Kharkov. It was just before midday: Elizabeth Francklin was at the table in the children's carriage with six-year-old Grand Duchess Olga and the waiter was bringing their pudding when there was a sudden jolt. The nurse took the frightened child on her knee, then came a violent impact and all three were thrown clear – their carriage derailed and was left hanging over a steep slope. 'The poor nursemaid Franklin was in a terrible state of fear and horror,' Tsaritsa Maria Feodorovna told her mother, 'for of course she was holding the little one in her arms as she flew but must have dropped her on the way, for she found herself alone on the ground and saw the little one already down from the steep slope running . . . and the poor waiter had his legs completely crushed by a stove that flew after him and fell on him.' At least one carriage had been crushed entirely and there were twenty-two dead and over thirty injured; the family themselves had had a miraculous escape. In bitter cold and rain the survivors did what they could until help came. When writing to her mother the Tsaritsa thought Elizabeth Francklin had not been hurt; in fact, the nurse had broken ribs and internal injuries, which she managed to conceal.[28]

A church was erected on the spot to give thanks for the family's survival and they kept on travelling, with the Tsaritsa's native Denmark also part of their annual round. In the next generation, Margaretta experienced the full programme of visits in Russia and in Europe. A lively minded, curious woman, she was not so keen a sightseer as Ada Leslie but she devoured information about the places she visited and the written accounts she left are heaving with detail. For her the Crimea was the greatest adventure, both for the breathtaking scenery and for the chance to encounter an extraordinary world, now long gone. 'In walking through Yalta,' she said, 'one hears so many different tongues, and sees so many nationalities that I was reminded of the day of Pentecost in Jerusalem. Here you meet a Turkish family, the women all closely veiled with the exception of one eye with which they closely scrutinise you. It makes you uncomfortable to see the one eye gazing at you and not to see anything in return. Again you will meet Tartars – lively looking people, tall, and generally slight and athletic looking . . . they all dye their hair a vivid red, and the married women blacken their teeth and paint the palms of their hands.'[29]

Margaretta was always fascinated by the people she encountered. Her chances to communicate with ordinary Russians were few, restricted by the security that surrounded the imperial family and by her own inability to speak the language. She must have found most of her information from the nursery maids and soldiers at Court, but she came away from Russia with a fund of stories and some were based on things she herself had seen. 'I have counted as many as twenty-one children all in one cabin', she wrote, 'and have been told that there are often more. . . . I have seen a woman yoked to a plough in company with the family cow, and driven by a man.'[30] The position, education and health of Russian women intrigued her; gipsy people caught her eye her too, appealing to her love of the supernatural. 'There are many gipsies in Russia', she wrote, 'and at Peterhoff I often witnessed their most extraordinary marriage ceremony.' She described how the gipsy families would form up in a procession of pony carts behind the groom and his bride, 'gorgeously dressed in a new print or muslin dress, a pair of white cotton gloves, and a piece of lace shaped like a three-cornered handkerchief with the corner hanging down behind, tied over her head and crowned with a wreath of artificial flowers'. The whole procession rode three times round in a circuit, and the marriage was made. 'It holds good,' Margaretta assured her readers, 'and is quite legal.'[31]

May T was equally intrigued by the gipsy people she met at Csurgó in Hungary, on the estate of the Karolyi family, where she stayed for several months before taking up her appointment at the Habsburg Court. There, she said, a gipsy man brought a lock of hair forward onto his forehead and tied flowers into it to indicate that he was saving to buy a bride. The plight of one such man, already widowed 'and not very attractive', moved her so much that she contributed to his savings and her hosts did the same. They were rather dismayed on seeing the bride: a sorry object whose hair had been shorn off and all her clothes taken away by her brothers, because they thought their father had accepted too little money for her. But it was the gipsy music May loved most, 'music which stirs one to the very soul, and searches out one's innermost heartaches'. She spent one afternoon with Count Michael Karolyi teaching the Csurgó gipsies airs from HMS *Pinafore*. It sounds wonderfully incongruous, but 'by tea-time they knew them all,' she said, 'and could Sir Arthur Sullivan have heard his music with the weird minor accompaniments they improvised for it, his soul would have been filled with joy, for it was surpassingly beautiful'.[32]

May had an extraordinary time in Hungary and Poland, countries that were then on the fringes of Europe, almost untouched by the rapid process of change. Stags fought under the windows of Castle Büsk, Count Badeni's Polish home, and in the winter packs of wolves prowled the park and it was unsafe to go out on foot. They killed a child from one of the villages: 'It is hard to believe that such things can happen so close to one', May wrote in her diary. She watched for wolves from the window for a whole evening but had 'a glimpse only of dark shadows flitting so quickly and silently over the snow that it was impossible to distinguish them. I feel quite creepy,' she said, 'and know I shall dream unpleasant dreams.'33 Margaretta also knew Poland, where the imperial family had a string of hunting lodges. She hated it. The vast Polish forests made her realise 'how terrible nature can be in her solitary places. The forest frightened me', she said, 'with its unknown possibilities of danger.'34

This was a primitive world, where traditional beliefs held strong. At the end of October, for the Feast of All Souls, May helped the Badenis to decorate their family tombs with candles in a hilltop cemetery outside Lemberg. The cemetery was crowded and as they drove home, 'we could see the lights from the hundreds of candles shining out through the darkness, like a shower of stars. For miles we could see them.'35 May thought this a beautiful custom, but she was not so impressed by the things that went on in Lemberg around Easter. She was awoken very early from her bed in the Governor's Palace on Easter Monday by screaming: in the street outside two girls were being dragged to a water pump by a group of young men, who proceeded to drench them before letting them go. Her maid told her 'the sprinkling' was a custom; Count Badeni seemed amused when she complained to him, but she thought no more about it until, at a luncheon party a few hours later, she was horrified to see the gentlemen suddenly begin to empty every available vessel of liquid, finger bowls included, over the ladies beside them. 'The table was a lake of running water,' she said. 'Exquisite creations of French millinery wilted and became masses of damp straw and muslin; toilettes from Vienna ran their wet colours into petticoats from Paris; powder disappeared and fringes hung in straight, unbecoming wisps.' May took refuge behind a large potted palm until a small man came rushing towards her, carafe in hand. Then she drew herself up to her full five foot ten. '"But Mademoiselle, it is the sprinkling," he stammered. "I decline to be sprinkled," I replied with withering scorn.' The Badenis thought her ridiculous and teased incessantly, but the spectacle had really brought out the English governess in May. 'It is bad enough in the stables,' she said, 'but I must say I think it disgusting in the drawing-room.'36

Other peoples' customs and habits were a constant reminder that this was not home. Much as she loved Athens, Ada Leslie found many things disturbing. The disposal of rubbish and even dead pets in the streets, for example, which everyone did as a matter of course, even the maids in the palace. 'One sees many things that are, to English eyes, painfully repulsive,' she said, 'such, for instance, as the custom of carrying the dead in open coffins through the streets. . . . It's a matter of religion with the Greeks, and they are proud to do today exactly the same as was done 19 hundred years ago.'[37] Within weeks of her arrival she had noticed that there were few women to be seen in the city. 'The reason is easily explained,' she told her cousin, 'as in all Eastern and southern lands, the women don't have a very good time of it. Amongst the poor classes they work very hard indeed, earning nearly all the money that maintains the family often times. Meanwhile the men spend most of their time smoking at the street corners, or sitting at dirty little tables outside the many cafés.'[38]

The East seemed to exert a fascination over those women who worked in Europe, only coming into occasional contact with that other, more mysterious world: like Doris Hincks, remarking on the Muslim dress she had seen in Bosnia, or Margaretta and the veiled Turkish women of the Crimea with their one, staring eye. But it was Kate Fox who produced the Eastern encounter to trump them all. In 1905, on her way to Russia with Prince and Princess Nicholas and their daughters, she was drawn into an official visit to the Sultan of Turkey in the Yildiz Palace in Constantinople, now Istanbul. She even spoke to the Sultan. This was not the original intention. The Greek party travelled by sea from Piraeus and, while the Prince and Princess went ashore to attend a religious ceremony and meet the Sultan, Kate stayed onboard ship with the two babies. It was almost bedtime when a private launch came up alongside bringing news that the Sultan had sent for the children to be his guests. Onshore one of his aides-de-camp was waiting with a carriage, 'and we had a very pretty drive through Constantinople, which was that night illuminated in honour of the anniversary of the Sultan's accession, and as it was getting dark we could see them beautifully'.

Kate settled the children and finally at a quarter past eleven a meal was brought to her room – Eastern ideas of time, as all the British women who worked in the East would attest, were not the same as those at home. Kate found it all rather 'Oriental' but the service was impressive: 'Two men brought a huge silver tray containing about twelve silver plates', she wrote, 'each loaded with food of various kinds (there were only two rusty knives and forks to eat all with!), and though I tasted everything they were very worried because I did not eat it all!' And she really appreciated the accommodation: 'The beds were very gorgeous, the pillow cases seemed too good to lie on; they were all tucks, insertion, ribbon and lace! The bedspreads too, were very elaborate; on my table there was a good supply of Turkish cigarettes, and on each washstand bottles of scent. In the morning I had to walk a very long way through the corridors to my bath, and was supplied with ever so many lovely towels with richly embroidered borders!'

In the morning Kate was free to explore the palace and she took a drive round the town in the afternoon. The Greek party was due to sail on to Odessa that evening and she was just getting the babies ready to return to their ship in time for bed when an officer came rushing into the room with news that the Sultan wanted to see them. The officer swept the elder Princess up in his arms and Kate had no choice but to hurry along behind him with the baby. 'His Majesty was very gracious speaking to me in French, through an interpreter,' she remembered, 'as he himself speaks nothing but Turkish. After that I left at once, and late that night was delighted on hearing . . . that the Sultan had presented me with a beautiful order called the Shepacat.'[39] Quite an honour, then, and Kate was right: the Order was a beautiful piece of official jewellery. The Order of Chefakat – not 'Shepacat' – the wonderfully named 'Order of Chastity (for Ladies)' was instituted by the Sultan Abdul Hamid II in 1880 and consisted of a five-pointed star in crimson enamel, edged with gold and with a small gold ball at the tip of each ray. In the centre a gold boss bore the Sultan's cipher; the star rested on a circular wreath of leaves and berries, enamelled in green and crimson, and the whole piece was mounted on another star studded with brilliants and hung from a star and crescent, again enamelled in crimson.[40] Kate may not have had many chances to wear her Order, but in that short meeting she must have made quite an impression on the Sultan.

Kate was not the only Englishwoman to enter the Sultan's palace and if Emmeline Lott could have heard her story she would probably have greeted it with a disapproving (and sceptical) sniff, though the Court of Sultan Abdul Aziz had seemed marginally less dreadful to her than the palaces of Egypt, where she lived out her nightmares before Kate was even born. At least the Sultan's food was edible, and there were echoes in his Court of the glamour that made the East seem so enticing. Even Emmeline devoted over seven pages of her first book to describing how wonderful the Egyptian princesses and harem ladies looked for their State visit to the Sultan's mother, in their richest silks, velvets and lace, dripping with gold and precious stones, 'like a galaxy of beauteous sprites, the denizens of a fairy land, and the attendants of two fairy queens'.[41] But it was Emmeline's firm contention that while others might be seduced by the glamorous exterior of life in the palaces of the Middle East, only she had penetrated into the interior and seen the squalor and depravity that lay behind the magic. She wrote to expose the harems, 'which cannot but be considered as secret institutions for the corruption of women'. Her books, published not long after her return to England, with the tantalising titles, *The English Governess in Egypt: Harem Life in Egypt and Constantinople* and *Nights in the Harem*, were a runaway success.

Emmeline crossed the Mediterranean from Marseilles to Alexandria on the steamer *Peleuse* in the spring of 1863, carrying letters of introduction to a bank in Alexandria: there, officials had arranged for her to go on by train to Cairo, on a first-class ticket. Nothing about the journey seems to have engaged her interest except the dark warnings issued by her travelling companions, a Greek merchant from Alexandria and a German from Frankfurt: 'your position as an English lady entitles you to receive every attention, yet at the same time you will be called upon to conform to many strange whims, fancies and customs, which may appear most singular and outlandish to your European notions; nay, many may even seem quite repugnant to your naturally sensitive feelings'.[42] At Tanteh their train was pulled into a siding to allow the passage of the Khedive's private dispatch train. Emmeline was intrigued to see 'the heads of several young ladies thrust out of the first-class carriage which was attached to the tender. My curiosity,' she said, 'was considerably excited when I saw that their cast of countenance was either Levantine or German. . . . I heard them distinctly conversing both in French and German.'

She asked the Greek merchant why this curious cargo was using the 'private despatch train' and the reply was coy: 'I cannot exactly tell you; but, in all probability, it is because it is always appropriated for the purpose of conveying all fair damsels who may chance to come on *flying* visits to H.H. Ismael Pacha. . . .'[43] Emmeline was convinced that this was her first encounter with the 'White Slave Trade', a dubious trafficking in the bodies and lives of innocent Western women: governesses, lured overseas by advertisements promising good positions in prominent families and then entrapped and sold. 'Many of the choicer plants from this foul soil were transplanted into the palaces of Egyptian Princes . . . many are still walled-up in these retreats and will pass away to the tomb under conditions which no mortal dare seek to unveil.'[44] It was a theme which Emmeline would often return to in her writing.

Once in Cairo, Emmeline spent one night in a hotel before being snatched away by a friend of the Khedive and held in his house for several weeks, comfortably but without access to the outside world. It later transpired that this was done to prevent her meeting with another Englishwoman in the hotel. The woman had been appointed to the position Emmeline was about to take up, then summarily dismissed by the Khedive for reasons which never became clear. Only after she left was Emmeline taken to the banks of the Nile for the short river crossing to the Ghezire Palace. She leaves us an irresistible picture: the English governess, tight and proper in her crinoline and black straw hat, clutching her bags and perched on the red and white damask divan of the Viceregal barge 'manned by twelve Arab boatmen, dressed like the ordinary Arabs but wearing turbans. The Viceregal standard, the everlasting crescent, floated at stem and stern.'[45] In a matter of minutes Emmeline had mounted the steps on the far bank and the doors of the harem closed behind her.

From this point, Emmeline's life became a constant struggle to maintain the standards of home in circumstances which to her seemed impossible. It didn't matter where she was; she might as well have been on the moon. She found the building and its inhabitants squalid and dirty. The servants intrigued as a way of life and were not above poisoning to secure their ends; protecting the little Pacha Ibrahim from poison was one of her stated duties. She hated the food and flatly refused to eat with her fingers: 'I could not, and would not, partake of my meals in that disgusting manner.'[46] She sensed that her virtue was under constant threat, even from the eunuchs. 'I doubted their infirmity of body and kept a watchful eye over them.' Once, she said, she was tricked into entering the Viceroy's bathroom and found him dressed only 'in his *pyjamas* "drawers"'. His principal wife and favourite concubines were busy 'drying his Viceregal's person with bath-towels' and he smiled when he saw her and beckoned her forward. What evil intentions lay behind that smile? Emmeline didn't wait to find out. Hastily dropping the little Pacha's hand, she bobbed a curtsy and fled.[47]

For their part, the Viceregal family treated Emmeline with respect and courtesy, doing their best to satisfy her requests, however bizarre they may have seemed. The harem ladies were fascinated by her clothes, especially the black straw hat, which was passed round from hand to hand, and the crinoline: 'At the earnest request of some of the ladies of the Harem, I rose from my seat, and walked up and down that noble hall, in order that they might see how European ladies generally paced up and down their rooms.'[48] A very similar scene was acted out in Bangkok at almost the same time, when Anna Leonowens encountered King Mongkut's many wives: 'they fingered my hair and dress,' she said, 'my collar, belt, and rings. One donned my hat and cloak, and made a promenade of the pavilion; another pounced upon my gloves and veil, and disguised herself in them, to the great delight of the little ones, who laughed boisterously'. The East clearly found the West intriguing too, but Anna had a degree of sympathy for the lives of the people there that Emmeline never tried to achieve.[49]

For most of her time in Egypt, Emmeline was locked inside the harem of the Ghezire Palace. Once, she went with the other inhabitants on a trip up the Nile on the Viceregal yacht – veiled, like the harem ladies themselves, but outside at least, and on the move. Otherwise she was condemned to share their seclusion and her health suffered. To help her, the family brought forward their annual move to the sea coast at Alexandria where the climate was more favourable. The eight-hour train journey in the company of the Princesses was mortifying to Emmeline. They took off their beautiful silk dresses and threw them in a heap on the floor. They squatted on the carpet to eat and 'tore the meat with their fingers like a set of cannibals', and – the final indignity, this – they emptied their chamber pots out of the train window. 'I thought their manners bad enough, in all conscience, *at home*; but now I had seen them *abroad*, and I never wished to have the honour of travelling with them again.'[50]

Emmeline Lott's constant tone of moral outrage is deliciously funny, though this was never her intention. But it is still something of a relief to turn to the writings of her successor Ellen Chennells, who describes the same Egyptian palaces and the same reigning family in tones so different that the connection is hard to recognise. Ellen arrived in Egypt in October 1871, six years after Emmeline left. She did not like the harem system any more than Emmeline, but where Emmeline saw the inhabitants as prisoners of a life with only two preoccupations – sex (which of course she did not name) and hashish – Ellen only attacked the harem for its stultifying boredom. 'On *fête* days,' she said, 'the impression is gorgeous; the magnificent dresses, the splendid apartments, the flashing of jewels, the open courts with the feathery palms, and the sound of falling waters, all produce a delightful effect. But on ordinary visits you were struck with the entire absence of anything to promote amusement or mental occupation. No books, music, or any little feminine work lying about.'[51] One senses a desire on her part to introduce a little tatting, embroidery or watercolour painting, to improve the dull lives of the harem ladies.

Of the moral aspects of the business, Ellen Chennells seemed entirely unaware. Either she was unwilling to judge the standards of another culture or, as a single lady, gently raised, she simply did not know about such things. In either case, there is a wonderful innocence about her response to the Khedive's having four wives. She admired the Princesses for living together in such harmony and told them so. 'That is because his Highness never shows any preference for one more than the others,' was the reply, 'if one is favoured to-day, the others have their turn tomorrow.' Miss Chennells was impressed. 'I thought him a wonderful man to keep the balance so even,' she said, 'and I think most people will be of my opinion.'[52] Emmeline Lott certainly would not have been!

Ellen Chennells's response to Egypt and its people was equally open-minded and warm. She wanted to see, to know and to admire, and she was luckier than Emmeline in that the terms of her employment did allow much more freedom, at least in the early years. She had been in Egypt a month when an outing to the Pyramids was proposed for the Grand Pacha Ibrahim and Princess Zeyneb and all the members of their educational establishment. It meant a very early start, but the morning was 'delightful, clear, and invigorating. We had a kind of brake, or *char-à-banc*,' Ellen said, 'very high above the dust, drawn by four horses, and the driver rode postillion.' They crossed the Nile on a bridge of boats and drove alongside an old branch of the river, on a two-year-old road built specially to allow the Empress of the French to visit the Pyramids. Before that, Ellen said, there was only a camel road that was frequently under water.

The royal children joined them at the Pyramids then, while one of the tutors climbed it, the rest of the party went on to see the Sphinx, 'of which little more than the giant head rises out of the sand. A man climbed up to the ear, which gave us a good idea of its proportions, as he looked a mere pigmy upon it.' Next, they visited the Third Pyramid and, while the ladies of the party debated whether they ought to go in, twelve-year-old Princess Zeyneb 'suddenly disappeared down the opening with surprising alacrity. Of course we all followed immediately,' Ellen said, '. . . and goodness knows how many Arabs! Some carried bits of candles; some dragged us along – and their help was needed! Sometimes we were in passages about three feet high, crawling like reptiles, sometimes going down steep inclines equally low, composed either of smooth slippery stone or of huge boulders, so that when you put out one foot you might have a yard to stretch before you had anything to plant it on. . . . You were always going up, or down, and generally on all-fours.'

It was an experience, though Ellen concluded that some other costume might have served her better: 'to enter the Pyramids in a crinoline and in a fashionable high bonnet was quite a mistake'. This did not, however, deter her from crawling into one of the tombs to admire the carvings on the wall, and, after lunch, from entering the Great Pyramid itself, carried unresisting (and with every appearance of pleasure) by three handsome Arabs. 'I must say these Bedouin Arabs are a fine race of men,' she said, 'tall, athletic fellows with intelligent countenances; and though in such close proximity, with an entire absence of fresh air, there was nothing more unpleasant than might have arisen in a London ballroom' – a nice reflection of life before deodorant.[53]

In her time in Egypt Ellen cruised on the Nile in a small boat – part of the flotilla that accompanied the Khedive's yacht. She visited the tombs at Sakkara and joined in donkey races in the desert – still in her crinoline and fashionable bonnet. She picnicked on the sand. She made a point of visiting whirling dervishes, whose performance she thought far superior to the howling ones. She delighted in Constantinople and the Bosphorus, 'the loveliest scenery in the world'.[54] Ellen was not blind to the frustrations and difficulties of living within someone else's culture. The standards were not always those of home: 'Had we known to what we should have been exposed,' she commented, during the Nile cruise, 'we would have brought with us some preserved meat in tins, some Huntley & Palmer's biscuits, tea, coffee, and sugar, a filter, and an Etna for boiling water. But we were told that everything would be provided for us, and this was our first experience.'[55] She simply chose to accept the difficulties, laughing or grumbling by turns as the occasion demanded, and always drinking in the sights and sounds unfolding round her.

Ada Leslie and Kate Fox both had the chance to see India; Ada on her first overseas appointment and Kate in the years following her enforced dismissal from Princess Nicholas's family. Ada sailed out from Liverpool late in 1883, full of excitement, to spend two years with the family of an Indian Army colonel. But the mother died during her voyage and on landing in Bombay, Ada discovered that she was to collect the children and take them back to England. She did have a chance to see something of the country, though, taking the mail train to Lucknow and staying with friends of the colonel before starting on the long journey home; 'I saw nearly everything worth seeing. . . . It's such fun here in India.'[56] She sailed for England with the children on the troopship *Jumna* with the 10th Hussars, enjoying herself thoroughly, 'what with Concerts, Sports, Entertainments, music and Dancing, the time passed away so quickly. On the 14th we had great fun as all the ladies received Valentines – and of course all the Officers pretend perfect ignorance.'[57]

Kate was sent out by the Norland Institute at the start of 1914 on an emergency placement, to collect a premature and sickly baby and his mother from Nowshera, a remote military station near the Afghan border, and bring them home to England. She sailed from Liverpool on the first available boat and, after a stormy passage, took the coastal steamer from Bombay to Karachi, then the Punjab express train across the Scind desert, and found herself some twenty-four hours later standing on a station platform at Lahore waiting for the train to Nowshera. 'I felt for the first time a little nervous,' she said, 'for I had been told by people who knew, that it was not safe to travel alone at night without a revolver.' But she got on the train, the inspector locked her into her compartment, and she arrived safely at Nowshera the next morning.

But safety at Nowshera was a relative commodity and Kate found the life there 'most exciting'. When the regiment marched away on duty everyone else had to move into the hotel for their own protection. It was blazing hot, there was very little water – making the care of a tiny baby rather difficult – but Kate had her pioneering hat pulled very firmly over her Norland bonnet. 'I think all these difficulties make the life so much more interesting,' she assured her fellow nurses, 'and also prove how one can manage without the luxuries one is inclined to call necessities, in more civilised lands. My bathroom had no curtain of any kind, so a piece of tissue paper had to be stuck on the window. Newspaper was wanted in many other ways, and was much too precious to be used as curtains.'58 Kate really proved her mettle on this journey. The baby's grandmother told Miss Sharman, 'She has achieved a most difficult task & bought a very delicate child to England under great difficulties & with no one to help her. . . . the Ship was overcrowded & the Dr useless. . . . My daughter wrote to me that she had been <u>such</u> a help and had never once fumbled altho' they were living in boxes & in deadly discomfort. I want to keep Miss Fox a few months until Baby is acclimatised.'59

From the sands of Egypt to the snows of Poland, with overheated German trains, Greek islands and the Afghan border, we have come a long way; but no British nurse or governess travelled quite so far, or had such life-changing experiences as Ethel Howard in her appointment to the Princes of Satsuma. Japan at the turn of the last century was changing rapidly yet was still fiercely proud of its own traditions. Ethel entered a world where everything was different. Her first sight of a man in a traditional kimono and wooden clogs, at Kobe, terrified her because as he ran towards her, wide sleeves flapping wildly, she was convinced that he had no arms. News from home took almost seven weeks to reach her. She rarely heard English spoken and understood no Japanese at first, yet, though she was given a collection of letters of introduction to British people, she was brave enough not to use them. 'I was a stranger,' she said, 'the first European woman who had ever resided in the family of a Japanese nobleman, and if I had visited many English families I might easily have been suspected of gossiping, which is abhorrent to the Japanese mind. I therefore resolved to wait, and to lead a secluded life, devoting all my time to the work itself, until I became better understood and could feel more trusted.'60 It was a lonely course to choose.

Ethel lived seven years in Japan. She saw the country from Kamakura to Hokkaido, Nikko to Nagasaki. At Nara, Japan's ancient capital, crowds turned out on the street simply to witness the sight of a Japanese Prince driving with a European lady, and the crush was terrible. She saw the Aino people of the far north, who lived apart from other Japanese and venerated the bear, and whose women tattooed moustaches on their lips. She enjoyed the famous tea ceremony, served by the eldest of the Shimadzu Princesses, 'I managed to drink off the full contents of the cup,' she said, 'but must confess that the after-effects of insomnia lasted two or three nights. The experience, however, was worth any amount of wakefulness. It left a calmness and gave a sense of peace not easily forgotten.'[61] The Princesses were not part of the Westernising experiment which entrusted their brothers to Ethel's care and they lived apart. The youngest fled in terror when she saw Ethel, her first ever European. But she was later persuaded to let Ethel see the traditional dolls brought out for her festival day, some of them hundreds of years old, and arranged on shelves with tiny portions of food and wine.

Ethel developed a taste for Japanese houses with their simple, clean lines. She liked their traditional beds too, then unknown in the West. 'I found them most comfortable,' she said, 'consisting as they do of soft, thick mattresses, called *futons*, covered with silk. They are kept in cupboards during the daytime, brought out at night, and laid on the tatami. Early in the morning the *futons* are carried away with magical celerity, put out of doors in the sun and air for a time, and then returned to the cupboards.'[62] Cut off from her own world, she grew so in tune with Japan and its ways that Western tourists became an irritation: 'I have come across tourists who either through ignorance or want of ordinary common sense and feeling have made me thoroughly ashamed and furious.'[63] Ethel saw earthquakes, typhoons and floods. She watched the construction of the Tokyo elevated railway and entered the closed world of the Emperor's private gardens. In later years her mind would often go back to her first awe-inspiring sight of Mount Fuji, from the deck of the ship that took her to Japan: 'The sun shining on its snow-clad slopes was a wonderful and never-to-be-forgotten sight. I remember how, as my heart sank with loneliness and fear, the Psalm kept ringing in my head, "I will lift up mine eyes unto the hills from whence cometh my help" – and often did I need it.'[64] A Japanese fellow passenger told her that sun on the mountain was considered a good omen for a new arrival: as she looked back on her 'seven wonderful years' she was sure that he was right.

ELEVEN

'A Wonderful Fifth Column'

REPRESENTING BRITAIN OVERSEAS

My wife and I had taken up our abode during the summer of 1918 at Lausanne. Our children's nurse, who was an Englishwoman, and who had served us with untiring devotion through all those trying times in Greece, was sent for one day by the British Consulate. Here, after being closely questioned about her employers, and cross-examined as to their private conversation, she was reminded that she was an Englishwoman and, as such, liable to be exposed to the severest consequences if she continued to offer her services to 'traitors to England'. She was threatened that unless she gave her employers notice at once she would be deprived of her passport. She came back to us in tears; naturally we had to let her go, not wishing to get her into further trouble on our account. She left the next day and we deeply regretted having to part with her. Identical measures had been applied to Queen Sophie's English nurse.[1]

Writing his memoirs in the 1920s, Prince Nicholas of Greece had good reason to feel bitter about the way his family was treated by Britain, France and their allies during and after the First World War. Greece had stood apart from the war as a neutral country, but as the fighting progressed there was a determined campaign, particularly from France, to denounce the Prince's brother King Constantine I as a closet supporter of the Germans. Constantine made an easy target; his wife Sophie was the Kaiser's younger sister. The Allied navies blockaded Greece. In the summer of 1916 Princess Nicholas confided her fury and unhappiness at the situation to Kate Fox: 'Poor Greece has been shamefully treated by the Powers who have lost no occasion to humiliate & insult her in every way,' she said, '& one must swallow it all & say nothing because one is small & weak! & that is called justice! . . . I'm so sorry for the King, it is dreadful for him.'[2] Ultimately the campaign paid off; the King was deposed and the rest of his family followed him into exile. Only his second son, Alexander, was left in uncomfortable isolation, as a puppet of the Allied powers.

And even exile, it seemed, was not punishment enough. In the closing months of the war, as Prince Nicholas described, official British attention turned towards the family's nurses, Elizabeth St John, Margaret Alison and Emily Roose, who remained faithful to the posts they had held for years. It probably never occurred to them that their loyalty to their own country could be questioned – but it was. 'I am very sorry to say that N. Margaret will be leaving us soon, she was <u>told</u> to do so!' Princess Nicholas remarked to Kate at the time. 'First it was St John & Roosie will probably be the next. I can't write all, but N. Margaret will tell you all about it – it is revolting! I suppose she will be leaving in about a month; I have not told the children yet, so please don't mention it if you write to them.'[3]

The British political establishment came very late to a realisation that British women working in royal households overseas could play a significant role for their country. And when the notion began to dawn its thrust went awry; British officials in the Greek case were seeing first an opportunity to gather incriminating evidence, then, a potential threat in the nurses' steadfast loyalty to the families who employed them. They failed to see that for generations women like Margaret Alison, Elizabeth St John and Emily Roose had played a benign role, quietly spreading British influence across the world as 'a wonderful fifth column planted into the most exclusive foreign nurseries and schoolrooms'.[4] 'Unacknowledged and unknown, that army of English Nannies and governesses were truly backstairs ambassadors,' the Romanian Princess Anne-Marie Callimachi commented in the aftermath of the Second World War, '. . . Had Herr Goebbels possessed such a weapon of penetration for his insidious ideas, he undoubtedly would have attempted to poison thousands of flexible young minds and had a try at the parents, too. As it was, overlooked and ignored by British officialdom their backstairs ambassadors remained a cohort of obscure freelances, unaware of the extraordinarily good work they were doing for their country.'[5] She was right, but to the British political establishment (all men) the world of the nursery and children was insignificant; only 'women's business'.

Queen Victoria could have advised them better. She had always valued the fashion that made important foreign families turn to Britain for their nurses and governesses and she encouraged it too. It created a latent fund of goodwill towards her country and, on a personal level, she knew intuitively that these women, so closely involved in the lives of their employers, could be an excellent source of information and advice if approached in the right way. She did not only use them in the context of marriages but generally, when she wanted a deeper understanding of a situation than the family members involved were prepared to give her. Discreet the nurses and governesses may have been, but they missed very little and they could be persuaded to speak, if they thought it was in their employers' best interests.

Over the generations their influence had spread in small ways. Wherever they went in the world, the nurses and governesses carried the language, customs, traditions and standards of home. This was expected; it was what you paid for when you employed an 'English' woman. Tsar Alexander II of Russia's granddaughter, Grand Duchess Maria Pavlovna, could have been speaking for almost every child brought up by an English nurse or governess when she remembered her own nursery years in the early 1890s. 'Nannie Fry and Lizzie Grove had brought to Russia all the habits of their native country;' she said; 'they ruled the nursery according to their own ideas and principles, and enjoyed an absolute sovereignty not only over my brother and me but over an innumerable retinue of Russian chambermaids, valets and assistant nurses. Until I was six years old I spoke hardly a word of Russian. The immediate household and all of the family spoke English to us.'[6]

Maria's cousin, Grand Duke Kirill, had Millicent Crofts to thank for the fact that his first language was English and this was not only true in Russia. Nursery English was spoken by children across Europe throughout the nineteenth century and later. Maria Pavlovna's mother was a Greek princess and her younger sister, Princess Marie of Greece, would later recall that 'In our babyhood, thanks to our English nurses, we all began by speaking English to each other. This did not last long. One day my father put his foot down, and ordered us to converse in Greek in the future.'[7] And Prince Adalbert of Prussia, third son of Kaiser Wilhelm II, caused consternation in his first lesson with a German tutor. Asked to name the emblem of Germany, the little boy said, quite correctly, 'Eagle'. But the tutor, not unnaturally assuming that the Kaiser's son would be speaking to him in German, thought he had heard '*Igel*' – 'hedgehog' – a very strange emblem for a proud imperial power.[8] In Austria in the 1890s the little Archduke Karl, who would go on to become the last Habsburg Emperor, learned to write in English before he wrote in German. All his other early lessons were in English too, under the direction of his governess Bridget Casey, whom he inherited from his young aunt Maria Annunciata. According to his mother's lady-in-waiting, he became so fluent that he would use English words quite unconsciously when he thought he was speaking German.

Spending all their time with the children, it was natural that the nurses would have talked about home, about their own families and experiences, and would have repeated the sayings, nursery rhymes, stories and songs that were part of a British childhood. Governesses must have fielded endless questions from the older children; how much more interesting, after all, for a child, to get 'Miss' telling stories about her home than to sit through the lessons she was trying to teach. The results could be amusing. One of the tutors at Queen Victoria's Court, late in 1866, was amazed to be greeted with, 'Are you a Regent Street swell?' from the lips of four-year-old Prince Heinrich of Prussia, the Queen's visiting grandson. It was left to little boy's mother to explain that when Emma Hobbs and May Hull brushed Heinrich's hair and dressed him in his best clothes they liked to say 'You look like a Regent Street swell' – clearly the idea had taken root, though the four-year-old could not have had any idea what it meant.[9]

Margaretta Eagar had no very high opinion of her singing voice but sometimes she had to oblige. Once, she said, Grand Duchess Tatiana was ill and unable to sleep. She asked Margaretta to sing for her, 'and I sang "Rock of Ages" till the poor little sufferer rebelled, and flatly refused to listen to it any more,' the nurse remembered, 'so I fell back upon "Villikins".' At that time, 'Villikins and his Dinah' had been a popular music-hall song in Britain for the best part of a century: to this day, most people would recognise the tune if they heard it. But a song less suited to the ears of a little Russian girl who cannot have been more than six or seven years old would be hard to imagine. 'Villikins' tells a story of unrequited love and cruel death in which poor Dinah, ordered by her father to marry a wealthy man she does not love, lies down in the garden and takes 'cold poison' only to be found, too late, by Villikins, her true lover. Little Tatiana was fascinated by the tragedy and the only thing in it that saddened her was the coldness of the poison: 'Why didn't she get her Nana to warm it for her? *You* would have warmed it for me, wouldn't you?'[10]

It is the sheer, joyous incongruity of some of these stories that gives them their appeal. As six-year-old Tatiana lay on her sickbed puzzling through the intricacies of Victorian romantic melodrama, some twenty years or so earlier, Millicent Crofts had thought 'the works of English literature, the first of which were *Barnaby Rudge* and *Oliver Twist*', suitable fare for her three little Russian Grand Dukes, all under ten years old.[11] And from Spain, the lesson plans of Annie Dutton and the exercise books of her youngest pupils give an extraordinarily detailed picture of the information that she thought appropriate to the children of King Alfonso XIII.

At eleven and ten years old, under Miss Dutton's direction, the little Infantes Juan and Gonzalo studied the great stories of English history: Bede's account of the conversion of England, Nelson's last fight at Trafalgar: '"They have done for me," he said . . . "Thank God I have done my duty." These were his last

words. The battle had been won; England was safe; and as brave a spirit as
ever lived had gone to his eternal rest.' Two years later the Infantes embarked
on a study of English literature few English boys their age could have matched.
Spanish princes they may have been, but by the time Miss Dutton had finished
with them they knew all about *Beowulf*, Caedmon's *Creation*, Layamon and
Robert of Gloucester, Langland, Chaucer and Geoffrey of Monmouth,
Marlowe, Ben Jonson, Beaumont and Fletcher, and other names, far more
obscure. Sometimes, thankfully, Annie Dutton fired their imagination with
simpler things, like stories of what English boys their age enjoyed doing. This is
apparent in a composition ten-year-old Gonzalo produced for his teacher in
1924: 'In England in the olden days and now too, when it snows the boys in
the schools fight snow-battles. How I should like to do this with Juannie
pelting him with snow balls and making him roll in the snow because it is
snowing very hard just now and I hope Nannie will let me go out and have a
good game.' ('Nannie' would have been the Scottish head nurse of the day,
Eugenie Doherty.)

Meanwhile, as the young Infantes grappled with English medieval literature,
their elder brother the Prince of the Asturias – the future King of Spain, so far
as anyone knew at the time – was treated to a course on the geography of
Britain which now seems quite breathtaking in its insularity. The British army,
Miss Dutton taught him, was 'Small, but brave and very efficient.' The navy
was 'Still superior to that of any other country', manufactured goods were
'More numerous and important than those of any other country', internal
communications 'Superior to those of any other country', domestic animals
'The finest in the world', and of the British people themselves she wrote;
'Owing to the insular position of England, the people are characterized by
strong national features. They are brave, enterprising and industrious; they are
remarkably attached to liberty, country and Home, and although very
hospitable they are reserved and proud to strangers.'

Annie Dutton's *Handy Reference Book to the Kings and Queens of England*,
which she herself composed especially for the Prince in 1922, when he was
fifteen, is a delight, sometimes rising to the heights of *1066 and All That* or the
Horrible Histories for the sheer oddity of its revelations, though Miss Dutton
would never have meant it to be funny. But her judgements are so
uncompromising. King John, she says, was 'Little less than a compilation of
vices polluted with meanness, cruelty, perjury and murder: a bad man, a worse
king and without dispute the most hated of all English monarchs.' Richard II
was 'handsome, but feminine', George I's 'tastes were low and degraded' while
George IV 'possessed talent but no virtue'. William IV was 'a bubbling old

gentleman with . . . a conically shaped head' and even Victoria (her pupils'
great-grandmother) 'was not remarkable for high development of any
specialized intellectual force'. And this unflattering chronicle of royalty is shot
through with quirky little insights: the history of the Morris dance, for
example, or the claim that Catherine of Braganza, wife of King Charles II,
introduced tea drinking to Britain, 'that temperate beverage' (hoorah!), or that,
in the reign of Mary Tudor, 'ladies were in the habit of carrying fans with
exceptionally long handles, in order to beat their daughters with, in case of
misbehaviour'.[12]

How useful any of this would have been to a future King of Spain is open to
question. But it is typical of the lessons that British governesses overseas were
teaching and, since the Spanish royal family liked and valued Annie Dutton
and employed her for fifteen years, from 1916 until the fall of the monarchy,
we have to assume that it is what they wanted their children to learn. The
unflinching confidence of some of Annie's statements may make modern
readers cringe – or laugh – but at the time it was accepted. Britain was a major
power and, while there were countries where the very British upbringing of
their future rulers came to be resented, for the most part the system passed
unquestioned. People wanted their children to be at ease with Britain and its
ways and they valued their nurses and governesses even for this fierce sense of
national pride – though it may have made them smile as well. 'Intensely loyal,
never assimilated, never conquered or convinced by anything un-British,'
Princess Callimachi said, 'they were a powerful influence.'[13] She recalled her
mother-in-law's governess Rebecca Paxton who had 'somehow strayed into the
wilds of Moldavia' when she was very young and stayed there, bringing up the
Callimachi children to maturity and then taking over the running of their
parents' house, making its inhabitants 'acutely conscious of England and as
loyal to that island as though it were a second homeland, and Miss Paxton an
official ambassador of the Empire'.[14]

Sometimes the women, particularly the nurses, passed on a few regional
peculiarities too. Nurses were renowned for dropping or misplacing their 'h's
in speech, a habit which always roused smiles (and usually disapproval) in
English society, where it was known as 'hatching'. Emma Hobbs was a
conspicuous offender. As she settled into the Kronprinzenpalais in Berlin at
the end of 1858 and prepared the nursery for its first royal baby, Emma kept
in touch by letter with Mary Anne Thurston, in England. One aspect of her
letters worried Mrs Thurston, who told the Queen, who in turn passed the
comment back to the expectant mother: 'Mrs Hobbs writes delighted with
everything but I am sorry to say she is a decided "hatcher" for she wrote to

Mrs Thurston (who is horrified at the prospect of the little individual speaking Cockney English) "I hear the Princess his getting on very well."'[15] And when, a few years later, the royal huntsman in Berlin could not find a hare to kill for the bizarre treatment the doctors suggested for baby Wilhelm's damaged arm, the Princess told her father, 'Mrs Hobbs exclaimed in indignation she could not understand why, as there were "Hoceans of airs running about the Place".'[16]

But if the thought of a small Prince of Prussia cheerfully dropping his 'h's caused alarm, imagine the reaction when the four little daughters of the last Tsar of Russia, picture perfect in their spotless broderie anglaise dresses and wide-brimmed hats, began to chatter away in a broad Irish (or was it Scottish?) accent. This was the situation King Edward VII encountered when he made the first visit of a British sovereign to Russia, meeting the imperial family on board ship off Reval in 1908. There are two theories about where the accent came from. If Irish, it must have been Margaretta Eagar's influence and if Scottish, from a tutor named John Epps. Either way, the King's remarks to the parents led to an English English tutor being appointed very smartly.

Within the Courts of Europe the employment of English nannies and governesses (including the Irish and Scottish ones) was a social matter. It was about equipping your children to feel comfortable on a level of society that was multinational; a level at which people had the means to travel freely, could converse in several languages and thought nothing of marrying across national boundaries. But beyond Europe these appointments always had a political edge. They were made by rulers from very different cultures who did aspire for themselves and their families to be conversant with that society but who also intended that, in the long term, appointing British women to teach their children would play a part in the modernising of their whole countries.

So, for example, in Egypt, which in the mid-nineteenth century was still part of the Turkish empire, with the Khedives ruling under the Sultan's authority. Emmeline Lott may have been the first European governess to live inside the harem, as she said, but she was certainly not the first Englishwoman to be employed by the Khedival family. The Greek merchant she met in the train on her way to Cairo when she first took up the appointment told her that the Western – predominantly French – education of the men of the family in recent years had started to bring about change. These princes, he said, 'surrounded themselves with foreign attendants, and even had English nurses for their children. This is the case with H.H. Mustapha Pacha, the heir presumptive to the Viceroyship, who not only treats that person with respect, but contributes most liberally to all her wants and requirements.'[17]

Nonetheless, Emmeline found herself a world that had hardly changed for centuries. She included an engraving of herself in her book, swathed from head to toe in robes like any other harem lady, with only her eyes on show, as a powerful testimony to the servitude expected of her. Emmeline left the country in 1865, her health broken but her notebook in hand, ready to make a second career from writing about her first. When Ellen Chennells arrived in Cairo in October 1871, Emmeline already had three best-selling books about her Egyptian experiences in print. It was surely no accident that one of the first things Ellen discovered was that the Khedival family was very angry about certain books describing the inner world of the harem. Her habit of keeping a diary made the royal children anxious to start with, but she assured them she had no intention of writing for publication. (This was a much later decision, she said, forced on her by circumstances when all those she had served at the palace were either dead or out of power. Her own savings had meanwhile been lost in a disastrous fall in the value of Egyptian bonds.)

But when she did write, the world Ellen described was a world under change. In the six years that passed between Emmeline's departure and Ellen's arrival things had already moved very quickly in Cairo. Soon after the publication of Emmeline's first book – perhaps by coincidence, perhaps not – the Khedive had taken steps to ensure that his son would have a British education *outside* the harem. He engaged a retired officer of the Indian Army, General Maclean, to teach the Pacha Ibrahim and established him, with his wife and family, in a house in Cairo. Ibrahim was sent out daily for his lessons but the Macleans did make courtesy visits to the palace, and the little Prince's mother took a liking to the General's eldest daughter. Miss Maclean was asked to teach Ibrahim's sister Zeyneb and, rather than admit Miss Maclean to the harem, the little Princess was sent out, like her brother, to spend her days at the Maclean's house. The first departure from custom the Macleans introduced, which caused some consternation, was to give Zeyneb precedence over her brother because she was a year older, even though she was a girl. They also gave equal treatment to the two slave children who shared the lessons, encouraging a freedom of expression the young master and mistress never resented.

In 1871 General and Miss Maclean left Cairo and a new staff was appointed: Mr Freeland, a married man with a young family, for Ibrahim, and Ellen Chennells for Zeyneb. A house was acquired for them all on the Choubrah Road in the most fashionable part of Cairo: 'The house was spacious and handsomely furnished, with every possible convenience,' Ellen wrote. 'We had all our separate suites of apartments, so as to enjoy privacy and social life at the same time.'[18]

Ellen paid tribute to the Khedive's attempts to improve the position of women in Egypt, 'but he knows that education must precede liberty,' she said, 'or it will become licence'.[19] She believed that the education of Princess Zeyneb was a part of this process. So far as she knew, no Muslim princess had ever been brought up outside the harem walls before and even for Zeyneb the experiment had to be short-lived. As a little girl the Princess wore Western dress and spent her days on the Choubrah Road, but at puberty she was locked inside the harem once again with Kopsès, her slave, for the rest of her life. Miss Chennells regretted this. She noticed how Kopsès particularly changed from a lively, intelligent, talkative girl, 'the free outspoken member of a free community', to 'the quiet, dignified Oriental, receiving notice from her superiors with profound respect' once she was in the harem.[20] And she felt sad for both girls 'because they had known what liberty was, and lost it just at the age when its deprivation would be felt the most.'[21] But when other people said it was wrong of the Khedive to subject his daughter to the experiment and then shut her away, Ellen disagreed. She believed he had gone as far as he could against the customs of his people: the sight of a young princess living outside the harem without the protection or company of the older women of her family who were still secluded, would never have been accepted, she said, in a Muslim country. 'By marrying her early, and then encouraging her gradually and innocently to introduce European customs, all was done that could reasonably be attempted; and had she lived, I believe a thorough change would in a few years have taken place in female society in Egypt.'[22]

Miss Chennells certainly did her best to be part of that change, encouraging Zeyneb to look beyond the walls that enclosed her. 'The Princess would ask me all sorts of questions about England,' she remembered, 'and whether I thought society would ever be the same in Egypt as it was with us. I told her I thought much would depend on herself. She was in a high position and would be looked up to as an example. If she by her conduct could show that liberty was not inconsistent with modesty and innocence, there was no doubt but a few years would bring about an entire revolution in the present system with regard to women. Their seclusion was not a Mahometan doctrine – it had existed in the East long before Mahomet; but in all countries, the more civilised a state became, the higher did women rise in the social scale.'[23] In the 1870s this last statement would have been fairly revolutionary teaching even in England.

Anna Leonowens shared wholeheartedly Ellen Chennells's belief that her influence could and should spread far beyond one royal child – or, in Anna's case, a large number of royal children. Anna was employed by King Mongkut explicitly as part of his gradual process of modernisation and change; to help open Siam to the best of the new developments then taking place in the West without overwhelming the country's distinctive character. Language was what the King most needed from Anna, for himself as much as his children, to assist him in his dealings with foreign governments. 'I have sixty-seven children,' he told her at their first meeting. '. . . You shall educate them, and as many of my wives, likewise, as may wish to learn English. And I have much correspondence in which you must assist me. And, moreover, I have much difficulty for reading and translating French letters; for French are fond of using gloomily deceiving terms. You must undertake; and you shall make all their murky sentences and gloomily deceiving propositions clear to me. And furthermore, I have by every mail foreign letters whose writing is not easily read by me. You shall copy on round hand, for my readily perusal thereof.'[24]

It was a responsible position, but in Anna Leonowens King Mongkut had taken on a competent linguist who was prepared to work long hours in his service. He had also taken on a strong-minded and hot-headed woman with firmly held views and very little patience; their clashes were frequent. Like Emmeline, Anna was contemptuous of a system that tied so many women to one man and, in her eyes, made little more than slaves of them. Then there was the parlous state of many actual slaves. For the first part of her time in Bangkok, very much against her will, Anna was installed with her young son Louis in the Nang Harm, the walled city within the King's palace which housed his children and dependent relatives under his care, together with the mothers of his children, a large number of concubines and an even larger number of young noblewomen given to the King by their families. It was part of Mongkut's royal duty to father as many children as possible on these last three groups of women, to strengthen the ties between the royal family and the nobility – but this was a concept no English governess could accept. Unlike Emmeline, though, Anna was not content to go home and write about it afterwards. She wanted to make a difference and she protested, loudly and often, when she thought an injustice was being done. In time people went to her with their grievances, not only against the King but also against judges and magistrates. When Anna left Bangkok in 1867 on a leave of absence that in fact proved permanent, the King's final words to her must have been heartfelt: 'I am often angry on you, and lose my temper, though I have large respect for you. But nevertheless you ought to know that you are difficult woman, and more difficult than generality.'[25]

Anna's own accounts of her years in Bangkok were heavily embroidered to suit the tastes and prejudices of a Western audience. Subsequent reworkings in a romanticised biography, a musical and three Hollywood films have so obscured her story – and enraged her critics – that her true legacy is hard to assess. King Mongkut was a far more enlightened and progressive ruler than she gave him credit for and the steady modernisation of his country would have taken place if Anna Leonowens had never set foot in Bangkok. But Anna was at the King's Court for nearly six years and she was a hard woman to ignore. She handled Mongkut's diplomatic correspondence when required and she gave lessons to his heir from the age of ten. Prince Chulalongkorn, who was a full brother of little Princess Fâ-ying, the enchanting eight-year-old who died of cholera, was a clever, thoughtful boy and Anna felt a strong attachment to him. 'He often deplored with me the cruelty with which the slaves were treated,' she said, 'and, young as he was, did much to inculcate kindness toward them among his immediate attendants. He was a conscientious lad, of pensive habit and gentle temper. . . . Speaking of slavery one day, he said to me: "These are not slaves, but nobles; they know how to bear. It is we, the princes, who have yet to learn which is the more noble, the oppressor or the oppressed."'[26]

Chulalongkorn succeeded his father not long after Anna left Bangkok and in his long reign he brought about many significant changes. The abolition of slavery in Thailand and the abandonment of the custom that required his people to prostrate themselves before him were just two examples of reforms that were dear to Anna's heart. His father had set such things in motion but it would hardly be fair to deny Anna some influence. Chulalongkorn certainly never forgot her and he was a good friend to her son Louis who held a trusted position at his Court. The King was reunited with Anna in a London hotel in August 1897, thirty years after their parting, and he greeted her with great affection: 'Oh Mem, what have you done with your beautiful curls?' They talked for a long time and Chulalongkorn told Anna he was sending his numerous sons and nephews overseas to be educated, and to acquire professional skills that could be useful to their country; skills like medicine and engineering. And though he also asked her why she had given the world such an unfair picture of his father, they parted friends. 'You have just met a very brave man,' Anna told her granddaughter, who was at the meeting. 'Accomplishing what he set out to do has cost him more than any of us realize.'[27]

For every Anna Leonowens or Emmeline Lott, who wrote about her experiences, there must have been a score of other women like them in the Middle and Far East who have left no record of their work. In 1862, the year Anna sailed up the Gulf of Siam and Emmeline Lott secured her appointment in Egypt, Emily Payne packed up her trunk and school books and set off for

Hsipaw, in the Shan district of the country the British would later call Burma, as governess to the children of a local Prince, the Sawbwa of Hsipaw. This was twenty years before the Shan provinces came under British control, but the Sawbwas of Hsipaw were the wealthiest princes in the area and they aspired to a modern, Western lifestyle. They were very British in sympathy and Emily may have obtained her appointment with them through British commercial interests as Anna did, through the Singapore branch of the British Borneo Company. But what adventures Emily had in the Sawbwa's family we may never know. She made her home with them and never saw England again, and the only memorial is the grave the family gave her in a little hilltop cemetery with a stone that reads simply 'EMILY PAYNE, Lady Governess'. In later years, though, visitors to the Grand Haw, the old palace in Hsipaw, were amazed to find a luxurious household run entirely on English lines. Perhaps this was Emily's legacy.

Burma may have been a world away but Japan was further still, and at the end of the 1800s the country was emerging painfully from centuries of isolation. The feudal system had been abolished by law but the mindset it produced in the country took longer to break, 'and it was in pursuance of the new policy', Ethel Howard wrote, 'that the appointment was made which placed me in charge of Prince Shimadzu and his young brothers.'[28] Ethel's appointment was a deliberate attempt to impose Western culture on the sons of one of Japan's most powerful noble families. There was no appointment more overtly political than hers, both for this reason and because it came at a significant moment in Japan's relationship with the world outside. In 1894 the Japanese emerged triumphant from a war with China only to find themselves forced by Western pressure to give back some of the land they had won. Russia stood in the way of further Japanese expansion; Japan needed a Western ally and chose Britain. Ethel was appointed while the talks were going on that would lead, a year later, to a formal Anglo-Japanese alliance. It cannot have been a coincidence. In Japan at least, her appointment was considered so groundbreaking that the press felt obliged to mask its true nature. On 20 February 1901, the Japanese *Times* reported that, 'One of the highest and most influential of the whole aristocracy of Japan has decided on having its children (especially its girls) brought up in the charge of an accomplished English lady.'[29]

The truth was that the girls were kept right away from Ethel in their ancestral home. The modernisation of their lives was never part of the plan: Ethel's brief was to transform the lives of Prince Tadashige and his brothers. Even in the West, the choice of a woman to take charge of five healthy boys, the eldest of whom was over fourteen, would have raised eyebrows. In Japan, as she was later to realise, it caused 'a commotion . . . the idea of a woman having anything to do with the sons of a Japanese nobleman being at the time of my arrival almost beyond endurance'.[30]

There seems little doubt that the Emperor himself had a hand in the experiment. His Master of Ceremonies and Court councillor, Mr Nagasaki, was present at Ethel's first meeting with her pupils and their gentlemen, 'the chief being a guardian uncle, who could not speak a word of English, and who looked very disapprovingly at me'.[31] Mr Nagasaki also introduced her to the head of the family's five guardians, the Marquis Matsukata, and acted as interpreter at all of their meetings; he was present too for Ethel's audiences with the Empress, who 'had always taken a lively interest in the progress made by the Prince and his brothers'.[32] But how did the appointment come about, and why Ethel Howard? She tells us only that she received a letter one day asking whether she would consider the position if offered. She never says who it came from, but she discussed it with Sir Edwin Arnold, the editor of the Daily Telegraph, and he urged her to accept. 'How beautiful it would be,' he said, 'if you could bring East and West together through the lives of these young noblemen.'[33]

Ethel's only previous experience of the East had been her teaching of King Chulalongkorn's nephew Prince Sitiphorn at home in England before she went to Berlin; this was hardly a qualification. Someone must have recommended her and the best clues probably lie in the circumstances surrounding her journey and her arrival in Japan. First, she was shown around her new home in Tokyo by Mrs Whitehead, the wife of the First Secretary to the British Legation; Mr and Mrs Whitehead already knew Ethel well because they were based in Berlin when she was working for the Kaiser's family. They certainly had a hand in choosing and furnishing the Tokyo house. Then, before reaching Tokyo, Ethel was entertained by the British Consul in the first Japanese port she reached and she mentions the support she received from Lord Sandwich. As far as she was concerned, he was just a fellow passenger, but he did often undertake diplomatic missions for Britain. And in her book, Ethel pays tribute to the 'generous help and encouragement' of Lady MacDonald, the British Ambassador's wife in Japan. Put together, these factors suggest that in Ethel's case at least, the British political establishment did play some part in her appointment.

But someone else played a more active part. Whoever sent the letter sounding Ethel out on her feelings about Japan, as soon as she accepted the position it was the Germans who sprang into action to smooth her path. A passage was booked for her on the German liner *Kiaouchou* and the Kaiserin at once telegraphed the captain, instructing him that Miss Howard was to receive special care on the voyage; Ethel also had the personal attention of Herr Ballin, the head of the shipping line. He promised her a free passage home if she found life in Japan too much to bear.[34] And soon after her arrival, the Kaiser sent a telegram to Prince Shimadzu, congratulating him on securing her services, 'and adding "which I deeply regret to have lost". In those days,' Ethel said, 'such a recommendation was of untold value, and I found this cable a great help. It seemed to complete the perfect confidence of the Guardians, though only time could justify their faith in me.'[35] She was to receive personal visits in Tokyo from the German Ambassador, Count d'Arco-Valley, and from the Chief of the German General Staff, Count von Waldersee, who 'insisted on having a photo taken with one of the boys on his shoulder, as he affirmed that the Kaiser would be most interested and gratified to receive such a picture of the East and West united'.[36] But if the Germans expected to gain some advantage from all this attention they would be disappointed. When a letter arrived for Ethel from the German Mistress of the Robes, 'telling me that His Majesty wished to hear all about my work with the Japanese Princes', Ethel had no doubt of where her duty lay. 'I followed the same rule in the Shimadzu family as I had at Potsdam, of silence as to the nature of my work,' she said. 'I wrote only expressing my thanks.'[37]

Like his grandmother Queen Victoria, Kaiser Wilhelm II was acutely aware of the important role entrusted to British nurses and governesses in training the rising generation of world leaders. Unlike her, he seemed to resent it. He and his wife were among the first to try to change the system in 1883, dismissing the English nurse their aunt Helena had chosen for their baby sons and appointing a German, much to the disgust of the Queen; 'I am indeed greatly shocked and grieved at the good English nurse being sent away,' she told his mother, 'and the German one taken instead. . . . I think it very wrong and foolish in two young people to pretend to know anything about the management of young children. One must depend so much upon one's nurse.'[38] The German nurse did last for a few years but British influence in the nursery was not so easy to avoid. In November 1886 Ada Leslie was brought in as nursery governess and in 1889 the redoubtable Miss Matcham took over as nurse. 'Nana' Matcham became so deeply rooted that in later years people assumed she had always been with the family and, though she still thought of herself as entirely English, her new home did affect her. Her language changed. In German the word for 'receive' is *bekommen*; Anne Topham was rather nonplussed to be told by Miss Matcham, when comparing Christmas presents, 'last year I became a set of teaspoons, and the year before I became a lovely silver teapot'.[39]

British women who worked at the Kaiser's Court were made to feel very conscious of their nationality and often quite uncomfortable about it. Ethel Howard believed it was from the German press and people that the anti-British feeling came. 'It was only too evident,' she said, 'that the German public thought that their Princes' upbringing, what with an English nurse and then an English governess, was rather too pro-British.'[40] But Anne Topham, who arrived in Germany at a time when mistrust between the two countries was on the increase, had a very different impression. It took her only a few days, she said, to discover that the Kaiser was 'very jealous of England . . . and it was a terrible disillusion for me. This man who had so often professed friendship for England was not really friendly at all, or at most his friendship was purely political and liable to change.'[41] She found herself called upon to answer for anything the English did to annoy him: English drinking habits, suffragettes – a particular hate of the Kaiser's because he simply couldn't understand them – 'He wants to know "what in heaven women want with a vote?"'[42]

At the time of Anne's arrival in Germany the Boer War, which had made England very unpopular in Europe, had entered its messy and apparently interminable final phase, 'and the Emperor's sneers at England's inability to finish the war were openly expressed to me in English'.[43] Anne tried to defend her country – the Kaiser called her 'the British Dreadnought' – but the constant sniping made her feel very isolated. Ethel may have had an easier time because she never tried to defend her country at all. Before she went to Berlin her father warned her to avoid discussing politics and the advice served her well. She would later say that the Kaiser was always kind to her but she was also aware that he tended to single her out 'as the laughing-stock of his Court'. Her German was poor; he looked for occasions to show her up for this in public, none more memorable than the formal luncheon when he took away her spoon and told her to ask the servant for another. When Ethel asked for a devil (*Teufel*) instead of a spoon (*Löffel*) the whole room erupted in helpless laughter and the incident even made the Berlin papers.[44]

The First World War made it inevitable that Germany would be the first place where British dominance of the world's nurseries was broken. And when hostilities ended, there was too deep a sense of injury on both sides for the old ties to be quickly restored. The Kaiser's daughter-in-law, Crown Princess Cecilie, looking back on the humiliation of defeat and the monarchy's fall, told a distant cousin that her only hope was, 'to bring up our children brave Germans, who will do their duty, whatever it may be'.[45] Writing her memoirs in the late 1920s, Cecilie did pay tribute to her own English nurse, Mary Jenkins, acknowledging that, 'although English was my first language I never suffered any ill effects from it. . . . The advantages I gained were permanent, that is to say, a thorough and perfectly natural knowledge of English, and with it probably also an appreciation of many English peculiarities', but she was aware that this could be unpopular with her readers.[46] 'Opinions may differ on the custom of placing English nurses in charge of royal nurseries,' she wrote. 'But it must be remembered that thirty or forty years ago the care given to children among us in Germany was not on as high a level as it was later. I myself deliberately broke with this custom for my children, but it is true only when the traditional English nurse had not been altogether successful with my first child. . . . With the active help of my mother-in-law, Kaiserin Auguste Viktoria . . . our hygienic arrangements and our experience in child-welfare have made rapid progress. I believe it is not an exaggeration for me to say that in this matter we have already surpassed the English.'[47]

But as the German royal families reassessed the upbringing they wanted for their children, in other parts of the world British nurses and governesses were quick to return. Some had never been away. The Egyptian royal family remained faithful to its British nurses. In the late 1930s and early '40s two Princess Christian nurses, Winifred Johnson and Sylvia Barber, looked after Princesses Ferial and Fawzia, the little daughters of King Farouk and Queen Farida and great-granddaughters of Emmeline Lott and Ellen Chennells's Khedive. At this later date the family still followed the same seasonal progress from Cairo to the seashore at Alexandria; both places Emmeline Lott had known and hated, though in Winifred and Sylvia's day there was no harem to trouble the sensibilities of a delicate Englishwoman. The King had one wife (at a time) and his baby daughters wore the clothes, played the games and could anticipate the freedoms of every other child of their class.

But the political establishment in Britain was far more aware by this time of the work being done by women like Winifred and Sylvia. The government may have taken an interest in their appointments: when a new nurse was sought for Queen Farida's third daughter Fadia, born at the end of 1943, government officials were certainly aware of what was happening. Approaches were made to the Norland Institute on the royal family's behalf and the selected nurse, Anne Chermside, was interviewed at the Home Office as well as the Egyptian Embassy before leaving to take up her post.

Anne was a farmer's daughter from Leamington Spa, born during the First World War, who earned her Norland training by doing a year's domestic work at the Institute first, in the months following her father's death. Girls who paid for their course at Norland in this way were known as 'maidens'. The tutors found Anne quiet and reserved at first, understandably, but she excelled in her training and held down two successful posts before the war. Then she took charge of the baby wing of the Dyrham Park Nursery near Bath, housing over seventy evacuee children from London. The chance to work for 'a prominent Egyptian family' was a opportunity she seized with pleasure. 'It was like a dream to me,' she said, 'going from war-weary England to sunny Egypt; the life was such a contrast to the preceding years.'[48] She had an uncomfortable flight to Cairo – passenger airlines were still a novelty then. There was no heating on board, only blankets, and the journey involved a series of very bumpy take-offs and landings. But the King was waiting to welcome her in person and the fabled luxury of the Abdin Palace seemed quite unreal after the privations of wartime Britain.

Like her Victorian predecessors, though, Anne found Cairo hot and dirty and she much preferred Alexandria, where she spent the first two months of her service with the Egyptian royal family: 'it is one of the most beautiful places I have ever seen'. The weather was perfect; she whiled away her mornings with the baby in the palace gardens and in the afternoons the elder Princesses would return from school to be joined by their friends, the exiled royal children of Greece, Princesses Sophie and Irene and Crown Prince Constantine. They swam and played on the beach, often with the Queen joining in as well, and when winter came the whole household returned to Cairo. It was a pattern of life that lasted until November 1948, when the King and Queen Farida divorced. Anne and Princess Fadia remained with the Queen until the little girl was eight years old, when Muslim law required her to return to her father.

By this time King Farouk had remarried and his new Queen, Narriman, was expecting a child. He offered Anne the position of nurse which she accepted gladly; on 16 January 1952 in the Abdin Palace she witnessed the birth of a Crown Prince, Ahmed Fuad. The days when royal nurses were discreetly ignored had long gone. Anne's picture appeared in the newspapers at home and the *Evening News* even interviewed her brother Robert, though he didn't tell them very much. To this day the reporter's frustration echoes through his bland words: 'Miss Chermside gets two months leave every two years; she was home last summer. She did not tell her family very much about her job but she likes it very much, says her brother.'[49]

Among those who visited the Abdin Palace to congratulate the King on the birth of his heir was General Sir Brian Robertson, Commander-in-Chief of the British Middle East Land Forces: his men fired a 21-gun salute in celebration beside the Suez Canal. The British had kept a strong military presence in the Middle East ever since the First World War, and the Egyptian royal children were not the only ones who lived under the protecting arm of the British army, cared for by British women. In April 1939 the young King Ghazi of Iraq died suddenly in a car crash, leaving the throne to his son Faisal, who was then only three years old. A cosseted, isolated child, it was said that up to the age of five Faisal was still fed by others, and was barely allowed even to walk on his own. Then he acquired an English governess. In her early thirties, Betty Sulman was teaching at her father's preparatory school in Sussex when the wife of a former ambassador to Iraq singled her out as a likely candidate for Faisal – it was a perceptive choice. Brisk, sporty and full of energy, Betty was glad to escape the staid respectability of Bexhill-on-Sea and she set off for Iraq with her cricket bat and reading primer. The year was 1940 and she passed through Paris just as the German army launched its invasion of France.

Betty swept away the pampering and fuss and brought other children into Faisal's life. She also persuaded the little boy's mother to take notice of him, telling her that a nightly visit to the nursery 'is not only your majesty's pleasure but also your duty'.[50] Under Betty's care Faisal blossomed and she found him a bright, endearing little boy, well able to do all the things that had been denied him before. She had a good time in Baghdad herself as well, making full use of all the social and sporting opportunities the Iraqi capital had to offer. She drove a borrowed Bentley with little regard to traffic regulations, and enjoyed riding. Once, she won the Iraqi army's five-furlong flat race, much to Faisal's delight. She attracted several admirers too, and finally accepted a proposal of marriage from John Morrison, an officer in British Intelligence.

But in the world around them, danger was growing. Faisal's grandfather Faisal I, King of the Hejaz, had fought alongside T.E. Lawrence in the Arab rising of 1916. It was the British who gave him the throne of the newly created country of Iraq in 1921 and he did not gain full independence until 1932. British involvement in Iraq remained strong but it was resented. When the Second World War broke out in the first months of young Faisal's reign, the Iraqi government was divided in its feelings towards Britain and at first it declared neutrality. Then, on the fall of France, public opinion changed and the leaders of the Pan-Arab movement called for an alliance with Nazi Germany. Secret negotiations began. In March 1941 Regent Abdul Illah, the King's uncle, was dismissed in a military coup. Everyone in the palace was arrested – even Betty. On securing her release, she found her way to the American legation where she was one of 200 people besieged for ten days with hardly any food or water; nothing daunted, it was Betty who took charge of distributing the meagre rations the legation could offer, keeping almost nothing back for herself.

Meanwhile, the British army made a decisive intervention and by the end of May the Iraqis surrendered. The Regent was reinstated with a moderate government under British protection and Iraq declared war on the Nazis. Betty may have returned to the palace at first, but she had lost nearly two stone in weight during the siege and it was after the traumas of the failed coup that she decided to resign her post and marry her fiancé – in later years her family would say that she 'bagged Dad in Baghdad'.[51] Faisal must have missed her but he still had a British nurse, Miss Borland, and by the end of 1942 Betty's successor had been chosen.

Despite her very Spanish-sounding name, Rosalind Ramirez was a Londoner, born in Acton. She owed the name to her Chilean stepfather, who took her to South America with her mother while she was still a small child. Few clues remain to her career before she went to Iraq; among her papers she kept photographs of a family in Braemar in Scotland, with herself pushing the pram, and she is also said to have visited Palestine and to have met members of King Faisal's Hashemite family. Whatever she had done before, in the spring of 1943 with the war at its height, she set off for Iraq and her new role as the King's governess. The British Council arranged her journey to Baghdad, almost certainly under military auspices. She appears to have stopped at Aden, Egypt and Damascus *en route* and a British Council member accompanied her, the 'most helpful & assiduous Ingham, my journey-mate', who later became 'rather annoyingly familiar, so that he had to be ticked off by me'.

This comment is taken from a diary record Rosalind started to keep soon after her arrival: it is tantalisingly brief, consisting of only three long entries made in a notebook while she was still staying in the rooms arranged for her in Baghdad's Sinbad Hotel. It shows her to have been sociable, amusing, quick in her judgements of people and rather overwhelmed by the amount of attention the British Council – an organisation set up in 1934 by the Foreign Office to promote cultural links with other countries – was showing her: 'by Jove I need every jot of rest I can get', she wrote, 'as the BC's idea is to trot me round here, there & everywhere making contacts – well, of course, I love it & never find it difficult but it does take a tremendous physical toll to talk & try to find links incessantly'.

Rosalind's photographs are the best remaining clue to her work with Faisal. They preserve glimpses of a very happy small boy in a perpetual summer, laughing into the camera, climbing trees, boating and playing games, cutting his birthday cake and tending the plants in his garden. She also kept cuttings from Iraqi and British forces' newspapers which show how closely the British Army was involved in Faisal's life. On his eighth birthday in May 1943, the boy King gave his first ever radio broadcast in both Arabic and English, sending his greetings, 'to all my friends in the British Empire and the United States. Some of you have fathers or brothers now serving in my kingdom,' he said. 'I want to send you a special greeting and to tell you that we are doing all we can to make them happy.' And for his ninth birthday, an article in the army paper *Trunk Call* described how, 'The Army and the RAF with memories of their own nine-year-olds, did their best to express some of the gratitude which all British service men here feel for the welcome extended to us by King Faisal and his people. . . . The Army gave him a garden switchback, constructed by the Royal Engineers and the RAF a "K" type collapsible rubber dinghy inflated by compressed air, and three model planes. . . .

'Little boys have a tremendous capacity for being thrilled and all those who had any part in constructing King Faisal's switchback will be gratified to know that he was <u>really</u> thrilled. In roughly thirty seconds he had broken away from the C-in-C, mounted the five foot platform and settled himself in one of the little trolley cars for the first Royal ride. He finished up in a rose bush and promptly came back for more.' In September 1943, *Parade*, a forces' magazine, featured a double-page spread of photographs of the King's daily life, showing him at work in his schoolroom with Rosalind. 'On the wall of the schoolroom there was a strange contrast in pictures. Some were paintings of little men and animals done by the King: others were reproductions of famous painters, including Van Gogh. He is fond of drawing and painting, his skill is that of the average small boy. . . . It is always a great temptation to be over flattering to royalty but one can say honestly that King Faisal is a very bright intelligent boy. . . . Many people foresee a brilliant future for him.'[52]

It was not to be. When the King was old enough for an English boarding school, Rosalind's appointment ended and she returned home. By the summer of 1947 she had found a new royal post as governess to Princes William and Richard of Gloucester, while Faisal went on to Harrow and Sandhurst. He never forgot her. In 1951 he gave her a signed photograph inscribed 'to Rosalind' and in 1952 he visited her with his mother. But Faisal would never have the opportunity to satisfy the hopes that rested on him. Once back in Iraq he fell victim to the chronic political instability which had beset his country from its foundation. In July 1958 he was assassinated with other members of his family and household in the military coup that established the Iraqi republic. 'Despite the best efforts of their foreign patrons,' an Arab writer, Fouad Ajami, remarked, 'the Hashemites with their English nannies and tutors and coachmen proved to be too refined for the brittle country. . . . Iraq was made of crueller stuff.'[53]

No one could doubt that Rosalind's appointment was political. Britain created the Hashemite kingdom of Iraq, Britain needed the boy King to grow up as a friend, thoroughly attuned to British ways. But in herself, she still preserved the same independence shown by generations of British nurses and governesses, who had had to forge their own way when their country took no official interest at all. Like Ethel Howard refusing to tell the Kaiser about her work with the Shimadzu princes; like Margaret Alison and Elizabeth St John, protecting the privacy of their Greek employers against threats from British Consular officials, Rosalind Ramirez declined to be used. On 17 May 1943 she attended a tea party at the British Embassy in Baghdad. There were a number of people there, but during the afternoon the Ambassador drew her aside for a private talk, 'the upshot of it being that I had a great work to perform for G B. I said I was afraid I was not political, purely educational & he seemed to think that was OK & just being myself I sh do good. I'm sure I hope so for I can't pretend.'[54]

TWELVE

'It's Only Bombs, Dear'

WITNESSES TO HISTORY

We lay at anchor several days in Sevastopol harbour, and made several excursions to the town and adjacent country. . . . We passed through the famous quarries where the English lay entrenched and so much desperate fighting took place. Beyond these quarries are the graveyards where lie the victims, or some of them, of the war. . . . We visited the English graveyard. The piece of ground was bought from Russia and is enclosed with a stone wall, the entrance is handsome, and the whole place is kept in beautiful order. There is a resident caretaker, a Russian, who keeps all trim, and plants and tends flowers and shrubs with great care. . . . But those graves! The inscriptions on them are sad beyond belief.[1]

The Crimean War ended seven years before Margaretta Eagar was born but she must have known the stories. On her first visit to the peninsula she looked forward to seeing the battlefield of the Alma and was disappointed that the only view she had was from the train window. So when the imperial family returned to the Crimea in 1902 and spent several days at anchor off Sevastopol in their yacht, she seized the opportunity to explore the town itself – the scene of a famous siege during the war – and the surrounding battlefields. Margaretta particularly wanted to find the grave of Hedley Vicars, a young captain of the 97th Regiment killed in a night attack in the Inkerman quarries. The posthumous publication of Captain Vicars's letters had made him a national hero, and in the years following his death it became fashionable to name boys after him. Margaretta managed to find him. 'He lies with his head to the wall', she wrote; 'his grave is well kept. He was only twenty-seven years of age. In so short a life we would have thought there was little room for distinction, but his name will long be remembered. . . .'[2]

Margaretta's interest in the war did not give offence to her companions at the Tsar's Court, even though their two countries had been enemies then and Russia had suffered a painful defeat. They were happy to show her the battlefields and to talk about what happened. They even teased her about it. Forty years on, the Crimean War was history, and the visit was a chance to see and to understand events their parents' generation had lived through.

For anyone with a sense of history, working at a royal Court had this added attraction of putting you in touch with the places where history was made and the people involved in its making. Miss Smith was often left in charge of the youngest Waldeck children while the elder ones toured the spas of Europe with their perpetually ailing mother. In the autumn of 1871, soon after the end of the Franco-Prussian war, sixteen-year-old Princess Pauline realised that her nurse would be on the spot to witness the return of the victorious German armies. 'Dearest Nanny', she wrote. 'How I envy you for being there to-day, we all wished so very much to see the entry of the troops. You must write us soon and tell us all about it.' The same letter passed on a nugget of royal gossip from the spa at Ischl: 'Only think Nanny what the people invent here', Pauline continued: 'the queen Isabelle of Spain was here and walked about with blue boots and red heels, and a gentleman told Herr von Padtburg, that she had become protestant and married an English lord!!!?'[3]

The exiled Queen Isabel II of Spain was a large, flamboyant woman whose doings always attracted interest. Even more so, the beautiful and remote figure of the Empress Elisabeth of Austria never failed to intrigue. She was so different from her reliable, hard-working husband; so glamorous and so unhappy, forever restless, moving from place to place and unwilling to be seen. It was something to be able to say that you had met her. Nellie Ryan was presented to her on a visit to Vienna and she was captivated: 'I remember she said how much she always admired the English, and everything that was English, and how much she regretted her inability to converse as fluently as she wished.' Nellie passed on the stories she had been told of the Empress's secret life of charity. 'She went into the poorest and darkest hovels,' she said, 'and no one ever knew that the kind, gentle lady was the same haughty and indifferent Empress who was so misjudged by many of her subjects.'[4]

But May T, as governess to the Empress's granddaughter, saw her in a very different light. May's first encounter with Empress Elisabeth happened by chance, in the imperial estate of Lainz which lay adjacent to the park of the summer palace at Schönbrunn. She and the little Archduchess had wandered further than they intended. The light was beginning to fade and they were hurrying home when 'we discerned a figure advancing rapidly towards us, all in black and heavily veiled; it seemed to float along, scarcely touching the ground. The Archduchess, in a panic, clung to me, gasping "Grandmama!",' May said. 'I was so startled that I almost forgot to curtsy, but habit is stronger than fright, and with the encumbrance of the clinging child, I did my utmost. The Empress did not turn her head, but seemed to breathe a "Good day", and passed, a black wraith in the twilight.'[5] On another occasion, May described how Erzsi and her mother, the widowed Crown Princess, were enjoying themselves in a hotel at Karersee in the Tyrol when they were told they would have to leave to make way for the Empress. 'It was a recognised fact,' May remarked, 'that she visited her dislike of her dead son's wife upon their child, the little Elizabeth, to such an extent that she never voluntarily saw her granddaughter and never spoke to her if she did see her.'[6]

With this experience, it was not surprising that May's reaction to the Empress's shocking death was one of curiosity rather than grief. Empress Elisabeth was stabbed in the heart by an Italian anarchist, Luigi Luccheni, on the shore of Lake Geneva in September 1898. May was in Vienna when the news broke. 'The excitement in the Royal Palace was indescribable,' she said. 'One man, an employé in the castle, went suddenly mad, and raved and shouted in the courtyard directly under the apartments of the Emperor for some time before he could be secured and got under control.'[7] When the body was brought back, members of the Court, including May, were required to attend the ceremony of 'Blessing the Corpse'. 'A plate of glass let into the coffin permitted us to look upon those beautiful features,' she remembered, 'beautiful in life, and now in death more lovely with an expression of deep and lasting peace upon them – the peace she had always been seeking, she had found at last. Alone she had lived of her own choice – alone she had died.'[8]

Both May and Nellie had their own story to tell about another famous Habsburg tragedy, the death of the imperial couple's only son, Crown Prince Rudolf, in his hunting lodge at Mayerling. Rudolf was found dead in his bedroom after shots had been heard in the early hours of 30 January 1889. With him was the body of his teenage mistress Baroness Marie Vetsera; her presence was concealed at first, but such a sensation could not be secret for long. Officially it was said that Rudolf had shot himself and most historians would agree, but so much was kept secret at the time that rumours abounded. Arriving at Court in the decade following the tragedy, Nellie was told that 'from proofs brought to the Empress it seems quite certain that murder, not suicide, was the cause'.[9]

May made no secret of her curiosity about Mayerling. 'I should, indeed, have been more than human,' she said, 'had I not, when the opportunity offered, endeavoured to probe the silence of all those who really knew.'[10] As governess to Rudolf's daughter she was able to meet several people who had been close to him and could have revealed exactly what happened if they chose.

But her constant probing questions produced a story quite different from the established version of events. They told her that Marie Vetsera had taken offence at the behaviour of some of Rudolf's drunken companions and had sought refuge in her room; that Rudolf was angry with them and a fight ensued which ended in someone striking him on the head with a champagne bottle, smashing his skull. Then one of the culprits shot Marie to prevent her from giving evidence. Perhaps May's informants, Rudolf's valet among them, and his doctor, just wanted to silence her questions.

Mayerling was a sensation for at least a century and May and Nellie were not unusual in their curiosity about it. But it seems there may have been an English governess who actually played a part in the tragedy. In the 1950s, the writer Bea Howe was given a story at second hand, said to have come from a committee member of the Queen Victoria Home for British Governesses in Vienna. It told how the Vetsera family held their daughter's governess, a Miss Crawford, responsible for the tragedy because she lost sight of Marie on the night the unfortunate girl slipped away to Mayerling. The governesses' home set up an inquiry to see if there had been professional neglect on Miss Crawford's part, but pronounced her innocent and the Vetseras provided her with a good pension on condition that she left Vienna and never spoke again about their daughter.[11] Is it possible? There are many investigations of Mayerling in print, none of which mention a Miss Crawford. But the Vetseras were the sort of family who would have employed an English governess and Marie was only seventeen. Perhaps there was a Miss Crawford and she took her secrets with her, discretion being always part of the governess's code.

In the summer of 1878 Kaiser Wilhelm I of Germany was severely injured in an assassination attempt, the second in the space of a few weeks. Augusta Byng received a graphic account of the aftermath of the attack from her pupil Princess Charlotte:

The day we arrived we were shown Grandpapa's cloak, helmet & sword, all 3 covered with blood. In the cloak alone, Uncle Fritz of Baden & I counted more than 80 wholes by the bullets; in the helmet they are innumerable. In the body of the Emperor there are above a hundred bullets, in his legs, arms, hips, hands, face, & head neck & back. He has asked repeatedly now to see Vicky of Baden & me, so Grandmama is going to take us in this morning. Henry saw him & says it is <u>dreadful</u> to see his head & face tied up & bandaged: he lies on a bed Mama gave him & cannot stir. The Empress is most kind to us all she looks like death, so pale, also the daughter. Poor Mama having much to do has a bad headache & poor Papa looks horrid

worried sad & tormented now that since 2 days he is made Regent, we never
see him, he is always occupied with the Ministers.[12]

But working at Court opened a window on sensations other than royal ones.
The world in which the nurses and governesses flourished was a world of
exciting and rapid change. Anne Topham saw the first cars arrive at the Neues
Palais in 1904, much against the will of the Kaiserin and her ladies who
thought the whole business very undignified. They converted rapidly to the
new form of transport, though: 'It was such a blessing to royalty to be able to
fly past their loyal subjects and escape recognition till they were fifty yards
farther on,' Anne said.[13]

In September 1909 the pioneering aviator Orville Wright flew his aeroplane
on the military exercise ground at Potsdam. Anne was there: 'He came along
buttoning up his leather jacket as he walked,' she remembered, 'a quiet,
taciturn individual who spoke in a rather soft, gentle voice when he spoke at
all, which was not often.'[14] Wright had really finished flying for the day when
the Kaiserin's party arrived but he went up again in their honour. The Kaiser
was not with them and he had yet to see an aeroplane in flight so, a week or so
later, Wright gave a demonstration especially for him. It was late in the day but
'Wright was waiting beside his machine,' Anne said, 'and after a word with the
Emperor put on his jacket and goggles, and in a few seconds the motor began
to hum steadily, the propellers whizzed round, and the huge machine moved
along smoothly and swiftly up into the darkening heavens. Its wide-spread
planes showed blackly for a moment against the intense sunset background,
then it went droning round the immense space, rising higher and higher
towards the stars, which were now shining brightly in the deep blue of the sky.
. . . At last it descended, dropping lightly within a few feet of us. The crowd on
the edge of the field cheered heartily.'[15]

While the imperial couple talked to Orville Wright and presented him with a
signed photograph of the Kaiser, Anne had a chance to talk to his sister, 'an
extremely charming woman who said that this was probably her brother's last
flight on German soil'.[16] It is hard now to realise how exciting all this must
have been. Anne described the intense anticipation in the household as the
Kaiserin's party prepared to go out for that first flight: 'The palace buzzed like
a hive', she recalled, 'while the footmen flew about summoning the ladies to get
ready at once.'[17] At the turn of the last century, so many familiar things were
only in their infancy. 'This year we have not left Greece,' Kate Fox told her
fellow Norlanders in 1906, 'and our chief excitement has been the Olympian
Games which took place in May, and were attended by members of the English

Royal Family, and also by many athletic celebrities from all parts of the world. I went several times, and it was, indeed, a most interesting sight to see the Stadium, which is built in white marble, and seats 70,000 people crowded, for the finish of the Marathon race.'[18]

The early years of the last century were also a time of mounting discontent. In the autumn of 1905, Kate was staying in the Vladimir Palace in St Petersburg when a strike by railway workers escalated rapidly into general unrest. It had been a violent year in Russia and that October the disturbances reached their climax. Kate's father was worried about her; so worried, in fact, that he wrote directly to Princess Nicholas. 'I got a letter from your father,' the Princess told her, 'he seems to be very anxious for you, poor man! I will try & answer as soon as I can & tell him there is no danger for "our daughters!" – If I have time I will try & see the Institute [Norland] and also your sister.'[19] A few weeks after this was written, Kate and the children left Russia for Grand Duchess Vladimir's family home at Schwerin in northern Germany.

The 1905 Revolution erupted during Russia's war with Japan, when a disillusioned country was reeling from a series of humiliating defeats. There were British women to witness events at both of the rival Courts. In St Petersburg, Margaretta Eagar watched the armies march away at the start of 1904. 'I had never seen such a sight before,' she said, 'and to my eyes they looked so badly provided for such a long journey, but the trains provided for their use were exceedingly comfortable.' The trains did not go far enough, however. Margaretta described the struggles that took place in the crossing of Lake Baikal, where the trains had to be abandoned because the ice would not bear their weight. Sledges were used instead and, despite all efforts to provide hot drinks and soup for the soldiers during the bitter crossing, many men froze to death. It was traditional for royal ladies to involve themselves and their Courts in relief work in wartime: Margaretta saw at first hand the well-intentioned working parties started by the Tsaritsa, in which society girls with very little idea of what they were doing tried to make shirts and other clothes for the troops.

She involved herself in a scheme to provide gift parcels for soldiers. Each parcel contained spare clothing – a shirt, socks, a woollen cap and a handkerchief – tobacco and cigarette papers, soap, tea, coffee and sugar, and materials to enable the men to write home: paper, envelopes and printed letter forms for men who could not write. Margaretta helped to pack the parcels and she collected donations for them from friends and acquaintances. She also drew the little Grand Duchesses into the cause. Together they folded and stamped the letter forms and slipped them into their envelopes. The children learned to do frame-knitting as well. 'They made scarves for the soldiers, and Olga and Tatiana crocheted caps indefatigably,' Margaretta said.[20] Even little Anastasia, at just two years and eight months old, 'frame-knitted, all by herself, two mufflers for the soldiers'.[21]

But the psychological effect of war on the children was extremely worrying for their nurse. Olga, the oldest, was eight years old when the war began, and she and her sisters absorbed the hostility and anger of the adult world without understanding it. 'It was very sad to me to witness the wrathful, vindictive spirit that the war raised in my little charges,' Margaretta recalled. One day, Olga looked up from her work and said, 'I hope the Russian soldiers will kill all the Japanese; not leave even one alive.' Five-year-old Maria, usually the most gentle of the children, reacted violently to a photograph of the Japanese Crown Prince's babies in her nurse's illustrated magazine; 'with a look of hatred coming into her sweet little face Marie slapped the picture with her open hand. "Horrid little people," said she; "they came and destroyed our poor ships and drowned our sailors."'[22]

A good nurse could not let this happen. Margaretta explained that babies could not be responsible for war and she challenged Olga particularly to think more deeply about the issues involved. 'I told her there were many little children and women in Japan, people who could not fight, and asked her if she really thought it would be good of the Russian soldiers to kill them.' The little girl then began to ask questions about the Japanese; the truth dawned gradually, as her nurse intended. 'I did not know that the Japs were people like ourselves.' From that day Olga 'never said again anything about being pleased to hear of the death of the Japanese'.[23]

The little Grand Duchesses were not alone in absorbing and repeating adult prejudice. Anne Topham saw the same thing happen in Berlin, though her charge, Viktoria Luise, was older and far less tractable than Olga and her sisters. Anne said that the German public were sympathetic to Japan when the war broke out; not so the Kaiser. At home he was deeply mistrustful of the 'yellow race', despite his public overtures to Japan. He was contemptuous of England for agreeing a Japanese alliance and he wanted to see a Russian victory. His twelve-year-old daughter 'used to ask the children who played with her if they were "Russians or Japanese", and was much grieved to find them all, without exception, on the side of Japan. "I am for the Russians," she would say; "first of all, because the Japanese are heathen; then because the sister of Tante Mimi (Princess Henry of Prussia) is Empress of Russia; thirdly, because if the Russians don't beat the Japanese *we* shall have to do it." It was easy to recognise the sentiments of "Papa",' Anne said.[24]

A world away from the prejudices of Europe, Ethel Howard gained a very different perspective on the war. 'If ever sorrows have been bravely and silently borne by a people individually,' she remembered, 'it was in those dark, sad days.'[25] The war had been expected in Tokyo for some time, she said, but its beginning came suddenly – it was the Japanese who opened hostilities with a surprise attack on the Russian base at Port Arthur. In the days and weeks that followed Ethel was struck by the incessant ringing of the bells of the newspaper sellers, which brought people rushing from their houses to hear the latest news from the front. The streets filled with small squads of soldiers – pathetically small, to Ethel's eye – 'drilling for all they were worth'. Temporary cavalry sheds went up along the roadsides and cavalry horses were broken in the public streets, risking life and limb from the tramcars that had, of necessity, to use the same streets, 'although in no instance did I ever see a rider who was not master of the situation'.[26]

The normal life of the nation stopped abruptly. Ethel was amazed by the transformed habits of the noble and royal ladies of Tokyo, who emerged from their centuries-old seclusion, abandoned their carriages to travel in the lower-class rickshaws, or even on public transport, and trained to care for the wounded. One of the older Shimadzu princesses, whose fragile, doll-like grace had impressed Ethel when they met, 'actually used a tram . . . and even discarded her lady attendant. She frequently washed the stained bandages of the wounded and disinfected them,' Ethel said, 'which was amazing when one saw her beautiful, delicate little hands, and knew the seclusion and inactivity of her past life.'[27]

The Tokyo house where Ethel lived with the Prince and his brothers was on a main crossroads and reminders of the cost of war passed daily beneath its windows. First came endless lines of rickshaws carrying the wounded from the station to the hospitals. All the men wore white kimonos, given to them at the station where the princesses and nobly-born ladies dressed their wounds. Military funerals also passed by almost every day; 'Even now Chopin's Funeral March sometimes rings in my ears in connection with this time, so often was it wafted in at our windows', Ethel wrote.[28] On one Sunday afternoon in May, the drowned officers and men of two Japanese warships were carried past in a single solemn procession.

For Ethel, the experience of the war was a profound one which taught her to know her hosts as she had not done before. Their culture was so different and in her attempts to be helpful she made many early mistakes. Once, wishing to show honour to Commander Hirosé, who sacrificed his life in an attempt to blockade Port Arthur, she made the three 'little brothers' stand to attention in an upper window as his funeral cortège passed the house. She learned soon after that this had caused grave offence because the Japanese considered it disrespectful to look down on the dead; all she could do was apologise. When told that a large number of sailors must be billeted in her house Ethel was apprehensive but she found the men absolutely silent and unobtrusive. She encouraged the boys to arrange an evening of entertainment for them as children might have done in similar circumstances in England, but it fell completely flat; the men 'seemed constrained and ill at ease, as if they would rather keep quiet while under the Prince's roof, or it may have been that they were too seriously engrossed in the war'.[29]

Since her arrival in Japan, Ethel had found the lack of visible emotion shown by the Japanese very hard to cope with. In wartime she judged it harshly. She saw many partings at the station and always they seemed to her to be cold, formal and loveless. Then, one day, she found herself in a train carriage with an officer who had just parted from his wife and child. He saluted them, she said, with no apparent emotion, then sat down as the train pulled away and raised his newspaper. She was shocked to see him fall back only moments later with 'one awful sob. . . . Mercifully, he recovered and pulled himself quickly together,' she said, 'and I saw no more signs of grief. But I had learned a lesson. It was an example of a Japanese farewell, the very coldness of which was the result of the deepest emotion. How often I have longed to know whether he ever returned!'[30]

There were lighter moments too. Ethel treasured the story of one Russian prisoner who was so grateful for the tea and food a Japanese soldier gave him that he kissed him, Russian fashion, only to be restrained and tied up. When the Japanese commander asked why the prisoner was tied the soldier explained, 'Sir – he tried to bite me.'[31] As her understanding of the Japanese grew, so Ethel was drawn deeper into their war effort on her own account. She helped to pack parcels for the troops, as Margaretta did, though these were Japanese-style parcels, lightweight paper bags, almost indestructible and each containing a toothbrush, soap and towel, chopsticks, tobacco and a pipe. On one single day, 9 February 1904, Ethel sent off 260 of these parcels to the front. She treasured the replies sent by some of the men, but still she did not feel she was doing enough. As the privations of the war increased, she wrote to the Shimadzu family guardians and asked them to stop her salary for the next six months. She suggested that the money might be given to the Red Cross instead, a gesture that was greatly appreciated.

As the country reached its lowest ebb, the Emperor issued an edict to his people: its words and meaning cut deep into Ethel's soul. She recalled how

Prince Tadashige handed her the translation. It read, 'Of you it is expected to accomplish the impossible.' 'Those words will go with me to the grave,' Ethel commented, years later.[32] And when the celebrations of victory finally came, Ethel Howard was privileged to be made as much part of them as if she had been Japanese. She met Admiral Togo, who masterminded his country's naval victory, and was struck 'with the wonderful expression of goodness and peace on his face'. She would afterwards count the meeting as one of her most treasured memories.[33]

Throughout the war Ethel tried to make the Shimadzu boys understand the full implications of what was happening – as Margaretta did in St Petersburg. Once it was over she wanted to take them on a visit to the battlefields. Prince Tadashige and the guardians gave their permission and, on 29 June 1907, the party set off; Ethel and the 'little brothers' with two gentlemen, an interpreter and two attendants, one male, one female. It was to be a long and uncomfortable journey across the sea and north into Korea and Manchuria. Conditions could be primitive there and friends protested to Ethel that the trip would be dangerous, but she was resolute. 'I believed it was essential for the development of the characters of these young boys.'[34]

Her expedition must have been approved of at the highest level. At Seoul, in Korea, the party was shown around the Emperor's palace by the Marquis Ito, architect of the Japanese constitution. At the port of Chemulpo (modern Inchon) they were invited to view Admiral Tomioka's flagship *Hashidate* and the Admiral gave them dinner on board. From Chemulpo they set off by launch for the boat that would take them to Dalny, and from there, Port Arthur was a further three-hour journey by train. 'There were plenty of battlefields to be seen between Dalny and Port Arthur,' Ethel said, 'miles of deep trenches made by the Japanese, and many mounds where the dead were buried . . . there was a man in the train who volunteered to explain things to us as we went along and who pointed out in the distance the famous 203 Metre Hill.'[35] A few days later they would drive out to the same battlefields and explore them on foot. At Port Arthur the head of the Japanese Admiralty, Admiral Hashimoto, gave a dinner for Ethel and the boys in what had once been a Russian school; he even arranged a programme of British band music to follow. Ethel found it all curiously moving; the familiar tunes, the talk of war and suffering and the battlefields and harbour of Port Arthur well within sight. 'What with the music of home and the stars overhead,' she said, 'one realized how short the distance is between life and death.'[36]

Few British nurses and governesses overseas would find themselves able to enter so closely into the emotions of their employers in wartime. For most, war

remained a crisis imposed by others which interfered with their real world.
A story of the Second World War describes how a nurse, asked about the noises
outside, replied, 'It's only bombs, dear, elbows off the table.' It may never have
happened, but it perfectly captures the attitude of most nurses to the subject of
war. The confusion was summed up in a long letter written by Isabel Sharman
of Norland in the early months of 1914. 'I am sure we ought each one to do
what we can to stem the flood of hate,' she told her nurses. 'We say we do not
hate the Germans, but every time we turn a joke against them or give voice to
our wishes for their humiliation, we fan the fire. . . . We must look forward to
the fact that the babies in the nursery to-day will, we hope, be friends with the
present German babies. The older children *will* play their war-games; but we
can lead their thoughts to understand that war can only be justified because
righteousness must come before peace, and above all things we must not allow
them to grow up to love war for war's sake.'[37]

The outbreak of the First World War had found many of her nurses – and
countless others like them – trapped in Germany or cut off, with enemy
territory between them and home. A few stayed put but most fled, across a
continent suddenly thrown into chaos. In the early days of the war the
transport systems of Europe were almost paralysed by people straining to reach
home in both directions across borders which had suddenly become hostile
frontiers. The issue of the *Norland Quarterly* which included Miss Sharman's
letter also printed accounts from those who had managed to reach home. They
told of road blocks, the arrest of prisoners and sporadic shooting in the streets.
Kate Fox was in Germany that summer. The outbreak of war found her at
Baden-Baden with her British employer and children and they failed to obtain
places on the last safe train home. With the declaration of war they were forced
to take refuge in the Baden sanatorium, under Red Cross protection.

Food grew scarce and anxiety mounted; then the Grand Duchess of Baden
obtained permission for a party of 'invalids' to leave under the protection of a
Greek doctor. That party consisted of Kate and her employer and children,
two South African ladies and their maid. They set off in two cars and drove
through the day, 'passing through magnificent scenery, which we were too
anxious to enjoy'. At Bad-Ems on the first night a hotel turned them away
because they were English; another took them in for a few hours, but they had
to leave at first light and they were told by the doctor to destroy any letters and
papers they might be carrying. 'During that day,' Kate said, 'we passed through
masses of troops, waggon-loads of beds and bedding for the Red Cross, etc.,
while at one place the gun carriages had to be drawn on one side to allow us to
pass. Here it was like a beehive, and we found we were only a few miles from

the frontier.' They reached Düsseldorf by midday and were warned by the doctor not to speak, as anyone found to be English would be in grave danger. It would have been wise to drive straight through the town but one of the cars ran out of petrol and the party was forced to stay while the drivers searched the surrounding countryside for a fresh supply.

The women passed a long, frightening night in a Düsseldorf hotel full of German soldiers. Rumours that English people were being shot at the border finally decided the doctor that he must find another way, and he bribed the captain of a Dutch boat to take his party to Holland by river. Several passengers were on board already and, once again, the doctor told the women to keep silent for their own safety. The others took refuge in the captain's cabin but Kate stayed on deck and watched the scenes at the military frontier, where customs officials and soldiers boarded the boat. It was a tense moment. The passengers' papers were examined and five Englishmen on the boat were arrested. Kate described the terror of their families and the cries of, 'The soldiers have taken Daddy, I want Daddy', from a little boy who refused to be comforted. Eventually the boat was allowed to continue its journey to Nijmegen in Holland. From there the women caught a train to The Hague, then took the first available boat home. It was a difficult, slow crossing, imperilled by mines, but they docked eventually, 'and we felt like embracing the first policeman we saw, it was so strange to feel safe again'.[38]

Some stories of escape had more sinister overtones. Hilda Maybury had only worked for the Grand Duke of Oldenburg for a few months when the war began and she told a tale of German duplicity, secret war plans and mounting hostility towards England. Late in July 1914 she was with the Oldenburg household on the Grand Duke's yacht anchored off Malmö in Sweden, where they had gone to visit an international armaments exhibition. When war was declared between Germany and France, she said, the attitude of her companions became increasingly hostile. Hilda was told that she could not send any letters unless the Grand Duke had read them. She had already been prevented from posting some letters and still had them. One of the Court ladies came to her cabin to take them, 'but I was too quick for her. I caught them from the table, tore them into countless bits, and flung them through the porthole into the open sea.'[39]

If the Grand Duke and his household had been wondering how to deal with Hilda Maybury, this melodramatic gesture would hardly have eased their fears. In the days that followed, she said, the Grand Duke became more polite and conciliatory, advising her that it would not be possible for her to leave but that, while she remained, she would be safe under his protection. She wrote two letters to her family which were read and dispatched but the post office sent them back. She felt like a prisoner. The family returned to Oldenburg and Hilda packed her belongings. 'My loneliness was terrible,' she said, 'for I had no one to turn to for advice. There was no British Consulate nearer than Hamburg, and it was forbidden to telegraph.'[40] Then Britain declared war on Germany. The Grand Duke's attitude changed and Hilda was banished to her room – a relief, in the circumstances, though it underlined how isolated she was. Then, on her first night under the new conditions, a local official came with two soldiers and demanded the returned letters. Hilda's rooms were searched; she was undressed by one of the Court ladies who went through all her clothes, then she was taken to a room at the top of a tower which was locked and guarded. The letters were found and removed for investigation and she was told that her fate would depend on the outcome.

Hilda's gesture on the yacht had come back to haunt her. It was only natural for the authorities to believe that someone who behaved like that must be hiding something: fortunately for Hilda, the returned letters were harmless and had already been read. So the Grand Duke made it possible for her to leave under escort to the Dutch border, with her full salary and travelling expenses. She sent him a note requesting the return of her passport, which was duly given, and at midnight she was taken from the palace. She carried a small portmanteau and dressing case and a hamper of food and she was promised that her luggage would be sent on – which it was, though it took a year to reach her.

Hilda's written account was very bitter, but the Grand Duke's people do seem to have done as much as they could to keep her safe and comfortable on the journey. The gentleman sent to escort her carried a picnic basket with sandwiches and wine. When the train stopped unexpectedly five miles short of the border he found a vehicle to drive the distance and even then would not leave her, but sought out the German border guard and explained the situation. The guard found a temporary refuge in the home of one of his companions, whose wife 'was wonderfully kind, and insisted on my lying on a couch in the kitchen'.[41] Still the escort stayed with Hilda until the next stage of her journey was arranged and he made sure she had the appropriate cash in hand. The village carrier was persuaded to take her by cart to Wynschoten from where she was able to catch a train to Rotterdam. There, for the first time, she heard accurate news and was able to organise the last stage of her journey.

Hilda Maybury's *Secrets of a German Royal Household* was only one of a series of books written during the war, when the prevailing feeling in England was fiercely anti-German. People wanted to read inside accounts of the

German royal houses which bolstered their prejudices. They wanted to be told that the Germans had been planning the war for years and had only pretended friendship; that Germans were brutal and harsh and ignorant. The anonymous *What I Found Out in the House of a German Prince* by 'an English governess' painted a picture even more chilling than Hilda's. Hilda at least did concede, however grudgingly, that the Grand Duke's people did their best to help her in the end. The 'English governess' had fewer scruples. She painted a picture of a country where even little children – her charges, aged six and under – were encouraged to play an elaborate game of bombing a large scale model of London (or St Petersburg or Paris; they could choose) from toy Zeppelins, egged on by their elders; 'Look at the white spots my bombs have left on important buildings! . . . Now watch the way I do it. I'm over Westminster Abbey . . .'[42]

Some clues remain to the author's identity. She was a Miss B and she tells us that her father was an English diplomat and her mother the daughter of a distinguished US naval officer. After an early childhood spent in America her family returned to England and she completed her education at Queen's College in London. She said that the Kaiser's brother, Prince Heinrich of Prussia – Emma Hobbs's little 'Regent Street swell' of the 1860s – recommended her to the German position, which she was offered in 1909. She took it because she was 'in the midst of a love affair which could not possibly end happily'.[43] Her employers' identity she left as vague as her own: a prince and princess distantly related to the Kaiser who employed Miss B to teach their two elder sons aged six and five years and an orphaned niece of seven; there was also a baby (with a Scottish nurse, 'Mrs M') and another son had been lost in infancy.

Whoever Miss B was, she painted a picture of a society in which everything was geared towards war. She described innocent-sounding individuals whom she was persuaded to introduce to relatives and friends at home, only to learn that they were spies. She claimed to have walked unsuspecting into a hotbed of anti-British feeling; 'in almost every German heart, north, south, east and west, a jealous hatred or else contempt of the British beat with the blood, a part of the German being'.[44] After four years she was finally stung into action by a book given to the eldest boy for Christmas, *Germany and the Next War*. 'It seemed to me a terrible book, a menace to the world . . . and made me wonder whether I ought not to repeat certain conversations I had heard, to someone in the British Embassy.'[45] She became, in short, a spy.

Miss B's first attempt to pass on information to an old friend in England about the things she had seen and heard, and the mysterious visitors who came to the Schloss, fell flat. Her friend was a retired ambassador and he thought her suspicions far-fetched. But when the children began to play at the invasion of Belgium in July 1914, confidently discussing Germany's strategic plans weeks before they would be brought into action, she felt that she had to act. She wrote a letter to the British Ambassador in Berlin telling him who she was, where she worked, what she had seen. Then she put it on the hall table with the ordinary post for the servant to collect. If the situation was as she described this was a stupid thing to do, but she seemed unconcerned. She expected a reply, or at least an official acknowledgement, but the days passed and nothing happened. Then the Princess's regular telegram with instructions about the children did not arrive. Newspapers were not delivered and silence fell around her.

On 4 August, the day Britain entered the war, an elderly uncle of the Princess arrived at the Schloss in the early hours of the morning. He accused Miss B of attempting to spy on the family and said he was there on his niece's request to take the children and their attendants away. Miss B must remain. She would receive all payments owing to her but she was not to see the children again and she should be grateful she was not handed to the police. She would not be allowed to leave but, like Hilda Maybury in Oldenburg, must stay under the family's protection until the war ended. Miss B spent the next six weeks in her room, eating only a bare minimum of food and feigning illness. Then, on the night of 15 September, she slipped out of the building at night and walked towards Coblenz, buying clothing to disguise herself on the way. Her German was good and no one suspected. From Coblenz she caught a Rhine steamer to the frontier, then crossed into Holland using her own old US passport. By October she had reached London.

Miss B and Hilda Maybury may have given an accurate account of what happened to them. Edith Keen also described being held under near house arrest for the first weeks of the war at Klein Glienicke, Prince Friedrich Leopold of Prussia's home. Prominent employers may have felt obliged to do something of the kind, particularly if they suspected their 'enemy' governess of passing on information about them; it would have happened to a German governess in this country too, as Hilda pointed out. But Edith did resist the idea that all Germans hated Britain. 'Wherever I went in Germany,' she said, 'I heard practically always friendly expressions about England. . . . I am certain that the war between England and Germany came as a tremendous surprise to many people in Germany.'[46] Nonetheless, she accused her employers of plotting and spying, and a fiercely anti-German feeling pervades her account, as it does Hilda's and Miss B's.

But other governesses stood against the tide and wrote well of their 'enemy' employers. Both Nellie Ryan and May T went on record in 1916, the year of the Somme and Verdun, to describe positive experiences in the homes of their Habsburg employers. Austria may not have aroused the same animosity in Britain as Germany did, but in 1916 it was still on the enemy side. Ethel Howard, Anne Topham and Lilian Brimble all took on the much harder task of writing fairly about the Kaiser's family. 'In the fierce light of the greatest conflagration of history,' Ethel wrote in the preface to *Potsdam Princes*, 'it is impossible for me to think of them now as I did then, but I have tried to write a true and unbiased account of my pupils as I found them.'[47]

And there were countless others like them who never went into print, but still felt, like Miss Sharman, that there was something precious in the old world and its ties of friendship that must be preserved. Nurse Kemence had left the Teck family by 1914 and was working in Kent, but on the outbreak of war her thoughts went back to her royal employers. She thought of the children's uncle, Duke Carl Eduard of Saxe-Coburg – once little 'Charlie' Albany whom Eliza Creak and Victoria Nicholls had nursed. He was a German prince in 1914, committed to his country's war effort despite his private feelings. His brother-in-law Prince Alexander was a high-ranking officer in the British army. In reply to a long letter from Princess Alice, Nurse Kemence wrote, 'this war is dreadful I do wish the Prince would not go, and how sorry I am for the poor Duke I hope he is fighting against the Russians, that is bad enough but it would be worse against the British, it is too cruel you cant hear a word about him, we must hope and trust he is safe and well'.[48]

Norland nurse Kathleen Wanstall was in a very sensitive position, caring for the children of a German diplomat, Prince Wilhelm of Stolberg-Wernigerode. Kathleen was a clergyman's daughter educated at St Margaret's, a school for clergy daughters in Bushey in Hertfordshire. She completed her training at Norland in February 1906 and joined the Stolberg-Wernigerodes at Schönberg in Hesse, the Princess's family home, in 1911. At that time the couple had a baby boy, Ludwig Christian, born in the previous year when his father was attached to the German Embassy in Rome. In January 1912 Kathleen shared the family's move to Vienna; Prince Wilhelm had a new job in the German Embassy there and his family set up home in a spacious flat on the Ströhgasse. 'The house and staircase make quite a palatial impression,' the Princess's mother commented in her diary some time later, 'and the flat looked inviting and comfortable with fine large parqueted corridors. Everywhere space and to spare, as the rooms extend over three sides on one floor. The children's rooms are particularly large, cheerful and attractive.

I was so glad to see everything from Rome again, but William has bought much that is new, furniture and pictures.'⁴⁹

The *Norland Quarterly* noted the birth of a second charge for Kathleen, a little girl, at the Villa Hein Reichenau, Lower Austria, on 18 September 1912. She was christened Anne Marie, and the only souvenir of Kathleen's feelings about her, her brother, and the whole experience of working for the Stolberg-Wernigerodes is a postcard she sent to Mildred Hastings of Norland late in 1913. 'We are staying with a Princess Reuss until Tuesday when we go to 22 Stroh Gasse, Vienna,' she said, 'I shall hope to write you a letter then. This photo was taken in August of my babes & their mother. Don't you think the wee girlie is rather sweet, she has always sucked those 2 fingers whenever she was sleepy or shy. The boy is an awful pickle but I am very fond of him, he was so pleased to have me back again after my holiday & told everybody even including the rabbits "Look my nanna's come back again." I had such a good holiday & such lovely weather.'⁵⁰

Unlike the majority of nurses working for German families, Kathleen did not go home on the outbreak of war. Despite the sensitivity of her position – an Englishwoman living and working in the house of a German diplomat in the Austrian capital in wartime – she stayed with the family and was still their nurse when baby Anne Marie, the 'wee girlie' died very suddenly at Christmas 1914, the first Christmas of the war. 'She was such a merry, unaffected child,' the grandmother wrote, 'full of the joy of being alive, and gifted with a wonderful voice for singing, Her hair was auburn, with a tinge of gold, the eyes large and clear with dark lashes.'⁵¹ It must have been a terrible shock and a lasting grief. Kathleen continued to care for Ludwig Christian, her 'awful pickle', throughout the war years.

Her fellow Norlander Lilian Eadie would have envied her. By the summer of 1914, Lilian had been happy in Darmstadt for nearly six years, in the palaces and hunting lodges Mary Ann Orchard, Madgie Jackson and Lilian Wilson once knew. She had no thought of leaving, nor did the family want to lose her. She was 'Nursie' and she was theirs. Lilian carried on working for them through the early months of the war and it was the Hesse government who finally insisted that she must go. They did not want the children of their Grand Duke to be cared for by an Englishwoman. For five-year-old Prince Ludwig, who had been looked after by Lilian Eadie all his life, the parting was traumatic. Over half a century later it was still vivid in his mind: 'I believe that the first great loss of my life was the parting from that ardently loved, kind, good woman.'⁵² Lilian was able to stay with him and his brother long enough to celebrate his sixth birthday on 20 November 1914; then she had to leave.

Three months into the war, the chaotic conditions experienced by others on the homeward journey had eased and there was no hint of danger. Arrangements were made for Lilian to travel with three other British ladies and a small boy, accompanied by a courier named Weil. They were told to pack their luggage on a Monday ready for collection in the afternoon. They were not to include any silver or gold, letters, photographs or newspapers, and not to carry any of these items on their person. After six years in Darmstadt Lilian had a great many treasured possessions which had to be left with the family.

The party left before seven o'clock the next morning and by evening had reached the Palast-Hotel Rheinischer Hof, opposite the main station in Hanover, from where Lilian sent two postcards. To the Grand Duchess she wrote, 'We have come so far on our journey safely, and everything so comfortable one would hardly know there is War, everybody has been so kind in making it so easy. It still hurts me to think I could not stay and be a help to Your Royal Highness. . . . There are so many things I would like to have said to you but at the last I could not.' And to Ludwig, her 'dear little Lu': 'It is the middle of the night and we are just waiting to go to the station and start once more. I have the little hearts on my chain, they are so sweet and I shall always wear them. I can just imagine you fast asleep in your cot. With lots of love and kisses from Nursie', and she added four of the very special kisses she had always used for the Hesse boys, '++oo'.[53]

By the next evening the party had reached Vlissingen and it was the turn of Ludwig's brother to receive a card. 'My darling Georgie', Lilian wrote. 'It is nearly two o'clock and very soon we shall be starting, to-morrow night we sleep on the steamer in the harbour and start early next morning, so all being well we shall be in London on Thursday evening. The man who is taking us is so nice, and looks after us well. With lots of love and kisses from Nursie. ++oo'[54]

By 28 November Lilian was back with her family at Topsham in Devon, still stunned by the unexpected effect of war on her life. She decided to take only temporary posts in the hope that it would end quickly and she could go back to Darmstadt, and she still exchanged letters with the boys and their mother, sending them through neutral Switzerland or the Netherlands: some were forwarded by the director of the Rijksmuseum in Amsterdam. Occasionally she found it comforting to talk to Joanne Rolestone, always the lynchpin of the Hesse family's nurses; she kept in contact with the Grand Duke's sister Princess Victoria in England too, and was used by her to pass on greetings. Lilian's heart remained in Darmstadt. She was constantly asking about the things the boys were doing and about their progress in lessons. Time and again she would say how much she missed them; 'they are not often out of my thoughts,' she told their mother, and 'I long for them both often, sometimes I wonder how ever I came away.' And when Ludwig's birthday came round again she told him, 'I shall be thinking of you, sometimes it does not seem long since you were a wee little baby, and Don was poking you all over to find out what you were made of. I can hardly believe you will be seven.'[55]

Two factors prompted Lilian's next move: the need for a regular income and the debilitating effect of being surrounded by anti-German sentiments she could not share. At the end of 1915 she was offered a permanent post in Russia, with a Countess Osten-Sacken at Tsarskoe Selo who had one small boy and another on the way. Lilian decided to accept, writing to the Grand Duchess to explain her reasons and adding, 'I know I shall often feel homesick, and not only for England. I still wish it had been my lot to stay and work for your Royal Highness.'[56] With no safe route overland she must have travelled by sea; a cold, difficult and dangerous journey in the second winter of the war. By February she was in Tsarskoe Selo and it was not long before she encountered someone who shared her regrets for the pre-war world. On 5/18 February the Tsaritsa Alexandra told her husband, 'Fancy only, I saw Miss Eady yesterday, Don & Loos nurse.' It was obvious just how much Lilian had needed a sympathetic audience; all her pent-up unhappiness was echoed in the Tsaritsa's letter: anxiety for her four brothers and her nephews at the front, the need to support her mother and the difficulty of finding a position, and always the agony of parting from the Hesses. Her continuing loyalty to them had caused real problems for her: 'In Engl. one got angry with her because she wld. not speak against the Germans but she had only received greatest kindness in Germany.'

For the Tsaritsa too, the meeting with Lilian Eadie brought back happier times. Twice they had met before: in 1910 when the imperial family spent three months in Hesse, and in 1912 when the Hesse family visited the Crimea. 'It was so nice seeing her,' the Tsaritsa told her husband, 'reminded me of old home & all & of Friedberg and Livadia especially.' She encouraged Lilian to visit often and to keep in touch with her maid, Magdalina 'Madelaine' Zanotti, 'so as to feel less lonely'.[57] This helped, but for Lilian the position with the Osten-Sackens would never be more than a job. She spent the summer in Finland with them and in autumn returned to a flat in St Petersburg, rechristened 'Petrograd' in wartime. Communicating with Darmstadt had been impossible all summer but in October and November she received letters and photos from the Hesse family. She wrote to thank them, anticipating her return to England when the winter was over and longing for the war's end. How could she know she was about to be at the centre of history's next great upheaval?

The Russian Revolution began in Petrograd in February 1917. It posed no immediate danger to a British nurse, but Lilian Eadie was ill and unable to travel. The Hesses heard no more from her until 9 November when she had just found her way to Norway from a capital in the throes of the Bolshevik takeover. It was said in her obituary notice in the *Norland Quarterly* that she escaped on the last train with the British Ambassador, but this cannot be – Sir George Buchanan did not leave until the following January. From Norway Lilian sent a letter and two postcards to Darmstadt while she waited for the ship back to England. There was a message she was desperate to pass on. 'About a week ago I saw Madeline Zanotti and heard from her that all the family were well,' she told the Grand Duchess of Hesse. 'I am sure Your Royal Highness will be glad to know, it is so very sad for them all.' She was referring to the imperial family, imprisoned at Tobolsk in Siberia, and she sent variations of the same message on postcards to the Grand Duchess and to the elder of the two Princes, presumably in the hope that at least one version would reach them.[58]

Neither she nor Madelaine could have known how far their confidence was misplaced. The Bolshevik Revolution had put the imperial family in jeopardy and, while Lilian was busy reassuring the Hesses, the prisoners in Tobolsk were casting around for a means of contacting relatives who might help them escape. They fastened their hopes on Madgie Jackson, the Tsaritsa's former governess. A letter was written to her, ostensibly by the English tutor Sydney Gibbes. The guards may have thought it no more than a long, chatty letter full of news; in fact, it gave a precise description of the house in which the family was being held. It described their daily life in detail and made reference to the British royal family by nicknames Madgie would have recognised. 'The Empress was sure that Miss Jackson would carry the letter to the Queen,' Gibbes told the British High Commissioner in Vladivostock eighteen months later, when he tried to find out why the attempt had failed.[59] He was able to establish that the letter arrived at the embassy in Petrograd and was sent out in the diplomatic bag; after that, the trail went cold.

Publication of this story in the 1970s led to a flurry of speculation about what had happened to the letter. The Tsaritsa placed absolute faith in Miss Jackson. If Queen Mary had received the letter from her, researchers reasoned, it should still be in the Royal Archives at Windsor. The fact that it was not seemed suspicious and has fed a number of conspiracy theories down the years. But the truth is tragically simple; the clue is in the letter itself – 'It is ages since you wrote. . . .'[60] In turning to Madgie Jackson, the Tsaritsa was remembering the strict, capable, loving woman of her girlhood, but by the end of 1917 Madgie was eighty-two and increasingly frail. The letter left Tobolsk on 15 December 1917 and had then to be forwarded to the Foreign Office in London, then sent on. On 28 January 1918 Margaret Hardcastle Jackson died. The causes given on her death certificate are 'valvular disease of the heart' and 'senility'. It was too late. Even if the letter had reached her before 28 January, she was past understanding what it said.

News of the family's murder at Ekaterinburg the following summer sent a profound shock through the nursing community. So many had known them: Lilian Eadie; Margaretta Eagar, whose rooms were full of framed photographs of the four little Grand Duchesses she still adored; did she, on hearing the news, remember the comment the eldest of those little girls had made to her stories of English history, with all that cutting-off of heads, 'I'm very glad I live now when people are so kind.'⁶¹ And Kate Fox, who had boasted to her fellow nurses in a letter to the *Norland Quarterly* in 1906, 'I saw . . . a good deal of the Imperial Family, having tea many times with the four little Grand Duchesses, and their brother, the infant Cezarewitch, at the Alexander Palace, situated in a lovely park, the country residence of the Emperor and Empress.'⁶² On 2 August 1918, two weeks after the murders, Princess Nicholas sent Kate a letter riven with incredulity and grief. 'We don't know what to believe about that dreadful news,' she said, 'somehow I can't think it is true, it seems too awful! Some people think it is true, others doubt it. Of course we only know what the papers say as we can't get any direct news from anyone there, no telegrams at all, & letters take several months to come & those are very rare. It is dreadful not to know the truth! Poor, poor things over there, those miserable girls! I think of them so much, what a sad youth & how dreadful to start life under those conditions! . . . Do you know that our dear old house in Zarskoe has been completely plundered & that it is inhabited by those fiends, as well as the house in town! somehow I can't grasp it yet. The situation & misery there must be altogether too awful.'⁶³

Other members of the imperial family did escape and several Englishwomen found their way to safety with them. A Miss Irwin became responsible for the children of the Tsar's cousin, Prince Ioann Konstantinovich, when their father was exiled to Siberia by the Bolsheviks and their mother decided to follow. She cared for four-year-old Vsevelod and his three-year-old sister Ekaterina in the Marble Palace in Petrograd, their grandmother's home. Eventually conditions became so bad that the whole group – the children's grandmother, Grand Duchess Elizaveta Mavrikievna, her two youngest children, the grandchildren, Miss Irwin and three other attendants – accepted an offer of help from Swedish diplomats and escaped by sea to Sweden. Margaret Neame, governess to seven-year-old George Brassov, the only son of the Tsar's younger brother Grand

Duke Mikhail, faced a much lonelier task in smuggling her young charge out of the country and in her case it was the Danes who provided the escape route.

Like Lilian Eadie, Margaret Neame had gone to Russia during the war, in May 1915, to take over the care of George and his half-sister 'Tata' Mamontov. She was a friend of the children's governess Edith Rata, Mrs Bennett, who was leaving to have a baby. Tata was in her rebellious teens and disliked Margaret, finding her too strict, but Margaret ignored the hostility and remained loyal to her new family in a time of increasing danger. After the Bolshevik Revolution she remarked in a letter home that things 'had come to such a pitch of terror that we were all praying and waiting anxiously for the arrival of the Germans, as we then knew we would be safe'.[64] The Germans never came. Grand Duke Mikhail was arrested on 7 March 1918. He shook hands with Margaret before leaving and she would always remember, 'the sad look in his eyes – so tired and ill . . .'.[65] After this it became imperative to get his son to safety. For five weeks Margaret hid with the little boy in the home of a Danish colonel who was negotiating a prisoner of war exchange. Then they boarded a Red Cross train full of German prisoners. Margaret carried papers identifying them as the wife and son of an Austrian officer. She took a considerable risk because neither she nor George spoke German, but they were lucky, crossing unchallenged into German-held territory at Pskov and then on to Berlin, where the Kaiser provided safe passage to Denmark.

Two British women were caught up in the dramas in the Crimea, where the Tsar's mother and sister and a large party of imperial cousins came within a whisker of being murdered. As nurse to the Tsar's great-niece, Princess Irina Yusupova, Zillah Henton had already been through more anxiety than most. Her charge's father, Prince Felix Yusupov, was at the heart of the conspiracy to kill Rasputin, the shady religious figure whose ascendancy over the Tsaritsa was blamed for so much of Russia's suffering. The conspirators had no doubt of the danger they faced and, as their plans began to take shape in the summer of 1916, Zillah, the baby and its mother were taken to the Yusupovs' Crimean estate at Koreis by the Prince's parents. Even there, the tension was palpable. Princess Irina Alexandrovna, the baby's mother, described a disturbing event just days before the murder: 'Something unbelievable's been going on with Baby,' she told her husband. 'A couple of nights ago she didn't sleep very well and kept repeating, "War, nanny, war!" The next day she was asked, "War or peace?" And Baby answered, "War!" The next day I said, "Say 'peace'." And she looked right at me and answered, "War!" It's very strange . . .'[66] Baby Irina was less than two years old when this happened. For her nurse, it must have been very worrying.

As a punishment for his part in the murder of Rasputin, Prince Felix was banished to Rakitnoïe near Kursk and his family hurried to join him. They left Zillah and the baby at Ai-Todor, the Crimean estate of the Tsar's sister, Grand Duchess Ksenia and her husband, the maternal grandparents. Zillah was warned that the baby's safety was in her hands and she was never to leave her; it must have been unnerving but at least at Ai-Todor she was not alone. The baby's young uncles were there with their tutors and their English governess Miss Coster, a steady, reassuring woman who had served the family some years and was devoted to them. After the Tsar's abdication a crowd marched on Ai-Todor wearing red ribbons. They wanted Zillah to wear one but she refused, asserting her loyalty to her own country. It was the Swiss tutor who defused the situation by leading the young Princes and Zillah, carrying baby Irina, out onto the balcony. He made a speech congratulating the crowd and telling them about his own origins in republican Switzerland. It worked and they went away happy.

Not long after this the party was joined by the Tsar's mother and sisters, the Yusupovs and various other members of the imperial family, who made their way to the Crimea and settled in their palaces along the coast. Miss Coster remained with her charges at Ai-Todor while Zillah and baby Irina went back to Koreis. A brief interval of peace followed but before long the palaces became subject to raids by hostile groups of sailors. In the autumn the Bolshevik Revolution hit the Crimea with chilling violence. Zillah was warned that they might have to leave at a moment's notice and she took to sitting up beside the baby's bed at night with a packed suitcase. In later years she would tell her family a story which surely relates to this time, of a night when Prince Yusupov came and tapped her on the shoulder and they left the house without speaking, she carrying the suitcase and he the child, walking for what felt like miles in the darkness to a vehicle which drove them to safety.

In February 1918 all the imperial prisoners were concentrated in one palace, Djulber, not far from Koreis; Miss Coster was in the party and all were kept under heavy guard. The Yusupovs remained at Koreis and Zillah helped them keep in touch with the prisoners. Only two visitors were allowed past the gates of Djulber, the doctor and two-year-old Irina. 'Her nurse took her to the gates of the park,' Prince Felix remembered, 'and the child entered it alone, with our letters pinned inside her coat. The answers reached us in the same way. Our little messenger never let us down.'[67]

The danger increased with an argument between two local Soviets about the fate of the prisoners. The nearest group, at Yalta, wanted blood. For several nights the guards at Djulber armed their prisoners and all stayed on watch together, and even at Koreis Prince Felix wrote of warnings of a general massacre and nights spent on watch on his father's roof. Ironically, all were saved by the arrival of German troops. For Miss Coster, imprisoned in the house, the ordeal had been one of isolation and the fear of murder. Zillah came much closer to the reality. In an interview for the *Yorkshire Post* in January 1936 she described a day when she had been sitting outdoors with the baby when she heard shooting. She found that three of the staff had been murdered: 'One of the men had tried to escape by crawling beneath the floor of a granary, but shots had been fired at him there until he was killed.'[68]

An uneasy peace returned under the Germans and the former prisoners returned to their homes. But with the signing of the Armistice the Germans were obliged to withdraw and, as Revolutionary troops closed in on the Crimea, the Dowager Tsaritsa bowed to the inevitable and accepted an offer of help from the British navy. On 7 April 1919 the ship HMS *Marlborough* anchored off Djulber and the imperial family and their attendants and friends made their way to the landing stage. When the ship sailed six days later, both Miss Coster and Zillah Henton were on board.

And finally, Marian Burgess. The tide of history that had washed her compatriots home in their various ways had landed her in Finland in the summer of 1917. Grand Duke Kirill was allowed to leave Petrograd because he swore allegiance to the Provisional Government. He settled his family in the small town of Porvoo (Borgå), using the local hotel-cum-cultural centre, the Suerahuone, or various houses belonging to friends. Burgie succumbed to typhoid soon after they arrived but she pulled through and refused to leave. She had not taken a holiday for six years but times were hard and, after an eight-year gap, the Grand Duchess was heavily pregnant with her third child. Prince Vladimir Kirillovich was born at Haikko Manor, just outside Porvoo, on 30 August and, once again, Burgie had a baby to care for. She sent the news to Margaret Alison in England who passed it on to Princess Nicholas; she, in turn told Kate Fox: 'She says that the baby is sweet but that the confinement was a very difficult one; however now both mother & child are quite well; I wonder when we shall see them all again.'[69]

Conditions deteriorated rapidly. The manor was subject to searches and in December 1917 civil war broke out in Finland: one battle was audible from Haikko. In Finland, as in the Crimea, the arrival of the Germans put an end to the fighting but the hardship did not end. Basic foods became scarce; in the summer of 1918 eleven-year-old Kira wrote to her aunt, 'Boy is so sweet. When he is hungry and Nana is preparing his lunch, the tears simply stream down his cheeks with hunger. We go for long walks and hunt for mushrooms in the woods.'[70] Not until autumn did conditions begin to ease. In November the Grand Duchess made her annual entry in Burgie's testimonial book and it expressed all they had suffered together since the Revolution. 'During these last two years', she wrote, 'Nurse Marian Burgess has remained faithfully at her post in spite of the greatest dangers, privations and miseries which we have had to endure. Weeks of sleepless nights – surrounded as we were by bloodshed and murder and terror – her courage never gave way. Living for nearly a year on starvation rations she managed by her untiring devotion to keep our three children in good health. By miracles of ingenuity she contrived to keep them clothed and fed. To me she has been a comfort and a friend such as one rarely meets. God bless her for all she has been to us during nigh upon 13 years.'[71]

But it was not over. As the First World War drew to a close an influenza epidemic spread across the Continent and populations weakened by war could offer little resistance. The disease is said to have claimed more victims than the war itself, and at the end of 1919 it reached Finland. The Kirill children succumbed and Marian Burgess nursed them; then she too fell ill. She was admitted to hospital on 17 December and on the 28th, she died: 'she had every possible care, but inflammation of the lungs developed, and there is no doubt that her constitution, weakened by all she had suffered, could not battle against such severe illness. The Grand Duchess was with her in the hospital when the end came, and wrote to Nurse Marian's family of the grief they felt in losing their nurse, whose devotion had made them all devoted to her.

'The snow was lying thick on the ground, and the coffin was taken on a sledge to a little church on the top of a steep hill by moonlight: "The light of the church window," the Grand Duchess wrote, "seemed to take the form of the cross and to be beckoning them on in their journey."'[72]

THIRTEEN

Living with the Memory

WHAT BECAME OF THE ROYAL NURSES AND GOVERNESSES

My darling Child
Fancy the little baby child whom I carried so often in my arms is 14 years old! A very happy birthday to you my pet. . . .

I so often wonder what you all are like now, and would treasure a new photograph of you all so much. Did you ever hear of Killarney? It is one of the most beautiful spots in the world. There are two ranges of mountains, 4 lakes studded with little islands, and the woods and flowers are beautiful. There are magnolias, rhododendrons, azaleas and eucalyptus all in full flower, and primroses and bluebells & cranebills all over the country. . . .

Dearest, I hope some day that you and your sisters may come to Ireland and see Killarney and all these beautiful places for yourselves.[1]

Life was not kind to Margaretta Eagar after she left St Petersburg in the autumn of 1904. In her published writing she maintained that the decision to leave was her own, for 'private and personal' reasons.[2] In fact she was dismissed. This is made plain by a comment in the Tsar's diary on 12 October: 'after many weeks of wavering Alix, strongly supported by myself and Princess Golitsina, at last decided to dismiss the Englishwoman, the children's nurse Miss Eagar. Maria Mikhailovna will tell her. This has caused trouble and dissention enough.'[3]

Nicholas II liked Margaretta at first and thoroughly approved her management of the nursery; the reason for his change of heart was almost certainly political. In 1904 Russia was suffering heavy losses in the war with Japan. Britain was not involved but was very pro-Japanese and it seems likely that there were powerful elements at Court – like Princess Maria Mikhailovna Golitsina, the Mistress of the Robes – who could not bear to see the long-awaited heir to the throne, born in that troubled summer, in the hands of a presumed enemy. Margaretta had done her best to help in Russia's war effort.

In June 1904 she had to go home because her mother was ill but Russia's troubles lay closest to her heart. On arrival in London she wrote to the Tsaritsa's trusted Madame Gueringer, 'There are lots of rumours here about Port Arthur. Please God the siege will end well soon and that this war will soon be over.'[4] But she had also tried to curb the children's hatred of the Japanese and it is easy to imagine how a misplaced 'Nana says . . .' from the lips of a little Grand Duchess could have inflamed feelings against her. The Tsar's comment, 'this has caused trouble and dissention enough' suggests that someone had been badgering him about it and, weighed down as he was by the war, he was simply glad to have the business done with.[5]

For Margaretta though, dismissal was a painful humiliation. It hurt even more to find rumours about her appearing in the British press. An English nurse was said to have been conveyed across the Russian border because she was caught stealing papers from the Tsar's study. This was too much and Margaretta fired off an angry letter to *The Times*: 'I now write as I am the only English nurse who has lately left Russia, to emphatically deny the truth of the story. . . . So far from being ignominiously dismissed, I received from the Empress a handsome money present, and a pension for my life was settled upon me. At Christmas I was the recipient of letters, cards and gifts from the Empress and the Imperial children. I need not say that the falsehood current in the papers has given much pain, not only to me, but to my friends.'[6] As far as the stealing goes, she was almost certainly telling the truth. The 'handsome money present' would have been the gratuity the Tsars normally gave to retiring employees but the dismissal was a fact, and it would always rankle.

Margaretta felt certain there had been a conspiracy against her – as there probably had – but over the years its nature became muddled. When asked to help with a privately printed genealogy of the Eagar family in the 1950s, her nephew Waldegrave stated that she 'was governess to the children of the Czar of Russia, until shortly after the birth of the Czarewitch, when she was replaced by a German intrigue', a bizarre idea which can only be a half-remembered version of the things Margaretta told him.[7] The next few years of her life were devoted to putting her story on record. She had already started with short pieces about Russia for *The Leisure Hour*, a magazine produced by one of the religious societies. Expanding on these pieces she wrote her memoirs, published in 1906. Her book opens with a very clear statement of her authority and trustworthiness: 'Shortly after the birth of the Czarovitch I said to the Empress that I often had thought of writing my memoirs. She encouraged me to do so, saying so many untruths had been published that it would be a relief to have an account of the Russian Court which was absolutely true. Hence this book.'[8]

Six Years at the Russian Court led to other writings. First there was the help Margaretta gave to Kellogg Durland with his articles on the Tsaritsa, which were published in America and in Britain and later appeared in book form; then her own pieces for the *Girl's Own Paper and Woman's Magazine*. Years later she almost certainly had a hand in a novel by Helen Eggleston Haskell, *Katrinka; the Story of a Russian Child*, which tells of a girl whose parents are sent to Siberia and who sets out to tell the Tsar, sure that he will bring them back if only she can speak to him. The book, published in New York in 1915, has several very Margaretta-ish elements: an affectionate focus on Tatiana, for example, and on the Tsaritsa, and a non-committal approach to the Tsar himself. Margaretta is actually mentioned in the book with profound regret by the little Grand Duchesses as they sing *Villikins and his Dinah*. Curiously, the story includes a German governess who replaced the 'governess' Miss Eagar; something which never happened except in the folklore of the Eagar family.

These publications helped to re-establish the status Margaretta had lost. She was somebody again – an authority on the Russian imperial family – but she still needed to earn a living. In 1906 or 1907 she took the lease on a boarding house in London, at 27 Holland Park Gardens. She employed domestic servants, filled the house with mementos of her time in Russia and brought her mother and invalid sister over from Ireland. The house was to provide for all their futures, but it went horribly wrong. It did not take Margaretta long to discover how different working life could be outside royal service. In St Petersburg she had been valued and treated with respect. Kings had gone out of their way to speak to her. But the keeper of a London boarding house was nobody in the eyes of its customers. Early in 1908 she heard from Madame Gueringer and all the regrets came flooding back. To have news of the Tsaritsa and the children and contact with the world that had cast her out, and with a sympathetic friend . . . She replied:

> I so often think of you, the blessed peacemaker, I wish I could see your sweet good face coming into my room again, but I suppose that never here in this world shall I see those who were so dear to me in Russia. In the next world however we shall meet again.
>
> I am very well – In spite of London fogs and the terrible pressure of the cares of this life. My mother and eldest sister live with me here, I have a boarding house. Dear Madame it is a <u>horrible</u> life. People are so impertinent here in England to women who have to work for their living; and I find the

work hard. So far the house has not ever paid its own expenses. I have got so thin with the perpetual running about, and the anxiety of trying to pay rent rates & taxes. These cost me about £200 a year that is Rs 2000, which is a great sum to make up.[9]

Margaretta ached for that other world. News that the King and Queen were going to drive past the end of Holland Park Gardens brought on a surge of nostalgic patriotism: 'I am so glad that Uncle Bertie, Auntie Alex, & Auntie Toria are going over to pay you all a visit,' she told Tatiana in a letter written for the little girl's eleventh birthday in June 1908. 'Do you know that they passed quite close to my house lately going to visit the Great Exhibition which has been opened here. And though they did not pass my house, but only the end of the street I put up flags, and put scarlet bunting with E R & a big gilt crown round my balcony . . . I wonder did they see it, but I am afraid not.'[10]

That September she heard of the death of Dr Korovin, who had helped her in the care of the imperial children and whom she remembered as a trusted friend. In November news that Grand Duke Alexei Alexandrovich, the Tsar's uncle, had died prompted her to write her only surviving letter to the Tsaritsa. 'Dear Madam,' it ran, 'I am so sorry to see by the papers that The Grand Duke Alexis is dead. Since I left Russia so many of the entourage of the Court have died. The Grand Duke was young to die. I remember how amused he always was at Olga when she was quite little, and today she is 13 years old. It seems incredible, I am so sorry her birthday festivities have been disturbed by this sad event. I hope Your Majesty is feeling better and stronger & that this sad event will not upset Your Majesty very badly.'[11]

The boarding house ran steadily downhill and by 1910 Margaretta was beside herself with worry. It spilled out even in a birthday letter to Grand Duchess Olga: 'My darling, What a great girl you are! Just 15 years old. I am so sorry not to be able to send you something better than the little work bag, but I have never had such a bad time in my life as I am undergoing at present. You know I have a Boarding House, and for three months it has been almost empty. And the expenses of rent, taxes, servants, gas coal &c are frightful. Pray for me my darlings that God will soon help me for I am in a sad way and all that are dependent on me. I am perfectly ill with anxiety and cannot sleep. My darling I am so sorry to trouble you with my troubles, but my heart is full of them.'[12] The weeks passed and things did not improve. To Madame Gueringer she wrote, 'I am at my wits end. I have even had to raise money on my jewellery. The house is taken on a lease and I cannot get rid of it unless

I become a bankrupt. I get so sick of it dear and of the English people. I made a great mistake, I think, in coming to London at all.' The good things in life all seemed to be happening somewhere else, to someone else – even her old friend Lilian Wilson: 'Did you hear that Miss Wilson who was with Princess Ella is married,' she wrote, adding, with a brave little flourish, 'I could have married since I came here but did not care for the man at all.'[13]

What happened next can only be guesswork. It would be pleasing to think that the Tsaritsa, who must have been told about the despairing content of these last two letters, stepped in to help Margaretta. Perhaps she did. Certainly someone did, for when we next meet Margaretta, six months later, in the 1911 letter to Tatiana extolling the virtues of Killarney, she is a changed woman, back in Ireland and staying with her married sister Jane Macleod in Baltinglass, County Wicklow, where her mother was also living. The boarding house and its debts were forgotten. In 1912 Margaretta suffered a serious accident which laid her up for some time. She was nearly fifty and had been lucky to survive, and the experience made her resolve to do something with her life again – 'I hope to see a great deal more of this world before I die.' By the following summer she had found her way to Hungary as English governess to a young boy. On Friday 13 June she wrote to Grand Duchess Maria:

My darling child,
Wednesday will be your birthday so I am writing to wish you a very happy one. I can hardly believe that it is fourteen years since I first saw you. You were a dear little baby in those days, and always so good and gentle. I wonder so much what you are like now.

Here I am teaching a boy of nine English, he speaks and reads fairly well, but his spelling is so queer, for he spells in the Hungarian fashion. He has no brothers or sisters so I play with him all day, and I think you would be amused if you had seen me yesterday breaking in a young donkey and today making hay. He is not a good boy, I am sorry to say, but I hope he will be better.

Martonvásár is not far from Budapest, and we came here in a steamer down the Danube, which as I am sure you know, is a very beautiful river. The steamer we came in goes all the way to the Black Sea, and they talk of going down there some day. It would be very nice. I believe we are going to Rüger in the Baltic this year, but it is not quite decided. We may go to Venice so I am seeing the world. . . .

Your loving old Nana who loves you very much
Margaretta Eagar.[14]

History's timing can be cruel. Margaretta was obviously happy when she wrote this letter. She was working again, in a job which gave her governess status and a chance to travel, but when war broke out in the following year she would have found her position compromised once more by other people's politics. No record survives of what she did. The collapse of the Russian monarchy in 1917 would have deprived her of her pension as well and that anxiety, followed so closely by the murder of the Tsaritsa and the four little girls she remembered with such love – who would never now have the chance to see Killarney – must have been devastating for her.

Through the 1920s and early '30s Margaretta's whereabouts are a mystery. Only her death certificate and will make it possible to piece together the end of her story. She died in The Grange Nursing Home at Keynsham near Bristol on 2 August 1936. They thought she was sixty-seven; in fact, she was a few days short of her seventy-third birthday. The entry under 'occupation' on her death certificate, 'of Ashley Grange, Bristol; Spinster, Governess', suggests that she was working until she was taken ill and this may explain why she had not given her true age.

She died an angry woman. Of her many nieces and nephews, the only relatives close to her at the end seem to have been her sister Jane's daughters, Muriel and Frances. Margaretta had favoured Frances, but at the start of 1936 they argued over the disposal of her belongings: the result was a will so furious that the officials of the Probate Registry must have felt their fingers burn when they touched it. Margaretta left everything to Muriel, save one item 'either my silver tea service, or the case of spoons whichever she likes' to a friend, Dr Lily Baker. She had little to leave in money – £218 before payment of duties; her nearest contemporary among the St Petersburg nurses, Frances Fry, left £1,146 when she died in 1934 – but there were also 'furniture, pictures and ornaments &c both in store and in Ireland'. Not wanting anyone to be in any doubt of her reasons Margaretta then launched into a diatribe against Muriel's sister: 'I leave nothing to my niece Frances Macleod because I spent nearly £400 on her education, travelling expenses and clothes . . . and also because of what she wrote to me recently which I cannot either forget or forgive – and also when I offered her certain of my things she ordered me to make a will & leave them to her. The will is now made.'[15]

Poor Margaretta, it was a sad end. Thankfully, few women found life so difficult and disappointing outside palace walls, though there were aspects of her experience which others shared. Even the boarding house. In the aftermath of the First World War a former Archduke of Austria fetched up in a seedy lodging house in Berlin. On learning who he was the landlady demanded payment in advance, saying, 'For over ten years I was in the Kaiser Wilhelm's household – as chief nurse to his children – and one thing I do know about hard-up royalties is that they never pay up, until they are forced.'[16] It can only have been Mrs Matcham. As the days passed, she regaled her new guest with stories of the Berlin nursery. She adored little Princess Viktoria Luise, she told him, and was scared of the Kaiser. Her admiration for the Kaiserin came close to worship. 'I could not help liking the woman for the admirable stoicism with which she faced her changed lot,' the Archduke wrote, '. . . she never complained, and her stern and forbidding manner would relax altogether when she spoke of her erstwhile charges.'[17]

Margaretta and Mrs Matcham, and others too, were damaged financially by the fall of the monarchies they had served. But there was a charity which might have helped them. From the 1840s the Governesses' Benevolent Institution had assisted retired governesses with no other means of support. Few women from royal service needed such help but there are some familiar names in the GBI lists. Hilda Maybury, briefly governess to the Oldenburg family in 1914, was helped by the charity, receiving an annuity of £30 and occasional smaller grants.[18] Lilian Eadie's sister Helen and Kate Ffolliott, sister of Anne Louisa Ffolliott who replaced Saxton Winter in Romania, also received annuities and grants: £6 a year was all Helen Eadie had when she applied for assistance.[19] The GBI could also provide accommodation. Their splendidly named 'Asylum for Decayed Governesses' in Kentish Town closed in 1867 but a home was opened in Chislehurst in 1872, comprising a complex of small houses. Queen Mary was patroness of the institute from 1910 and when the exiled Queen of Greece wrote to her in 1924 requesting help for Katherine Howard Nicholls, her daughters' former governess, the Queen was pleased to help.[20] She spoke to the institute's secretary and Miss Nicholls was awarded house no. 12 and, in the following year, a grant of £24.[21]

Anne Chermside was lucky in that the Egyptian royal family still needed her in exile and still had the means to pay her. She had lived through the dynasty's darkest moments and shared their danger. When Crown Prince Fuad was only ten days old there were riots in Cairo: 'The sky grew steadily darker with the smoke from the burning town', Anne wrote, 'and ashes began falling on the Palace balconies – gunfire could be heard all around us.' For two nights she slept on the floor in her uniform and there was a machine-gun post under the nursery windows. In June the family moved to Alexandria and were in the Ras-el-Tin Palace by the harbour when they woke one July morning to find themselves surrounded by soldiers. The King was forced to abdicate in favour of his son and the whole family left that same day onboard the royal yacht *Mahroussa*. 'I think one of the most moving scenes I saw was the Royal Standard being taken down over the Palace for the last time,' Anne said.[22] She retired only when the children were grown up, but was invited back in 1978 to nurse King Fuad's eldest child. She died in November 1988, while visiting Princess Fadia in Switzerland.

Women whose employing families kept their thrones – or who lived and died before the upheavals of the twentieth century – were looked after very well in retirement. Some stayed with their royal families – like Mary Barnes, who brought up Prince Otto of Wied. She became nurse to the Baden family and was cared for by them. She is buried today in their family crypt in the chapel at Mainau in Switzerland. The Mecklenburg-Schwerin family's nurse Mary Jenkins lived out her days with them, as her youngest charge Duchess Cecilie, Crown Princess of Prussia, remembered: 'She had a snug little flat in the Alexandrine Palace, opening on to the Old Garden. We used to spend many hours of sociable talk with the old lady, who passed the evening of her life there in peace and undisturbed by anyone. She spoke a quite peculiar blend of German and English, which often contributed to our amusement. . . . She died in the year 1917 at the age of eighty-eight, and is buried in the cemetery at Ludwigslust; my brother and sister and I regularly visit her grave.'[23]

Kathleen Wanstall spent the First World War in the household of the German diplomat Prince Wilhelm of Stolberg-Wernigerode, and returned home when the war ended. In December 1920 she became nurse to the newborn Princess Antoinette of Monaco. Kathleen also cared for Prince Rainier, who was born in 1923 – 'my big boy', she would call him in later years – and she provided stability in an otherwise troubled family. In 1950, as sovereign Prince of Monaco, Prince Rainier honoured his old nurse with the *Chevalier de l'Ordre de Saint Charles*, a move which was very popular in Monaco where Kathleen was well known (her reputed refusal to speak French obviously did not count against her). Princess Antoinette married in 1951 and Kathleen, then in her sixties, went on to care for her three children, passing naturally, as the Princess said in a letter to Norland, from nanny to granny. In the final year of her life she was bedridden with arteriosclerosis and the family nursed her; she died in May 1967. She was such a respected figure in Monaco that her funeral filled the English Church to overflowing.

Two stalwarts of the Russian imperial family, Elizabeth Francklin and Mary Ann Orchard, became good friends in their later years. Elizabeth was in a strange position. The distance that had worried her between her charge, Grand

Duchess Olga Alexandrovna, and Tsaritsa Maria Feodorovna, the child's mother, deepened with the years. The Tsaritsa did not have the time to devote to Olga that she had given her older children, but she came to resent the love her daughter felt for Elizabeth Francklin. She accused the nurse of being too indulgent and too affectionate and finally, in the late 1890s, she tried to replace her with a lady-in-waiting. But Olga would not hear of it. Well into her rebellious teens, she threatened to run away or to do something scandalous in revenge. She also brought the young Tsar, her brother, into the argument on her side. So Elizabeth Francklin stayed, hated by Maria Feodorovna and increasingly denied the gifts and favours the family usually gave their servants, but absolutely secure in Olga's affections.

Mary Ann Orchard, 'Orchie', came into their lives at the end of 1894, when her charge Princess Alix of Hesse was married to the Tsar. Orchie's attachment to Alix was as deep as Elizabeth Francklin's to Olga and she helped to dress her Princess for the wedding in the elaborate costume traditional at the Russian Court. Alix's sister Irène described the preparations: Alix 'was led into the room where the Bride is dressed, & there the diadem (a lovely shape) the crown, the earrings, the diamonds for neck & arms were put on, the orange blossoms & myrtle, & the big cloak of "drap d'or" with a cape bordered with Ermine like the whole cloak, Aunt Minny's maids Orchie & Madeleine assisting'. When it was over the newly-weds moved straight into the Anichkov Palace with Tsaritsa Maria Feodorovna, 'Aunt Minny', and Irène was one of several members of the bride's family who visited them there. 'Alicky had already put up lots of her frames, nick-nacks &c,' she told Queen Victoria, 'and Orchie was busy bustling about with the rest of all her things, clothes &c – it looked so home like.'[24]

It did not always feel like home, though, with three separate groups of people trying to live together as one family under the Anichkov roof. To the tensions that already existed between Maria Feodorovna, Olga and Mrs Francklin were soon added new stresses between Maria Feodorovna and her daughter-in-law. Only the two nurses struck an instant bond and, as the months passed, their greatest pleasure was to sit and reminisce over the teacups about 'their' children, allowing Orchie to expand at length on her favourite subject – Princess Alix. Her pride was complete when Alix's first child, Grand Duchess Olga Nikolaevna, was born a year after the marriage. Orchie was given overall control of the nursery and the baby adored her; when Princess Louis of Battenberg was in Russia in the spring of 1896 she told Queen Victoria, 'The baby is magnificent – a bright intelligent little soul – she is especially fond of Orchie smiling broadly whenever she catches sight of her.'[25]

But Orchie's days of actual nursing were long past. In the autumn of 1899 she returned to England and she made her will in Dorchester on 13 September before returning to Russia; her health deteriorated steadily. The Tsaritsa saw that she was well cared for and in 1903 the family took her with them when they went to Darmstadt, where she had lived for so long. 'Mrs Orchard is here,' Margaretta told Mme Gueringer in October 1903. 'I think she seems better but her memory is not good. She forgets so much and her nose is so <u>purple</u>, I'm afraid it's the heart which causes that. She is always very happy.'[26] The following spring the Tsaritsa sent her other resident invalid, her lady-in-waiting Princess Orbeliani, to the spa at Nauheim. She told a friend: 'Orchie goes with her, as she is failing rapidly – she understands little, remembers nothing & is becoming childish, but Nauheim has always done her gout and heart good. It's very sad to see her so.'[27] Sometime after this, Mary Ann Orchard returned to England. It has been said that she left Russia 'in a huff' but, given the state of her health, that sounds unlikely; she was no longer capable of arranging a journey or of travelling alone.[28] She did return somehow, though, and she died at Forest Gate in Essex on 8 August 1906. 'I miss my dear old Orchie so much, as you can imagine,' the Tsaritsa wrote. 'But her sufferings are over now and one could not wish it otherwise.'[29]

Orchie's friendship with Elizabeth Francklin was not forgotten. While the official will disposed of her money and property in England, there must have been a second document dealing with belongings she left in Russia: this was dealt with by the Tsaritsa's office. On 29 October Elizabeth wrote to Madame Gueringer: 'In answer to your letter telling me of the bequest in my dear old friend Miss Orchard's will, of an easy chair which she has left to me, I shall feel greatly obliged if you will kindly have it sent to me here.' 'Here' was the palace of Gatchina, where Olga Alexandrovna still had apartments, though she had married a Prince of Oldenburg in 1901 and she and 'Nana' had moved out of the Anichkov Palace. Their home – Elizabeth Francklin's St Petersburg home for the rest of her life – was the Oldenburg mansion on Sergeevskaya Street.

In comparison with Mary Ann Orchard, and with most other nurses and governesses overseas, Elizabeth Francklin had a very full family life which coexisted with her life in royal service. She had been in Russia three or four years when her elder son, Thomas, decided to follow her and found work with an English company in St Petersburg. In October 1886, realising that her daughter Annie's marriage was failing and concerned for her grandchildren, Elizabeth paid their fares to Russia and rented a flat in Gatchina town. She hired a servant to look after them. A divorce soon followed and Elizabeth encouraged her daughter to stay on and earn her living by teaching English.

Thomas Francklin married a Russian girl and in time Annie also remarried. The grandchildren were sometimes allowed to play with Olga, though Elizabeth made them mind their manners and address Olga by her title. Her grandson George remembered teas in the imperial nursery with bread and the golden syrup his grandmother ordered specially from England; bread before cake was Elizabeth Francklin's invariable rule and at Christmas she made the plum puddings herself. She insisted that her family should remember they were English, but as time passed Russia gently took them over.

To the Grand Duchess, Elizabeth Francklin remained 'Nana' and no matter how grown up she became, obeying Nana was a way of life. A note Olga sent to her mother was auctioned some time ago. Written in 1910, when Elizabeth Francklin was seventy-three years old and Olga nearly thirty, it read, 'I am sorry to say that I cough & sneeze – principally – because of the cough – Nana says I must not go out. I perspire every minute so it would be too easy to catch a chill – which might turn out badly for me – so I, with great resignation must stay indoors!'[30] The relationship never changed until the day Elizabeth Francklin died, peacefully in her sleep, in April 1913. She was seventy-eight years old. An obituary appeared in the Russian press: it gave a fanciful account of her origins, but her family treasured it. 'Mrs Franklin', it read, 'came from an ancient aristocratic English family. She received an excellent medical education and had a wide clientele in the highest circles in England. She came to Russia in 1882, on the invitation of the Russian Imperial Court. The Queen Dowager Alexandra, widow of the late King Edward VII, knew Mrs. Franklin personally, and graciously allowed her to go to Russia.'[31]

The British royal family did not keep retired nurses and governesses in house, but they did make provision for them. Of the women who played key roles in bringing up Queen Victoria's large family, Mary Anne Thurston was made housekeeper at Windsor on her retirement from the nursery in 1865, with a salary and a £50 a year nurse's pension. When she retired as housekeeper in 1868 the pension rose to £150, half each from the Privy Purse and from the Lord Chamberlain's Department, and she was offered rooms at Cumberland Lodge.[32] In the late 1880s when her health began to fail she was living in Kensington Palace, where the Queen visited her on several occasions.

'Old May', Marianne Hull, had entered the royal nursery in 1842 when the Prince of Wales was a month old and she stayed until 1858, when she left to marry Charles Hull, the Queen's Messenger. At that time the Queen called her 'the most faithful, devoted being one could imagine & much beloved by the children'.[33] May was often called back to act as temporary nurse to the grandchildren, sometimes going overseas: the *Windsor & Eton Express* noted at the time of her death that she 'was a great favourite . . . with all the Royal Family, all of whom continually presented her with valuable gifts, until her residence became quite a treasure house of mementos'.[34] The end came in September 1888. The Queen was in Balmoral at the time but Mrs Hull's doctor kept her fully informed and the news touched the whole royal family. 'I was so sorry to hear of old May's death,' Prince Alfred told his mother. 'I shall miss seeing her in the corridor at Windsor before dinner where she always came when any of us were on a visit. I am suggesting to Bertie that we should creat[e] some memorial of her grave.'[35] In the event, as *The Times* reported on 30 August 1889, the Queen's surviving children provided the memorial stone in Clewer Churchyard, which was inscribed with their seven names.

From medieval times the Queen Consort or Queen Dowager in England had the power to appoint deserving ladies to the sisterhood of St Katherine's Hospital, a charitable foundation akin to an almshouse. By the mid-nineteenth century there was no hospital as such, just three small houses in St Katherine's Precinct, on the outer circle of Regent's Park. As there was no Queen Consort or Queen Dowager either, the houses were in Queen Victoria's gift. A vacancy came up in 1860 and the Queen contacted her children's governess Sarah Anne Hildyard. 'There are 3 sisters,' she told her, 'each of whom have a small House . . . which they may let if they please, with an income of 200 a year. Now, it struck us dear Miss Hildyard, that this may be a convenience to yourself in after times & also to your Sisters, who possibly might like to live there & then be near to you, & yet <u>not</u> actually in London.'[36] (Curious to think of a time when Regent's Park was 'not actually in London' . . .)

Miss Hildyard accepted gratefully – 'I could hardly have chosen a spot where I should more like to dwell hereafter' – and when she retired five years later St Katherine's became her home.[37] She lived there until her death in May 1889 when the house, no. 8 St Katherine's Precinct, passed to Margaret Hardcastle Jackson. 'Madgie' was promised the first vacancy at St Katherine's in 1888, when the Queen insisted that it was time for her to retire from Darmstadt. The Princesses visited from time to time and Madgie was able to keep her hand in as a governess too: Victoria, Princess Louis of Battenberg, often employed her to teach the four Battenberg children and she prepared the eldest of them, Princess Alice (later Princess Andrew of Greece), for confirmation. As the years passed, the Tsaritsa also valued Madgie's advice, writing from Russia for suggested reading matter for the four Grand Duchesses: 'If you know of any interesting historical books for girls, could you tell me, as I read to them and they have begun reading English for themselves.'[38]

When Marianne Green's appointment in Berlin ended, Kaiserin Friedrich's first thought was that her skills might find employment outside teaching. She wrote to Sir Philip Owen, director of the South Kensington Museum, about Marianne, 'She must return to England – & is naturally anxious to have some work to do – either as a secretary to another writing a book – or to an institution – or as a Lady Decoder in the British Museum, to anyone writing a work. – Perhaps you might know of an opening of this kind for her as you see & meet so many people.' It appears that he did not. Marianne had no home of her own and no surviving family; Queen Victoria promised her the next vacancy in St Katherine's and, after a fruitless stay in London, the governess took herself to Schwerin to teach Duchess Alexandrine, the elder sister of Duchess Cecilie and a future Queen of Denmark. By 1897 she had retired from there and was living in the cottages at Clewer, Windsor, where 'old May' Hull had lived, when the vacancy finally occurred. On the death of Lady Anne Loftus, Marianne Green moved into no. 7 St Katherine's Precinct, becoming Madgie Jackson's next-door neighbour.

For a later generation of the British royal family, Charlotte 'Lalla' Bill would always occupy a special place. The children of King George V and Queen Mary were all attached to her, and her commitment to Prince John was something the King and Queen would never forget. She was given a pension of £120 after Prince John's death. In 1923 the royal couple particularly wanted to appoint her housekeeper at Buckingham Palace but she was unsure. The housekeeper's salary was £150 and Lalla asked if she could receive this and keep her pension; loyal though she was, she was also very canny and she pointed out that if she took an outside job she would have both salary and pension intact.[39] This caused some debate in the Privy Purse Office. Paying a pension and a salary at once from the same source was no longer done in the public services and officials decided, with the King's approval, to offer £180 for the housekeeper's post, rising to £200, with board wages and allowances extra and with an assurance that on retirement the whole of her service would be taken into account and her pension would be based on her final salary.[40]

Lalla agreed, and she worked as housekeeper for three years before deciding to retire. Again, this posed problems. The upper age limit for the job was seventy and she was only fifty-three; also she had chosen to leave, which should have made her ineligible for a pension. But hers was a special case, and as 'she came back into service not at her own request but, if anything, with some reluctance' the Keeper of the Privy Purse and the King's Treasurer agreed to set the rules aside and pay a pension of £144. 'As I told you,' the Keeper remarked in a memo to the Deputy Treasurer, 'Mrs Bill's case must necessarily be treated exceptionally. Her long and devoted service to Prince John entitles her to special consideration.'[41]

Housekeeping – even on the scale of Buckingham Palace – may have had no appeal for a woman whose real interests lay in childcare. In the years between Prince John's death and the appointment at the Palace, Lalla Bill had several chances to take a royal baby in her arms again. Princess Mary, whom she had nursed almost from birth, married Henry, Viscount Lascelles in 1922 and in 1923 gave birth to her first child. Lalla was there to see that all went smoothly. On 8 February – the day after the birth – Queen Mary told Queen Alexandra: 'we waited in a little sitting room near her bed room, until Mary's maid came & knocked at the door & merely announced "A boy". I flew off the sofa & went into Mary's dressing room where I met Harry Lascelles & we fell into each others arms with joy! . . . Lalla is looking after the baby & is very happy.'[42] Lalla also attended the birth of Princess Mary's second child and in January 1925 was in Bermuda with Lady Patricia Ramsay – 'Patsy' of Connaught – and her five-year-old son Alexander. 'Our grounds lie behind the house on rising ground,' Lady Patricia told Queen Mary, '& our drive comes up past an enclosed brackish lagoon, which belongs to the place too. It is really very pretty, & Lalla keeps on saying how much she thinks you would like it. I do wish you could be spirited here secretly to have a look at it!'[43]

Then came the appointment at Buckingham Palace and after that, Lalla Bill disappears for a few years. According to the writer Ursula Bloom, who knew her well, she lived in Norfolk through the 1930s and '40s and Queen Mary would visit whenever she was at Sandringham. The abdication crisis of 1936 was a real blow to the King's former nurse. Ursula Bloom said that she saw Lalla in tears then, for the first and only time, because 'it was so awful for his mother. . . . But you could never make him do something that he didn't really want to do.' Lalla worried about the new King; 'He was never a strong baby, never really too sturdy as a little boy, and the strain of it will be too much for him!'[44]

Late in 1950 Queen Mary wrote to King George VI to suggest that Lalla Bill might be offered a vacant cottage at West Newton, near Sandringham. 'My darling Mama,' he replied. 'Thank you so much for your letter about Lalla. It did come as a surprise but a very nice one & I think she would be a perfect person to have in the village. She knows many people here still & they all like her. . . . The cottage will have to be repainted & cleaned & Lalla should choose the colours. I will write to her & offer her the accommodation if you would kindly let me have her address. There is no one waiting for it at the moment & Lalla is the very person to go there.'[45]

Lalla accepted the offer and was reunited with many old friends. Winifred Thomas's aunt Lizzie Stratton lived not far away, widowed and increasingly frail but reluctant to leave the home she had shared with her late husband. Lalla and Mabel Butcher, a former housekeeper at Sandringham, kept an eye on her. Once, Winifred wrote to Lalla from India: there had been an article on Sandringham in the *Picture Post*, which must have brought back memories. 'Dear Little Winnie,' ran the reply. 'As such I knew you in the long ago days – it was nice to receive your letter. I am glad you were amused at P. Post & it would be nice for you seeing the picture of the old place again.' It was a long letter, mostly aimed to reassure Winifred about her aunt, but Lalla also had news of her own: 'Well now', she wrote, 'on Jan 10th Mrs Butcher & I we are doing a tour to Chille on the Renia del Pacifico – for 10 weeks, it will be nice to get where it is warm.' She promised to see Mrs Stratton before they left.[46]

Mary Cottage, West Newton, was Lalla Bill's home until 1959, when she went to live with a niece in Hampshire. She died in St Mark's Hospital in Maidenhead, aged eighty-nine, and characteristically, apart from a few specific bequests to family members, she left almost half of her estate to the Church of England Children's Society.

Former nurses and governesses often kept in touch with the royal families who had employed them. For most the royal appointment was the defining moment of their lives and the one they would have returned to if they could. Mary Green, 'Nana' to the first three of Queen Marie of Romania's children in the 1890s and early 1900s, lived out her retirement in a cottage in Windsor. She christened it 'Mignon', the nickname of her youngest charge. In about 1919 Marie paid her a surprise visit: 'she nearly fainted with joy,' the Queen wrote, 'she had not expected us. As profuse of words as in the olden days, she wept, laughed and exclaimed, blessing and scolding us in turns. She had endless questions to ask, tales to tell, souvenirs to dig up. It all poured forth in a comic jumble of 'H'-less words. . . . Of course, we had to accept a cup of tea and sat down in a small parlour, the walls of which were lined with royal family photographs, representing all of us at different stages of our lives. . . . It was no easy matter to tear ourselves away from her loquacious hospitality.'[47]

Queen Marie would not have considered visiting her arch-enemy Saxton Winter, whose name she had done so much to blacken, but others did. Queen Wilhelmina retained great affection for her former governess, as did the grown-up children of the Maule family whom Saxton had taught before she went to the Netherlands. After leaving Romania, Saxton Winter lived with her sister Nancy at 39 South Road, Saffron Walden. In 1935 Queen Wilhelmina visited and a newspaper photographer captured the scene by the gate as the Queen was about to leave: Wilhelmina herself in profile beside a tiny, bent figure with white hair, hardly visible between the heads of the watching crowd. A second elderly lady in a buttoned-up cardigan, standing at a respectful distance and smiling benignly, was probably Nancy. Both sisters had only months to live. Saxton Winter died on 29 January 1936, aged eighty-one. It may have been her executor and former pupil, Hugh Patrick Guerin Maule, who wrote the brief obituary which appeared in *The Times* on Friday the 31st: 'Miss Elizabeth Saxton Winter, formerly governess for 10 years to the Queen of the Netherlands, and beloved friend of many old pupils, died at her home at Saffron Walden, Essex, on Wednesday, after lying unconscious for a week. Her sister, Miss Nancy Hodges Winter, with whom she lived in retirement, died on Wednesday last week.'

Emily Roose was forced into retirement in her fifties, suffering from severe arthritis and osteoporosis. She moved to South Africa for the climate and to be near her sister Ellen, 'Nell', who looked after her, though her health was in a far more precarious state than her letters to her former charges ever admitted. She was almost bedridden, unable to walk and in constant pain. One day she broke a rib simply because her sister's foot slipped as she helped her from a chair and they collided: 'poor Nell was very upset, but not me,' she wrote, 'I cheered her by telling her the story of Polleana – do you remember the book, always be glad things are not worse if you break <u>one</u> rib, be thankful it is not 2!'[48] This refusal to give in was typical of 'Roosie'.

   This letter is one of a bundle from 'Old Nana' to Princess Cecile, the third of Emily Roose's five charges, preserved by the Hesse family. They cover the period from January 1931 to June 1933; twenty-four long and often rambling letters which bear witness to Roosie's courage in the face of debilitating illness and to her abiding love for 'her' five children, Margarita, Theodora, Cecile, Sophie and Philip of Greece. She was writing to the others too, and to their grandmother, their mother, their father; occasionally to Cecile's mother-in-law the Grand Duchess of Hesse and to some of the other former nurses of the Greek royal family; not, perhaps, to Kate Fox, her old rival, though she did look back with fondness on the weeks they had spent together on Corfu, their last weeks in Greece. 'Do you remember when Philip was born & you sisters how delighted you were,' she asked Princess Cecile. 'I go through all those old times again, & do hope & pray I can walk again, it is so lazy to feel well & only sit still.'[49] Able to do so little for herself, Roosie lived through her letters and the contact they brought with the world she had belonged to for so long.

The family's news was endlessly fascinating to her. The first of the letters was written before Cecile's wedding to the Hereditary Grand Duke of Hesse – Lilian Wilson and Lilian Eadie's little 'Georgie', though at over six feet five no one would have called him 'little' any more. Princess Sophie had married a few weeks before and the elder sisters were also engaged. 'I shall picture you on the second of Feb in your wedding gown and naturally long to be near you all', Roosie wrote. 'But I know I am better here, until I can skip and be useful again.'[50] In April 1931, after Princess Margarita's wedding, she said, 'I thought of you all on the 20th & Margarita I pictured in her wedding dress & Philip carrying her train. He must be quite clever with it after having 3 sisters married so near.'[51] When Cecile's first child was born in late October Roosie was beside herself: 'I wish I could express the joy I felt for you when I got the happy telegram this morning at 9 o'clock. I gave such a shout Nell came rushing, left her hot iron & burnt the dress, I said never mind the old frock, my Princess Cecile has a son & my dear would you believe it, I forgot the old tight knees and started getting up better. . . . Oh! how I longed to be near you, just a peep of joy – I can imagine the excitement at Wolfsgarten & your husband's happiness.'[52]

The thought of the baby she had carried holding a baby of her own brought back a flood of memories. Roosie told the Princess how, when she was born, her mother had expected a son with such confidence that 'we talked of the kind of suits you should wear at 3 years old'.[53] Later she sent Cecile of photo of herself at five months old so that she could see how like her the baby was, and she wished for 'my old nursery book to send you. How interested you would have been now you have a baby. I used to write every day from the day you were all born, things you eat & when you started spinich egg, orange juice etc some of the doings would be amusing – I must have left the book in "Mon Repos"', she wrote, 'I remember Mrs Blowes telling me I left a few books in my cupboard.'[54]

The photographs the family sent her were a constant delight. Nell's son framed some of them for her room: 'I can see them when I am in bed,' she said, 'doctor & Parson always have a good look at all & admire them, last week the Matron & Sister from the hospital I was in, came again & their first words doctor told us you had some new pictures of your Princesses.'[55] Other photographs and the most recent letters and postcards never left her side: Nell called them her 'luggage' and whenever she was well enough to be helped out onto the veranda to sit in the sun; or later, when she took herself out in a wheelchair, she kept them with her. 'How you would laugh to see me with all my packets, when I move all the pictures and knitting bag go with me. . . . It is pleasant & I write letters & when people come I entertain them – first look at all my pictures, out comes my packet tied carefully with a piece of your pink hair ribbon. When you had long hair & a big bow tied on the side you used to be very particular about the bow being just right.'[56]

She was still 'Nana', handing out good advice, trying valiantly to knit knickers for the babies – though the arthritis in her fingers made this a real struggle – and everything seemed to remind her of the children; of something they said or did, or of some small incident in the nursery. 'It is still summer here & 12 pineapples for a shilling', she wrote on 3 March 1932, 'makes me long to send some to Philip, he told me once, he loved me nearly as much as pineapple', and a year later, 'Philip gave me pleasure again another letter this mail, and full of fun. Did I remember when I called him to get up quick Easter morning & while I was out of the room he dressed & got in to bed again – when I got back & found him in bed I began to scold, then out Philip jumped all ready dressed! Then the fun to laugh at me. He wrote rather large said not to tire my eyes, bless him!'[57]

The early 1930s were not an easy time for Prince Andrew of Greece's family, scattered and in exile as they were, but they never forgot to keep Roosie supplied with the news, the photographs, the little gifts that helped her to carry on, and they also provided more practical support. Their letters almost always carried gifts of money. One Christmas Cecile's husband sent her £200; the children's aunt, Queen Louise of Sweden, and their grandmother Victoria, Marchioness of Milford Haven – once Princess Louis of Battenberg – also made gifts to her. A mention of anything she needed, whether for living expenses or medical treatment, always produced a quick response. 'Oh! if I could only see you all', she wrote. 'When I can walk again, I shall want to fly.'[58]

Nell's health gave out at the end of 1932 and she had to go into a convalescent home, while her sister was moved to another address, with other carers. After June 1933 there are no more letters and no clue to what became of Emily Roose: it may be that she had died.

Caring for dependent relatives as Nell cared for Emily was often the lot of single women. Millicent Crofts looked after her mother and Beatrice Todd had to give up nursing to care for a succession of relatives. When the Waldeck family's 'Nana' Smith heard that her father was ill at home in Huntingdon in 1872 she felt obliged to go to him, though she was very unhappy about it. The Princess applauded her decision: 'I think you are quite right in the course you have undertaken, of sticking to the wish to remain near your elderly father & of not accepting any situation, that will take you from him. Surely a blessing will rest on that intention!' She then tried to console 'Nana' with the thought of an imminent birth in the family, her brother's child: 'I can quite fancy the happy look you will have when the baby lies in yr arms.'[59]

A few of the single nurses whose stories we have followed did find husbands, albeit rather late in life. Lilian Wilson left the Hesse nursery in September 1908 after thirteen years to marry Wilhelm Scharmann, an accountant in the Grand Duke's treasury whom she must have known for some time. She was forty-four. He was thirty-two and had previously lived with his mother. Being married to a Court official meant that Lilian was still close at hand and could stand in as nurse to the Princes if needed; after one such return in 1910 she told their mother, 'it is strange that for the too short a time I had there I should miss them so, last night again I thought I heard them calling me'.[60] In 1919 she and Wilhelm moved into a house on the Bessunger Strasse in Darmstadt. The city records contain no further mention of Lilian, though Wilhelm lived there until the 1940s.

Her successor Lilian Eadie went home to Devon after her escape from Russia, finally resigned to the fact that 'Georgie' and 'Lu' were too old for a nurse. But they did not forget her and, during a holiday in Switzerland with Prince and Princess Andrew of Greece and their family, they wrote letters to be brought back to England for Lilian by one of the cousins. Lilian was thrilled, both with the letters and the accompanying photographs: 'what a difference to the small boys I left, but the faces are just the same'.[61] In November 1921 she wrote to her little 'Georgie', now 'My dear Prince Don' for his birthday: 'I can hardly believe you are 15 years old, don't expect I should know you now. I often think about you and little Lu, and the old days in Darmstadt and Wolfsgarten, and wish we could have them all over again.' She had been ill, she said, and had gone to stay with a cousin in Guildford. 'My cousin here is a Scout master and I help him often with the boys, last week we had over 100 boys to tea, it was some work to cut bread and butter and find buns for all those boys, and you should have heard the noise that went on in the Hall. I have a very soft place in my heart for all small boys, and especially for two I said goodbye to in Darmstadt some years ago.'[62]

Lilian Eadie was on the threshold of a new life, though perhaps she did not realise it. Five years later, in 1926, at the age of fifty-one, she married her Scout-master cousin, Harold Vivian Jeffery, who was also managing director of a gun maker and sports shop in Guildford High Street. The rest of her life was devoted to him and to his Scouts and she made quite a name for herself in the Guildford area. She found expression for her artistic talents too, designing a commemorative window for the town's Centenary Hall, which is mentioned in her obituaries. But echoes from that other world were never far away. Lilian's obituary in the *Norland Quarterly* spoke of her grief at the murder of the Tsar and his family: 'she had grown very fond of all the girls and the little boy'. How much more would she have felt the tragic events of November 1937 when 'Don', the Hereditary Grand Duke of Hesse, his wife Princess Cecile, their two young sons and Grand Duchess Eleonore were all killed in a plane crash near Ostende on the way to Prince Ludwig's wedding. Lilian's affection for them had never dimmed and she may even have attended the funeral. She certainly kept in contact with Darmstadt and she received a letter from Prince Ludwig shortly before her death in March 1967, at the age of ninety-one.

There were some, too, who gave a lie to the myth that being a governess was death to all hope of marriage. Throughout her time in royal service, Ada Leslie was keen on Reginald Castle, whom she seems to have met on her visit to India in 1883. He joined the Indian Police Service not long afterwards and over the years made several attempts to see Ada: she always put him off – 'One has to keep many of one's affairs quite quiet, you know.'[63] And he waited, and waited. When Ada decided to leave the household of the Crown Princess of Greece in the summer of 1893 he obviously felt he had waited long enough. He proposed marriage and was accepted and, by the end of 1894, Ada had joined him in Burma where he was then serving. Her last letter to her cousin Pollie was written from Burma on 5 December 1894; after this nothing more is known of her.

Ethel Howard married a Mr H.A. Bell, sometime after leaving Japan in 1908. They visited the country together, perhaps on honeymoon, and were welcomed as honoured guests by Prince Tadashige, who was married by then with two small children of his own. The dedication of Ethel's *Japanese Memories* 'to the memory of my beloved husband' shows that Mr Bell must have died sometime before 1918 and there is only one further reference to Ethel herself. From October 1922 until March 1923 Prince Tadashige Shimadzu and his wife were in Britain on an extended visit. On 28 March they gave a reception in London and *The Times* lists Ethel among the guests. Tadashige became Japanese Naval Attaché in London in 1931; Ethel would have been so proud.

Those who did not marry sometimes branched out in other directions – like Jane Potts, governess to the Albany family. She left them at the start of 1901. 'I can't realise that I am not coming back,' she told Princess Alice of Albany, 'that that delightful chapter in my life is closed – closed with the century – I shall miss you more than I can say – I shall miss the arguments, when I tried to convince you against your will, and you would not be convinced. You always bore & forebore with me – & I am very grateful – I can truly say those 10 years were good for me & they were the <u>happiest</u> in my teaching life.'[64] She opened an exclusive girls' school in Eastbourne; in time Alice's daughter Princess May of Teck would be one of her pupils.

Other women chose to write about their experiences, as Kaiser Wilhelm II pointed out when he met the mysterious Miss B for the first time: '"Well," he said, "I suppose by this time you have begun to make notes for the great book?" I had to show my stupidity by asking what book his Majesty referred to? "Why, the book you will write about Us," he explained in his rather grating voice. "Of course you will do it. They all do."'[65] In his case he was right, most of them did: Ethel Howard, Anne Topham, Lilian Brimble . . . The published memoirs of May T, Nellie Ryan, Margaretta Eagar, Anna Bicknell, Anna Leonowens, Emmeline Lott and others provide lasting evidence of the work they did. There should have been one more name to list. In 1945 the Registrar of Norland wrote to Kate Fox to wish her luck with her proposed memoirs. On 19 February 1948 the principal's secretary told Kate, 'Miss Blakeney has read the beginning of your memoirs, and was so fascinated with them that she took the liberty of reading some of your manuscripts to the students in training. Miss Blakeney would like to know if she may have some more of your manuscript; meanwhile, she is keeping your valuable document very carefully until she hears from you again.'[66]

It was never published. If only . . . Kate Fox had been everywhere and met everyone, and she was proud of it. After her return to Princess Nicholas's family in 1921 she stayed with them, or at least close to them, for the rest of her life: she saw all three Princesses married and stood in occasionally as nurse to the next generation. She was probably annoying at times. She did tend to dine out on her royal connection, but the family seem to have tolerated her with great affection like a slightly trying elderly aunt, and they valued her years of unbroken loyalty. Kate died on 19 November 1949 in Iver Cottage Hospital, near to Princess Marina, Duchess of Kent's home at 'Coppins', leaving a formidable catalogue of valuable items given to her by royalty, mostly bequeathed back to royalty in her will. The Duchess of Kent attended the funeral with her sister Olga, Princess Paul of Yugoslavia and, when the service was over, they visited Kate's sister Jessie, who was in hospital. And Kate's manuscript? It seems to have vanished without trace.

'Foxie', 'Roosie' and 'Burgie', Lalla Bill, Nana Bell and Miss Byng, Ethel Howard, Mary Anne Thurston and the Lilians, Wilson, Brimble and Eadie –

for generations all types and conditions of British women took on the care of royal children, at home and overseas. To the sometimes rarified atmosphere of royal Courts they brought the down-to-earth, trusted values of home, coupled with real love for the children. When little Prince Berthold of Baden, charge of nurse Beatrice Halls, was asked his name he is supposed to have replied, 'In German my name is Berthold. In English my names are "sweetheart" and "darling".'[67] British nurses and governesses were valued and sought after and they performed an incalculable service, both to the families who employed them and to their own country. From sisters Pauline Gessler and Sarah Nichols in the 1770s to Anne Chermside, who was still working for the Egyptian royal family in the 1970s, they represent two centuries of honest, loving service and their voices echo down the years. . . .

'My life has been most interesting, but before I touch on the best side of it, I should like to say to those who imagine that a Royal post must certainly be everything that is desirable, that it is in many ways very much like an ordinary one, except that the responsibilities are heavier. . . .'[68]

'Do you know that often when I am tired and worn out with the worries of my position, I think of you with more or less envy – you with your husband and dear little girls and pretty home – I faraway in a foreign country for ever tucking my legs under other people's tables. However we cannot have everything. I have had many wishes gratified in seeing other lands. . . .'[69]

'I dreamt the other night I was in the Palace, and I saw all the beds as plainly & little white robed figures, who were very reluctant to lie down – May God bless and protect them always. . . .'[70]

'I prefer, while endeavouring to forget some things, merely to remember many sunshiny hours spent with boys, who, to whatever family they belonged, were to me just children, loving and beloved. . . .'[71]

APPENDIX

Nurses and Governesses

Adams, Mary – Nurse to the children of Princess Louis of Battenberg, with family in Malta 1891. (Not to be confused with Mary Adams from London, born 12 July 1845, dresser to Princess Alice, then to Princess Louis, 1874–86/7, afterwards to Queen Victoria.)

Agar, Miss – Governess to Christian Victor and Albert of Schleswig-Holstein, early 1870s.

Agnes, Miss – Governess to the daughters of Queen Isabel of Spain in exile in Geneva, 1870. Agnes was possibly her Christian name.

Alison, Margaret Jane – Nurse, Norland trained from September 1899. With Princess Nicholas of Greece 1913–18. With Princess Wiasemsky from 1923. Born 22 January 1867, educated Girls' College, Huddersfield, and private school; hospital training, Birmingham Orthopaedic. Died 1950.

Aplin, Frances Mary – Nurse, Norland trained from September 1895. Under Kate Fox in the nursery of Princess Nicholas. Born 1 April 1877, educated Wimbledon High School.

Atkinson, Miss – Governess to the elder sons of Kaiser Wilhelm II until December 1895; resigned due to ill health.

B, Miss – Governess to the children of Prince V and Princess L in Germany; daughter of an English diplomat and his American wife, educated Queen's College. Anonymous author of *What I Found Out in the House of a German Prince*.

Bailie (Bailey), Emma – Nurse to the Hesse family under Mary Ann Orchard, c. 1869–70. Became nurse to the Erbach-Schönberg children, afterwards housekeeper at Schönberg. Died Schönberg 1919, aged 74.

Barber, Sylvia Kathleen – Nurse, Princess Christian trained, leaving college May 1935; 1940 with the Egyptian royal family in Cairo. Married a Mr Hay, went to New Zealand.

Barnes, Mary – Nurse to the Wied family, especially Prince Otto, from 1848. Then to the Baden family, 31 December 1815–15 July 1879; buried in the Badens' private crypt at Mainau, Switzerland.

Bell, Anne – Nurse to Crown Prince Felipe of Spain, 1960s

Bell, 'Nana' – Nurse to the daughters of Grand Duke Georgi Mikhailovich of Russia, early 1900s to 1920s, then to the future King Peter of Yugoslavia from September 1923; then to the family of Don Arturo Edwards in Chile in 1930s, where she died. Born c. 1870s, possibly Harrogate area.

Bicknell, Anna – Governess to the daughters of the Duc de Tascher de la Pagerie, Grand Master of Empress Eugénie's household, 1856–65. Left in failing health after serious carriage accident. Author of *Life in the Tuileries under the Second Empire*.

Bill, Charlotte 'Lalla' – Nurse to the children of George V and Queen Mary, 1896–1919, head nurse from 1 July 1900. Born Maidenhead 1875, daughter of William James and

Annie Bill. First appointment with the Purdey family, Taplow. Nursery maid at Marlborough House 1895. Other short-term royal appointments and from April 1926 housekeeper at Buckingham Palace. Retired 1 May 1928, lived in Norfolk. Died 1964.

Blackburn, Mary – Nurse to the children of the Prince and Princess of Wales from late 1860s. A Mary Ann Blackburn, aged 60, born Wisbech, Cambridgeshire, is listed on 1901 census, as monthly nurse to a family in Belsize Park, Hampstead.

Borland, Miss – Nurse to King Faisal of Iraq, mid–late 1940s.

Bowman, Jeanne – Nurse, Norland trained. With HRH Princess Michel de Bourbon (Princess Yolande de Broglie-Revel, sister-in-law of Queen Anne of Romania) in 1955.

Boyd, Miss – Governess to Princesses Alexandra and Marie of Greece, 1870s/80s under their German governess Countess Groben.

Brimble, (Ethel) Lilian – Governess to Crown Prince Wilhelm of Prussia's sons, 1911–14. Born 1877, Plaistow, Kent, daughter of Edward Henry Brimble, mahogany merchant, and his wife Agnes Edith. Three years in Mecklenburg pre-1910. Wrote *In the Eyrie of the Hohenzollern Eagle*. Still living in 1933 when she was traced through the London *Evening Standard* and met her former charge, Prince Louis Ferdinand, in London.

Brock, Mrs 'Boppy' – Nurse to Princess (later Queen) Victoria, presumably from birth, 1819 onwards.

Brompton, Miss – Nurse to the children of King Victor Emanuel and Queen Elena of Italy, early 1900s.

Brooke, Edith Elizabeth – Nurse, Norland trained, from July 1911. Under-nurse to Constance Sadler in the Mecklenburg-Schwerin nurseries from 1912; became ill shortly before the First World War; was able to return to the family briefly though forced to leave again in wartime – still listed in Schwerin in December 1914. Born 14 February 1882, a barrister's daughter. Two years' previous experience as a governess, a German teaching qualification and two years' helping in Sutton High School (where she herself had been a pupil). Still alive in 1929/30 when Miss Sadler met the Mecklenburg-Schwerins again.

Brotherstone, Mrs – Nurse; monthly nurse/midwife, late nineteenth century.

Bunting, Gertrude – Nurse to the Prince of the Asturias, 15 June 1907–6 November 1908. Died of a stroke, 6 November 1908, buried in the municipal cemetery of Our Lady of the Almudena for 200 pesetas; this and the undertakers' account for 482 pesetas 50 was paid by the Spanish Court. Possibly the Gertrude Bunting christened on 22 September 1861 in Cranfield, Buckinghamshire, daughter of Anthony and Elizabeth Bunting; listed on 1881 census, aged 19, as governess in the house of Henry R. Brand, MP and Magistrate, at Temple Duisley, Hitchin.

Burgess, (Alexandra) Marian, 'Burgie' – Nurse, Norland trained, from July 1901. Nursed the children of Grand Duke and Grand Duchess Kirill of Russia from 1907. Born 10 January 1874, daughter of a wholesale provision merchant, Alexander Burgess and wife Hannah. Lived in Gateshead, educated at Church High School, Newcastle. Exiled to Finland with family during Russian Revolution, died of influenza in 1919 while still in service. Twin Kathleen Burgess was also a Norlander (died 4 June 1945).

Butler, Miss – Music teacher to the Edinburgh princesses during their time on Malta, late 1880s.

Butler, Annie – Nurse to the future King Olav of Norway until 1911; said to have been dismissed for her part in suffragette demonstrations (though this was possibly another nurse). Taken on again by the family for four months from September 1937 to teach King Olav's daughters English.

Byng, Augusta Maria, 'Spin' or 'Minnie' – Governess to the children of Crown Prince and Princess of Prussia from spring 1870. Born Staines, *c.* 1830, daughter of William Bateman Byng and his wife Ann Boyack; sisters Anne Matilda Watson Byng (married Edward Skegg, Frederick Curtis), Julia Byng, brother Henry. Diagnosed with cancer September 1881, returned to Staines. Died March 1882, aged 52.

Carver, Harriett E. – Nurse to Princess Christian's children at Frogmore; listed on 1871 census, from Middlesex, aged 19.

Casey, Bridget, 'Miss Bride' – Governess to Archduchess Annunziata, then to Archduke Karl (later Emperor of Austria), 1880s/90s. Said to have had a moral influence which lasted long after she had left him to become a Benedictine oblate. (He was canonised in 2004.)

Chapman, Marjorie – Nurse to Prince and Princess Henry of Battenberg's children, 1889–1900. Afterwards married a Mr Sheddon.

Chapman, Susan – Nurse to the Duke and Duchess of Connaught's children, 1881–90. Appointed 1891 to Linen Room at Windsor, retired 1896. Christened 17 March 1845, Geddington, Northamptonshire, daughter of Charles Chapman, gamekeeper and his wife Mary Ann. Died second quarter of 1898, shortly after her father, whom she nursed.

Chennells, Ellen – Governess to Princess Zeyneb at the Court of Ismael Pasha, Khedive of Egypt, from October 1871 for five years. Possibly the Ellen Chennells listed on the 1851 census as governess at 33 Grosvenor Place, London, aged 32 and born St Luke's Chelsea. Author of *Recollections of an Egyptian Princess by Her English Governess*.

Chermside, Anne – Nurse, Norland trained, entering as a 'Maiden' in 1931. Employed by King Farouk of Egypt in October 1945 and shared the royal family's escape into exile. Born 11 October 1915, a farmer's daughter from Leamington Spa. Died very suddenly while visiting Princess Fadia in Switzerland, 8 November 1988.

Christie, Eugenia – Nurse to the future Tsar Alexander II and his sisters, from 1818; left to marry in 1830.

Clark, Mrs – Nurse; monthly nurse to Queen Victoria in 1840s, appears to have worked in the household under name of 'Mrs Roberts'. Born *c.* 1806, entered Hanking household, Hampshire, as nursemaid in 1824; left to marry, 1826. Husband 'very cruel & dissolute'; left him after birth of their son, 1828. Persuaded to return, left again *c.* 1830. Trained as a monthly nurse at Lying-in Hospital. In the royal household from 27 November 1840. Died 1849.

Clark, Mrs – Nurse; monthly nurse to Princess Alice, the Princess of Wales and other members of Queen Victoria's family at home and abroad from 1863 to 1872.

Collenette, (Constance) Irene – Nurse, Norland trained from October 1896. With Grand Duchess Kirill for a few months in 1907; with Beatrice, Princess Alfonso of Orléans-Borbón, from 1910 for ten years. Rejoined Kirill family in 1920 for six years, following the death of Marian Burgess. Born 8 March 1877, Guernsey, the daughter of a chemist and scientist, Adolphus Collenette. Educated Ladies College, Guernsey. Retired June 1945. Died 5 February 1956, aged 79.

Collins, Eliza – Nurse to Queen Victoria's family, late 1840s, sketched by Winterhalter.

Collins, Margaret – Governess to the Hanover Princesses, 1850s; cousin to Pauline Harriet Stewart who took over from her when she married Count Georg Bremer of Cadenburg.

Colquhoun, Molly – Nurse, Norland trained, from 30 September 1926. Two years with Princess Casimir Poniatowski, 1931–3. A vicar's daughter, born 19 December 1907.

Conway, Mrs – Nurse to the Prince of the Asturias and Infante Jaime, 28 November 1908 (three weeks after Gertrude Bunting's death).

Coombs (Combe), Alexandra – Governess to the daughters of Grand Duke Georgi Mikhailovich of Russia, daughter of Henry Coombs, a British businessman working in Russia. Lived in an old people's home in England in the 1950s.

Copeland, Miss – Governess; nursery governess to Prince Hansel of Pless from 1904.

Coster, Miss – Governess to the sons of Grand Duchess Ksenia and Grand Duke Alexander Mikhailovich, 1910s. Shared the family's imprisonment in Crimea during the Russian Revolution and their escape on HMS *Marlborough*, 1919.

Crawford, Miss – Governess to Baroness Marie Vetsera, implicated in the tragedy of Mayerling, 1880s.

Creak, Eliza – Nurse to the Albany children, 1880s. Dismissed March 1886 after arguments with the Duchess of Albany. Married a Mr Stockham in March 1908. Possibly the Eliza Creak listed on 1881 census as born in Ely in *c.* 1850, nursemaid in house of George Shelts Pennant, JP, Wicken, Northamptonshire.

Crofts, Millicent – Nurse to the children of Grand Duke Vladimir Alexandrovich, 1876–86, dismissed by their mother. Born London, Bloomsbury, 13 August 1852, daughter of William Crofts, printer, and his wife Anne Elizabeth Strutton; great-niece of Catherine Strutton. On 1901 census in Walton Road, Wavendon, Buckinghamshire with her 73-year-old widowed mother. At Princess Marina's wedding, 1934. Died 8 May 1941.

Croisdale, Violet Mary – Nurse, Princess Christian trained, left college 1912. December 1930, 1932 with HRH Princess George of Greece, at St Cloud, then Paris. Resigned by December 1938.

Crowther, Sylvia Mary, 'Crowdy' – Nurse, Princess Christian trained, left college 1914. Nurse to Prince Tomislav of Yugoslavia from 1927 and to the future King Peter after Nana Bell; his grandmother Queen Marie didn't like her, believing she was too close to his mother – had her dismissed. In Bradford by December 1935. Died June 1971.

Davenport, Georgina – Nurse to King Alfonso XIII of Spain until end July 1896.

Davies, Miss – Nurse to Prince Friedrich Karl and Princess Margarete of Hesse-Cassel's sons in 1894, when the Princess wrote to ask her old nurse Mrs Wakelin to vet Edith Davies, a sister of her children's nurse, for Crown Princess Sophie in Athens, who was said to be having trouble with nurses.

Delaney, Emma – Governess/companion to the daughters of Queen Isabel II of Spain, late 1870s, early '80s; the next generation called her 'Miss Emma'.

Digby, Gwendoline – Nurse, Norland trained, from July 1905. With Princess Yusupov, 1923. Born 25 January 1881, the daughter of a banker and East India merchant, educated at private school. Died 13 June 1962, aged 81.

Dodd, Kate Emily – Nurse, Norland trained, from October 1901. With Princess Thurn and Taxis, 1908. Daughter of Alfred George Dodd, agent in the Limerick district for the Great Western Railway Company, educated at private school.

Doherty, Eugenie – Nurse to the children of King Alfonso XIII of Spain, 1911–26.

Doherty, Martha – Nurse to the daughters of King Alfonso XIII of Spain, 1919–29. Her sister Catherine Doherty is also mentioned in her personnel file in Madrid.

Douglas, Julie – Governess to the daughters of Prince Georg Viktor and Princess Helene of Waldeck, 1870s. Married Reverend P. Acland.

Draper, Miss Elinor – Governess to Princess Mary Adelaide of Cambridge from 1840.

Duncan, Lilian Mary – Nurse, Norland trained, from April 1903. With the Maharani Horkar of Indore in 1910. Born 16 March 1884, daughter of a tea merchant.

Dutton, Annie Mary – Governess/English teacher to the children of King Alfonso XIII of Spain, 1916–31. An inscription to her on a 1928 photo of Infanta Beatriz suggests that Miss Dutton was a Red Cross nurse at some time before she worked for the family.

Dyer, Miss – Governess to Tata Mamontov, stepdaughter of Grand Duke Mikhail Alexandrovich at Knebworth, autumn 1913, in place of Miss Rata. Taught her the piano.

Eadie, Elizabeth, 'Lilian' – Nurse, Norland trained from October 1894. Nurse to Georg Donatus and Ludwig of Hesse, 1908–14. Born Plymouth 18 April 1875, educated Exeter High School; daughter of James and Helen Eadie of Topsham, Devonshire. Father a bank manager. The 1901 census shows her as nurse to the baby daughter of Sir Henry F. Lambert, Bart, of Stamford House, Enville, in Staffordshire, with her elder sister Helen Mary as governess in same household. Married Harold Vivian Jeffery in 1926. Died 19 March 1967 after a long illness, aged 91.

Eagar, Margaretta Alexandra – Nurse to the daughters of Tsar Nicholas II, appointed late 1898, in Russia from February 1899. Born Limerick, 12 August 1863, daughter of Francis McGillycuddy Eagar and Frances Margaret Holden. Father became governor of Limerick Prison. Trained at the Royal Hospital, Belfast, was also in France. Dismissed October 1904. Opened boarding house in Holland Park Gardens which ran into debt. Governess in Hungary 1913. Author of *Six Years at the Russian Court* and various articles. Died Grange Nursing Home, Keynsham, Bristol, 2 August 1936.

Ede, Miss – Nurse to Princess Elizabeth of Yugoslavia, daughter of Prince Paul and Princess Olga, from late 1930s; supported the family in Second World War and shared their exile in Kenya. Helped Neil Balfour and Sally Mackay write a biography of Prince Paul; praised in their acknowledgements for having 'been able to recollect certain events with such perfect clarity'.

Eusden (Euston), Mary – Governess to Princes Willem and Maurits of the Netherlands, sons of King Willem III and Queen Sophie, 1840s; later companion and English reader to Queen Sophie.

Evans, Alice – Nurse to the elder sons of King Alfonso XIII of Spain, the Prince of the Asturias and Prince Jaime, 15 June 1907–18 February 1914; later maid to their mother Queen Ena.

Everard, Miss – Governess to the children of King Peter of Serbia, 1880s.

Ffolliott, Anne Louisa – Governess to Prince Carol of Romania, taking over from Saxton Elizabeth Winter, April 1900. Not Irish as Queen Marie claimed: born Bethnal Green, September quarter 1862, daughter of William Folliott, a fabric designer, and his wife Jane, both from Middlesex, living in Dagenham in 1881.

Foster, Nannie – Nurse to Princess Alexandra of Greece, 1920s; friendly with Emily Roose. Left in 1926.

Fox, Jessie – Nurse, Norland trained, from 3 December 1893. Assistant nurse to Princess Nicholas of Greece's daughters from December 1906. Died 4 August 1950.

Fox, Kate Frances – Nurse, Norland trained from December 1894. With Prince and Princess Nicholas of Greece and their daughters; dismissed 1913, returned to the family in 1921 and remained with them as companion/assistant and nurse to grandchildren for the rest of her life. Born 9 May 1870, educated by governess, then Marlborough College, Exeter. Daughter of Charles Fox, newspaper publisher and his wife Ellen, one of three sisters. Keen photographer. Presented with Order of Chefakat by the Sultan, Order of St Sava by Prince Paul of Yugoslavia. Wrote memoirs, now lost. Died 19 November 1949.

Francklin, Elizabeth Sophia – Nurse to Grand Duchess Olga Alexandrovna of Russia from 1882. Previously monthly nurse. Christened 19 October 1834, parish church, Toddington, Bedfordshire; daughter of Joseph Smith Cook, innkeeper, and his wife Ann. Married Thomas William Francklin, grocer, in the parish church at Upton cum Chalvey, 8 April 1858; three children, Thomas, Walter and Annie, who married John Froud in 1879. Died April 1913 in Sergeevskaya Street, St Petersburg (Grand Duchess Olga's house); buried in Gatchina cemetery.

Fraser, Fanny – Governess to Princess Marie Louise of Bourbon Parma, eldest daughter of Duke Robert of Parma and future Queen of Bulgaria, from late 1870s; became lady-in-waiting on Marie Louise's marriage.

Fry, Frances – Nurse to the children of Grand Duke Pavel Alexandrovich of Russia 1889 to 1898; possibly also to their cousin Princess Nina Georgievna, elder daughter of Grand Duke Georgi Mikhailovich, born June 1901; her will included a 'Gold Chain Bracelet with "Nina" marked on it in Rubies Sapphires and Diamonds' and another gold and pearl brooch given by the child's mother. Born Newington, London, June quarter 1850 with twin, Jane, the children of Henry Fry, paper hanger and his wife Caroline Georgiana Randall; three other children. Henry Fry died in 1857; Frances and Jane afterwards placed in Female Orphan Asylum, Lambeth. Died Brighton, 18 June 1934.

Garnsey, Hannah – Nurse to the children of Alice, Princess Louis of Hesse under Mary Ann Orchard, 1872–4.

Geddes, Kathleen – Nurse, Norland trained from October 1920. Nurse to the grandchildren of Archduke Karl Stefan at Zywiec in Poland 1927–9. Roman Catholic, daughter of a bank inspector.

Gessler, Pauline – Nurse to the future Tsar Alexander I of Russia from 1777. Born 1740s, presumed to be the daughter of John Primrose, son of the Jacobite Sir Archibald Primrose, executed at Carlisle in 1746. Sister of Sarah Nichols. Married to Johann Gessler, Alexander's valet.

Gibb, Grace Isobel – Nurse, Norland trained from July 1906. From December 1907, Norland probationer with Princess Nicholas of Greece. In 1909 in family of Madame de Mumm, a position Princess Nicholas found for her. Born 1 July 1874, father in the shipping business. Died suddenly, 24 Feb 1942.

Gibson, Mrs – Nurse to Prince Lennart of Sweden. Dismissed for drugging the baby with morphine.

Girdlestone, Mrs – Nurse to the children of the Duke and Duchess of Teck, 1860s/70s.

Goode, Mrs – Nurse to Prince and Princess Henry of Battenberg's children until June 1889.

Graham, Maria (later Lady Calcott) – Governess to Dona Maria da Gloria in Brazil. Widow of Captain Thomas Graham, RN, arrived Brazil 13 March 1823. Appointment lasted only a year, ended by Court conspiracy. Married Augustus Wall Calcott, February 1827. Wrote various travel books and *Little Arthur's History of England*. Died 1842.

Graves, Louisa – Governess to the daughters of Alice, Princess Louis of Hesse, 1873–7. From a naval family. Had a sister, Constance, who taught the Hesse children music.

Green, Annie – Nurse to the Edinburgh children; listed on the 1881 Windsor Castle census as a widow, 19 years old and from Ashford.

Green, Marianne Elizabeth – Governess to the daughters of Crown Prince and Princess of Prussia, then to Duchess Alexandrine of Mecklenburg-Schwerin. Born 1 January 1847 in Nayland, Suffolk, daughter of the Reverend Charles Wade Green and his wife Mary Ann Brough. To Berlin in October 1881 on three-month trial to replace Miss Byng. Secretarial work for the Crown Prince. Stayed until 1 May 1889. In 1897 became a sister of St Katherine's, living at no. 7 St Katherine's Precinct.

Green, Mary A. – Nurse to the children of Crown Princess, later Queen, Marie of Romania, 1890s to early 1900s. Said also to have nursed royal children in England and Russia. Lived in Windsor in 1919. Queen Marie is said to have written to 'Nana' Green every week until she died.

Green, Mrs Rosa (née Foster) – Nurse; as monthly nurse, attended Princess Mary, Duchess of York (later Queen Mary) from May 1894 until the birth of Prince Henry in 1900. Also present when Prince John was born, 1905. Attended Queen Maud of Norway and Princess Alexander of Teck; travelled to Coburg for the Duchess of Saxe-Coburg. Attended Queen Ena of Spain in 1907. Visited by George V and Queen Mary at Adelaide Cottage, Windsor, in 1931.

Greenleaf, Rose – Nurse, Norland trained from December 1893. Nurse to Princess Galitzine in Tiflis, 1915 in Caucasus. Born 22 September 1872 in Greenwich, gave no family details to Norland Register.

Grove, Lizzie – Nurse under Frances Fry in Grand Duke Pavel's household, 1890s.

Halls, Beatrice Bevington – Nurse, Norland trained from July 1895. Nurse to the children of Princess Max of Baden from 1906. Born 24 December 1876, a vicar's daughter from King's Lynn, educated at King's Lynn High School.

Hammersley, Miss – Governess to Princess Marie-Josée of Belgium, 1920s.

Hardy, Hazel – Nurse, Norland trained from 31 December 1931. With Princess Elizabeth of Yugoslavia as relief nurse, April 1948.

?, Harriet – Nurse to the children of Prince Alexander of Hesse and Princess Battenberg in Verona, pre-1857. Moved with the family to Padua.

Haskew, Helen Mary – Nurse, Norland trained from January 1914. With Princess Cantacuzene in Switzerland. Father was an iron merchant.

Hawes, Mrs Catherine Anne (née Samuel) – Nurse; second nurse to the children of Crown Princess of Prussia under Mrs Wakelin from 1869. This may have been her second appointment to the family; it is suggested that she worked for them before as an under-nurse and left in 1866/7 to be married. Possible previous appointment to family of the photographer Oscar Rejlander.

Henton, Zillah 'Hentie' – Nurse to Princess Irina Felixovna Yusupova, granddaughter of Grand Duchess Ksenia. Worked in St Petersburg from 1906, possibly for a family connected to the Court. Born 17 December 1866, Inner Street, Spittlegate, Grantham, the ninth of thirteen children. In 1881 at age of 14 worked as errand girl. Trained at Queen Charlotte's Hospital. Then in family of the Reverend G.T. Whitehead of West Burton. To Crimea in 1916, escaped on HMS *Marlborough*. Died 24 October 1940.

Hickling, 'Nanny' – Nurse to Prince Paul Romanovsky-Ilyinsky (born London, 1928; only son of Frances Fry's little Grand Duke Dmitri Pavlovich). Accompanied her charge to America in 1939.

Higgenbottom, Miss 'Miss Higg' – Governess to Grand Duchess Alexandra Nikolaevna of Russia, 1830s and '40s.

Hildyard, Sarah Anne – Governess to the children of Queen Victoria from 1847. Born *c.* 1811 in Lincolnshire, a clergyman's daughter. Retired 1865, becoming a sister of St Katherine's. Died in May 1889.

Hincks, Doris Wynne – Nurse, Norland trained from October 1922. Nurse to the children of Queen Marie of Yugoslavia from 1930. Born 22 June 1902, the daughter of a civil and electrical engineer; educated Queen's School, Chester. Died 22 June 1937 after sudden illness requiring two operations.

Hinman, (Gertrude) Marion 'Marie' – Nurse, Norland trained from October 1913. From 1920 with family of Prince Christian of Hesse-Philippsthal-Barchfeld. Daughter of a commercial traveller, educated County High School, Wellingborough and in Germany.

Hobbs, Emma – Nurse to the elder children of the Crown Princess of Prussia, appointed autumn 1858. Previously at Lady Scott's. Born 1826/7, daughter of John Hobbs, wharfinger; married Jesse Skinner, 18 October, Southborough, near Tunbridge Wells.

Hobbs, Georgina – Nurse assistant, but principally maid to the Crown Princess of Prussia, appointed December 1857. Sister of Emma Hobbs.

Hobbs, Penelope – Nursery maid to children of the Crown Princess of Prussia from 1869; niece of Emma and Georgina Hobbs.

Howard, Ethel – Governess to the Kaiser's children 1895–8, having previously taught the King of Siam's nephew. Then to Prince Shimadzu and his brothers in Japan, 1901–8. Born early 1870s. Married H.A. Bell after 1908; he died by 1918. Wrote *Potsdam Princes* and *Japanese Memories*.

Howard, Sophia – Governess of Princess Mary Adelaide of Cambridge to 1847.

Howe, 'Nannie' – Nurse to Crown Prince Alexander of Yugoslavia from August 1945. Retired in 1948 when his family went to New York.

Hughes, Miss – Nurse to Grand Duchess Alexandra Alexandrovna, 1843. Possibly Margaret Hughes, afterwards married Thomas Isherwood.

Hughes, Ellen – Nurse to Princess Victoria of Battenberg's children, 1890s. In October 1891 went with family to Malta. In Darmstadt with them in 1892. Listed as 'kinderfrau' in Darmstadt, 'Hof-und Staatskalendar', 1896–1900.

Hughes, Henrietta 'Etta' – Governess/English teacher to the sisters of King Alfonso XIII, 22 November 1890–7 July 1898. The 1881 census lists two possibles: Henrietta Huges, governess aged 35 from Norwich, working in the Hospital School in Great Yarmouth run by her aunt Charlotte Goffin, and Hettie M. Hughes aged 17, born in Bristol and a student at the University of Bristol, living with her parents Walter and Alicia at 7 Cownfield Road, Clifton, Gloucestershire.

Hull, Miss – Governess to Princess Irene of Greece, appointed late 1919/early 1920.

Hull, Marianne 'Old May' – Nurse to Queen Victoria's children 1842–58 and relief nurse to the grandchildren. Born Marianne/Mary Anne Cripps, 1811; married Charles Hull, Queen's Messenger in 1858. Widowed 1869. Died in 1888, buried in Clewer churchyard.

Inglis, Fanny Erskine – Governess to the daughters of Queen Isabel of Spain, 1861–76. Daughter of an impoverished nobleman (descended from Earls of Buchan), brought up in Paris, moved to America with mother and sisters after father's death. Taught in her mother's school in Boston. Married His Excellency Don Calderon de la Barca, Spanish Ambassador, becoming the Marquesa de Calderon de la Barca. With him to Mexico, becoming governess on his return to Madrid; went into to exile with Queen Isabel.

Inman, Miss – Nurse to Prince (later King) Boris of Bulgaria, chosen by Queen Victoria and Princess Beatrice, 1890s.

Innocent, Ellen – Nurse; monthly nurse used by various princesses, 1860s. Married a Mr Wolmersley.

Irwin, Miss – Nurse to Prince Ioann Konstantinovich of Russia's children from 1914.

Isherwood, Miss – Nurse to Tsesarevich Nikolai Alexandrovich of Russia, 1844.

Jackson, Margaret Hardcastle 'Madgie' – Governess to Princess Luise Margarete of Prussia, then to the daughters of Princess Alice, Grand Duchess of Hesse. Born London 20 September 1837. With Lady Maud Herbert until the latter's conversion to Catholicism. Sister of St Katherine's from May 1889, at no. 8. Died 28 January 1918.

Jackson, 'Nannie' – Nurse to Princess Alexandra of Greece in exile in Italy from about 1926. From Yorkshire; her sister worked as nurse for a family in Rome.

Jenkins, Mary – Nurse to the Mecklenburg-Schwerin children, 1880s. Born c. 1829. Lived in retirement in the family's care; died 1917, buried at Ludwigslust.

Johnson, Winifred Mary – Nurse, Princess Christian trained, leaving college in 1925. With the Queen of Egypt, at Montazah Palace, Alexandria, 1938. Married Mr Crisp by December 1941 but still with royal family; by December 1946 in New Zealand.

Johnston, Euphemia – Nurse; monthly nurse to Princess Christian in 1867, Princess Alice in 1874, the Duchess of Edinburgh in 1874/5. From Scotland, born c. 1824, began her career as a 27-year-old widow with three small children to support. Trained Maternity Hospital, Edinburgh c. 1850. The 1881 census lists a Euphemia Johnson, born 1824 in Scotland, at St Mildmay Medical Mission Hospital, London.

Jones, Mrs – Nurse to the children of Princess Louis of Battenberg, 1890s.

'Kate' – Governess to King Michael of Romania's daughters, 1950s.

Keen, Edith – Governess/companion to Princess Victoria Margarete of Prussia, early 1900s.

Kemence, A. – Nurse to the children of Alice, Princess Alexander of Teck, 1910/11, possibly 1907–13. Almost certainly one of two sisters, Amelia Ann or Laura Ada Kemence, daughters of Anthony and Esther Kemence from Hedgerley, Buckinghamshire, both of whom were nurses.

Kempthorne, Mrs – Nurse; head nurse to the Princess Royal, Britain, November 1840.

Kennedy, Mrs – Nurse to Grand Duke Mikhail Pavlovich of Russia, from 1798. Born Miss Ramsbottom, governess and Italian teacher to Mikhail's elder sisters. Married the chaplain to the English Church in St Petersburg.

Kidd, Alice M. – Nurse; nursery maid to the Duchess of Fife in Brighton, 1901, aged 20 and from Lonsdale, Barton Manor, Kirkby.

King, Lucie – Governess to Duchess Cecilie of Mecklenburg-Schwerin, 1880s. Previously taught in Imperial Gymnasium in St Petersburg; had German/Italian ancestry through her mother and was fluent in four languages.

Kitz, Emma – Governess to Alice, Princess Louis of Hesse's children, 1870s. Could have been German, though she wrote to the Princess in fluent English.

Knight, Mrs Clara – Nurse to Bowes-Lyon family, then to Princess Elizabeth and Princess Margaret Rose, 1923–46.

Lavater, Fanny – Governess to Marie of Nassau (later Princess of Wied). Born *c.* 1813, French father, English mother. Dismissed for defending her charge from an unjust punishment, later returned as her companion and remained with her. Died in 1877.

Lena, Miss – Governess to Tata Mamontov 1910–11. From Ireland.

Leonowens, Anna – Governess/English teacher to the family of King Mongkut of Siam, 1862–7. Born Ahmadnagar, India, 6 November 1831, married Thomas Owens, Christmas Day 1849 in Poona. Four children, two of whom survived. To New York in 1867, opening a school on Staten Island, giving lecture tours and writing memoirs, *The English Governess at the Siamese Court* and *The Romance of the Harem*. Later moved to Halifax, Nova Scotia to live with her married daughter; active in fields of art education, social reform, and women's suffrage. Died on 19 January 1915. Later the subject of a romanticised biography, a stage musical and three Hollywood films.

Leslie, Ada – Governess to the sons of Kaiser Wilhelm II, 1886–7/8. Born Islington, London, March 1861, daughter of William Leslie, printer, and his wife Sarah. Joined household of Kaiserin Friedrich in 1888 and was lady-in-waiting to Sophie, Crown Princess of Greece from autumn 1889. Left in 1893 and married Reginald Castle; last heard of in Burma, 1894.

Lilly, Mrs – Nurse; monthly nurse to Queen Victoria through all nine confinements.

Long, Mrs – Nurse to Prince Christopher of Greece from 1888.

Lorne, Miss – Nurse to the children of Crown Princess Sophie of Greece, early 1890s, dismissed for being too strict.

Lott, Emmeline – Governess to the Grand Pasha Ibrahim, son of the Khedive of Egypt, engaged in 1862 by the Khedive's London agent. In Egypt 1863–5. Claimed to have often met Queen Victoria and Prince Albert as a child in the private grounds of Frogmore and Windsor. Wrote *The English Governess in Egypt*, *Nights in the Harem* and *The Grand Pacha's Cruise on the Nile*.

Lukyn, Edith Barbara – Nurse, Norland trained from May 1923. With the Duchesse delle Puglie at Miramare, Trieste from 1931, Duchess of Aosta from 1936. A dentist's daughter, born 17 October 1905; Roman Catholic, educated Marist Convent, Richmond.

Lunn, 'Nannie' – Nurse to Crown Prince Alexander of Yugoslavia from 1948.

Lyon, Jane – Nurse to Tsar Nicholas I of Russia, 1790s/early 1800s. Born *c.* 1779, daughter of a Scottish artist in Russia. Left to marry in 1803; lived in the Anichkov Palace in widowhood.

Macdonald, Miss – Nurse to Princess Elizabeth of Yugoslavia (daughter of Prince Paul), late 1930s.

Mace, Caroline Elizabeth, 'Bessie' – Nurse, Norland trained from December 1896. With Princess Radziwill. Born 2 October 1875, daughter of a wholesale druggist.

McElligot, Nora – Governess to Princess Marie Adelaide of Luxembourg, 1900s, later to Prince Timo of Saxony, 1930s.

Maclean, Miss – Governess to Princess Zeyneb, daughter of the Khedive, 1866–71 (her father General Maclean was tutor to the Khedive's son, Ibrahim Pasha).

Macmillan, Charlotte – Nurse to the children of Princess Eugenie of Greece from 1939.

McMillan, Miss – Governess to the children of Prince René of Bourbon Parma and Princess Margarethe of Denmark, 1930s/40s.

Marr, Ida, 'Mimarr' – Governess to Princess Ileana of Romania, from late 1920.

Mary, Miss – Nurse to the infant King Alfonso XIII from birth, 1886.

Matcham, Mrs – Nurse to the children of Kaiser Wilhelm II, 1889–1902. Kept a run-down boarding house in Berlin, 1919.

Matzow, Ellen Julie, 'Smatzo' – Nurse, from Norway, Princess Christian trained, left college September 1931. With the sons of Queen Marie of Yugoslavia from 1932, under Sylvia Crowther. Married Crown Prince Peter's tutor, Cecil Parrott, 12 June 1935 at Trondheim.

Maybury, Hilda Clara Harriet – Governess to the children of the Grand Duke of Oldenburg 1914. Born 18 March 1875, daughter of Charles Maybury, manufacturing chemist, and his wife Teresa. November 1935 applied for GBI assistance as a serious eye complaint made further work impossible. Wrote *Secrets of a German Royal Household*.

Meier, Ilse Frieda Bathildis – Nurse, Norland trained from April 1899. With Princess Oskar of Prussia from 1915, also with Princess Joachim. Born 9 September 1877, daughter of a merchant from Bremen, educated in England. Returned to England in 1920s.

Metzger, Gladys Marie – Nurse, Norland trained from April 1913. With Alice, Princess Andrew of Greece, 1914–15. Born 15 April 1892, educated at Barnet Grammar School; father a secretary.

Miller, Mignon St John Mitchell – Nurse, Norland trained from October 1907. With 'A Prince or Count of Austria'. Born 11 October 1888; gentleman's daughter.

Millington, Mrs – Nurse to Prince Waldemar of Prussia from 1889.

Milne, Leila – Governess to the Connaughts, late 1880s/90s, then to Princess Elisabeta of Romania from *c*. 1907.

Moffatt, Elizabeth – Nurse to Princesses Victoria and Elisabeth of Hesse 1863–6. Born Durham, *c*. 1835. Listed at Frogmore House with Princess Christian's family on 1871 census.

Neame, Margaret – Governess to George Brassov, son of Grand Duke Mikhail Alexandrovich of Russia from May 1915; escaped with her charge in April 1918.

Newman, Florence – Nurse, Norland trained from July 1895. With Margarete, Princess Friedrich Karl of Hesse, 1907. Died 13 July 1921, after an illness.

Nicholls, Katherine Howard – Governess to Princess Helen of Greece, early 1900s. Born December quarter 1868, Wandsworth. In 1881 was one of twenty-six pupils in a school at 17 Cedars Road, Clapham. Applied for GBI assistance in 1923; Queen Mary helped to place her in the home at Chiselhurst, 1925. Died 9 July 1936.

Nicholls, Victoria – Nurse to the 2nd Duke of Albany and Princess Alice from 1886.

Nichols, 'Mrs' – Nurse; wet nurse to the infant 2nd Duke of Albany, August 1884. Presumably unmarried as Queen Victoria gave special instruction to call her 'Mrs'.

Possibly the same as Victoria Nicholls (above), though this is never stated.

Nichols, Sarah – Nurse to Grand Duke Konstantin Pavlovich of Russia from late 1770s. Born 1748; presumed to be the daughter of John Primrose, son of the Jacobite Sir Archibald Primrose, executed at Carlisle in 1746. Sister of Pauline Gessler. Died in St Petersburg, 1799, aged 51.

Noon, Beatrice – Nurse to the Prince of the Asturias, 1910. Said to have become pregnant by King Alfonso XIII in 1915.

Odgers, Marie – Nurse, Norland trained from October 1894. With the Duchess of Saxe-Coburg, 1906–7; with Countess Hochberg, 1909–10. Born 5 April 1867 in Cornwall, a gentleman's daughter (Mr Billing Odgers). Educated at private school; 1899–1904 with Mrs Bruce Ismay, Sandheys, Mossley Hill, Liverpool. Died 16 August 1949.

Orchard, Mary Ann 'Orchie' – Nurse to the children of Alice, Grand Duchess of Hesse from 1866 to 1886/7. Remained with the family and accompanied Princess Alix to Russia in 1894. Born in Dublin, 20 March 1830. Family connection also with Dorset. Died August 1906, buried in Manor Park Cemetery, Sebert Road, Forest Gate, London.

Page, Miss – Governess to Prince George and Princess Augusta of Cambridge, 1825.

Palmer, Christine Mary 'May' – Nurse, Norland trained from March 1896. With Princess Thurn and Taxis from 1909. Born 6 May 1875, daughter of a spice merchant; educated at private school.

Paterson, Mrs – Nurse; monthly nurse, later nineteenth century, with Caroline Mathilde of Schleswig-Holstein, Kaiserin Auguste Viktoria, and Irène, Princess Heinrich of Prussia.

Paxton, Rebecca – Governess to the daughters of Princess Zenaide Callimachi in Moldavia from 1860s/70s; later took over management of household.

Payne, Emily – Governess to the children of the Sawbwa of Hsipaw in Burma from *c*. 1862 until her death.

Pegley, Mrs – Nurse; monthly nurse to Queen Victoria, 1840s. Frequently sketched by the Queen.

Peters, Mrs Elizabeth – Nurse, head nurse to the children of Duke and Duchess of York, 1894–April 1897. Left the royal household to marry.

Pickard, Agnes – Nurse to the children of Duke and Duchess of Edinburgh, under Mrs Pitcaithley. Listed 1881 as a widow, aged 34 and from Barnstaple in Devon.

Pickens, Lily – Nurse to André and Alexander Bariatinsky, sons of Princess Katherine Yurievsky, early 1900s. Looked after Princess Yurievsky in early 1920s.

Pinkerton, Helen – Governess to Grand Duke Nikolai Nikolaievich, 1840s. Born Edinburgh in 1818, possibly related to Reverend Robert Pinkerton of the Edinburgh Missionary Society who worked in the Caucasus, and wrote travel books on Russia. Married Ludwig Marguardt, Saxon landscape gardener and botanist in 1835. Died in 1905.

Pitcaithley, Annie – Nurse to the children of Duke and Duchess of Edinburgh from 1875. Born 1840 from Banff in Scotland; married and widowed. Died of cancer while in service, 15 November 1884.

Plunkett, Constance Mary – Nurse, Norland trained from January 1920. With Prince Gabriel de Bourbon in Cannes, 1930. Born 21 July 1891, daughter of a surgeon dentist; Roman Catholic, educated at La Sainte Union de Sacré Coeur Convent, Highgate Road. Served as a VAD in France, Salonika and England, also two years' experience as governess.

Potts, Jane – Governess; 'Finishing governess' to Princess Elisabeth of Waldeck, then to Princess Alice and the 2nd Duke of Albany, 1890–end 1900. Born *c.* 1854 in Cumberland. Afterward, in 1901 opened exclusive girls' school in Eastbourne.

Pullman, Ann – Nurse to Queen Victoria's family, 1858–68. Born *c.* 1833 in Devonshire. Later worked in the Linen Room at Buckingham Palace.

Ramirez, Rosalind – Governess to King Faisal of Iraq from May 1943, then to Prince William and Prince Richard of Gloucester. Born Acton, West London, grew up in South America. Wrote an account of an experiment in mime with the young Princes at St James's, *It Began in a Palace*; also contributed to memorial book for Prince William of Gloucester.

Rata, Edith 'Ratafia' – Governess to Tata Mamontov, stepdaughter of Grand Duke Mikhail Alexandrovich from 1911. Married the groom Mr Bennett at St Mary's Church, Knebworth, 13 August 1914, before returning to Russia with the Grand Duke's family.

Reichenbach, Madame – Governess/English teacher to Princess Marie Bonaparte, early 1890s. Irish, but married to a Prussian tutor.

Ritchie, Miss – Governess to Princess Samatsingi in Poona, late 1880s.

Robb, Katherine Mary – Nurse, Norland trained from October 1904. With Margarete, Princess Friedrich Karl of Prussia, 1905. Born 11 August 1883, daughter of John Robb, Doctor of Medicine and Surgeon Lieutenant-Colonel in the Indian Medical Service; educated Blackheath High School and Aberdeen High School.

Roberts, Mrs – Nurse; monthly nurse to Queen Victoria 1840s. Real name probably Clark, q.v.

Roberts, Ada E. – Nurse; head nurse in the household of the Duchess of Fife, April 1901, 25 years old, single and from Denbridge, Acton Park.

Roberts, Susan Frances – Nurse, Princess Christian trained, leaving college in 1917. With Princess Paul of Yugoslavia, 1930.

Robson, Miss – Governess to the Connaught children, September 1890.

Rolestone, Joanne – Nurse, to the children of Alice, Princess Louis of Hesse under Mary Ann Orchard, 1874–86/7. First governess appointed for Victoria, Princess Louis of Battenberg's children, *c.* 1892.

Roose, Emily – Nurse to Prince and Princess Andrew of Greece's children, 1905–*c.* 1930. Born *c.* 1872, Devonport, the daughter of a boot maker, James Roose and his wife Helen. 'Nurse domestic' at 57 Egerton Grove Kensington, 1901, to the children of Herbert W. Savory, Commander, RN, and his American wife Kate. Crippled by arthritis and osteoporosis while still in her fifties, lived in retirement in South Africa.

Rowles, Naomi Floyd 'Rowley' – Nurse, Norland trained from January 1922. With the grandchildren of Archduke Karl Stefan of Habsburg at Zywiec in Poland in 1926. Born 12 September 1902, daughter of a dentist from Dover. Roman Catholic, educated at St Ursula's Convent, Dover.

Ryan, Nellie – Governess/companion? In the household of Archduke Karl Stefan from late 1890s. No official job title given, but she seems to have been associated with the children, especially the daughters.

Sadler, (Emma) Constance – Nurse, Norland trained from July 1907. With the Mecklenburg-Schwerin family, 1912–14. Born 20 September 1876, a gentleman's daughter; ten years' experience of Sunday School teaching. Forced to leave Schwerin by war; kept contact with family and met again in Garmisch 1929/30. Died 2 December 1959.

St John, Elizabeth Alix – Nurse, Princess Christian trained, one of the original intake as nurse no. 9. With Queen Sophie of Greece 1913–18, then nurse to King Michael of Romania from 1921. Born Finchampstead, Berkshire, September quarter 1869, with twin, Edward. Died December quarter 1961.

Salmond, Catherine Welsh, 'Gertie' – Nurse, Norland trained from March 1894. With Sophie, Crown Princess of Greece 1902–5, then with Princess Marie Anna of Schaumburg-Lippe. Born 12 February 1875, a farmer's daughter from Arbroath, Scotland.

Savell/Saville, Mrs – Governess to Grand Duchess Elena Vladimirovna (later Princess Nicholas of Greece), from late 1880s. In England in early 1900s, in contact with Princess Nicholas and Kate Fox. Possibly to be identified with:

Savile, Mrs – Governess to Duchess Cecilie of Mecklenburg-Schwerin 1892–8.

Scott, Miss – Nurse to the children of Prince Pedro de Alcántara including Isabelle, the future Countess of Paris, from 1911.

Shaw, Miss – Nurse to the Prince Imperial, France, 1850s.

Slade, Maud Adeline – Nurse, Norland trained from June 1894. With Princess Yourievsky in France, 1908–9. Born 31 July 1876, the daughter of a clerk.

Sly, Mrs – Nurse; head nurse to Queen Victoria's children, 1840–5.

Smith, Miss – Nurse to the children of Prince Georg Viktor of Waldeck, 1850s–72. From Huntingdon.

Smith, Miss – Governess to Prince Alexander of Yugoslavia, 1920s.

Smith, Thirza – Nurse to the children of Princess Friedrich Leopold of Prussia, 1890–1901, then to Lexel, second son of Daisy, Princess of Pless, early 1900s.

Smyth, Alice Janet Scott – Nurse, Princess Christian trained, left January 1916. With Princess Mafalda, Princess Philipp of Hesse from 1929, then with the Crown Princess of Italy from 1934. From Nadnagedh, Burton Post, County Donegal.

Southby, May – Governess to Princess Marina Chavchavadze in Russia, early 1900s.

Southey, Mrs – Nurse to the Princess Royal, November 1840, dismissed after the birth of the Prince of Wales. Sister of the poet Shelley.

Spence, Helen Caroline Ken – Nurse, Norland trained from January 1893. First 'royal' Norlander, chosen within first year of institute's existence by Kaiserin Friedrich for her daughter Sophie, Crown Princess of Greece, as '2nd to a lady nurse' at £20 a year. Born 22 May 1874, daughter of a master mariner from Newcastle upon Tyne.

Stainthorpe, Josephine – Nurse to the children of King Alfonso XIII of Spain, 1 July 1916–22 September 1918, when she died in service.

Stainton, Anne – Nurse, Princess Christian trained, left September 1904. In Romania with Elizabeth St John, caring for King Michael from 1921; with Princess Mafalda, Princess Philipp of Hesse from 1927.

Stewart, Pauline Harriet, 'Hartie' – Governess/companion to daughters of King George V of Hanover from February 1860. Married Lieutenant-Colonel Otto von Klenck in 1865 and remained in Hanover.

Street, Miss – Governess/English teacher to the children of the exiled Empress Zita of Austria-Hungary at Lequieto 1923–9; stayed in Spain when family moved to Belgium.

Strutton, Catherine 'Kitty' – Nurse to the children of Alexander II of Russia from 1845. Born 26 March, christened 6 October 1811, St John's Hackney, London, the daughter of

George Strutton, bricklayer, and wife Elizabeth. Great-aunt of Millicent Crofts. Died Winter Palace, 10 March 1891, funeral at English Church in St Petersburg, buried Smolenska Cemetery on Vassilevsky island.

Sulman, Betty – Governess to King Faisal II of Iraq from 1940, when he was five, until the pro-Nazi coup in 1941. Married John Morrison.

Sutton, Kitty – Governess to the future Queen Carola of Saxony in Vienna, 1840s.

T, Miss May – Governess to Wanda Badeni, daughter of the Governor of Austrian Poland, from October 1892, then to Archduchess Elisabeth of Austria, 1895–8. Roman Catholic with early thoughts of vocation. Said to have been the first lady in Vienna to have been seen riding a bicycle in public, with permission of the Crown Princess. Later with Ursula Challoner, daughter of 1st Baron Gisborough. Wrote *Recollections of a Royal Governess*.

Taylor, Mrs – Governess (probably nursery governess) to Prince Roman and Princess Nadejda, younger children of Grand Duke Peter Nikolaevich of Russia, early 1900s.

Taylor, Constance Marjory – Nurse, Princess Christian trained, left September 1929. With Maharani Sahiba of Bastur State, Jagdalpur, India, 1934.

Thorpe, Mrs – Nurse to the children of Crown Princess Sophie of Greece.

Throckmorton, Miss – Nurse to Archduchess Marie Valerie of Austria, 1868–74. Frequently clashed with Countess Festetics, the Empress's lady-in-waiting; dismissed, reputedly for gossiping.

Thurston, Mrs Mary Anne – Nurse to the children of Queen Victoria, appointed spring 1845 aged 35; from Suffolk, widowed with a daughter. Housekeeper at Windsor 1865. Died at Kensington Palace September 1896.

Todd, (Edith) Beatrice – Nurse, Norland trained from December 1896. With Princess Irène, Princess Heinrich of Prussia from 1902. Born 21 December 1872; father a clerk in the Ecclesiastical Commissions Office, educated High School, Eaton Square. Died 4 April 1959.

Topham, Anne – Governess to Princess Viktoria Luise of Prussia, August 1902–December 1909. Born Derby 1864, second child of Thomas Topham, tenant farmer in Mackworth, Derbyshire. Educated Moravian School, Ockbrook. Keen photographer. Wrote *Memories of the Fatherland, Daphne in the Fatherland, Daphne in Paris, Memories of the Kaiser's Court, The Golden Moment, The Beginning and the End, The Tale of Thomas Truelove*, and *Chronicles of the Prussian Court*, also magazine and newspaper articles. Died 12 December 1927, aged 63.

Trevellyan, Miss – Governess to Tata Mamontov, stepdaughter of Grand Duke Mikhail Alexandrovich, 1917–18.

W, Mrs – Governess to Archduchess Elisabeth Marie of Austria, *c.* 1890–5.

Wakelin, Mrs Mary Ann – Nurse to the children of the Crown Princess of Prussia in Berlin, from October 1869, also to her granddaughter Feodora of Saxe-Meiningen, 1879. Born Mary Ann Conway, 2 April 1837/8; a widow with two children, Gertrude and John, at the time of her appointment. Gertrude educated at Kaiserin Augusta's school at Charlottenburg, went on to be governess to Sybil Coke (friend of Queen Mary). Mrs W remarried 1886, to William Morter of Hampstead.

Walker, Miss – Governess to the future Kaiserin Augusta Viktoria, 1870s/80s, later principal of the Royal School at Bath. Living in Buckinghamshire in late 1890s.

Walker, Jane – Governess to two eldest daughters of Archduke Ferdinand of Austria (?Peter Ferdinand or Josef Ferdinand); worked for the resistance in the Second World War, saving the lives of escaping POWs in Warsaw.

Walkley, Louisa – Nurse; head nurse to the children of the Prince and Princess of Wales, October 1872; retired 1 January 1881, died 11 August 1895.

Wallace, Pamela – Nurse to the children of King Juan Carlos of Spain, 1960s.

Wanstall, Kathleen Churchill – Nurse, Norland trained from April 1904. With Princess Wilhelm of Stolberg Wernigerode 1911–18. Nurse to the children of the Hereditary Princess of Monaco from 1921. Born 30 January 1886, daughter of the vicar of Condover. Educated at St Margaret's, a clergy daughters' school in Bushey. Created Chevalier of the Order of St Charles by Prince Rainier of Monaco in April 1950. Nurse to the family of Princess Antoinette of Monaco. Died of arteriosclerosis on 9 May 1967, aged 81, at the home of Princess Antoinette.

Wells, Monica – Nurse to the children of King Juan Carlos of Spain, 1960s.

Wilkinson, Florence Mary – Nurse, college trained, looked after the son of Princess Anne-Marie Callimachi in Romania, early 1900s.

Wilson, Mrs – Nurse, the married sister of Eliza Creak, who provided temporary cover in the Duchess of Albany's nursery in the summer of 1886.

Wilson, Elizabeth Jane 'Lilian' – Nurse to Princess Elisabeth of Hesse, 1895–1903, then to Hereditary Grand Duke Georg Donatus, 1906–8. Born Traphton, Northamptonshire, 20 April 1864, daughter of Edward Wilson, railway porter, and his wife Emma. Married Wilhelm Scharmann, Buchhalter with the Grand Duke's Kabinettskasse, in September 1908. Wilhelm, twelve years younger than Lilian, had previously lived with his mother. Last listed address in Darmstadt records 381 Bessunger Strasse: moved there in 1919. Wilhelm listed there until 1943; no further reference to Lilian.

Wilson, Marie Bennet 'Minnie' – Nurse, Norland trained from July 1900. With Princess Paul of Yugoslavia, 1926–9. Born Belfast 14 January 1877, daughter of a flour merchant and mill owner.

Wiltshire, Agnes – Nurse to the children of Crown Princess Margarete of Sweden, 1906–28. 'Her little home was full of family photographs – of our family, memories from Sweden, and a lot of cake tins.' (Sigvard Bernadotte, *Erindringer* (Forum, Copenhagen, 1975), p. 12.)

Winter, Saxton Elizabeth – Governess to Queen Wilhelmina of the Netherlands from 1 February 1886 to 2 November 1896. Born Portland, Dorset, 1855, daughter of a butcher; educated Royal Asylum of St Anne's Society, Streatham Hill, London. With Princess Marie of Wied, July 1897–8. Appointed winter 1898 by Queen Elisabeth of Romania for Crown Prince Carol; left April 1900. Sent Carol a Christmas present in 1900 which remains in the possession of his family, with her inscription. Pension of £150 p.a. from Queen Wilhelmina, rising to £250 in 1929. Died Saffron Walden, 29 January 1936.

Wood, Amy – Nurse, Norland trained from April 1901. Sent to Berlin on the request of the Crown Princess but 'the honour . . . was of brief duration'. Born 11 March 1873, a doctor's daughter.

Woodfield, Miss 'Nini' – Nurse to Queen Marie of Romania's younger children, early 1900s.

Notes

MANUSCRIPT AND ARCHIVAL SOURCES

RA   Royal Archives, Windsor Castle. QVJ references are taken from Queen Victoria's Journal.
HSD GF   Hessisches Staatsarchiv Darmstadt, Grossherzogliches Familienarchiv.
NKH   Netherlands, Koninklijk Hausarchief.
GARF   State Archive of the Russian Federation.
MPN AGP   Madrid Patrimonio Nacional, Archivo General de Palacio.
LMA   London Metropolitan Archive.
            Archive of Norland College (formerly the Norland Institute).
            Nord Anglia College (for Princess Christian's).
Letters of Ada Leslie to Mary Anne Galsworthy by permission of Mr Francis Barnard

Chapter One, pp. 1–19

1. Larissa Yermilova, *The Last Tsar* (Bournemouth, Parkstone Planeta, 1996), p. 57.
2. Lady Augusta, Stanley, *Later Letters of Lady Augusta Stanley, 1864–1876* (London, Jonathan Cape, 1929), p. 218.
3. GARF F.655 L.1 F.2155, Catherine Strutton to Grand Duchess Maria Pavlovna, 27 December 1886.
4. *The Times*, 14 March 1891.
5. Quoted in Jacques Ferrand *Nianias, Souvenirs* (Paris, Ferrand, 1999), p. 13, in French, from *Dvorianskoie Sobranie* no. 9, 1998, pp. 31–2.
6. GARF F.655 L.1 F.2155, Catherine Strutton to Grand Duchess Maria Pavlovna, 27 December 1886; when Richard Strutton, Kitty's youngest brother, married, he was not able to sign his name.
7. The origins of the two nurses are explored in some detail in 'Marginalia: An Anglo-Russian Medley' by Professor A.G. Cross in *SEER*, vol. 70, no. 7 (October 1992), pp. 719–21.
8. *Ibid.*, p. 719.
9. Quoted in Emmanuel Ducamp (ed.), *The Winter Palace* (Paris, Alain de Gourcuff, 1994), p. 19; because this is a translation, it is impossible to guess at the significance of the words 'nanny' and 'nurse' or the distinction Nicholas I intended when he used them.
10. A.G. Cross (ed.), *An English Lady at the Court of Catherine the Great* (Cambridge, Crest Publications, 1989), p. 52.

11. *Ibid.*, p. 7.

12. *Ibid.*, p. 83.

13. *Ibid.*, p. 77.

14. E.A. Brayley Hodgetts, *The Court of Russia in the Nineteenth Century*, vol. I (London, Methuen, 1908), p. 147.

15. Quoted in the above, p. 143.

16. Elizaveta P. Renne, 'Bridging Two Empires: Christina Robertson and the Court of St Petersburg', in *An Imperial Collection; Women Artists from the State Hermitage Museum* (exhibition catalogue, London, Merrell, 2003), p. 92.

17. *Ibid.*, p. 93.

18. W.A.L. Seaman and J.R. Sewell (eds), *The Russian Journal of Lady Londonderry, 1836–37* (London, John Murray, 1973), p. 54.

19. Olga, Queen of Württemberg, *Traum der Jugend goldner Stern* (Pfullingen, Verlag Günther Neske, 1955), p. 207; 'Miss' and 'dear little girl' are in English in the original German text.

20. Quoted in Harvey Pitcher, *When Miss Emmie was in Russia* (London, John Murray, 1977), p. 5.

21. *Ibid.*, p. 6.

22. RA VIC/M16/3, Dr Locock concerning Mrs Roberts (Mrs Clark), 27 November 1840. The document was mounted into one of the contemporary household books. On the mount, apparently in Queen Victoria's handwriting, the heading is repeated 'Dr Locock concerning Mrs Roberts' with no mention of Mrs Clark.

23. Cecil Woodham-Smith, *Queen Victoria* (Bungay, Book Club Associates edn, 1973), p. 275 for reference to Prince Albert; various references to Mrs Roberts in RA QVJ.

24. RA QVJ, 4 April 1863.

25. RA QVJ, 9 January 1864.

26. RA QVJ, 13 January 1864.

27. RA QVJ, 13 December 1864.

28. Alice, Princess of Great Britain, Grand Duchess of Hesse, *Letters to Her Majesty The Queen* (London, John Murray, 1897), p. 163.

29. Marie, Princess zu Erbach-Schönberg, Princess of Battenberg, *Reminiscences* (London, George Allen & Unwin, 1925), pp. 117–18.

30. Princess Alice, *Letters to Her Majesty The Queen*, p. 208.

31. RA VIC/Add. U143/2, Queen Victoria to Princess Alice, 21 May 1864.

32. RA VIC/Add. C26/35, Victoria, Princess Royal, Crown Princess of Prussia to Lady Caroline Barrington, 22 August 1867.

33. RA PP/VIC/MB/2.

34. RA VIC/Add. A 24/82, Queen Victoria to the Duchess of Sutherland, 24 April 1867, quoted in Barbara E. Mortimer, 'The Nurse in Edinburgh *c.* 1760–1860: the impact of commerce and professionalism', unpublished DPhil thesis, University of Edinburgh, 2002.

35. *Ibid.*, p. 298.

36. Richard Hough (ed.), *Advice to a Granddaughter* (London, Heinemann, 1975), p. 98.

37. RA VIC/Z91/21, Princess Irène of Hesse (Princess Heinrich of Prussia) to Queen Victoria, 1 March 1889.

38. Arthur Gould Lee, *The Empress Frederick Writes to Sophie* (London, Faber & Faber, 1955), p. 134.

39. RA GV/CC45/305, Queen Victoria Eugenie of Spain to Mary, Princess of Wales, 14 June 1907.

40. The spelling of the name, 'Francklin' with the 'c' is original and appears on official documents, including the marriage certificate. It is also the way Elizabeth herself signed her name, though over the years biographers and historians have constantly made it 'Franklin'.

41. GARF F.642 L1 F2846, Elizabeth Francklin to Empress Maria Feodorovna, 1 September, no year given. The names mentioned are the older imperial children, Olga's brothers and sister.

42. GARF F.642 L1 F2846, Same to same, 23 June 1887.

Chapter Two, pp. 20–42

1. GARF F1463 L1 F647, Emily Loch to Empress Alexandra Feodorovna, 7 December 1898.

2. Andrei Maylunas and Sergei Mironenko (eds), *A Lifelong Passion* (London, Weidenfeld & Nicolson, 1996), p. 133. The translator here has chosen the word 'nanny'; the Tsar would probably have used 'bonne', maybe the Russian 'niania'; in the English of the day, this would have been 'nurse'.

3. Mary Lutyens (ed.), *Lady Lytton's Court Diary* (London, Rupert Hart-Davis, 1961), p. 79.

4. GARF F.1463 L1 F647, Emily Loch to Empress Alexandra Feodorovna, 5 December 1898. The 'wife of the Scotch Minister in London' who recommended Margaretta was probably her sister Frances, whose husband, the Revd George Hanson, headed the Presbyterian Church in the capital – he was, in fact, Irish. Emily Loch does not seem to have been aware of the connection.

5. GARF F.1463 L1 F647, Emily Loch to Empress Alexandra Feodorovna, 7 December 1898.

6. Quoted in Edward Frank Eager, *The Eager Family in the County of Kerry* (privately printed, Dublin, 1958), p. 38. This may not be a reference to the *London Times*. The spelling of McGillycuddy varies between different sources and individuals.

7. GARF F.1463 L1 F647, 'Miss Eagar's testimonials copies'.

8. HSD GF D24 N5 35–2, Princess Louis of Battenberg to Grand Duke Ernst Ludwig of Hesse, 22 January 1895.

9. RA VIC/Z21, Irène, Princess Heinrich of Prussia to Queen Victoria, 1 March 1889.

10. RA VIC/Add. PP/953, December 1857.

11. John C.G. Röhl, *Young Wilhelm; the Kaiser's Early Life* (Cambridge University Press, 1998), p. 118; Roger Fulford (ed.), *Dearest Child: Letters between Queen Victoria and the Princess Royal 1858–1861* (London, Evans, 1964), p. 166.

12. RA VIC/Z7/10, Princess Royal to Queen Victoria, 18 September 1858.

13. RA VIC/Add. U32/10, Queen Victoria to the Princess Royal, 19 January 1859.
14. RA VIC/Z7/54, Princess Royal to Queen Victoria, 18 December 1858.
15. RA VIC/Z11/10, Princess Royal to Queen Victoria, 10 May 1861.
16. Fulford (ed.), *Dearest Child*, p. 333.
17. RA EB71.
18. GARF F.1463 L1 F647, Emily Loch to Empress Alexandra Feodorovna, 30 January 1899.
19. MPN AGP c.1150 e.25.
20. M. Eagar, *Six Years at the Russian Court* (London, Hurst & Blackett, 1906), pp. 1–2.
21. *Ibid.*, p. 3.
22. *Ibid.*, p. 5.
23. Penelope Stokes, *Norland, 1892–1992* (Hungerford, Norland College, 1992), p. 12.
24. *Norland Quarterly*, no. 49 (September 1913).
25. *Ibid.*, no. 18 (Christmas 1901).
26. *Ibid.*, no. 108 (Christmas 1934).
27. Unpublished letter in Norland Archives.
28. *Norland Quarterly*, no. 29 (Christmas 1906).
29. Mildred Hastings Album, Norland Archive.
30. RA MDK/PRIV/Kate Fox, Princess Nicholas to Kate Fox, 19 October/1 November 1907.
31. *Norland Quarterly*, no. 94 (Spring 1930).
32. *Ibid.*, no. 41 (Christmas 1910).
33. *History of the Princess Christian College* (privately printed, Manchester, 1950s), p. 2.
34. Stokes, *Norland*, p. 41.
35. Graf Heinrich von Spreti (ed.), *Alix an Gretchen; Briefe der Zarin Alexandra Feodorovna an Freiin Margarethe v. Fabrice* (privately printed, Germany, 2003), pp. 149–50.
36. *Norland Quarterly*, no. 32 (Christmas 1907).
37. *Princess Christian College*, 4th Annual Report (Machester, 1908).
38. Roger Fulford (ed.), *Dearest Mama: Letters between Queen Victoria and the Crown Princess of Prussia 1861–1864* (London, Evans, 1968), p. 88.
39. *Ibid.*, p. 95.
40. Roger Fulford (ed.), *Your Dear Letter: Private Correspondence of Queen Victoria and the Crown Princess of Prussia 1865–1871* (London, Evans, 1971), pp. 167–8; 'the Baron' was Baron Stockmar, 'Sir James' the royal doctor Sir James Clark and 'Lady Caroline', Lady Caroline Barrington, the Superintendent of the Royal Nurseries.
41. Eagar, *Six Years at the Russian Court*, p. 267.
42. Edward J. Bing (ed.), *The Letters of Tsar Nicholas and Empress Marie* (London, Ivor Nicolson & Watson, 1937), p. 146.
43. M. Eagar, 'Further Glimpses of the Tsaritsa's Little Girls', in the *Girl's Own Paper and Woman's Magazine*, vol. XXX (1909), p. 536.
44. *Norland Quarterly*, no. 90 (Christmas 1928).
45. *Ibid.*, no. 25 (Summer 1904).

46. RA MDK/PRIV/Kate Fox, Princess Nicholas to Kate Fox, 3/16 June 1909.
47. RA MDK/PRIV/Kate Fox, Same to same, 9/22 April 1910.
48. RA MDK/PRIV/Kate Fox, Same to same, 14/27 April 1910.
49. RA MDK/PRIV/Kate Fox, Same to same, 19 January/1 February 1915.
50. RA MDK/PRIV/Kate Fox, Same to same, 11/24 April 1915.
51. RA MDK/PRIV/Kate Fox, Same to same, 12/25 November 1915.
52. RA MDK/PRIV/Kate Fox, Same to same, 27 December/9 January 1919–20; 14 November 1920.

Chapter Three, pp. 43–62

1. Anna Bicknell, *Life in the Tuileries under the Second Empire* (London, T. Fisher Unwin, 1895), p. 15.
2. *Ibid.*, p. 13.
3. Elizabeth Cuthbert, 'A Perfect Godsend; A Scotswoman at the Court of Hanover', in *Royalty Digest*, vol. VII, 1998, p. 226.
4. Anon. (Miss May T), *Recollections of a Royal Governess* (New York, Appleton, 1916), pp. 6–7.
5. *Ibid.*, p. 114.
6. *Ibid.*, p. 228.
7. *Ibid.*, p. 168.
8. Ethel Howard, *Potsdam Princes* (London, Methuen, 1916), p. 13.
9. *Ibid.*, p. 4.
10. Fulford (ed.), *Your Dear Letter*, p. 88.
11. *Ibid.*, pp. 271–2.
12. Princess Charlotte of Prussia to Augusta Byng, 3 July 1874; private collection.
13. Victoria, Princess of Prussia, *My Memoirs* (London, Eveleigh Nash and Grayson, 1929), p. 9.
14. *Windsor & Eton Express*, 10 February 1837; genealogy.rootsweb website.
15. Crown Princess of Prussia to Augusta Byng, 11 September 1881; private collection.
16. *Ibid.*, 14 September 1881.
17. Princess Victoria of Prussia to Augusta Byng, 18 November 1881; private collection.
18. LMA GBI1938 4459/A/O3/019.
19. RA VIC/Add. A15/ 4778, Crown Princess Victoria to the Duchess of Connaught, 24 February 1887.
20. Roger Fulford (ed.), *Darling Child: Private Correspondence of Queen Victoria and the Crown Princess of Prussia 1871–1878* (London, Evans, 1976), p. 255.
21. Princess Alice, *Letters to Her Majesty The Queen*, p. 233.
22. HRH Princess Wilhelmina of the Netherlands, *Lonely But Not Alone* (London, Hutchinson, 1960), p. 26.
23. RA VIC/Add. A15/4778, Crown Princess of Prussia to the Duchess of Connaught, 24 February 1887.
24. Ada E. Leslie to Mary Anne Galsworthy, 23 November 1883.
25. Same to same, 26 November 1886.

26. Same to same, 3 March 1891.
27. Anne Topham, *Memories of the Kaiser's Court* (London, Methuen, 1914), p. 13.
28. E.L. Brimble, *In the Eyrie of the Hohenzollern Eagle* (London, New York, Toronto, Hodder & Stoughton, nd), pp. 253–4.
29. Quoted in Bea Howe, *A Galaxy of Governesses* (London, Derek Verschoyle, 1954), p. 138.
30. *Ibid.*, p. 141.
31. Elizabeth Baigent and Lois K. Yorke; entry on Anna Leonowens in the *New Dictionary of National Biography* (Oxford University Press, 2004).
32. Anna Harriette Leonowens, *The English Governess at the Siamese Court* (Folio Society, 1980; originally published 1870), p. 19.
33. RA VIC/Add. A30/1790, Princess Emma of Waldeck to Miss Smith, 12 October 1878.
34. Princess Wilhelmina, *Lonely But Not Alone*, p. 37.
35. Anne Topham, *Chronicles of the Prussian Court* (London, Hutchinson, 1926), pp. 51–2.
36. Howard, *Potsdam Princes*, p. 41.
37. *Ibid.*, p. 23.
38. *Ibid.*, p. 41.
39. *Ibid.*, p. 42.
40. Brimble, *Hohenzollern Eagle*, p. 223.
41. *Ibid.*, pp. 223–8.
42. RA VIC/Z11/8, Princess Royal to Queen Victoria, 3 May 1861.
43. Topham, *Memories of the Kaiser's Court*, pp. 23–4.

Chapter Four, pp. 63–87

1. HIH the Grand Duke Cyril (Kirill), *My Life in Russia's Service – Then and Now* (London, Selwyn & Blount, 1939), p. 14.
2. Stella King, *Princess Marina, Her Life and Times* (London, Cassell, 1969), pp. 39–40.
3. Marie, Grand Duchess of Russia, *Things I Remember* (London, Cassell, 1930), pp. 10–11, 13.
4. *Ibid.*, p. 34.
5. Eagar, *Six Years at the Russian Court*, pp. 21–2.
6. *Ibid.*, p. 9.
7. The Duke of Windsor, *A Family Album* (London, Cassell, 1960), p. 23.
8. Fulford (ed.), *Dearest Mama*, p. 194.
9. RA VIC/Add. U407, Queen Victoria to Jane, Lady Moreton, lady-in-waiting to the Duchess of Albany, 5 August 1884.
10. Fulford (ed.), *Darling Child*, p. 159.
11. Gerard Noel, *Ena; Spain's English Queen* (London, Constable, 1984), p. 137.
12. Maylunas and Mironenko (eds), *A Lifelong Passion*, p. 130.
13. RA MDK/PRIV/Kate Fox's private letters, undated account of Ray Barton.
14. RA MDK/PRIV/Kate Fox, Princess Nicholas to Kate Fox, 4/17 April 1914 – it was a girl.

15. RA MDK/PRIV/Kate Fox, Same to same, 11/24 May 1914; Pavlo was the future King Paul of the Hellenes.
16. RA GV/FF3/ACA/14, Nurse Kemence to Princess Alice of Teck, 29 March (1910).
17. *Norland Quarterly* (August 1926).
18. RA VIC/Z7/10, Victoria, Princess Royal to Queen Victoria, 18 September 1858.
19. Fulford (ed.), *Your Dear Letter*, pp. 168–9.
20. *Ibid.*, p. 172.
21. *Norland Quarterly*, no. 41 (Christmas 1910).
22. HSD GF D24 Nr.75/5, 'Old Nana' to Princess Cecile, 6 October 1931. Cecile's husband was the Hereditary Grand Duke George Donatus of Hesse, one of Lilian Eadie's 'little Princes'.
23. Ellen Chennells, *Recollections of an Egyptian Princess by her English Governess*, vol. II (London, William Blackwood, 1893), pp. 65–6.
24. *Norland Quarterly*, no. 12 (December 1899).
25. *Ibid.*, no. 11 (March 1899).
26. RA/MDK/PRIV/Kate Fox, Kate Fox to Princess Nicholas, 5/8 October and 11/14 October 1921.
27. RA/MDK/PRIV/Kate Fox, 'Tittums' to Kate Fox, 21 October 1921. There are two theories about who Tittums was, Princess Margarita or Princess Irène of Greece. Here it seems more likely to be Margarita as Irène is referred to independently in the letter.
28. RA/MDK/PRIV/Kate Fox, Princess Nicholas to Kate Fox, 18 June/1 July 1910.
29. RA VIC/Add. A30/1783, Princess of Waldeck to Nana (Miss Smith), 5 February 1867.
30. RA VIC/Add. A30/1782, Princess Sophie of Waldeck to same, 6 October 1866.
31. Fulford (ed.), *Dearest Mama*, p. 176.
32. RA/MDK/PRIV/Kate Fox's private letters, account of M.E. Penson, 15 June 1903.
33. RA/MDK/PRIV/Kate Fox, Princess Nicholas to Kate Fox, 14/27 November 1905.
34. Fulford (ed.), *Dearest Mama*, pp. 207–8.
35. *Ibid.*, p. 210.
36. Grand Duchess Marie, *Things I Remember*, p. 39.
37. Topham, *Memories of the Kaiser's Court*, pp. 163–6.
38. HSD GF D24 44/7a; Lilian Wilson to the Grand Duchess of Hesse, 23 June 1907.
39. Grand Duchess Marie, *Things I Remember*, p. 37.
40. Kellogg Durland, *Royal Romances of Today* (London, T. Werner Laurie, nd, *c.* 1911), p. 91.
41. RA/MDK/PRIV/Kate Fox, Princess Nicholas to Kate Fox, 1/14 March 1916 and Princess Marina to same, undated card found in a letter written by Princess Nicholas, 31 March/13 April 1915.
42. Miss E. Saxton Winter, 'Training Wilhelmina to be a Queen', in the *Girl's Own Paper and Woman's Magazine*, vol. XXX (1909), pp. 327–8, 399.
43. RA/MDK/PRIV/Kate Fox, Princess Nicholas to Kate Fox, 14/27 November 1905.
44. Princess Wilhelmina, *Lonely But Not Alone*, p. 38.
45. Anne Topham, *A Distant Thunder* (selections from the writings of Anne Topham, edited by Wendy Reid Crisp, New York, New Chapter Press, 1992), p. 80.
46. *Ibid.*, pp. 151–2.

47. Anon., *Recollections of a Royal Governess*, p. 147.

48. Howard, *Potsdam Princes*, p. 52.

49. *Norland Quarterly*, no. 18 (March 1902).

50. RA VIC/Z260/1–2, Queen Victoria's Reflections 1847–59. The Queen's sentence structure reads rather oddly to modern eyes. The 'short religious ones' refers of course to the lessons, not the children.

51. Eagar, 'Further Glimpses of the Tsaritsa's Little Girls', p. 367.

52. HSD GF D24 44/7, Georg Donatus and Ludwig of Hesse to their parents, 18 October 1913.

53. Cuthbert, 'A Perfect Godsend', p. 226.

54. Bicknell, *Life in the Tuileries*, p. 20.

55. Topham, *Memories of the Kaiser's Court*, p. 52.

56. Winter, 'Training Wilhelmina to be Queen', p. 595.

57. *Ibid.*, p. 401.

58. Anon., *Recollections of a Royal Governess*, p. 198.

59. Marie, Queen of Romania, *The Story of My Life*, vol. 1 (London, Cassell, 1934–5), p. 60.

60. HSD GF Abt. D24 Konv 26/2, Princess Victoria to Princess Alice, 14 September 1875.

61. Eagar, 'Further Glimpses of the Tsaritsa's Little Girls', pp. 366–7.

62. Topham, *Memories of the Kaiser's Court*, p. 23.

63. Howard, *Potsdam Princes*, pp. 66–7.

64. HRH The Duke of Windsor, KG, *A King's Story* (London, Cassell, 1951), p. 7.

65. Arthur Gould Lee, *The Empress Frederick Writes to Sophie* (London, Faber & Faber, 1955), p. 241.

66. Ursula Bloom, *The Royal Baby* (London, Robert Hale, 1975), p. 94.

67. An opinion supported by seven different midwives. Too early an introduction of cow's milk could cause permanent damage; feeding in a badly sprung pram would cause nothing worse than indigestion.

68. RA/MDK/PRIV/Kate Fox, Princess Nicholas to Kate Fox, 14/27 November 1905.

69. RA GV/CC1/162, the Duke of York to the Duchess of York, 10 August 1896.

70. Alexandra, Queen of Yugoslavia, *For a King's Love* (London, Odhams, 1956), p. 142.

71. *Norland Quarterly*, no. 19 (September 1902).

72. *Ibid.*, no. 33 (March 1908).

73. RA VIC/Z260/7, Queen Victoria's Reflections 1847–1859; memo, 3 January 1847.

74. Fulford (ed.), *Your Dear Letter*, p. 189.

75. RA VIC/Add. C26, Crown Princess Victoria to Lady Caroline Barrington, 31 May 1868; the figures were annual salaries.

76. RA EB71, Prince of Wales Household Appointments Book.

77. Baroness de Stoeckl, *Not All Vanity* (London, John Murray, 1950), p. 47.

78. *Norland Quarterly*, nos 6 and 7 (September and December 1897).

79. Topham, *A Distant Thunder*, p. 131.

80. Eagar, *Six Years at the Russian Court*, p. 266.

81. Ethel Howard, *Japanese Memories* (London, Hutchinson, 1918), p. 64.

Chapter Five, pp. 88–109

1. The *P.C. Magazine*, 1925; Elizabeth Alix St John and Anne Stainton.
2. *Ibid.*, 1927; Anne Stainton.
3. *The Norland Quarterly*, no. 98 (Summer 1931).
4. The Hon. Mrs Hugh Wyndham (ed.), *Correspondence of Sarah Spencer, Lady Lyttelton* (London, John Murray, 1912), pp. 333–4.
5. Brimble, *Hohenzollern Eagle*, p. 170.
6. *Ibid.*, p. 173.
7. Bicknell, *Life in the Tuileries*, p. 144.
8. *Ibid.*, pp. 107–8. The Prince was still a boy when his father lost his throne. At the age of 23 he died, serving with the British army in the Zulu Wars on his own insistence.
9. Eagar, *Six Years at the Russian Court*, p. 186.
10. *Ibid.*, p. 120.
11. Brimble, *Hohenzollern Eagle*, p. 171.
12. Eagar, *Six Years at the Russian Court*, pp. 86–7.
13. *Ibid.*, p. 160.
14. Anon., *Recollections of a Royal Governess*, pp. 132–3.
15. *Ibid.*, pp. 248–50.
16. Brimble, *Hohenzollern Eagle*, pp. 171–2.
17. Prince Louis Ferdinand of Prussia, *The Rebel Prince* (Chicago, Henry Regnery Company, 1952), p. 12.
18. Brimble, *Hohenzollern Eagle*, pp. 19–20.
19. *Girl's Own Paper and Woman's Magazine*, vol. XXX (1909), p. 535.
20. Margaretta Eagar, 'More about the Little Grand Duchesses of Russia', the *Girl's Own Paper and Woman's Magazine*, vol. XXX (1909), p. 535.
21. Eagar, 'Further Glimpses of the Tsaritsa's Little Girls', p. 367.
22. Eagar, 'More about the Little Grand Duchesses of Russia', p. 536.
23. *Ibid.*, p. 536.
24. Eagar, 'Further Glimpses of the Tsaritsa's Little Girls', p. 367.
25. *Ibid.*
26. Durland, *Royal Romances*, pp. 198–203. Most of Margaretta Eagar's anecdotes about Anastasia appear in this book, which was an expanded version of Durland's magazine articles. According to Durland, the story about the Dowager Tsaritsa related to her birthday, but the mention of picking flowers makes her name day more likely. Her birthday was in November, her name day in July, and in Russia name days were given more prominence.
27. Howard, *Potsdam Princes*, pp. 29–31.
28. *Ibid.*, p. 32.
29. *Ibid.*, pp. 33–4.
30. *Ibid.*, p. 34.
31. *Ibid.*, p. 37.
32. *Ibid.*, pp. 85–6.
33. Winter, 'Training Wilhelmina to be Queen', p. 329.

34. HSD GF Abt. D24 44/7a, Lilian Wilson to the Grand Duchess of Hesse, 28 June 1907.

35. HSD GF Abt. D24 44/7a, Same to same, 3 April 1908.

36. HSD GF Abt. D24 44/7a, Same to same, 6 April 1908.

37. HSD GF Abt. D24 44/7a, Same to same, 13 April 1908.

38. HSD GF Abt. D24 44/7a, Same to same, 25 April 1908.

39. HSD GF Abt. D24 44/7a, Same to same, 3 May 1908.

40. HSD GF Abt. D24 44/7c, Lilian Eadie to the Grand Duchess of Hesse, 10 June 1911.

41. HSD GF Abt. D24 44/7c, Same (as 'Georgie') to same, 22 June 1911.

42. HSD GF Abt. D24 44/7c, Same to same, 27 June 1911.

43. RA MDK/PRIV/Kate Fox, Princess Nicholas to Kate Fox, 14/27 November 1905.

44. Halldis Bomhoff, *Min lille prins – Dagbok fra kronprins Olavs første skoletid* (Oslo, Gyldendal Norsk Forlag A/S, 1992), p. 20. I am indebted to Trond Noren Isaksen for this reference, and for all the information on Miss Butler.

45. Topham, *Distant Thunder*, p. 82.

46. RA MDK/PRIV/Kate Fox, Princess Nicholas to Kate Fox, 28 October 1911.

47. *Norland Quarterly*, no. 32 (Christmas 1907).

48. RA MDK/PRIV/Kate Fox, Princess Nicholas to Kate Fox, 19 October/1 November 1907.

49. RA MDK/PRIV/Kate Fox, Same to same, 3/16 June 1909.

50. RA MDK/PRIV/Kate Fox, Same to same, 20 October/2 November 1913.

51. RA MDK/PRIV/Kate Fox, Same to same, 2/15 June 1920.

52. RA MDK/PRIV/Kate Fox, Kate Fox to Princess Nicholas, 5/18 October 1921; 'Vuttut' was the nursery nickname of Princess Elizabeth of Greece.

53. RA MDK/PRIV/Kate Fox, Same to same, 11/24 October 1921.

54. RA MDK/PRIV/Kate Fox, Same to same, 5/18 October 1921.

55. RA MDK/PRIV/Kate Fox, Same to same, 11/24 October 1921.

56. RA MDK/PRIV/Kate Fox, Princess Olga to Princess Nicholas, 24 October/6 November 1921.

57. RA MDK/PRIV/Kate Fox, Kate Fox to same, 11/24 October 1921.

58. HSD GF Abt. D24 Konv 26/2, Louisa Graves to Princess Alice, 2 November 1876.

59. RA GV/FF3/ACA/14, Nurse Kemence to Princess Alice, 29 October (1911).

60. HSD GF Abt. D24 Konv 44/7c, Lilian Eadie to the Grand Duchess of Hesse, 6 December 1911.

61. HSD GF Abt. D24 Konv 75/5, 'Old Nana' to Princess Cecile, 26 November 1931.

62. Emmeline Lott, *The Governess in Egypt; Harem Life in Egypt and Constantinople* (London, Richard Bentley, 1865), vol. I, p. 75.

63. *Ibid.*, p. 154.

64. *Ibid.*, p. 161.

65. Howe, *A Galaxy of Governesses*, p. 144.

66. Lott, *The Governess in Egypt*, pp. 285–6.

67. Ellen Chennells, *Recollections of an Egyptian Princess by her English Governess* (London, William Blackwood, 1893), vol. I, pp. 4–5.

68. *Ibid.*, p. 5.

69. Howard, *Japanese Memories*, p. 75.

70. *Ibid.*, pp. 169–70.
71. *Ibid.*, p. 170.
72. *Ibid.*, p. 30.
73. *Ibid.*, pp. 30–1.
74. *Ibid.*, p. 63.
75. *Ibid.*, p. 66.
76. *Ibid.*, p. 282.
77. Durland, *Royal Romances*, pp. 100–1.
78. Baroness de Stoeckl, *My Dear Marquis* (London, John Murray, 1952), p. 125.
79. Baroness de Stoeckl, *Not All Vanity* (London, John Murray, 1950), p. 78.
80. Winter, 'Training Wilhelmina to be Queen', p. 401.
81. Brimble, *Hohenzollern Eagle*, p. 192.

Chapter Six, pp. 110–29

1. Brimble, *Hohenzollern Eagle*, p. 74.
2. *Ibid.*, p. 72.
3. *Ibid.*, p. 55–6.
4. *Ibid.*, p. 70.
5. *Ibid.*, p. 127.
6. Nathalie Majolier, *Stepdaughter of Imperial Russia* (London, Stanley Paul & Co., 1940), pp. 39–40.
7. de Stoeckl, *My Dear Marquis*, pp. 170–1.
8. Nellie Ryan, *My Years at the Austrian Court* (London, John Lane, 1916), pp. 83–4.
9. *Ibid.*, pp. 84–5.
10. *Ibid.*, p. 129.
11. See p. 84.
12. 20 November 1896: 'Before tea we went into the nursery. Nicky and Alix sat in the play pen and played with their daughter!' Maylunas and Mironenko (eds), *A Lifelong Passion*, p. 154.
13. Information and quotations from a collection of nine lesson plans, exercise books and a classroom diary preserved by Miss A.M. Dutton and now in private hands. Don Javier Vales Failde was a royal chaplain who had taught religion to the Prince of the Asturias from 1916 to 1918.
14. RA MDK/PRIV/Kate Fox, Kate Fox to Princess Nicholas, 5/18 October 1921.
15. Emile Burns (trans.), *The Memoirs of the Crown Princess Cecilie* (London, Victor Gollancz, 1931), p. 119.
16. Crown Princess of Prussia to Augusta Byng, 19 November 1872; private collection.
17. Same to same, undated; private collection.
18. 'To Dear Miss Green', *The Times*, 8 December 1961.
19. Winter, 'Training Wilhelmina to be a Queen', p. 400.
20. Fulford, *Dearest Child*, pp. 289, 291.
21. *Ibid.*, p. 322.
22. RA VIC/Add. A15/2739, Princess Alice to Queen Victoria, 14 March 1878.

23. RA VIC/Add. A15/2740, Margaret Hardcastle Jackson to Princess Alice, 13 March 1878.

24. RA VIC/Z87/33, Princess Victoria of Hesse to Queen Victoria, 6 April 1881.

25. Richard Hough (ed.), *Advice to a Granddaughter* (London, Heinemann, 1975), p. 89.

26. RA VIC/Add. U166/31, Princess Victoria of Battenberg to Queen Victoria, 12 March 1887.

27. RA VIC/Add. A30/248, Queen Victoria to Sir Robert Collins, 12 July 1890. It was usual for the Queen to refer to herself in the third person when writing to a member of the household.

28. RA VIC/Add. A30/1740, Helene, Duchess of Albany to Sir Robert Collins, 19 September (1890).

29. RA VIC/Add. A30/1741, Same to same, 21 September 1890.

30. Anon., *Recollections of a Royal Governess*, p. 129.

31. HSD GF Abt. D24 Konv 44/7a, Lilian Wilson to the Grand Duchess of Hesse, 23 June 1907.

32. Eagar, *Six Years at the Russian Court*, p. 145.

33. RA MDK/PRIV/Kate Fox, Princess Nicholas to Kate Fox, 25 June 1910.

34. RA MDK/PRIV/Kate Fox, Princess Victoria to Kate Fox, 2 July 1910.

35. Fulford (ed.), *Your Dear Letter*, pp. 237–8ff.

36. Cuthbert, 'A Perfect Godsend', p. 230.

37. *Ibid.*, p. 227.

38. RA PP/VIC/Add. 2604.

39. RA VIC/Add. U32/46, Queen Victoria to Kaiserin Friedrich, 15 September 1896.

40. RA VIC/Z32/27, Crown Princess of Prussia to Queen Victoria, 26 March 1879.

41. Queen Marie, *Story of My Life*, vol. II, p. 83.

42. RA MDK/PRIV/Kate Fox, Princess Nicholas to Kate Fox, 14/27 November 1905.

43. Preben Ulstrup, 'The Danish Royal Family and the Russian Imperial Family', *Treasures of Russia – Imperial Gifts* (exhibition catalogue from the Amalienborg Palace, The Royal Silver Room, 2002), p. 121.

44. RA MDK/PRIV/Kate Fox, Queen Olga to Kate Fox, 20 September/3 October 1908.

45. RA MDK/PRIV/Kate Fox, Prince Nicholas to Kate Fox, 29 August 1910.

46. RA MDK/PRIV/Kate Fox, Princess Nicholas to Kate Fox, 14/27 November 1905.

47. RA MDK/PRIV/Kate Fox, Same to same, 3/16 March 1909.

48. RA MDK/PRIV/Kate Fox, Same to same, 31 October/13 November 1911.

49. Howe, *A Galaxy of Governesses*, p. 149.

50. Crown Princess of Prussia to Augusta Byng, 19 November 1872; private collection.

51. Same to same, undated, *c.* 1873; private collection.

52. Same to same, 25 August 1881; private collection.

53. RA VIC/Z35/37, Victoria, Princess Royal, Crown Princess of Prussia to Queen Victoria, 29 August 1881.

54. Fulford (ed.), *Your Dear Letter*, p. 271.

55. Crown Princess of Prussia to Augusta Byng, 3 September 1881; private collection.

56. Same to same, 11 September 1881; private collection.

57. Same to same, details from several letters, September 1881–January 1882; private collection.

58. Same to same, 20 January 1882; private collection.
59. Same to same, 27 February 1882; private collection.
60. Same to Frederick Curtis, 28 December 1890; private collection.

Chapter Seven, pp. 130–49

1. HSD GF Abt. D24 Nr.1815, Souvenir Album.
2. Date and place of birth from official records in the State Archive in Darmstadt; family details from her will, which also suggests a strong connection to Dorset. At death, Mary Ann Orchard owned three cottages at Fordington in Dorset.
3. Princess Alice, *Letters to Her Majesty The Queen*, p. 138.
4. Alice, Princess, *Grossherzogin von Hessen und bei Rhein; Mittheilungen aus Ihrem Leben und aus Ihren Briefen* (Darmstadt, Arnold Bergsträsser, 1884), p. 302. This letter of 20 April 1872 was omitted from the English edition of the Princess's letters and only appears in the (earlier) German translation. 'Stahl', literally 'steel' probably refers to the 'grey powder' used in Leopold's treatment. It was a mixture of mercury and chalk used as a purgative for children. 'Sir William' was the Queen's doctor Sir William Jenner.
5. Princess Alice, *Letters to Her Majesty The Queen*, p. 227.
6. RA VIC/Add. U/155, Princess Alice to Queen Victoria, 15 November 1878.
7. RA VIC/Add. U/157, Same to same, 19 November 1878.
8. RA VIC/Z87/49, Princess Victoria of Hesse to Queen Victoria, 3 August 1881.
9. RA VIC/Z174/9, Princess Irène to Queen Victoria, 11 March 1892.
10. RA QVJ, 27 April 1892.
11. Speaight, Richard N., *Memoirs of a Court Photographer* (London, Hurst & Blackett, 1926), pp. 89, 90.
12. MPN AGP Caja 16695/Exp.16, Personnel file of Miss Gertrude Bunting.
13. RA GV/FF3/ACA/14, Nurse Kemence to Princess Alice of Teck, 7 December (1911).
14. RA VIC/Z91/95, Princess Irène to Queen Victoria, 15 May 1894.
15. Norland College Archive.
16. *Norland Quarterly*, no. 33 (March 1908); the letter is dated December 1907, from Beatrice's home in Sussex.
17. Carmen Sylva, HM Queen Elisabeth of Roumania, *From Memory's Shrine* (London, Sampson Low, Marston & Co., nd), p. 168.
18. *Ibid.*, p. 169.
19. *Ibid.*, pp. 246–9.
20. *Ibid.*, p. 172.
21. RA GV/CC 10/225, Prince Albert to Queen Mary, 24 May 1916.
22. *The Times*, Court Circular, 4 August 1905.
23. de Stoeckl, *My Dear Marquis*, p. 113; HRH Princess Alice, *For My Grandchildren*, p. 78; Bing (ed.), *Letters of Tsar Nicholas and Tsaritsa Marie*, p. 243.
24. *The Times*, 23 May 1910.
25. *The Times*, Court Circular, 18 July 1911.
26. Sarah Bradford, *George VI* (London, Weidenfeld & Nicolson, 1989), p. 51.
27. *The Times*, Court Circular, 5 May 1914.

28. RA GVI/PRIV/CSP/01/11, Queen Mary to Prince Albert, letters May–July 1916.
29. Bloom, *Royal Baby*, p. 96.
30. *Daily Mail*, 20 February 1998, letter from F. Hollingsworth, Thomas Haverly's grandchild.
31. RA GV, Queen Mary's Diary, 1917.
32. RA GV/AA 60/313, quoted in Stephen Poliakoff, *The Lost Prince* (London, Methuen, 2003), p. xxxiv.
33. Rupert Godfrey (ed.), *Letters from a Prince* (London, Little, Brown & Company, 1998), p. 129.
34. All references to the Prince's death and funeral from RA GV, Queen Mary's Diary.
35. Leonowens, *The English Governess at the Siamese Court*, p. 98.
36. *Ibid.*, p. 19.
37. *Ibid.*, p. 99.
38. *Ibid.*, p. 100.
39. *Ibid.*, pp. 101–2.
40. *Ibid.*, p. 102.
41. Eagar, 'More about the Little Grand Duchesses of Russia', the *Girl's Own Paper and Woman's Magazine*, vol. xxx, p. 535.
42. Eagar, *Six Years at the Russian Court*, p. 181.
43. Meriel Buchanan, *Diplomacy and Foreign Courts* (London, Hutchinson, nd), p. 27.
44. Meriel Buchanan, *Queen Victoria's Relations* (London, Cassell, 1954), p. 37.
45. GARF F.625 L.1 F.358, Margaretta Eagar to Madame Gueringer, 14/27 October 1903.
46. Eagar, *Six Years at the Russian Court*, p. 189.
47. *Ibid.*, p. 192.
48. Quoted in Preben Ulstrup, 'The Danish Royal Family and the Russian Imperial Family', in *Treasures of Russia – Imperial Gifts*, p. 128.
49. HSD GF Abt. D24 Nr. 39/1.

Chapter Eight, pp. 150–73

1. Norland Archive, Kate Fox to Miss Sharman, 14 April 1913.
2. RA MDK/PRIV/Kate Fox, Charles Fox to Kate Fox, 30 March 1913.
3. RA MDK/PRIV/Kate Fox, Princess Nicholas of Greece to Kate Fox, 5/18 July 1910.
4. RA MDK/PRIV/Kate Fox, Same to same, 3/16 June 1909.
5. RA MDK/PRIV/Kate Fox, Same to same, 28 October 1911.
6. RA MDK/PRIV/Kate Fox, Same to same, 9–22 October 1910.
7. RA MDK/PRIV/Kate Fox, postcard, Prince Nicholas to Kate Fox, October 1912.
8. RA MDK/PRIV/Kate Fox, Princess Nicholas to Kate Fox, 3/16 January 1913.
9. RA MDK/PRIV/Kate Fox, Same to same, 25 January/7 February 1913.
10. RA MDK/PRIV/Kate Fox, Same to same, 8/21 January 1913; the Grand Duchess's words are quoted by her daughter.
11. RA MDK/PRIV/Kate Fox, Prince Nicholas to Kate Fox, 29 January/14 February 1913. This letter in the Prince's own hand, clearly dated, was found among Kate's papers enclosed in a letter of 1921. In July 1913, as the emotional temperature rose, Kate

complained that she had not received a word of support from the Prince. It seems possible that this letter was withheld in St Petersburg and rediscovered after the Grand Duchess's death.

12. RA MDK/PRIV/Kate Fox, Princess Nicholas to Kate Fox, 16 February/1 March 1913.
13. RA MDK/PRIV/Kate Fox, Same to same, 25 March/9 April 1913.
14. Norland Archive, Lady Ailsa to Miss Sharman, 1 July 1899.
15. RA MDK/PRIV/Kate Fox, Princess Nicholas to Kate Fox, 8/21 April 1913.
16. RA MDK/PRIV/Kate Fox, Prince Christopher to same, 15 October 1913.
17. RA MDK/PRIV/Kate Fox, Princess Nicholas to same, 21 June 1913.
18. RA MDK/PRIV/Kate Fox, Same to same, 24 September/7 October 1913 and passim.
19. RA MDK/PRIV/Kate Fox, Same to same, 8/21 October 1913.
20. RA MDK/PRIV/Kate Fox, Same to same, 1/14 September 1913.
21. RA VIC/Add. C22/59, Duke of Connaught to Francis Knollys, 17 April 1902.
22. RA VIC/Add. A15/3455, Prince Arthur to Queen Victoria, 30 August 1881.
23. RA VIC/Add. A15/3554, Mary Egerton to Queen Victoria, 20 March 1882.
24. RA VIC/Add. A15/4164, Queen Victoria to Prince Arthur, 18 January 1884.
25. Mary Howard McClintock, *The Queen Thanks Sir Howard* (London, John Murray, 1945), p. 224.
26. RA VIC/Add. A15/4164, Queen Victoria to Prince Arthur, 18 January 1884.
27. Elizabeth Longford (ed.), *Darling Loosy* (London, Weidenfeld & Nicolson, 1991), p. 228.
28. *Ibid.*, p. 229.
29. Longford (ed.), *Darling Loosy*, p. 234.
30. RA VIC/Add. A15/4164, Queen Victoria to Prince Arthur, 18 January 1884.
31. RA VIC/Add. A15/5619, Same to same, 16 September 1890.
32. RA VIC/Add. A15/5624, Same to the Duchess of Roxburghe, 19 September 1890.
33. RA PP/VIC/CSP/1896/13909.
34. RA VIC/Add. C22/59.
35. Princess Alice, *For My Grandchildren*, p. 62.
36. RA VIC/Z266/30, Duchess of Albany to Queen Victoria, 23 July 1886.
37. RA VIC/Z266/31, Same to same, 28 July 1886.
38. RA VIC/Z266/30, Same to same, 23 July 1886.
39. RA VIC/Z266/31, Same to same, 28 July 1886.
40. Princess Alice, *For My Grandchildren*, p. 62. It is not clear whether there was any connection between 'Nanna', Victoria Nicholls, and the unmarried mother 'Mrs' Nichols who was Prince Charles Edward's wet nurse two years earlier (see pp. 66–7).
41. RA VIC/Add. MSS A30/232, Queen Victoria to Sir Robert Collins, 22 September 1886.
42. Ricardo Mateos Sainz de Medrano, 'The Others; The illegitimate children of Kings Alfonso XII & Alfonso XIII', in *Royalty Digest*, vol. XII, 2003, pp. 144–7.
43. Hilda Maybury, *Secrets of a German Royal Household* (London, Skeffington & Son, nd, ?1919), pp. 15–16.
44. *Ibid.*, p. 36.
45. *Ibid.*, p. 52.
46. *Ibid.*, p. 76.

47. Ernst Ludwig, Grossherzog von Hessen und bei Rhein, *Erinnertes* (Darmstadt, Eduard Roether Verlag, 1983), pp. 56–7.
48. Marie, Duchess of Coburg to Crown Princess Marie of Romania, 12 February 1902. I am indebted to Mr John Wimbles for this reference.
49. Queen Marie, *Story of My Life*, vol. II, p. 141.
50. *Ibid.*, p. 142.
51. *Ibid.*, p. 140.
52. Princess Wilhelmina, *Lonely But Not Alone*, p. 45.
53. NKH Nr. A50-VIIc-S, Elizabeth Saxton Winter to Queen Wilhelmina, 1 October 1898.
54. Quoted in Paul D. Quinlan, *The Playboy King* (Westport, Greenwood Press, 1995), p. 16.
55. NKH, Nr. A50-VIIc-S, Elizabeth Saxton Winter to Queen Wilhelmina, 1 May 1899.
56. Queen Marie, *Story of My Life*, vol. II, p. 142 and NKH, Nr. A50-VIIc-S, Elizabeth Saxton Winter to Queen Wilhelmina, 1 May 1899.
57. Queen Marie, *Story of My Life*, vol. II, pp. 82–3.
58. Bodleian Library MS Eng d. 2350, Max Müller Papers f.1, Queen Elisabeth to Mrs Max Müller, 21 April 1900.
59. Queen Marie, *Story of My Life*, vol. II, p. 145.
60. Quinlan, *Playboy King*, p. 17. Quinlan gives two sources for this: a Romanian author and a letter written by Marie to her father-in-law in December 1897.
61. Queen Marie, *Story of My Life*, vol. II, p. 139.
62. Both letters quoted Quinlan, *Playboy King*, pp. 15, 16.
63. Quinlan, *Playboy King*, p. 17 and note.
64. Marie, Duchess of Coburg to Elizabeth Saxton Winter, undated.
65. Marie, Duchess of Coburg to Crown Princess Marie, 9/22 January 1902. I am indebted to Mr John Wimbles for these two references.
66. Quoted in Quinlan, *Playboy King*, p. 18.
67. Bodleian Library MS Eng d. 2350, Max Müller Papers f.1, Queen Elisabeth to Mrs Max Müller, 21 April 1900.
68. *Ibid.*
69. *Ibid.*
70. Elizabeth Burgoyne, *Carmen Sylva* (London, Thornton Butterworth, 1940), p. 189.

Chapter Nine, pp. 174–94

1. Howard, *Potsdam Princes*, pp. 172, 177.
2. *Ibid.*, p. 7.
3. Bicknell, *Life in the Tuileries*, p. 17.
4. Anon., *Recollections of a Royal Governess*, p. 132.
5. *Ibid.*, p. 136.
6. Quoted in Howe, *A Galaxy of Governesses*, p. 147.
7. Maybury, *Secrets of a German Royal Household*, p. 38.
8. Howard, *Potsdam Princes*, p. 169.
9. *Ibid.*, p. 89.

10. *Ibid.*, pp. 125–7.

11. *Ibid.*, p. 176.

12. Anon., *Recollections of a Royal Governess*, p. 166.

13. Topham, *A Distant Thunder*, p. 31.

14. Howard, *Potsdam Princes*, p. 114.

15. *Ibid.*, p. 164.

16. *Ibid.*, p. 163.

17. Bicknell, *Life in the Tuileries*, p. 124.

18. Howard, *Potsdam Princes*, pp. 181–2.

19. Maybury, *Secrets of a German Royal Household*, p. 48.

20. Howard, *Potsdam Princes*, p. 162.

21. Ryan, *Austrian Court*, pp. 224–30.

22. Howard, *Potsdam Princes*, p. 177–8.

23. *Ibid.*, p. 9.

24. Anon., *Recollections of a Royal Governess*, p. 134.

25. Bicknell, *Life in the Tuileries*, p. 30.

26. Topham, *A Distant Thunder*, p. 240.

27. Brimble, *Hohenzollern Eagle*, pp. 216–17.

28. Eagar, *Six Years at the Russian Court*, pp. 48, 207–8.

29. Bicknell, *Life in the Tuileries*, pp. 30–1.

30. Wyndham, *Correspondence of Sarah Spencer*, p. 326.

31. Fulford (ed.), *Your Dear Letter*, p. 190; 'Ditta' and 'Vicky' were two of the children, Princesses Charlotte and Victoria of Prussia.

32. *Ibid.*, p. 276.

33. Brimble, *Hohenzollern Eagle*, p. 96.

34. May T quotation from *Recollections of a Royal Governess*, p. 135.

35. Ada Leslie to Mary Anne Galsworthy, 27 November 1888.

36. Same to same, 22 December 1888.

37. Winter, 'Training Wilhelmina to be a Queen', p. 517.

38. Ada E. Leslie to Mary Anne Galsworthy, Potsdam, 7 March 1887.

39. Brimble, *Hohenzollern Eagle*, p. 132.

40. Eagar, *Six Years at the Russian Court*, pp. 49–50; Brimble, *Hohenzollern Eagle*, p. 135.

41. Ryan, *Austrian Court*, p. 212; the name day was the festival of the saint after whom the person was named, and it was celebrated at Roman Catholic and Orthodox Courts.

42. Topham, *A Distant Thunder*, p. 94.

43. *Ibid.*, pp. 94–5.

44. Ryan, *Austrian Court*, p. 31.

45. Ada Leslie to Mary Anne Galsworthy, 1 December 1889.

46. Topham, *A Distant Thunder*, pp. 269–70.

47. Eagar, *Six Years at the Russian Court*, p. 90.

48. Anon., *Recollections of a Royal Governess*, p. 196.

49. NKH, Nr. A50-VIIc-S, Elizabeth Saxton Winter to Queen Wilhelmina, 1 May 1899.

50. Howard, *Potsdam Princes*, p. 162.

51. Topham, *Memories of the Kaiser's Court*, p. 99.

52. *Ibid.*, pp. 127–8.
53. Eagar, *Six Years at the Russian Court*, p. 35.
54. Howard, *Potsdam Princes*, p. 161.
55. Ada Leslie to Mary Anne Galsworthy, 7 March 1887.
56. Eagar, *Six Years at the Russian Court*, p. 84.
57. Ada Leslie to Mary Anne Galsworthy, 7 March 1887.
58. Brimble, *Hohenzollern Eagle*, pp. 144–5.
59. Howard, *Potsdam Princes*, p. 270.
60. Brimble, *Hohenzollern Eagle*, pp. 144–5.
61. Howard, *Potsdam Princes*, pp. 272, 274.

Chapter Ten, pp. 195–216

1. Lott, *Governess in Egypt*, vol. II, pp. 210–11.
2. J. Rogerson to Dr Brown, 15/26 April 1800; Dr Charles Brown Papers, private collection. A note on the letter states that it was received in May.
3. Stanley, *Later Letters of Lady Augusta Stanley*, p. 199.
4. Winter, 'Training Wilhelmina to be a Queen', p. 400.
5. RA GV/FF3/ACA/14; Jane Potts to Princess Alice of Albany, 4 January 1901.
6. Topham, *A Distant Thunder*, p. 46.
7. Winter, 'Training Wilhelmina to be Queen', p. 400.
8. Same to same, 24 May 1892.
9. Anon., *Recollections of a Royal Governess*, pp. 1–2.
10. Howard, *Potsdam Princes*, p. 5.
11. Topham, *A Distant Thunder*, p. 1.
12. Anon., *Recollections of a Royal Governess*, pp. 85–6.
13. Fulford (ed.), *Your Dear Letter*, p. 36.
14. Ryan, *Austrian Court*, p. 174.
15. Ada Leslie to Mary Anne Galsworthy, 1 December 1889.
16. Same to same, 26 November 1886.
17. Winter, 'Training Wilhelmina to be Queen', p. 400.
18. Doris Hincks, letter in the *Norland Quarterly*, no. 96 (Christmas 1930).
19. Same to same, 16 December 1890.
20. Ada Leslie to Mary Anne Galsworthy, 31 March 1890.
21. *Ibid.*
22. HRH Prince Nicholas of Greece, *My Fifty Years* (London, Huchinson, nd, *c.* 1926), p. 33.
23. HRH Prince Christopher of Greece, *Memoirs* (London, The Right Book Club, 1938), p. 46.
24. Ada Leslie to Mary Anne Galsworthy, 1 May 1890.
25. Same to same, 19 March 1893.
26. Same to same, 17 August 1891.
27. Eagar, *Six Years at the Russian Court*, pp. 122–3.
28. Letter quoted in the exhibition catalogue *Treasures of Russia – Imperial Gifts*, pp. 237–40.

29. Eagar, *Six Years at the Russian Court*, pp. 126–7.
30. *Ibid.*, p. 73.
31. *Ibid.*, pp. 82–3.
32. Anon., *Recollections of a Royal Governess*, p. 105.
33. *Ibid.*, p. 29.
34. Eagar, *Six Years at the Russian Court*, p. 113.
35. Anon., *Recollections of a Royal Governess*, p. 27.
36. *Ibid.*, pp. 51–3.
37. Ada Leslie to Mary Anne Galsworthy, 2 February 1891.
38. Ada Leslie to Mary Ann Galsworthy, 3 March 1890.
39. Kate Fox, letter to the *Norland Quarterly*, no. 29 (Christmas 1906).
40. Taprell Dorling, *Ribbons and Medals* (London, Philip, 1957), p. 265.
41. Lott, *Governess in Egypt*, vol. II, pp. 239–46.
42. *Ibid.*, vol. I, pp. 12–13.
43. *Ibid.*, vol. I, pp. 4–5.
44. Emmeline Lott, *Nights in the Harem*, quoted in Howe, *A Galaxy of Governesses*, p. 177.
45. Lott, *Governess in Egypt*, vol. I, pp. 64–5.
46. *Ibid.*, vol. II, p. 197.
47. *Ibid.*, vol. I, pp. 275–6.
48. *Ibid.*, p. 97.
49. Leonowens, *English Governess at the Siamese Court*, p. 77.
50. Lott, *Governess in Egypt*, vol. II, p. 52.
51. Chennells, *An Egyptian Princess by her English Governess*, vol. I, p. 8.
52. *Ibid.*, p. 9.
53. *Ibid.*, pp. 18–24.
54. *Ibid.*, p. 114.
55. *Ibid.*, p. 61.
56. Ada Leslie to Mary Anne Galsworthy, 30 January 1884.
57. Same to same, 12 April 1884.
58. Kate Fox letter in the *Norland Quarterly*, no. 52 (July 1914).
59. Helen E. Ogilvie to Miss Sharman, Norland Archive.
60. Howard, *Japanese Memories*, p. 30.
61. *Ibid.*, p. 100.
62. *Ibid.*, p. 128.
63. *Ibid.*, p. 133.
64. *Ibid.*, p. 15.

Chapter Eleven, pp. 217–37

1. Prince Nicholas, *My Fifty Years*, pp. 279–80.
2. RA MDK/PRIV/Kate Fox, Princess Nicholas to Kate Fox, 15/28 June 1916.
3. RA MDK/PRIV/Kate Fox, Same to same, 20 July/2 August 1918; in fact, Emily Roose was not told to leave, probably because Prince and Princess Andrew were closer to the British royal family than the others.

4. Howe, *A Galaxy of Governesses*, p. 15.
5. Princess Anne-Marie Callimachi, *Yesterday Was Mine* (London, Falcon Press, 1952), p. 236.
6. Grand Duchess Marie, *Things I Remember*, p. 11.
7. HI and RH Grand Duchess George, *A Romanov Diary* (New York, Atlantic International, 1988), p. 3.
8. Topham, *A Distant Thunder*, p. 257.
9. Fulford (ed.), *Your Dear Letter*, pp. 108n., 112.
10. Eagar, *Six Years at the Russian Court*, p. 271.
11. Grand Duke Cyril, *My Life in Russia's Service*, p. 13.
12. Information and quotations from a collection of lesson plans, exercise books and a classroom diary preserved by Miss A.M. Dutton and now in private hands.
13. Callimachi, *Yesterday was Mine*, p. 237.
14. *Ibid.*, pp. 235–6.
15. Fulford (ed.), *Dearest Child*, p. 154.
16. RA VIC/Z3/32, Victoria, Princess Royal to Prince Albert, 30 July 1860.
17. Lott, *Governess in Egypt*, vol. I, p. 10.
18. Chennells, *An Egyptian Princess by her English Governess*, vol. I, p. 3.
19. *Ibid.*, p. 73.
20. *Ibid.*, p. 64.
21. *Ibid.*, p. 211.
22. *Ibid.*, p. 212.
23. *Ibid.*, p. 165.
24. Leonowens, *English Governess at the Siamese Court*, p. 59.
25. *Ibid.*, p. 210.
26. *Ibid.*, p. 211.
27. Leslie Smith Dow, *Anna Leonowens: A Life Beyond The King and I* (Nova Scotia, Pottersfield Press, 1991), p. 123. Anna Fyshe, the granddaughter, left a diary account of the meeting.
28. Howard, *Japanese Memories*, p. 9.
29. *Ibid.*, p. 11.
30. *Ibid.*, p. 12.
31. *Ibid.*, p. 20.
32. *Ibid.*, p. 285.
33. *Ibid.*, p. 13.
34. Howard, *Potsdam Princes*, pp. 136–7.
35. Howard, *Japanese Memories*, p. 36.
36. Howard, *Potsdam Princes*, p. 19.
37. Howard, *Japanese Memories*, p. 36.
38. Fulford (ed.), *Beloved Mama*, p. 146.
39. Topham, *Memories of the Kaiser's Court*, p. 25.
40. Howard, *Potsdam Princes*, p. 171.
41. Topham, *Chronicles of the Prussian Court*, p. 18.
42. Topham, *Memories of the Kaiser's Court*, p. 292.

43. Topham, *Chronicles of the Prussian Court*, p. 18.
44. Howard, *Potsdam Princes*, p. 123.
45. Prince Christopher, *Memoirs*, pp. 271–2.
46. Burns (trans.), *Crown Princess Cecilie*, pp. 107–8.
47. *Ibid.*, p. 107.
48. Anne Chermside letter in the *Norland Quarterly* (10 July 1954).
49. *Evening News*, 16 January 1952; cutting in Norland Archive.
50. *The Times*, 25 May 2003; Betty Morrison obituary.
51. *Ibid.*
52. All quotations from and about Rosalind Ramirez are taken from her own papers, now in the collection of Konstantin Eggert.
53. Quoted in Richard Beeston, 'The Last King of Iraq', *Sunday Times Magazine*, 14 February 2004.
54. Ramirez Papers.

Chapter Twelve, pp. 238–62

1. Eagar, *Six Years at the Russian Court*, pp. 165–6.
2. *Ibid.*, p. 167.
3. RA VIC/Add. A30/1784, Princess Pauline of Waldeck to Miss Smith, 26 September 1871.
4. Ryan, *Austrian Court*, p. 30.
5. Anon., *Recollections of a Royal Governess*, p. 202.
6. *Ibid.*, p. 201.
7. *Ibid.*, p. 305.
8. *Ibid.*, p. 307.
9. Ryan, *Austrian Court*, p. 37.
10. Anon., *Recollections of a Royal Governess*, p. 157.
11. Howe, *A Galaxy of Governesses*, p. 154.
12. Princess Charlotte of Prussia to Augusta Byng, 6 June 1878; private collection.
13. Topham, *Chronicles of the Prussian Court*, p. 159.
14. Topham, *Memories of the Kaiser's Court*, p. 177.
15. *Ibid.*, p. 178.
16. *Ibid.*, p. 179.
17. *Ibid.*, p. 176.
18. *Norland Quarterly*, no. 29 (December 1906); Kate Fox letter, 31 October 1906.
19. RA MDK/PRIV/Kate Fox, Princess Nicholas to Kate Fox, 30 October/12 November 1905.
20. Eagar, *Six Years at the Russian Court*, p. 199.
21. Eagar, 'Further Glimpses of the Tsaritsa's Little Girls', p. 366.
22. Eagar, *Six Years at the Russian Court*, p. 201.
23. *Ibid.*, pp. 201–2.
24. Topham, *Chronicles of the Prussian Court*, p. 172.
25. Howard, *Japanese Memories*, p. 172.

26. *Ibid.*, p. 173.
27. *Ibid.*, pp. 173–4.
28. *Ibid.*, p. 175.
29. *Ibid.*, p. 178.
30. *Ibid.*, p. 177.
31. *Ibid.*, p. 65.
32. *Ibid.*, p. 184.
33. *Ibid.*, pp. 189–90.
34. *Ibid.*, p. 217.
35. *Ibid.*, p. 234.
36. *Ibid.*, p. 236.
37. *Norland Quarterly*, no. 53 (Christmas 1914), principal's letter.
38. *Ibid.*, Kate Fox's letter.
39. Maybury, *Secrets of a German Royal Household*, p. 133.
40. *Ibid.*, p. 142.
41. *Ibid.*, p. 153.
42. Anon. (an English Governess), *What I Found Out in the House of a German Prince* (Chapman & Hall, Ltd, 1915), p. 25.
43. *Ibid.*, p. 7.
44. *Ibid.*, pp. 40–1.
45. *Ibid.*, p. 182.
46. Edith Keen, *Seven Years at the Prussian Court* (London, Eveleigh Nash, 1916; reprinted *Royalty Digest*, 1997), p. 47.
47. Howard, *Potsdam Princes*, p. v.
48. RA GV/FF3/ACA/14, Nurse Kemence to Princess Alice of Teck, 30 August 1914.
49. Marie of Battenberg, *Reminiscences*, p. 369.
50. Norland Archive, Mildred Hastings's album.
51. Marie of Battenberg, *Reminiscences*, p. 374.
52. From *Erinnerungen eines Darmstädters*, the text of Prince Ludwig's last talk, given at the Hessischen Landesmuseum in April 1968 and afterwards published by Eduard Roether Verlag. No dates or page numbers.
53. HSD GF Abt. D24 Nr. 58/8 and Nr. 75/4, travelling instructions and two undated postcards.
54. HSD GF Abt. D24 Nr. 75/4, undated postcard.
55. HSD GF Abt. D24 Nr. 58/8, L.E. Eadie to the Grand Duchess, 26 April 1915, 26 June 1915; Nr. 75/4, L.E. Eadie to Prince Ludwig, 16 November 1915. 'Don' was a family nickname for Ludwig's brother Georg Donatus, which gradually took over from 'Georgie' as he grew older.
56. HSD GF Abt. D24 Nr. 58/8, L.E. Eadie to the Grand Duchess, 2 January 1916.
57. Joseph T. Fuhrmann (ed.), *The Complete Wartime Correspondence of Tsar Nicholas II and the Empress Alexandra* (Westport, Connecticut, Greenwood Press, 1999), p. 382.
58. HSD GF Abt. D24 Nr. 58/8 and Nr. 75/4, two postcards, 9 November 1917; letter to the Grand Duchess 12 November 1917.
59. J.C. Trewin, *Tutor to the Tsarevich* (London, Macmillan, 1975), p. 91.

60. *Ibid.*, p. 90.
61. Eagar, *Six Years at the Russian Court*, p. 161. When Margaretta Eagar put these words into print, she could have had no idea how ironic they would later sound.
62. Kate Fox letter in the *Norland Quarterly*, no. 29 (Christmas 1906).
63. RA MDK/PRIV/Kate Fox, Princess Nicholas to Kate Fox, 20 July/2 August 1918.
64. Rosemary and Donald Crawford, *Michael and Natasha* (London, Weidenfeld & Nicolson, 1997), p. 338.
65. *Ibid.*, p. 339.
66. Edvard Radzinsky, *Rasputin* (London, Weidenfeld & Nicolson, 2000), p. 447.
67. Felix Youssoupoff, *Lost Splendour* (London, Jonathan Cape, 1953), p. 266.
68. 'The Revolution in Russia; Former English Nurse's Experiences', *Yorkshire Post*, 18 January 1936.
69. RA MDK/PRIV/Kate Fox, Princess Nicholas to Kate Fox, 15/28 January 1918.
70. Quoted in John Van Der Kiste, *Princess Victoria Melita* (Stroud, Alan Sutton, 1991), p. 135.
71. Quoted in the *Norland Quarterly*, no. 66 (June 1920).
72. *Norland Quarterly*, no. 66 (June 1920); Marian Burgess's obituary, unsigned but written by Mildred Hastings.

Chapter Thirteen, pp. 263–84

1. GARF F.651 L.1 F.326, Margaretta Eagar to Grand Duchess Tatiana, 5 June 1911.
2. Eagar, *Six Years at the Russian Court*, p. 283.
3. Nicholas II, *Dnevniki Imperatora Nikolaya II* (Moscow, Orbita, 1991), p. 231.
4. GARF F.625 L.1 F.358, Margaretta Eagar to Madame Gueringer, 13 July 1904.
5. It may also be significant that the dismissal came a few weeks after doctors had noticed that the little Tsesarevich (who would prove to have haemophilia) was bleeding from the navel. This seems less likely because the reality of his condition did not sink in for some time – and Princess Golitsina is unlikely to have known about it.
6. *The Times*, 6 January 1905.
7. Eager, *The Eager Family in the County of Kerry*, p. 40.
8. Eager, *Six Years at the Russian Court*, opening note.
9. GARF F.625 L.1 F.358, Margaretta Eagar to Madame Gueringer, 3 February 1908.
10. GARF F.651 L.1 F.326, Same to Grand Duchess Tatiana, 4 June 1908.
11. GARF F.625 L.1 F.358, Same to the Tsaritsa, 16 November 1908.
12. GARF F.651 L.1 F.326, Same to Grand Duchess Olga, 7 November 1910.
13. GARF F.625 L.1 F.358, Same to Madame Gueringer, 6 December 1910.
14. GARF F.651 L.1 F.326, Same to Grand Duchess Maria(?), 13 June 1913. This letter is filed in GARF as a letter to Tatiana – as, indeed, is the letter of 7 November 1910. In that case the '15 years old' gives the game away; this letter is more difficult to be certain about because Wednesday 18 June was actually Anastasia's birthday. As she would not have been fourteen in 1913 but only twelve, and as it is hard to imagine anyone describing Anastasia as 'so good and gentle', I've given it to Maria, whose 14th birthday by the Western calendar was 26 June.

15. Will of Margaretta Eagar, 29 February 1936, administration granted 27 April 1937.
16. Leopold Wölfling, *My Life Story; From Archduke to Grocer* (New York, E.P. Dutton, 1931), p. 240.
17. *Ibid.*, p. 241.
18. LMA: GBI 1934–8, 4459/N/04/004; GBI 1938, 4459/D/01/005; GBI 1934, 4459/D/01/008.
19. LMA: GBI 1931–34, 4459/N/04/003; GBI 1934–8, 4459/N/04/004.
20. RA GV/CC 8/288, Queen Mary to King George V, 28 November 1924.
21. LMA: GBI Book K/ LMA, 4459/A/01/011.
22. Anne Chermside, letter to the *Norland Quarterly* (10 July 1954).
23. Burns (trans.), *Memoirs of the Crown Princess Cecilie*, p. 111.
24. RA VIC Z91/112, Irène, Princess Heinrich of Prussia to Queen Victoria, 1 December 1894.
25. RA VIC Add. U166/127, Victoria, Princess Louis of Battenberg to Queen Victoria, 20 May 1896.
26. GARF F.625 L.1 F.358, Margaretta Eagar to Madame Gueringer, 14/27 October 1903, in French.
27. von Spreti, *Alix an Gretchen*, pp. 145–6; Tsaritsa Alexandra to Gretchen von Pfuhlstein (née Fabrice), 4/17 May 1904, in German.
28. Vorres, *The Last Grand Duchess*, p. 107.
29. *Ibid.*, p. 170, Same to same, 29 September/10 October 1906, in German.
30. Copy in private collection.
31. Antonia Ridge, *Grandma Went to Russia* (London, Faber & Faber, 1959), p. 131.
32. RA PP/VIC/MB, 30 March 1865, 1 January 1869.
33. RA QVJ, 5 July 1858.
34. RA VIC Z197/57, Death notices for Mary Anne Hull.
35. RA VIC Z191/19, Prince Alfred to Queen Victoria, 7 October 1888.
36. RA VIC M18/45, Queen Victoria to Miss Hildyard, 9 July 1860.
37. RA VIC M18/46, Miss Hildyard to Queen Victoria, 9 July 1860.
38. Buxhoeveden, *Life and Tragedy of Alexandra Feodorovna*, p. 129.
39. RA E.O./Pen/3/4/9; Memo from the Keeper of the Privy Purse to the Deputy Treasurer to the King, 19 April 1923.
40. RA E.O./Pen/3/4/9; Memo from the Deputy Treasurer to the Keeper of the Privy Purse, 19 April 1923; unattributed memo, 5 November 1925.
41. RA E.O./Pen/3/4/9, Note to the King's Treasurer relating to Mrs Bill's pension on retirement, 23 March 1928; Keeper of the Privy Purse to Deputy Treasurer, 28 March 1928.
42. RA PS/GV/O.2548/46, Queen Mary to Queen Alexandra, 8 February 1923.
43. RA GV/CC 45/672, Lady Patricia Ramsay to Queen Mary, 6 January 1925.
44. Bloom, *Royal Baby*, p. 100.
45. RA GV/CC 14/16, King George VI to Queen Mary, 3 December 1950.
46. Letter in Anne Sharp collection.
47. Diana Mandache (ed.), *Later Chapters of My Life; The Lost Memoir of Queen Marie of Romania* (Stroud, Sutton Publishing, 2004), pp. 46–7.

48. HSD GF Abt. D24 Nr. 75/5, 'Old Nana' Roose to Hereditary Grand Duchess Cecile of Hesse, 3 December 1931.
49. HSD GF Abt. D24 Nr. 75/5, Same to same, 3 December 1931.
50. HSD GF Abt. D24 Nr. 75/5, Same to same, 12 January 1931.
51. HSD GF Abt. D24 Nr. 75/5, Same to same, 29 April 1931.
52. HSD GF Abt. D24 Nr. 75/5, Same to same, 24 October 1931.
53. HSD GF Abt. D24 Nr. 75/5, Same letter.
54. HSD GF Abt. D24 Nr. 75/5, Same to same, 3 December 1931.
55. HSD GF Abt. D24 Nr. 75/5, Same to same, 29 April 1931.
56. HSD GF Abt. D24 Nr. 75/5, Same to same, 8 June 1933.
57. HSD GF Abt. D24 Nr. 75/5, Same.
58. HSD GF Abt. D24 Nr. 75/5, Same to same, 26 November 1931.
59. RA VIC/Add. A30/1784, Princess of Waldeck to Nana Smith, 22 December 1872.
60. HSD GF Abt. D24 Konv 44/7b, Nana Scharmann to the Grand Duchess of Hesse, 17 June 1910.
61. HSD GF Abt. D24 Konv 58/8, Lilian Eadie to Princes Georg Donatus and Ludwig, 10 September 1919.
62. HSD GF Abt. D24 Konv 75/4, Lilian Eadie to Prince Georg Donatus of Hesse, letter undated but written for the Prince's fifteenth birthday, 8 November 1921.
63. Ada Leslie to Mary Anne Galsworthy, 16 December 1889; private collection.
64. RA GV/FF3/ACA/14, Jane Potts to Princess Alice of Albany, 4 January 1901.
65. Anon., *Household of a German Prince*, p. 60.
66. Norland Archive, principal's secretary to Kate Fox, 19 February 1948.
67. Norland Archive, Mildred Hastings's papers.
68. Kate Fox letter in the *Norland Quarterly*, no. 29 (Christmas 1906).
69. Ada Leslie to Mary Anne Galsworthy, 31 March 1890; private collection.
70. GARF F.655 L2 F46, Millicent Crofts to Grand Duchess Vladimir, 25 January 1916.
71. Brimble, *Hohenzollern Eagle*, p. 254.

Bibliography

Anon. (Miss May T), *Recollections of a Royal Governess*, New York, Appleton, 1916

Anon. (An English Governess), *What I Found Out in the House of a German Prince*, London, Chapman & Hall Ltd, 1915

Annual Reports of the Princess Christian College, Manchester

Albert, Harold A., *Queen Victoria's Sister*, London, Robert Hale, 1967

Alexandra, Queen of Yugoslavia, *For a King's Love*, London, Odhams, 1956

Alice, Princess, *Grossherzogin von Hessen und bei Rhein; Mittheilungen aus Ihrem Leben und aus Ihren Briefen*, Darmstadt, Arnold Bergsträsser, 1884

Alice, Princess, Countess of Athlone, *For My Granchildren*, London, Evans, 1966

Alice, Princess of Great Britain, Grand Duchess of Hesse, *Letters to Her Majesty The Queen*, London, John Murray, 1897

Bertin, Celia, *Marie Bonaparte; A Life*, London, Quartet Books, 1983

Bicknell, Anna, *Life in the Tuileries under the Second Empire*, London, T. Fisher Unwin, 1895

Bing, Edward J. (ed.), *The Letters of Tsar Nicholas and Empress Marie*, London, Ivor Nicolson & Watson, 1937

Bloom, Ursula, *The Royal Baby*, London, Robert Hale, 1975

van Braam, Elisabeth et al., *In Royal Array; Queen Wilhelmina, 1880–1962*, Zwolle, Waanders, 1998

Brimble, E.L., *In the Eyrie of the Hohenzollern Eagle*, London, New York, Toronto, Hodder & Stoughton, nd

Burns, Emile (trans.), *The Memoirs of the Crown Princess Cecilie*, London, Victor Gollancz, 1931

Buxhoeveden, Baroness Sophie, *The Life and Tragedy of Alexandra Feodorovna, Empress of Russia*, London, Longmans, Green and Co., 1918

Callimachi, Princess Anne-Marie, *Yesterday Was Mine*, London, Falcon Press, 1952

Carmen Sylva (HM Queen Elisabeth of Roumania), *From Memory's Shrine*, London, Sampson Low, Marston & Co., nd

Chennells, Ellen, *Recollections of an Egyptian Princess by her English Governess*, 2 vols, London, William Blackwood, 1893

Christian Ludwig, Herzog zu Mecklenburg, *Erzählungen aus Meinem Leben*, Schwerin, Stock & Stern, 1998

Christopher, HRH, Prince of Greece, *Memoirs*, London, The Right Book Club, 1938

Corti, Count, *Elizabeth, Empress of Austria*, London, Thornton Butterworth, 1936

Crawford, Rosemary and Donald, *Michael and Natasha*, London, Weidenfeld & Nicolson, 1997

Crosse, A.G., 'An Anglo-Russian Medley: Semen Vorontsov's Other Son, Charles Cameron's Daughter, Grand Duke Alexander Pavlovich's English Playmate, and Not Forgetting His English Nurse,' in *SEER*, vol. 70, no. 4 (October 1992)

——, *An English Lady at the Court of Catherine the Great*, Cambridge, Crest Publications, 1989

——, 'Early Miss Emmies: English nannies, governesses and companions in pre-Emancipation Russia', *New Zealand Slavonic Journal*, no. 1 (1981)

Cyril (Kirill), HIH the Grand Duke, *My Life in Russia's Service – Then and Now*, London, Selwyn & Blount, 1939

Dow, Leslie Smith, *Anna Leonowens: A Life Beyond The King and I*, Nova Scotia, Pottersfield Press, 1991

Durland, Kellogg, *Royal Romances of Today*, London, T. Werner Laurie, nd, *c.* 1911

Eagar, M., *Six Years at the Russian Court*, London, Hurst & Blackett, 1906

——, 'Further Glimpses of the Tsaritsa's Little Girls' and 'More about the Little Grand Duchesses of Russia', in the *Girl's Own Paper and Woman's Magazine*, vol. XXX (1909)

Eager, E.F., *The Eager Family in the County of Kerry*, Dublin, privately printed, 1958

Elsberry, Terence, *Marie of Romania*, London, Cassell, 1972

Ernst Ludwig, Grossherzog von Hessen und bei Rhein, *Erinnertes*, Darmstadt, Eduard Roether Verlag, 1983

Feigl, Erich (ed.), *Kasier Karl I; Persönliche Aufzeichnungen, Zeugnisse und Dokumente*, Munich, Amalthea, 1984

Ferrand, Jaques, *Nianias; Souvenirs*, Paris, Ferrand, 1999

Fulford, Roger (ed.), *Beloved Mama: Private Correspondence of Queen Victoria and the German Crown Princess 1878–1885*, London, Evans, 1981

——, *Darling Child: Private Correspondence of Queen Victoria and the Crown Princess of Prussia 1871–1878*, London, Evans, 1976

——, *Dearest Child: Letters between Queen Victoria and the Princess Royal 1858–1861*, London, Evans, 1964

——, *Dearest Mama: Letters between Queen Victoria and the Crown Princess of Prussia 1861–1864*, London, Evans, 1968

——, *Your Dear Letter: Private Correspondence of Queen Victoria and the Crown Princess of Prussia 1865–1871*, London, Evans, 1971

Gathorne-Hardy, Jonathan, *The Rise and Fall of the British Nanny*, London, Weidenfeld & Nicolson, 1993 edn

George, HI and RH Grand Duchess, *A Romanov Diary*, New York, Atlantic International, 1988

Gibbs, Mary Ann, *The Years of the Nannies*, London, Hutchinson, 1960

Girl's Own Paper and Woman's Magazine, 1880s–1920s

Gould Lee, Arthur, *The Empress Frederick Writes to Sophie*, London, Faber & Faber, 1955

Groeneveld, Phillippe, *Konigin Wilhelmina*, Zaltbommel, Europese Bibliotheek, 1990

Hamann, Brigitte, *The Reluctant Empress*, Berlin, Ullstein, 1982

History of the Princess Christian College, Manchester, privately printed, 1950s

Hough, Richard, *Louis and Victoria*, London, Hutchinson, 1974

—— (ed.), *Advice to a Granddaughter*, London, Heinemann, 1975

Howard, Ethel, *Potsdam Princes*, London, Methuen, 1916

——, *Japanese Memories*, London, Hutchinson, 1918

Howe, Bea, *A Galaxy of Governesses*, London, Derek Verschoyle, 1954

Jackman, Sydney W. and Hella Haasse (eds), *A Stranger in The Hague; the Letters of Queen Sophie of the Netherlands to Lady Malet 1842–1877*, Durham and London, Duke University Press, 1989

Keen, Edith, *Seven Years at the Prussian Court*, London, Eveleigh Nash, 1916; reprinted *Royalty Digest*, 1997

King, Stella, *Princess Marina, Her Life and Times*, London, Cassell, 1969

Larisch, Countess Marie, *My Past*, London, Eveleigh Nash, 1913

Leonowens, Anna Harriette, *The English Governess at the Siamese Court*, London, Folio Society, 1980, originally published 1870

Lott, Emmeline, *The Governess in Egypt; Harem Life in Egypt and Constantinople*, 2 vols, London, Richard Bentley, 1865

Louis Ferdinand of Prussia, Prince, *The Rebel Prince*, Chicago, Henry Regnery Company, 1952

Ludwig Ferdinand of Bavaria, HRH Princess, *Through Four Revolutions 1862–1933*, London, John Murray, 1933

Lutyens, Mary (ed.), *Lady Lytton's Court Diary*, London, Rupert Hart-Davis, 1961

Majolier, Nathalie, *Stepdaughter of Imperial Russia*, London, Stanley Paul & Co., 1940

Mandache, Diana (ed.), *Later Chapters of My Life; The Lost Memoir of Queen Marie of Romania*, Stroud, Sutton Publishing, 2004

Marie, Grand Duchess of Russia, *Things I Remember*, London, Cassell, 1930

Marie, Princess zu Erbach-Schönberg, Princess of Battenberg, *Reminiscences*, London, George Allen & Unwin, 1925

Marie, Queen of Romania, *The Story of My Life*, London, Cassell, 3 vols, 1934–5

Mateos Sainz de Medrano, Ricardo, 'The Others; The illegitimate children of Kings Alfonso XII & Alfonso XIII', in *Royalty Digest*, vol. XII (2002–3)

Maybury, Hilda, *Secrets of a German Royal Household*, London, Skeffington & Son, nd, ?1919

Maylunas, Andrei and Sergei Mironenko (eds), *A Lifelong Passion*, London, Weidenfeld & Nicolson, 1996

Mortimer, Barbara E. 'The Nurse in Edinburgh *c.* 1760–1860: the impact of commerce and professionalism', unpublished DPhil thesis, University of Edinburgh, 2002

Nicholas of Greece, Prince, HRH, *My Fifty Years*, London, Huchinson, nd, *c.* 1926

Noel, Gerard, *Princess Alice*, London, Constable, 1974

——, *Ena; Spain's English Queen*, London, Constable, 1984

Obolensky, Serge, *One Man in His Time*, London, Hutchinson, 1960

Olga, Queen of Württemberg, *Traum der Jugend goldner Stern*, Pfullingen, Verlag Günther Neske, 1955

O'Shaughnessy, Edith, *Marie Adelaide, Grand Duchess of Luxemburg, Duchess of Nassau*, New York, Jonathan Cape and Robert Ballou, 1932

Pakula, Hannah, *The Last Romantic, A Biography of Queen Marie of Romania*, London, Weidenfeld & Nicolson, 1984

Parrott, Cecil, *The Tightrope*, London, Faber & Faber, 1975

Paul of Hohenzollern-Roumania, *Prince, King Carol II*, London, Methuen, 1988

Peter II, King of Yugoslavia, *A King's Heritage*, London, Cassell, 1955

Phenix, Patricia, *Olga Romanov; Russia's Last Grand Duchess*, Canada, Viking, 1999

Pitcher, Harvey, *When Miss Emmie was in Russia; English Governeses before, during and after the October Revolution*, London, John Murray, 1977

Poliakoff, S., *The Lost Prince*, London, Methuen, 2003

Pope-Hennessey, James, *Queen Mary*, London, George Allen & Unwin, 1959

Quinlan, Paul D., *The Playboy King*, Westport, Connecticut, Greenwood Press, 1995

Radu, Prince of Hohenzollern-Veringen, *Anne of Romania; A War, An Exile, A Life*, Bucharest, Romanian Cultural Foundation Publishing House, 2002

Ramer, Carole J., *The Final Photo of the Romanovs*, Lakeside, California, Aarenssen Publishing Company, 1998

Ramme, Agatha (ed.), *Beloved and Darling Child; Last Letters between Queen Victoria and her Eldest Daughter, 1886–1901*, Stroud, Alan Sutton, 1990

Renne, Elizaveta P., 'Bridging Two Empires: Christina Robertson and the Court of St Petersburg', in *An Imperial Collection: Women Artists from the State Hermitage Museum*, exhibition catalogue, London, Merrell, 2003

Ridge, Antonia, *Grandma Went to Russia*, London, Faber & Faber, 1959

Robinson, Jane, *Wayward Women; a Guide to Women Travellers*, Oxford, Oxford University Press, 1990

Röhl, John C.G., *Young Wilhelm; the Kaiser's Early Life*, Cambridge, Cambridge University Press, 1998

Rutter, Owen, *Portrait of a Painter; The Authorized Life of Philip de László*, London, de László Foundation, 2003

Ryan, Nellie, *My Years at the Austrian Court*, London, John Lane, 1916

Seaman, W.A.L. and J.R. Sewell (eds), *The Russian Journal of Lady Londonderry, 1836–37*, London, John Murray, 1973

Speaight, Richard N., *Memoirs of a Court Photographer*, London, Hurst & Blackett, 1926

von Spreti, Graf Heinrich (ed.), *Alix an Gretchen; Briefe der Zarin Alexandra Feodorovna an Freiin Margarethe v. Fabrice*, privately printed, 2003

Stanley, Lady Augusta, *Letters of Lady August Stanley, 1849–1863*, London, Gerald Howe, 1927

——, *Later Letters of Lady August Stanley, 1864–1876*, London, Jonathan Cape, 1929

de Stoeckl, Baroness, *My Dear Marquis*, London, John Murray, 1952

——, *Not All Vanity*, London, John Murray, 1950

Stokes, Penelope, *Norland, 1892–1992*, Hungerford, Norland College, 1992

Sylva, Carmen, HM Queen Elisabeth of Romania, *From Memory's Shrine*, London, Sampson, Low, Marston & Co., nd

Topham, Anne, *Memories of the Kaiser's Court*, London, Methuen, 1914

——, *Chronicles of the Prussian Court*, London, Hutchinson, 1926

——, *A Distant Thunder*, selections from the writings of Anne Topham, edited by Wendy Reid Crisp, New York, New Chapter Press, 1992

Treasures of Russia – Imperial Gifts, exhibition catalogue from the Amalienborg Palace, the Royal Silver Room, 2002

Trewin, J.C., *Tutor to the Tsarevich; An Intimate Portrait of the Last Days of the Russian Imperial Family Compiled from the Papers of Charles Sydney Gibbes*, London, Macmillan, 1975

Vickers, Hugo, *Alice, Princess Andrew of Greece*, London, Hamish Hamilton, 2000

Victoria, Princess of Prussia, *My Memoirs*, London, Eveleigh Nash and Grayson, 1929

Viktoria Luise, HRH Princess of Prussia, *The Kaiser's Daughter*, London, W.H. Allen, 1987

Vorres, Ian, *The Last Grand Duchess*, London, Hutchinson, 1964

Weissensteiner, Friedrich, *Die Rote Erzherzogin*, Munich, Piper, 1993

Wilhelmina, HRH Princess of the Netherlands, *Lonely But Not Alone*, London, Hutchinson, 1960

Windsor, The Duke of, *A Family Album*, London, Cassell, 1960

Winter, Miss E. Saxton, 'Training Wilhelmina to be a Queen', in the *Girl's Own Paper and Woman's Magazine*, vol. XXX (1909)

Wölfling, Leopold, *My Life Story: from Archduke to Grocer*, New York, E.P. Dutton, 1931

Woodham-Smith, Cecil, *Queen Victoria; Her Life and Times*, Book Club Associates edn, 1973

Wyndham, The Hon. Mrs Hugh (ed.), *Correspondence of Sarah Spencer, Lady Lyttelton*, London, John Murray, 1912

Index

Royalty indexed in family groups, by country then by Christian name and titles. Others indexed by surname. Princesses are indexed under their married name if this occurs in the text.

Acland, Revd Peter, 58, 289
Adams, Mary, 25, 285
Ailsa, Marchioness of, 156
Ajami, Fouad, 236
Alexander, Euphemia, 14
Alison, Margaret, 40–2, 157, 158, 217–18, 237, 261, 285
Arco-Valley, Count, 230
Arnold, Sir Edwin, 229
Atkinson, Miss, 53, 60, 285
Austria-Hungary: Elisabeth Marie, 'Erzsi', Archduchess, 44, 78, 80–1, 92–3, 175, 239–40; Elisabeth, Empress, 239–40; Franz Josef, Emperor, 80–1, 175, 188, 190–1; Karl Stefan, Archduke, 69, 112–13, 179–80, 193, 199–200, 290; Karl, Emperor, 219; Maria Annunciata, Archduchess, 219; Maria Teresa, Archduchess, 113, 187; Marie Valerie, Archduchess, 299; Rudolf, Crown Prince, 44, 240–1; Stephanie, Crown Princess, 45, 116

B, Miss, 184, 251–2, 283, 285
Baden: Berthold, Prince, 284; Friedrich II, Grand Duke, 241; Luise, Grand Duchess, 191; Marie Louise, Princess Max, 34, 35; Viktoria, Princess (later Queen of Sweden), 241
Badeni, Count, 44, 207; Countess, 199; Wanda, 188, 199
Badger, Revd George Percy, 56–7
Bailie, Emma, xiii, 131, 285
Baird, Emily, 15
Ballin, Herr, 230
Barber, Sylvia, 232, 285
Bariatinsky, Marie, Princess, 21
Barnes, Mary, 136–8, 144, 168, 196, 270, 285
Barrington, Lady Caroline, 38, 85, 122
Barron, Billy, 112

Barton, Ray, children's outfitter, 67–8
Beale, Dorothea, 49
Bell, 'Nana', xi, 40, 70, 108, 285
Bell, H.A., 282
Bennett, Kate, 142
Bicknell, Anna, 43, 51, 79–80, 90–1, 175, 178, 181–2, 183–4, 283, 285
Bill, Charlotte, 'Lalla', 28, 52, 66, 79, 82–3, 85, 138–44, 275–7, 285–6; family background, 28
Blakeney, Miss, 283
Bloom, Ursula, 83, 276
Bomhoff, Halldis, 100
Borland, Miss, 235, 285
Bowman, Dr, 143
Brassov, George, 258–9
Brazil: Leopoldina, Empress, 55, 105, 126–7, 176; Maria da Glória, Princess, 55, 105; Pedro I, Emperor, 55, 176
Brett family, 18
Brimble, (Ethel) Lilian, 54, 61–2, 90, 91, 93, 96, 98, 109, 110–11, 182, 184, 186–7, 193–4, 253, 283, 286
Brompton, Miss, 101, 286
Brontë sisters, 44
Brotherstone, Mrs, 159, 286
Brown, Dr Charles, 196
Brown, Miss, 8
Buchanan, Sir George, 147, 257
Buchanan, Meriel, 147
Buhman, Eugeniu, 171
Bunting, Gertrude, 134, 286
Burgess, Marian, 34, 35, 71, 72, 101, 157, 261–2, 286
Buss, Frances, 49
Butcher, George, 29
Butcher, Mabel, 277
Butler, Annie, 100, 286–7

Butler, Captain, 141
Byng, Augusta Maria, 47–8, 115, 123, 127–9, 287; family background, 47–8; sisters, 128–9

Callimachi, Anne-Marie, Princess, 218, 222
Calot, Dr, 153, 155, 157
Cantacuzino, Zizi, 170–1
Casey, Bridget, 219, 287
Castle, Reginald, 282
Chaliapin, Feodor, 111–12
Chaloner, Ursula, 45
Chapman, Marjorie, 134, 287
Chapman, Susan, 159–63, 287
Chennells, Ellen, 70, 106, 212–14, 224–5, 232, 287
Chermside, Anne, 232–3, 284, 287; family, 233, 287
Cheveley, Mrs, 6
Chorinsky, Count, 180, 200
Christie, Eugenia, 8, 196, 287
Clark, Mrs, 12–14, 15, 131, 287
Clark, Mrs (Mrs Roberts), 10–11, 287
Clarke, Doris, 89, 109
Coke, Sybil, 123
Collenette, Irene, 34, 35, 39, 69–70, 101, 102, 287
Collins, Margaret, 44, 288
Collins, Sir Robert, 119, 164
Conway, Mrs, 134, 288
Coombs, Alexandra, 108, 112, 288
Coster, Miss, 260–1, 288
Cotton, Violet, 28
Crawford, Marion, xii
Crawford, Miss, 241, 288
Creak, Eliza, 163–4, 253, 288
Crofts, Millicent, 'Milly', 2–3, 52, 64, 152–3, 158, 219, 220, 280, 284, 288; family, 2, 288
Croisdale, Violet Mary, 37, 288
Crowther, Sylvia, 170, 288
Curtis, Frederick, 129

Dalton, Canon, 143
Darcourt, Octavie, 47
Denmark: Christian IX, King, 117, 197
Dimsdale, Baron Thomas and Baroness Elizabeth, 4–6, 29, 76, 195, 197
Dobeneck, Sophie, Baroness von, 46
Doherty, Eugenie, 29, 134, 221, 289
Doherty, Martha, 134, 289
Douglas, Julie (later Mrs Acland), 50–1, 119, 289
Duncan, Lilian, 34, 289

Durland, Kellogg, 76, 94, 108, 265
Dutton, Annie Mary, 114, 220–2, 289

Eadie, Elizabeth, 'Lilian' (later Mrs Jeffery), 35, 37, 39, 70, 75, 79, 99–100, 104–5, 254–7, 258, 269, 279, 281–2, 289; family, 269, 289
Eagar, Margaretta, x, 20–6, 28–9, 30–1, 38, 39, 65–6, 75, 79, 81, 86, 91, 94–6, 120, 146, 147–9, 180–2, 182–3, 187, 190, 192, 204, 205–6, 207, 220, 223, 238–9, 243–4, 247, 258, 263–8, 272, 283, 289; family, 23–4, 267, 264, 265, 268, 289, 303 n.4
Edgworth, Maria, 55
Edwards, Catherine, 122
Egypt: Ahmed Fuad, Crown Prince, 233, 269–70; Fadia, Princess, 232, 233, 270; Farida, Queen, 232, 233; Farouk, King, 232, 233–4, 269–70; Fawzia, Princess, 232; Ferial, Princess, 232; Ibrahim, Grand Pacha, 105–6, 195, 211, 213, 224; Ismael Pacha, Khedive, 105, 195, 210–12, 224–5; Kopsès (slave of Princess Zeyneb), 106, 224–5; Mustafa Pacha, 223; Narriman, Queen, 233–4; Zeyneb, Princess, 106, 213, 224–5
Elphinstone, Lady, 160
Emery, Miss, 195–6
Epps, John, 223
Erbach-Schönberg: Marie, Princess Gustav, xiii, 253–4; Maximilian, Prince, xiii
Evans, Alice, 134, 165, 289
Ewen, Mr, 28–9

Fabrice, Gretchen, 36
Ffolliott, Anne Louisa, 172–3, 269, 289; family, 172, 269, 289
Finch, Frederick, 85
Fox, Jessie, 33, 34, 71, 84–5, 283, 290
Fox, Kate, x, xii, 33, 34, 35, 37, 39, 40–1, 64, 67–8, 70, 71, 72–3, 76, 78, 83, 100–4, 114–15, 120–1, 124–6, 150–9, 173, 208–9, 214–15, 217, 242–3, 248, 258, 261, 278, 283, 284, 290; family, 33, 125, 150–1, 157, 243, 290
France: Eugénie, Empress, 184; Napoleon, Prince Imperial, 90–1
Francklin, Elizabeth, ix, 17–19, 59, 158, 205, 270–3, 290; family, 17–18, 272–3, 290
Freeland, Mr, 224
Froebel, Friedrich, 31
Fry, Frances, 12–13, 27–8, 64–5, 76, 219, 268, 290; family, 27–8, 290
Fürstenburg, Prince, 189

Galsworthy, Mary Anne, 'Pollie', 52

Gaskell, Mrs, 44

Germany: *see also* Prussia and individual States, Auguste Viktoria, Kaiserin, 15, 37, 46, 61, 62, 73, 81–2, 111, 177, 178–9, 192, 193, 229–30, 232, 242, 269; Augusta, Kaiserin, 122–3, 241; Friedrich III, Kaiser (also Crown Prince of Prussia), 26, 52, 115–16, 241–2; Victoria, Kaiserin Friedrich (Princess Royal of Great Britain, Crown Princess of Prussia), 10, 11, 14, 15, 16, 26, 32, 38, 46–7, 48–9, 51–2, 53, 62, 67, 69, 72, 74, 89–90, 115–16, 117, 121, 123–4, 127–9, 164, 184, 185, 188–9, 199, 241, 269; Wilhelm I, Kaiser, 241–2; Wilhelm II, Kaiser, 52, 53, 72, 75, 96, 100, 101, 177, 178, 179, 187–8, 189–90, 191–2, 193, 194, 219, 223, 230–1, 237, 244, 269, 283

Gessler, Pauline, 4–5, 284, 290; Johann, 4

Gibb, Grace, 34, 290

Gibbes, Sydney, 257–8

Golitsina, Maria Mikhailovna, Princess, 263, 323 n.5

Governesses' Benevolent Institution, 269

Graham, Maria (Lady Calcott), 55–6, 78, 105, 126–7, 176, 196, 291

Grancy, Wilhelmine, Baroness, 118

Graves, Louisa, 81, 104, 291

Great Britain: Albert Victor of Wales, Prince, 12; Albert, Prince Consort, 11, 38, 184; Alexander of Battenberg, Prince, 186; Alexander of Teck, Prince (later Earl of Athlone), 253; Alexandra, Princess of Wales and later Queen, 12, 13, 14, 18, 23, 28, 117, 120, 140, 142, 143, 266, 273, 276, 286; Alfred, Prince, Duke of Edinburgh (later Duke of Saxe-Coburg), 67, 196, 274, 291; Alice of Albany, Princess (later Princess Alexander of Teck and Countess of Athlone), 68–9, 104, 119, 135, 140, 163–4, 197, 253, 282–3; Arthur of Connaught, Prince, 125, 160–2; Arthur, Prince, Duke of Connaught, 117–18, 159–63; Beatrice, Princess Henry of Battenberg, 29, 129, 161, 290, 293; Christian Victor, Prince of Schleswig-Holstein, 69, 285; Christian, Prince of Schleswig-Holstein, 104, 196; Edward VII, King, 11, 89–90, 100, 120, 139, 223, 266, 286; Edward VIII, King (later Duke of Windsor), 17, 66, 82–3, 143, 276; George V, King, 13, 66, 83–4, 138, 139, 140, 142, 275–7; George VI, King (Prince Albert), 17, 138, 141, 276; George, Prince, Duke of

Kent, 138, 140, 141, 143; Helena Victoria, Princess of Schleswig-Holstein 21, 36; Helena, 'Lenchen', Princess Christian of Schleswig-Holstein, 15, 36, 53, 54, 73, 129, 230, 287; Helene, Princess, Duchess of Albany (Princess of Waldeck), 50–1, 72, 73, 119, 163–4; Henry 'Liko' of Battenberg, Prince, 161; Henry, Prince, Duke of Gloucester, 17, 138, 141, 143; John, Prince, 17, 83, 138–44, 275, 276; Leopold of Battenberg, Prince, 134; Leopold, Prince, Duke of Albany, 66, 131–2, 133, 134, 163–4; Louis of Battenberg, Prince (later Lord Mountbatten), 16; Louis of Battenberg, Prince, 40; Louise, Princess, Duchess of Argyll, 37, 161; Luise Margarete, Princess, Duchess of Connaught (Princess of Prussia), 50, 51–2, 117, 159–63; Marina, Princess, Duchess of Kent (Princess of Greece), 35, 40, 76, 86, 101, 102–4, 114–15, 125, 150, 153–8; Mary, Princess (also of York, and later Viscountess Lascelles), 17, 139, 143, 276; Mary, Queen (also Princess of Teck and Duchess of York), 14, 17, 28, 66, 82–4, 122, 138, 139, 140, 142, 143–4, 257–8, 269, 275–7; Maurice of Teck, Prince, 68; May of Teck, Princess, 69, 283; Patricia, 'Patsy' of Connaught, Princess (later Lady Patricia Ramsay), 161, 276; Philip, Prince, Duke of Edinburgh (Prince of Greece), 40, 102–4, 105, 278, 279, 280; Richard, 2nd Duke of Gloucester, xii, 236, 297; Rupert of Teck, Prince, 69, 104, 134, 135; Victoria, Princess (also of Wales), 13, 120–1, 139, 141, 143, 266; Victoria, Princess Louis of Battenberg, Marchioness of Milford Haven (Princess of Hesse-Darmstadt), 12, 13, 16, 25, 81, 98, 104, 118, 131, 132, 135, 255, 271, 274, 280; Victoria, Queen, xii, 11, 12, 13, 14, 15, 16, 20, 21, 26–7, 38, 50, 62, 66–7, 69, 73, 78–9, 85, 116–19, 121, 122, 131, 132, 159–64, 185–6, 196, 218–19, 222–3, 273–4, 275, 286, 293, 308 n.50, 312 n.27; William of Gloucester, Prince, xii, 236, 297

Greece: Alexander, King of the Hellenes, 103, 217; Alexandra, Princess, 103, 289; Alice, Princess Andrew (Princess of Battenberg), 40–2, 68, 147, 274; Andrew, Prince, 40, 147; Aspasia Manos (wife of King Alexander), 103; Christopher, Prince, 40, 120, 157, 204; Constantine I, King of the Hellenes (previously Crown Prince and Duke of Sparta), 40, 139,

217; Constantine, Crown Prince (later King Constantine II), 233; Elena, Princess Nicholas (Grand Duchess Elena Vladimirovna of Russia), 33, 34, 35, 40–3, 67–8, 71, 73, 77, 83, 100–2, 114–15, 120, 124–6, 150–9, 208, 217–18, 258, 261, 283; Elizabeth, Princess, 35, 40, 41, 67, 73, 101, 102–4, 150, 153–6, 158, 208–9; Eugenie, Princess, 37; George I, King of the Hellenes, 40, 124–5, 155, 197–8; George, Prince, 40; Irene, Princess, 233; Katherine, Princess, 37, 38, 42; Margarita, Princess, 40, 41, 71, 102–4, 278, 279, 307 n.27; Marie, Princess George, 37; Nicholas, Prince, 40, 101, 125, 153–4, 155, 204, 208, 217–18, 283, 314–15 n.11; Olga, Queen, 40, 125; Paul, King of the Hellenes, 73; Peter, Prince, 37; Sophie, Crown Princess and later Queen (Princess of Prussia), 16, 32, 37, 40, 53, 188–9, 201, 203–4, 269, 282; Sophie, Princess (daughter of Prince Andrew), 102–4, 233; Sophie, Princess (later Queen of Spain), 217; Theodora, Princess, 40, 41, 102–4, 278
Green, Marianne Elizabeth, 48–9, 52, 115–16, 275, 291
Green, Mary A., 124, 169–70, 277, 291
Green, Mrs Rosa, 17, 291
Grove, Elizabeth, 'Lizzie', 64, 219, 291
Gueringer, Maria Feodorovna, 30, 147, 264, 265–6, 272

Haft, Frau, 123
Halls, Beatrice, 34, 35, 284, 291
Hanking, Mrs, 10
Hanover: Ernst August, Crown Prince, later Duke of Cumberland, 122; Frederica, Princess, 44, 121; George V, King, 121–2; Mary, Princess, 44, 121; Mary, Queen, 44, 121–2
Hansell, Henry, 85, 138
Hashimoto, Admiral, 247
Haskell, Helen Eggleston, 265
Hastings, Mildred, 31, 34, 35, 135, 254
Haverly, Elsie, 143; Thomas, 142
Hawes, Catherine Anne, 184, 291
Henton, Zillah, 259–61, 291–2
Hesse-Cassel: Mafalda, Princess Phillipp (Princess of Italy), 88–9; Margarete, Princess Friedrich Karl (Princess of Prussia), 34, 35, 288; Moritz (Maurice), Prince, 88–9
Hesse-Darmstadt: Alice, Princess Louis and later Grand Duchess (Princess of Great Britain), 12, 13, 14, 50, 66, 67, 81, 118, 120, 130–3, 290, 291; Cecile, Hereditary Grand Duchess (Princess of Greece), 40, 70, 102–4, 105, 278–80, 282; Eleonore, Grand Duchess, 35, 37, 70, 75, 98–100, 104–5, 120, 254, 255, 256, 257, 278, 282; Elisabeth, Princess (daughter of Grand Duke Ernst Ludwig), 25, 75, 94, 146–9, 166–7; Elisabeth, Princess (daughter of Grand Duke Ludwig IV), 13, 104, 118, 131, 132; Ernst Ludwig, Grand Duke, 13, 25, 35, 75, 98, 99, 104, 131, 146, 147–9, 254; Friedrich Wilhelm, 'Fritzie', 14, 130, 131–2, 146; Georg Donatus, Hereditary Grand Duke, 75, 79, 97–100, 104, 105, 140, 254, 255, 256, 257, 279, 280, 281, 282, 322 n.55; Ludwig Ernst Andreas, Prince (birth of) 279; Ludwig IV (Louis), Grand Duke, 118, 132, 133; Ludwig, Prince, 79, 99–100, 104, 105, 254, 255, 256, 281, 282; Marie, Princess, 132
Higgenbottom, Miss, 8–9, 196, 292
Hildyard, Sarah Anne, 'Tilla', 74, 85, 274, 292
Hincks, Doris, 202–3, 208, 292
Hirosé, Commander, 245
Hobbs, Emma (later Mrs Skinner), 26–7, 38, 62, 69, 72, 117, 121, 122, 123, 127, 159, 184, 220, 222–3, 251, 292; family, 27
Hobbs, Georgina, 26–7, 38, 127, 292
Hofmeister, Dr, 14
Holden family, 24
Howard, Ethel, xi, 45–6, 51, 53, 54, 60, 78, 82, 86, 96–7, 106–8, 110, 174, 176–7, 178–9, 181, 185, 191, 192, 193–4, 198, 200, 215–16, 228–30, 231, 237, 244–7, 253, 282, 283, 292; family, 45, 292
Howe, Bea, 241
Howe, Nannie, 84, 292
Hsipaw, Sawbwa, 278
Hughes, Ellen, 25, 292
Hughes, Miss, 4, 292
Hull, Marianne (née Cripps), 'Old May', 199, 220, 273–4, 293

Indore, Maharani of, 34
Innocent, Ellen, 12, 14, 293
Iraq: Abdul Illah, Regent, 234; Faisal I, King of the Hejaz, 234; Faisal II, King, xii, 234–7; Ghazi, King, 234
Irwin, Miss, 258, 293
Irwin, Mr, 149
Isherwood, Miss, 4, 293; family, 4

Italy: Elena, Queen, 88, 89; royal children, 101
Ito, Marquis, 247

Jackson, Margaret Hardcastle, 'Madgie', 49–50, 117–18, 120, 254, 256–8, 274, 293
Japan: Akinoshin Shimadzu, 107, 245–6, 247; Hirohito, Emperor, 108; Junnosuke Shimadzu, 107, 245–6, 247; Shimadzu Princesses, 216, 228, 245; Tadashige Shimadzu, Prince of Satsuma, 78, 106–7, 228–9, 230, 247, 282; Tomijiro Shimadzu, 107; Yonosuke Shimadzu, 107–8, 245–6, 247
Jeffery, Harold Vivian, 281–2
Jenkins, Mary, 231–2, 270, 293
Johnson, Winifred, 232, 293
Johnston, Euphemia, 14–15, 293
Jones, Mrs, 25, 293
Justice, Elizabeth, 9

Karolyi, Countess, 45, 206
Karolyi, Michael, Count, 206
Kaulbach, Friedrich August von, 169
Keen, Edith, 179, 252, 293
Kemence, Nurse A., 68–9, 104, 134, 135, 140, 253, 293
Kennedy, Mrs (Miss Ramsbottom), 6, 8, 196, 293
King, Lucie, 115, 294
Kitz, Emma, 104, 294
Knight, Clara, xii, 294
Knollys, Francis, 159, 163
Kohl, J.G., 9
Korovin, Dr, 266

La Harpe, Frédéric, 4
Lascelles, Henry, Viscount, 276; George (birth of), 276
Lehzen, Baroness, 119
Leigh, Lady, 27
Leiningen, Marie, Princess, 12
Leo XII, Pope, 45
Leonowens, Anna, xii, 56–7, 144–6, 211, 225–7, 283, 294; family, 56–7, 226, 227, 294
Leslie, Ada, 52–3, 57, 61, 185–6, 188–9, 192–3, 200–1, 203–4, 208, 214, 230, 282, 284, 294; family, 52, 53, 294, 320 n.27
Liddell, Georgiana, 48
Lieven, Countess, 7
Lilly, Mrs, 14, 294
Loch, Emily, 20–3, 28, 29, 36
Locock, Dr, 11, 12

Londonderry, Lady, 8
Lord, Emily (later Mrs Ward), 31–2, 35
Lott, Emmeline, 105–6, 195, 209–12, 223–4, 232, 283, 294
Luccheni, Luigi, 240
Lyon, Jane, 6–8, 204, 294
Lyon, R. Cuthbert G., 138, 141–2
Lyttelton, Lady, 89–90, 184
Lytton, Lady, 21

Macclesfield, Lady, 12
McDonald, Annie, 162
MacDonald, Lady, 229
Mackintosh, Mrs, 66
Maclean, General and Miss, 224
Mamontov, Natalia, 'Tata', 111–12, 259
Manby, Dr, 143
Matcham, Mrs, 60–1, 62, 81–2, 230, 269, 295
Matsukata, Marquis, 229
Maule family, 59, 277, 278
Maybury, Hilda, 165–6, 176, 179, 249–50, 252, 269, 295
Mecklenburg-Schwerin: Alexandra, Grand Duchess, 34, 35; Alexandrine, Duchess (later Queen of Denmark), 275; Alexandrine, Princess Wilhelm of, 85
Merry del Val, Madame, 45; Monseigneur, 45
Metzger, Gladys, 41–2, 295
Millington, Mrs, 135, 295
Moffatt, Elizabeth, 131, 295
Monaco: Antoinette, Princess, 270; Rainier, Prince, 270
Morier, Lady, 3
Morrison, John, 234

Nagasaki, Mr, 229
Neame, Margaret, 258–9, 295
Netherlands: Alexander, Prince, 58; Emma, Queen (Princess of Waldeck), 50–1, 57–8, 76, 116, 168, 171, 172, 186, 196–7; Wilhelmina, Queen, 58, 60, 75, 76–7, 78, 80, 97, 108–9, 116, 168, 169, 172, 186, 191, 196–7, 202, 277–8; Willem III, King, 57–8, 289
Newman, Florence, 34, 295
Nicholls, Katherine Howard, 269, 295
Nicholls, Victoria (nurse to the Albanys), 164, 253, 295, 315 n.40
Nichols, Mrs (wet nurse), 67, 295–6, 315 n.40
Nichols, Sarah, 4–5, 284, 260
Noon, Beatrice, 134, 165, 260

Norland Institute, 31–6, 39–40, 44, 86, 214, 215, 232, 243, 248, 283

Norway: Haakon, King, 100, 101; Maud, Queen, 100, 143; Olav, Crown Prince (later King: born Prince Alexander of Denmark), 100–1, 139, 141, 143

Odgers, Marie, 34, 260

Offenberg, Baron, 150, 156

Oldenburg: Altburg and Ingeborg, Princesses, 165–6; Friedrich August, Grand Duke, 165–6, 249–50

Orbeliani, Sonia, Princess, 272

Orchard, Mary Ann, 39, 130–4, 135, 144, 146, 159, 254, 270–2, 260, 313 n.2; family, 131, 260

Orsini, Felice, 183

Osten-Sacken, Countess, 256

Owen, Sir Philip, 275

Palmer, Christine Mary, 'May', 39–40, 296

Paterson, Mrs, 15–16, 296

Paxton, Rebecca, 222, 296

Payne, Emily, xii, 227–8, 296

Penson, M.E., 'Juvenile Outfitter', 72–3

Perrin, Mademoiselle, 155

Peters, Elizabeth, 82–3, 84, 296

Pinkerton, Helen, 196, 296

Pitcaithley, Annie, 81, 296

Pope-Hennessey, James, 82–3

Potts, Jane, 119, 197, 282–3, 297

Primrose, Archibald and John, 4

Princess Christian College, 36–8, 44, 86

Prussia: *see also* Germany, Adalbert, Prince, 96–7, 98, 193, 219; August Wilhelm, Prince, 61–2, 96–7; Cecilie, Crown Princess, 35, 54, 115, 231, 270, 275; Eitel Freidrich, Prince, 96–7, 108–9, 193; Friedrich Karl, Prince, 50, 117; Friedrich Leopold, Prince, 252; Friedrich, Prince (son of Crown Prince Wilhelm), 186–7; Heinrich, 'Henry', Prince, 98–100, 135, 199, 219, 241, 251; Heinrich, Prince (son of Prince Heinrich and Princess Irène), 135; Hubertus, Prince, 111; Irène, Princess Heinrich (Princess of Hesse-Darmstadt), 15–16, 25, 33, 98–100, 118, 131, 133, 135, 244, 271; Joachim, Prince, 61, 62, 78, 97, 193; Louis Ferdinand, Prince, 54, 61–2, 90, 91, 93, 110–11; Margarete, Princess (daughter of Prince Friedrich Leopold), 179; Marianne, Princess Friedrich Karl, 50, 117; Oskar, Prince, 60, 97, 176, 193;

Sigismund, Prince (son of Prince Heinrich and Princess Irène), 135; Victoria, Princess, 47, 115, 184; Viktoria Luise, Princess, 54, 60, 75, 78, 80, 189, 193, 244, 269; Waldemar, Prince (son of Kaiser Friedrich III), 47, 115, 123; Waldemar, Prince (son of Prince Heinrich and Princess Irène), 16, 98, 135; Wilhelm, Crown Prince (son of Kaiser Wilhelm II), 53, 96–7, 108–9, 110–11, 193; Wilhelm, Prince, 54, 61–2, 90, 91, 109, 110–11

Pullman, Anne, 85, 297

Purdey family, 28

Pushkin, Alexander, 9

Queen's College, London, 49

Quiñones de Léon, Juana Alfonsa Milán, 165

Quiñones de Léon, Señor, 165

Ramirez, Rosalind, xii, 235–7, 297

Ramsay, Alexander, 276

Rasputin, Grigory, 259

Rata, Edith (later Mrs Bennett), 111–12, 259, 297

Robb, Katherine, 34, 297

Robertson, Sir Brian, General, 233

Rodd, Rennell, 115

Rogerson, Dr John, 6, 195–6

Rolestone, Joanne, 135, 255, 297

Romania: Carol I, King, 168–9, 170, 171, 172; Carol, Prince (later King Carol II), 169–70, 172–3; Elisabeth, Queen (Princess of Wied), 136, 137–8, 168–9, 170, 171–2, 173; Helen, Crown Princess (Princess of Greece), 38; Marie, Queen (Princess of Edinburgh and Saxe-Coburg), 15, 73, 124, 168–73, 191, 277, 288; Michael, Prince and later King, 38, 88–9

Roose, Emily, 40–2, 70, 78, 102–4, 105, 218, 278–80, 297, 319 n.12; family, 40, 278–80, 297

Rowles, Naomi, 69, 297

Roxburghe, Duchess, 159, 160, 162

Ruspoli, Princess, 33

Russia: Alexander I, Tsar, 4–5; Alexander II, Tsar, 1, 2, 8, 64; Alexander III, Tsar, 1, 3, 4, 10, 205; Alexandra Alexandrovna, Grand Duchess, 4; Alexandra Feodorovna, Empress (Princess Alix of Hesse), 20–3, 29, 36–7, 38, 39, 67, 73, 79, 104, 113, 118, 120, 132, 133, 134, 147, 148, 149, 182–3, 190, 192, 193, 223, 256–8, 263, 264, 265, 266, 271–2, 274, 267, 311 n.12; Alexandra Feodorovna, Empress (wife Nicholas I), 4; Alexandra Nikolaevna, Grand Duchess,

8–9; Alexei Alexandrovich, Grand Duke, 1, 266; Alexei Nikolaevich, Tsesarevich, 108, 258, 263, 264, 323 n.5; Anastasia Nikolaevna, Grand Duchess, 81, 95–6, 148–9, 223, 243–4, 258, 323 n.14; Boris Vladimirovich, Grand Duke, 170, 171; Catherine the Great, Empress, 4–6, 195; Dmitri Pavlovich, Grand Duke, 12–13, 64–5, 95; Ekaterina Ioannovna, Princess, 258; Elizaveta Mavrikievna, Grand Duchess, 73, 258; Ioann Konstantinovich, Prince, 258; Kira Kirillovna, Princess, 35, 73, 101–2, 261–2; Kirill Vladimirovich, Grand Duke, 63–4, 71, 101, 152, 153, 170, 219, 261–2; Konstantin Pavlovich, Grand Duke, 4–5; Ksenia Alexandrovna, Grand Duchess, 67, 259, 260; Maria Alexandrovna, Tsaritsa, 204; Maria Feodorovna, Empress (wife of Tsar Paul), 7, 8; Maria Feodorovna, Tsaritsa (wife of Tsar Alexander III), 1, 2, 18, 19, 95, 125, 139, 205, 259, 260, 271, 309 n.26; Maria Nikolaevna, Grand Duchess (daughter of Nicholas II), 95, 148–9, 183, 187, 223, 243–4, 258, 267, 323 n.14; Maria Pavlovna, Grand Duchess (daughter of Grand Duke Pavel), 28, 64–5, 74, 76, 95, 219; Maria Pavlovna, Grand Duchess Vladimir (Duchess of Mecklenburg-Schwerin), 3, 125, 150–9, 243; Marie Georgievna, Grand Duchess Georgi Mikhailovich (Princess of Greece), 40, 86, 112, 154–5, 219; Marie Kirillovna, Princess, 35, 101–2, 261–2; Mikhail Alexandrovich, Grand Duke, 111–12, 259; Mikhail Nikolaevich, Grand Duke, 4, 8; Mikhail Pavlovich, Grand Duke, 6; Nicholas I, Tsar, 6–8, 74; Nicholas II, Tsar, 13, 20, 34, 67, 95, 113, 147, 149, 192, 223, 263–4, 265, 311 n.12; Nikolai Alexandrovich, Tsesarevich, 4; Nikolai Nikolaevich, Grand Duke, 8; Olga Alexandrovna, Grand Duchess, 18–19, 125, 158, 205, 270–1, 272, 273; Olga Nikolaevna, Grand Duchess, 23, 65, 67, 79, 91–2, 94, 147–9, 223, 243–4, 258, 266, 271; Paul, Tsar, 4, 7, 8; Pavel Alexandrovich, Grand Duke, 1, 12, 27, 75; Sergei Alexandrovich, Grand Duke, 1, 3; Tatiana Nikolaevna, Grand Duchess, 22, 65, 94–5, 147–9, 220, 223, 243–4, 258, 265, 266, 267; Victoria Feodorovna, Grand Duchess Kirill (Princess Victoria Melita of Edinburgh and Saxe-Coburg, Grand Duchess of Hesse-Darmstadt), 34, 35, 146, 151, 157, 166–8, 170,

261–2; Vladimir Alexandrovich, Grand Duke, 1, 63, 126, 151; Vladimir Kirillovich, Prince, 102, 261–2; Vsevelod Ioannovich, Prince, 258
Ryan, Nellie, 112–13, 179, 181, 187, 199–200, 239, 240, 253, 283, 297

Sadler, Constance, 34, 35, 297
St John, Elizabeth Alix, 37–8, 40, 42, 88–9, 218, 237, 298; family background, 37–8, 298
Salmond, Catherine Welsh, 'Gertie', 32–3, 40, 73, 77, 298
Sandwich, Lord, 229
Saville, Mrs, 125, 298
Savoury, Commander Herbert, RN, 40
Saxe-Altenburg, Prince, 192–3
Saxe-Coburg: Alfred, Prince (also of Edinburgh), 15; Carl Eduard (Charles Edward), Duke, 2nd Duke of Albany, 66, 163–4, 253; Maria Alexandrovna, Duchess (Grand Duchess of Russia and Duchess of Edinburgh), 2, 15, 67, 73, 74, 167–8, 170, 171–2; Viktoria Adelheid, Duchess, 17, 34
Saxe-Meiningen: Bernhard, Prince, 123; Charlotte, Princess (Princess Bernhard), 47, 123, 184, 241–2; Feodora, Princess, 123
Saxony, Crown Prince and Princess (Archduchess Louise of Austria-Tuscany), 188
Scharmann, Wilhelm, 281
Schaumburg-Lippe, Marie Anna, Princess Georg II, 73
Schleswig-Holstein-Augustenburg, Ernst Günther, Duke, 176
Schleswig-Holstein-Glücksburg: Caroline Mathilde, Duchess, 'Calma', 16, 22, 98; May, Princess, 78
Scott, Lady, 26, 27
Seymour, Lady William, 25
Sharman, Isabel, 31, 33, 41, 150, 151, 156, 157–8, 215, 248, 253
Shaw, Miss, 90–1, 298
Siam (Thailand): Chulalongkorn, King, 227; Fâ-ying, Princess, 145–6, 227; Maha Mongkut, Rama IV, King, 57, 144–6, 225–7; Sitphorn, Prince, 46
Simpson, Hilda, 142
Simpson, Dr James Young, 15
Sly, Mrs, 90, 298
Smith, 'Nana', x, 58, 72, 163, 164, 239, 280–1, 298
Smyth, Alice, 89, 298

Spain: Alfonso XIII, King, 114, 134, 165; Alfonso, Prince of the Asturias, 29, 76, 108, 134, 221; Alvaro, Prince of Orléans-Borbón, 35, 69–70; Beatrice, Princess Alfonso of Orléans-Borbón (Princess of Edinburgh and Saxe-Coburg), 34; Ena (Victoria Eugenia), Queen (Princess of Battenberg), 17, 67, 134, 165, 186; Gonzalo, Infante, 114, 134, 220–1; Isabel II, Queen, 239, 285, 288, 293; Jaime, Infante, 108; Juan, Infante, 114, 220–1; Maria Cristina, Queen, 114

Speaight, Richard, 134

Spence, Helen Caroline Ken, 32, 298

Stainthorpe, Josephine, 134, 298

Stainton, Anne, 88–9, 298

Stanley, Augusta, Lady, 196

Stewart, Pauline Harriet, 'Hartie' (later von Klenck), 44, 79, 121–2, 298; family, 44, 121–2, 298

Stoeckl, Agnes, Baroness, 86

Stolberg, Countess, 188

Stolberg-Wernigerode: Anne-Marie, Princess, 254; Ludwig Christian, Prince, 253–4; Wilhelm, Prince, 253–4

Stratton, George and Lizzie, 140, 141, 277

Strutton, Catherine, 'Kitty', 1–4, 10, 15, 74, 196, 204–5, 298–9; family, 2–3, 298–9

Sullivan, Arthur, Sir, 206

Sulman, Betty (later Mrs Morrison), 234, 299

Sweden: Louise, Queen (Princess of Battenberg), 280; Margaret, Crown Princess (Princess Margaret, 'Daisy' of Connaught), 37, 160–2, 300; Sigvard, Prince, 300

T, May, xi, 44–5, 51, 54, 78, 80–1, 92–3, 116, 119, 175, 177, 181, 185, 188, 190–1, 198, 199, 206–7, 239–41, 253, 283, 299; family, 45, 299

Talleyrand, Marquise de, 33

Tashcher de la Pagerie, family, 43, 80

Thadden, Fraulein von, 60

Thomas, Frederick, 141

Thomas, Winifred, 140–4, 277

Thurn and Taxis, Princess, 39, 288

Thurston, Mary Anne, 26, 27, 69, 79, 122, 131–2, 134, 163, 222–3, 273, 299; granddaughters, 122

Tiutcheva, Anna, 2

Todd, Beatrice, 33, 85, 135, 144, 147, 280, 299

Togo, Admiral, 247

Tolstoy, Countess (Princess of Holstein-Beck), 196

Tolstoy, Countess Alexandrine, 2

Tomioka, Admiral, 247

Topham, Anne, 54, 60, 62, 75, 78, 81–2, 86, 101, 177, 182, 187–8, 189–90, 191–2, 197, 198, 230, 242, 244, 253, 283, 299; family, 299

Turkey: Abdul Aziz, Sultan, 209; Abdul Hamid II, Sultan, 208–9

Vales Failde, Don Javier, 114, 311 n.13

Vetsera, Marie, Baroness, 240–1

Vicars, Hedley, 238

Wakelin, Mary Ann, 122–3, 299; family, 122–4, 299

Waldeck: Elisabeth, Princess, 119; Friedrich, Prince, 72; Georg Viktor, Prince, 50–1; Helene, Princess (wife of Prince Georg Viktor), 50–1, 72, 239, 280–1; Marie, Princess, 50–1; Pauline, Princess, 50–1, 239; Sophie, Princess, 72

Waldersee, Count, 230

Walker, Miss, 46, 51, 299

Wanstall, Kathleen, 253–4, 270, 300; family, 300

Wenham, Mrs, 18

Wheeler-Bennett, John, Sir, 82–3

Wied: Hermann, Prince, 136; Luise and Elisabeth, Princesses, 168; Marie, Princess (Princess of Nassau), 136, 137, 294; Marie, Princess (Princess of the Netherlands), 168, 171; Otto, Prince, 136–8; Wilhelm, Prince, 136, 168, 171

Wilson, Elizabeth Jane, 'Lilian', 25–6, 35, 38, 75, 97–9, 120, 146–9, 166–8, 254, 267, 279, 281, 300; family background, 26, 300

Wilson, Mrs (née Creak), 163, 300

Winter, Saxton Elizabeth, 57–60, 75, 76–7, 78, 80, 97, 108–9, 116, 168–73, 186, 191, 196–7, 201–2, 277–8, 300; family, 58–9, 277–8, 300

Wood, Amy, 35, 300

Wright, Orville, 242

Yugoslavia: Alexandra, Queen (Princess of Greece), 84, 103; Olga, Princess Paul of (Princess of Greece), 33, 35, 40, 41, 72–3, 77, 102–4, 150, 153–6, 158, 208–9, 289; Peter II, King, 84, 285; Tomislav, Prince, 202, 285

Yusupov: Felix, Prince (father), 259–61; Felix, Prince (son), 259–61; Irina Alexandrovna (Princess of Russia), 259–61; Irina, Princess, 259–62

Zanotti, Magdalina 'Madelaine', 256–7, 271